# ECOPRAGMATICS

*EDWARD T. WIMBERLEY*
*AND*
*SCOTT PELLEGRINO*

# ECOPRAGMATICS

*EDWARD T. WIMBERLEY*
*AND*
*SCOTT PELLEGRINO*

First published in 2014 in Champaign, Illinois, USA
by Common Ground Publishing LLC
as part of the On Sustainability book series

Library of Congress Cataloging-in-Publication Data

Wimberley, Edward T.
  Ecopragmatics / Edward T. Wimberley and Scott Pellegrino.
    pages cm
  Includes bibliographical references and index.
  ISBN 978-1-61229-612-8 (pbk : alk. paper) ISBN 978-1-61229-613-5 (pdf)
  1. Deep ecology--United States. 2. Environmentalism--United States. 3. Environmental policy--
United States--Citizen participation. 4. Human ecology--United States. I. Pellegrino, Scott. II. Title.

  GE197.W56 2014
  304.20973--dc23

                    2014035687

Cover image photo credit: Published courtesy of Florida Gulf Coast University

# Table of Contents

**Introduction to Ecopragmatics: We Can't Dance Together.... (Or Even Agree on the Tune!)** ........................................................................1
The World's Gone Crazy Environmental Cotillion .........................................1
Deep Ecology, Environmental Activism, and Radicalism................................4
Conservationism ...............................................................................................5
Public Equivocality: The American Environmental Values Survey (AEVS)...7
National Surveys and Polls: More Environmental Tepidity ...........................9
Dancing Together to a Tune of Our Own Making.........................................13
Ecopragmatics: Can-do and Compromise ...................................................15
Principles of Ecopragmatics .........................................................................18
Ecopragmatics & Environmental Imagining ...............................................21
First: Carefully Consider the Case................................................................22
Second: Reconsider the Five Principles of Ecopragmatics...........................22
Third: Frame and If Necessary Re-Frame the Case Employing an Ecological Metaphor ........................................................................................................23
Fourth: Specify the Thematic Perspective on the Problem and Develop a Tentative Conclusion......................................................................................24
Fifth: Develop a Strategy for Pursuing a Resolution to the Case Problem .....24
Sixth: Review Your Analysis and Conclusions .............................................24
Book Outline ..................................................................................................25
Dewey, Rorty, Minteer, and Other Pragmatic Thinkers ...............................29

**Chapter 1: Straight Talk—The Pragmatism of William James** ........30
The Problem with Philosophers......................................................................30
Consequences and Metaphor.........................................................................32
The Pinball Wizard Metaphor and Streams of Consciousness ......................39
Truth through Consequences ..........................................................................41
Pragmatism, Utilitarianism, and Relativism ................................................43
Comparing the Explicit Method of Dewey with the Metaphorical Method of James ..............................................................................................................46
Imagining Cash-value: Deciphering the Jamesian Metaphorical Method ...49
Policy Analytic Frameworks: James and Dewey ..........................................50
Imagining's Brief Departure from James: Dewey and Communitarianism.52
Jamesian Imagining versus Dewey's Empirical Method ..............................54

**Chapter 2: The L&N Don't Stop Here Anymore—Coal and Craig, Colorado** ...........................................................................................56
When the L&N Don't Stop There Anymore: Clean Air and Coal in Colorado ........................................................................................................56
Imagining: The Case of Craig, Colorado—Case Summary.........................57
Preliminary Analysis: Key Stakeholders ......................................................60
Exteriorities and Interiorities ........................................................................62
Processes and Perspectives............................................................................68
Opportunities, Costs, Biases, and Potential Pitfalls.....................................71
Novel Ideas and Approaches versus Tried and True .....................................74

Tentative Problem Identification and the Five Attitudinal Principles of
Ecopragmatics ........................................................................................77
Principle One: Be Outcome Oriented ......................................................78
Principle Two: Be Mindful.......................................................................79
Principle Three: Thoughtfully Discriminate............................................79
Principle Four: Be Grounded in Past Experiences...................................80
Principle Five: Be Open to New Experiences...........................................81
Imaginating as Stream of Consciousness.................................................81

## Chapter 3: Simplify—Interiority, Exteriority, and Necessary Anthropocentrism...................................................................................83

Simplification: Unbundling Interiority and Exteriority ...........................83
Nested Ecology and Integral Theory ........................................................85
Order from Chaos .....................................................................................88
The Relationship between Interiority and Exteriority: Big Coal ..............90
Integral Ecology .......................................................................................91
Re-framing: Walking in Another's Shoes ................................................93
Walking in Another's Shoes: Approaching Coal from the Perspective of the
Coal Industry ...........................................................................................95
Ecopratmatics, Interiority, and Exteriority .............................................98
A Second Case Illustration: The Floridan Aquifer ..................................99

## Chapter 4: Cool Water—The Floridan Aquifer and Groundwater Resources........................................................................................... 101

Water, Water, Everywhere... ..................................................................101
The Floridan Aquifer ..............................................................................103
The Depletion of Groundwater Resources..............................................104
Florida Groundwater Regulators: State Water Management Districts.........107
Suwannee River Water Management District (SRWMD)............................109
Buckeye, PCS Phosphate, and the Jacksonville Electric Authority (JEA) ...113
Two Industries Consume 80% of Daily Reported Groundwater .................119
Environmental Advocacy Stakeholders...................................................123
Earthjustice and Federal Litigation against USEPA Over Water Nutrient
Limits......................................................................................................125
Actions and Intentions: Exteriorities and Interiorities ..........................128
Florida's Governor's Response ...............................................................133

## Chapter 5: Stand inside My Shoes—Framing and Reframing Seemingly Intractable Environmental Issues.....................................135

If I Could Be You (And You Me) ............................................................135
Satisficing and Bounded Rationality ......................................................136
The Limits of Rational Decision-making and Decision Frames...............137
Decision Framing and Hardening of the Categories................................141
Framing and the Limits of Rationality: Moral Psychology Research..........142
Accommodation and Compromise ..........................................................144
Framing and Reframing 101: A Survival Scenario..................................145
Intuitive Versus Deliberative Imaginating..............................................148
Competing Frames: A Frame-logic Paradigm .........................................151
Framing and Reframing Seemingly Intractable Environmental Issues.........154

Identifying Stakeholders and Developing Framing Themes ........................ 159

**Chapter 6: Gyppo Loggers and Spotted Owls ................................. 164**
Gyppo Loggers, the Northern Spotted Owl, and the End of a Way of Life .. 164
The Steady Decline of the Timber Industry in the Pacific Northwest ......... 165
Regulatory Impacts upon Timber Production in Washington and Oregon ... 167
The Northwest Forest Plan and WOPR ......................................................... 171
Loggers, Environmentalists, Regulators, and Timberland Industry ............ 173
Loggers ......................................................................................................... 175
Environmentalists ......................................................................................... 178
Regulators ..................................................................................................... 182
The Timber Industry ..................................................................................... 186
A Language Frame to Accessing Federal Land for Lumber Processing ...... 189
Identity Framing on the Basis of the Degree of Anthropocentrism ............. 201
Employing a Risk Frame-logic: Bargaining to Share Risks ....................... 206
Rationale Versus the Process for Achieving a Frame-fit ............................. 210

**Chapter 7: Let's Work Together—Individual Freedom and**
**Community Need ................................................................................. 212**
Intuition and Community ............................................................................. 212
Winning Hearts and Minds ........................................................................... 215
Avoiding Analysis Paralysis ......................................................................... 217
Intuition and Social Ecology ....................................................................... 220
Balancing Individual Freedom and Community Needs ............................... 222

**Chapter 8: Oil and Water—The Green Tea Coalition .................... 225**
Imaginating and Communitarianism ............................................................ 225
Oil and Water: The Green Tea Coalition ...................................................... 226
Pertinent State Legislation ........................................................................... 227
Utility Scale Solar Energy and the Residential Solar Energy Producer:
Costs ............................................................................................................. 229
Solar Energy Waste Products ....................................................................... 230
Solar Power in Georgia: Disposal, Treatment and Recycling
Considerations .............................................................................................. 232
The Adequacy of Georgia's Electric Grid System ...................................... 234
Environmental Communitarianism at Work ................................................. 237

**Chapter 9: Going Home—From Olmsted to the Carolina Thread**
**Trail ..................................................................................................... 241**
On Being Unwittingly Pragmatic ................................................................ 241
A Tradition of Greenways ............................................................................ 242
Regional Stewardship and the Carolina Thread Trail .................................. 244
From Environmental Summit to Open Spaces Framework Plan: Voices &
Choices ......................................................................................................... 247
A State of the Region Report, Open Spaces Conservation and the Carolina
Thread Trail .................................................................................................. 252
The Charlotte-Mecklenburg Community Foundation's Environmental
Committee ..................................................................................................... 256
The Carolina Thread Trail ............................................................................ 258
What Makes the Carolina Thread Trail Unique and Worthy of Emulating? 260

Imaginating the Carolina Thread Trail ...........................................................263
Necessary Anthropocentrism and Householding Principles .........................268
A Communitarian Approach to Regional Economic and Environmental
Planning ...........................................................................................................268
Conclusion .......................................................................................................269

**Chapter References .............................................................................271**
Introduction: Introduction to Ecopragmatics ...............................................271
Chapter 1: Straight Talk .................................................................................276
Chapter 2: The L&N Don't Stop Here Anymore ...........................................279
Chapter 3: Simplify ........................................................................................287
Chapter 4: Cool Water ....................................................................................289
Chapter 5:  Stand Inside My Shoes ................................................................295
Chapter 6: Gyppo Loggers and Spotted Owls ...............................................299
Chapter 7: Let's Work Together .....................................................................306
Chapter 8: Oil and Water ................................................................................309
Chapter 9: Going Home ..................................................................................313

# Preface and Acknowledgements

Every book has a source somewhere and for us that source was the classroom where we were consistently sensing a general degree of cynicism and hopelessness regarding the serious environmental problems of our day. The student's sense of hopelessness, as we quickly learned, emanated from many places: the textbooks they were reading, the comments and positions of their professors, the news stories they were viewing on television and online, the philosophical perspectives they were acquiring from the journals and proceedings of conferences they were attending and the perspectives they had acquired in their home communities from among family, friends, community leaders and more.

As we considered this sad state of affairs we found ourselves likewise buffeted between the extremes of the modern world of environmentalists, preservations, conservationists, anarchists and more. As we considered what we could do to help navigate this world of extremes and absolutes, we revisited the work of the pragmatists, and upon reviewing that body of literature again, realized that a pragmatic approach to environmental problems might be the tool we had been looking for – an antidote to the balkanization of contemporary discussions and debates over important environmental issues and an approach to problem solving that students, policymakers and community leaders might fruitfully learn and apply across a lifetime of environmental and civic service and engagement. To that end, we reacquainted ourselves with John Dewey and William James and in the process realized that the metaphorical and psychological style and orientation of James might be well suited to persuading contemporary and budding policymakers that common ground and common cause may yet be found among disparate opinions and interests if only participants could learn to interact with another on an ongoing basis openly, intuitively and civilly. What follows is a tentative effort to present that pragmatic vision philosophically and practically combining narrative methodologies interspersed with illustrative case studies.

We would like to thank those who helped us with writing this book. They include Ben Minteer of Arizona State University whose own work on environmental pragmatics in the style of John Dewey inspired us to pen a similar approach based upon William James. We would like to thank Amitai Etzioni for his work on communitarianism that we have found to be so very useful in understanding and solving environmental problems. Similarly we are indebted to the late Herbert Simon and James March formerly of Carnegie-Mellon University for their contributions to decision-making theory. However, we would like to extend our particular gratitude to the moral psychologist Jonothan Haidt whose work on rational decision making has convinced us that successful negotiations pertinent to our most import environmental issue simply must occur locally and recognize the importance of the intuitive processes that shape values and philosophies and determine how or if rational discussion and inquiry will follow. To these important persons and others who must go unnamed we extend our deepest gratitude and appreciation.

# Introduction to Ecopragmatics: We Can't Dance Together…. (Or Even Agree on the Tune!)

It's the world's gone crazy cotillion
The ladies are dancin' alone
Side men all want to be front men
And the front men all want to go home.

*It's the World Gone Crazy (Cotillion)*
Waylon Jennings and Shel Silverstein

## The World's Gone Crazy Environmental Cotillion

Few would disagree that when it comes to contemporary environmental issues it's as though "the world has gone crazy!" If environmental political discourse, policymaking and planning can in any way be compared to participating in a cotillion ball where couples dance together, take new partners, learn new steps and moves, and cooperate with the instructions of a "caller" who directs the dance, then we can only conclude – based upon the current state of environmental affairs – that we have forgotten how to dance together and can't even agree on the tune. At a time when the nation and the world are facing a staggering array of major environmental challenges - climate change, dwindling supplies of freshwater, depleted fisheries, desertification, overpopulation, disease, and hunger - to name but a few – our leaders are deadlocked, our political discourse is at a standstill, our citizens are confused, the quality of our public discourse appears to be hopelessly balkanized and our people and planet are suffering.

In the midst of this crisis environmental philosophers and ethicists practice their art within the confines of the academy largely isolated and insulated from the demands and *vicissitudes* of the world around them. Arguably the product of their efforts *ought* to be contributing to the resolution of environmental problems. Unfortunately they are largely impotent in their capacity to influence the public policy debate for the simple reason that their presence is not significantly felt in the public square given their preference to practice their professions within the university and its environs. Insulated as they are within the culture of the university they largely write their philosophies for themselves and others who share their views and publish their work in a range of journals sympathetic to their perspectives knowing that the editorial polices of these journals are influenced by like-minded academics. The product of their habits and proclivities is intellectual balkanization, intolerance for ideas that differ from their own, indifference to hostility for those who would criticize their ideas or present alternative perspectives and – most importantly – irrelevance of their ideas relative to the public discourse that occurs beyond the gates of their academies and beyond earshot of their windows and doors. These issues: balkanization, polarization, politicization, insularity, the stultification of scholarship across philosophical lines, intolerance of intellectual discourse, bias and a growing irrelevancy to the environmental policy process in the world beyond the academy have been discussed or criticized in one way or another by many scholars and commentators (Wimberley, 2012; Zygmunt, 2006; Bookchin, 2005; Guha, 2005; Rosebraugh, 2004; Zimmerman, 2003; Keulartz, 1999; Clark, 1996, Fox 1989).

Criticizing these cloistered environmental philosophers and their ideological kin, however, can prove hazardous. In some cases, daring to disagree with a particular environmental philosophy can result in the offender being labeled "anti-environmental" (Jacques, Dunlap & Freeman, 2008) or finding oneself accused of engaging in "brownlash"- "a deliberate misstatement of scientific findings designed to support an anti-environmental world view and political agenda" (Ehrlich & Ehrlich, 1998, p. 13). In still other cases holding opinions at odds with "established" environmental thought can result in vilification and efforts to have the offending party fired or censured.

The most recent and disturbing example of this were the efforts to have Danish associate professor Bjorn Lomborg fired following the release of his book *The Skeptical Environmentalist* (2001). Following publication of the book – whose content did not question the reality of anthropocentric global warming but rather questioned the utility of the steps that were being proposed to deal with it – Lomborg was attacked from all quarters in the environmental movement and was eventually censured by the Danish Committee on Scientific Dishonesty for publishing content that was "clearly contrary to the standards of good scientific practice." Lomborg was later cleared of these charges following a backlash of protest from scientists and academics worldwide (Houlder & MacCarthy, 2003).

Louisiana State University (LSU) coastal scientist Ivor van Heerden found himself in similar circumstances following the Hurricane Katrina disaster. As chairman of the state's independent Team Louisiana Investigation, van Heerden criticized the U.S. Corps of Engineers for poorly engineering the levees designed to protect New Orleans. Louisiana State University terminated him as a research professor in May 2010 following the publication of his comments regarding the New Orleans levee system. Dr. van Heerden is currently litigating his dismissal claiming LSU punished him for being the whistle blower who exposed the failures of the U.S. Corps of Engineers in designing and maintaining the New Orleans levee system (Scheifstein, 2009).

However, those who have investigated the van Heerden firing more closely attribute his termination to "classic campus politics: jealousies, rivalries and professional disputes," professor van Heerden's sometimes abrasive personality, and the threat he posed to future federal funding for wetlands research – much of it through the Corps of Engineers. According to investigative reporter Annette Sisco of the Picayune-Times,

> van Heerden's real danger to LSU was his threat to funding. The federal government is the largest source of research funding for universities, and LSU was lining up tens of millions of dollars for coastal and wetlands work -- much of which might be partnered with the corps. Having one of its professors lobbing bombs at the feds made some at the university fear for the LSU pocketbook. That's why members of Team Louisiana, as well as researchers from other universities, were warned to shut up or risk their careers. Fortunately for all of us they decided their ethics -- as professors, engineers and citizens -- compelled them to continue to work for the public good. (Sisco, 2009)

The politically "correct" position for van Heerden to have taken in the aftermath of Hurricane Katrina was to go along with the dominant narrative of the time which was to portray Katrina was a "storm-of-the-century" type phenomena, likely attributed to global warming – as Vice President Al Gore reiterated in his award winning film *An Inconvenient Truth* (Guggenheim, 2006) – whose carnage could not be laid at the feet of any particular group beyond the criticism directed toward FEMA and the administration of then President George W. Bush who were accused of failing to adequately respond to the disaster in a timely fashion. Van Heerden chose the politically incorrect option following Katrina and in the world of environmental academia prioritizing the politically "incorrect" over the "correct" can be perilous indeed.

Academic jealousy and intolerance is but one of a number of issues endemic to the environmental movement in part because there are so many environmental philosophies and camps whose adherents are drawn from among a broad array of professional backgrounds. Dealing with these diverse interests is inherently difficult precisely because of their diverse and often divergent interests. The common theme among most – but not all - groups is their corporate failure to exert significant influence upon the environmental policy scene. In other words – employing the "dance" metaphor we began this introduction with - they have either not been invited to the dance or for one reason or another have chosen not to participate. Regardless of "why" or "whether" they have chosen to participate or not, their absence from the environmental policy dance means they are irrelevant to the activities that will occur therein. Failure to participate in the "dance" of environmental policy implies an unwillingness to associate or work with others who bring different ideas and values regarding how the dance should proceed, what tunes will be played, who will lead and who will follow, what pace the dance will assume and who will leave the dance with whom.

Consequently, when environmental philosophers, ethicists and others choose to excuse themselves from interacting with people from a variety of backgrounds who are imbued with a variety of ideas about the relationship of humans to the environment, they unilaterally cede the floor to those who will choose to participate, call the tune, lead, follow, maneuver, doe-see-doe, dance and leave with either old or new partners – it's their choice since they have chosen to "dance." Wallflowers *forgo* these opportunities. Even so, among the many philosophical camps that could be dancing two stand out: deep ecology and conservationism.

## Deep Ecology, Environmental Activism, and Radicalism

Deep ecologists are the most influential school of environmental thought today particularly in terms of their relative impact upon academics, administrators, students, and, indirectly (by virtue of their activism and radicalism), policymakers (Luke, 2002). The typical deep ecologist assumes an eco-centric outlook toward nature and humanity and acquires an anti-anthropocentric perspective regarding human involvement in the environment. As a result, deep ecologists risk being construed as misanthropic - regarding humans as an ecological problem best solved by segregating them to the greatest degree possible from nature (Bookchin, 1987; Sessions, 1995).

Deep ecologists take pride in differentiating their values from those of other environmental schools, and sometimes their zeal to protect the environment can be interpreted as intolerance or arrogance particularly when ensconced within the more radical enclaves of the deep ecology movement (Zimmerman & Taylor, 2005; Taylor, 1997). Unlike the "light-green" or "shallow ecologists," who principally confine themselves to ameliorating existing environmental problems, deep ecologists see themselves as acting proactively and preventively orienting their efforts toward the entire planet rather than toward people alone (Naess, 1973; Orton, 2006; Clark, 1996). They also embrace a philosophy - reinforced by a platform of shared beliefs – that effectively politicizes adherents (Sessions, 1995).

Deep ecologists are particularly committed to pursuing an ethic that is eco-centric - not anthropocentric. Thus they tend to bestow their deepest condemnation upon those they perceive as blatantly anthropocentric in their environmental views and actions – i.e. those believing in the legitimacy of humans living in the natural world and utilizing its resources to achieve their own sustenance, happiness and security. To the purveyors of deep green ecology those who don't share their eco-centric, politically and economically revisionist values run the risk of being considered unenlightened, uninformed, retrograde, demeaning to the sanctity of mother earth and a threat to people and the planet. Therefore in the minds of deep ecologists eco-centrism represents enlightened thought while anthropocentrism is regarded as comparatively unenlightened, primitive, offensive and even dangerous (Steiner, 2010; Stead, 2010; Williamson, 2007; O'Hara, 1999, White, 1967).

Deep ecologists are a diverse group and their ideas are arguably the most influential of all the environmental philosophies. However they are unsympathetic regarding existing human culture, economy and government. As a consequence their discontent has in part informed the values of environmental activists and radicals (Sussman, 2012; Taylor, 2008; Cramer, 1998).

Radical environmental thinkers and writers, as exemplified by the work of Erick Jensen, Aric McBay and Lierre Keith (Jensen, McBay & Keith, 2011) are anarchistic, seeking to replace the current political and economic system with a new (though ill-defined) alternative that is friendlier to the environment and more prescriptive of human initiative, discretion and freedom. Consequently, their philosophy tends to be misanthropic and antagonistic toward all other environmental philosophies and often conflicts with current law and civic values and practices. Adherents of this philosophy principally see themselves as activists and revolutionaries and the coterie of devotees with whom they interact largely share their radical and insular perspective.

Most notable among the radical environmentalists are those associated with Greenpeace, the Animal Liberation Front, Sea Shepherd and the Ruckus Society to name but a few. Sadly, it is not uncommon to hear calls for violence from among the environmental radical community. For instance, eco-journalist and activists Steve Zwick recently published an article on *Forbes* online in which said the following regarding climate change skeptics:

> We know who the active denialists are – not the people who buy the lies, mind you, but the people who create the lies. Let's start keeping track of them now, and when the famines come, let's make them pay. Let's let their houses burn. Let's swap their safe land for submerged islands. Let's force them to bear the cost of rising food prices. They broke the climate. Why should the rest of us have to pay for it? (Zwick, 2012)

Similarly, Finnish environmental activist Pentti Linkola, in *Extinguish Humans, Save the World,* translated into English as *Can Life Prevail?* (2009) reflects upon the ecological state of the planet by observing that:

> The crippling human cover spread over the layer of the Earth must forcibly be made lighter: breathing holes must be punctured in this blanket and the ecological footprint of man brushed away. Forms of boastful consumption must be violently crushed, the natality of the species violently controlled and the number of those already born violently reduced - by any means necessary. (Linkola, 2009, p. 170)

The values of these and other similar groups place them at odds with those who deal with business and economic organizations, corporations and non-governmental organizations (NGOs) – particularly in the areas of energy, agriculture, forestry, chemicals, mining, and finance. Accordingly, they find themselves at odds with conservationists – those with comparatively anthropocentric values dedicated to employing human ingenuity and technology to manage and maintain a wide array of natural resources and habitats upon which humans depend.

## Conservationism

Within the academy those dedicated to a conservation ethic can principally (though not exclusively) be found within schools of agriculture, forestry and mining, as well as among those employed in schools of engineering, business and architecture. Conservationism also includes chemists, biologists, physicists, lawyers, business people and other professionals who assume a stewardship and resource management perspective regarding their work regardless of whether they labor within or beyond the walls of the academy. These scientists and professionals, representing a vast array of disciplines, apply their conservationist values in their work on behalf of farmers, miners, foresters, corporations, governments and communities.

Conservationists address a wide range of problems to include genetically engineering crops to resist drought, disease-prevention, pest control, and cropland irrigation. They are also involved in energy conservation, energy development of all kinds, and technology innovation. Meanwhile other conservation professionals manage our forests, farms, fisheries, wetlands and recreational and drinking water resources. As a group, conservationists follow in the footsteps of an illustrious line of forbearers to include Theodore Roosevelt, Gifford Pinchot, Aldo Leopold and George Perkins Marsh. However, regardless of where they work, conservation-minded professionals seek to help people live better utilizing fewer natural resources so as to insure that a comparable set of resources will be indefinitely available to their descendants.

At the heart of the conservationist's beliefs is optimism relative to human adaptability and ingenuity, the richness, diversity and resilience of nature and the capacity of humans to wisely manage and utilize natural resources for human benefit while indefinitely sustaining resources for future generations. Therefore conservationists are blatantly anthropocentric – person-oriented - meaning that they are most comfortable with the idea of humans living in nature and utilizing its resources – providing they do so for the benefit of the many and not just the few and that they utilize natural resources in such a way that they will also be available to future generations of citizens.

Conservationists found outside of academic environmental or ecological studies programs readily collaborate with agricultural, business, and corporate interests. Situated as they are within the university and the community, conservationists have comparatively little interaction with their intellectual kin committed to deep-ecology, eco-feminism, environmental radicalism, environmental aestheticism or the like. In so doing, they bear no hostility toward other environmentalist camps – indeed they may be largely indifferent to their divergent values. Thus the distance they maintain from members of the environmentalist community is principally motivated by what they do and with whom they collaborate and engage in business – not ideology.

Generally speaking the values of conservationists are more applied and utilitarian than is the case for the bulk of their "environmentalist" colleagues (Haider & Jax, 2007). Therefore, they find little common ground or common cause among academic and activist environmentalists, preferring instead to collaborate with agriculture, energy, and corporate interests that contribute to their conservationist interests and initiatives. This collaboration inevitably results in their being criticized and vilified by environmental activists and radicals (Hassoun, 2011; O'Hara, 2007; Hoffman & Sandelands, 2005). The net effect is that the conservationists, like virtually every environmentally oriented profession or discipline within the academy and beyond, tend to talk among themselves, contributing in their own unique way to the balkanization of environmental philosophy, ethics and values.

Sadly, once philosophical camps become balkanized and distrustful or disdainful of those with divergent environmental interests communication, dialogue and growth cease and entropy and decay sets in producing stalemate. This, I believe, is the current state of environmental philosophy and ethics in the academy. Intellectual efforts have become insular and self-serving. Cross-pollination of ideas has ceased – except for those occurring within any particular philosophical camp. Moreover, too often students are being educated to be activists, radicals or revolutionaries rather than for collaboration, dialogue, consensus seeking, compromise and change. The net effect of all these forces is that environmental philosophy has rendered itself irrelevant to the pressing environmental issues of the world and has done so during a period in which public support for environmentalism and environmentalists is tepid at best.

## Public Equivocality: The American Environmental Values Survey (AEVS)

Returning to the "dance" metaphor, it's worth noting that academics are not the only parties absenting themselves from the cotillion. Citizens are also sitting the dance out and a number of recent surveys and polls provide insight regarding why. One of the most important contemporary surveys to document the public's environmental opinions is the 2005 American Environmental Values Survey (AEVS) (Gunns, 2006). This comprehensive 240-item survey was distributed to some 4,000 people and completed by approximately 1,500 respondents. The survey yielded many interesting results, but among findings reported, those most salient to our discussion are the respondents top 11 ranked priorities to include (1) "Americans' environmental concerns are divergent and polarized," (3) "Issue complexity has paralyzed many Americans," (7) "Competing priorities effect all groups of Americans," (8) "There are three major environmental issue groupings (pollution, planetary threat; human ecology) among Americans," (10) "Environmental responsibility is getting more personal," and (11) "Environmentalism and Environmentalists have an image problem."

It is not surprising to learn that Americans are polarized in their environmental concerns. The personal values of citizens are bifurcated, perceiving the natural environment as either a place for recreation, hunting, hiking or camping or alternately seeing it as wilderness. Understandably, those perceiving nature as wilderness favor keeping humans out of nature whereas those perceiving nature in more utilitarian terms favor human use of nature.

The respondents' polarized environmental worldviews likely contribute to their equally polarized perceptions of environmentalists and environmentalism. Accordingly the survey's findings classify the interests of environmentalists and environmentalism as falling into one of three issue clusters:

1. Destruction of the Planet: A concern for the destruction of natural and wilderness areas, food chains, rainforests, ozone, and extinction of endangered species. These issues are conceptual and global; most Americans cannot relate to them. These issues are most effective for use with well-educated, successful, and self-confident segments of the American public.
2. Polluted Resources: A concern for polluted resources (water, air, soil), pesticides in food, nuclear waste disposal, and toxic waste. These are

more visible, easier to understand, and more accepted issues among most Americans. (One barrier: some groups believe pollution problems have been solved.) Focusing on polluted resources is most effective in messaging to lower- income, less educated and self-confident Americans.
3.   Human Ecology: A concern for uniquely human challenges such as traffic congestion, population growth, noise pollution, and urban sprawl. All Americans relate to these issues (Gunns, 2006, p. 12).

Respondents reported that they were also overwhelmed by the complexity of environmental issues presented to them on a daily basis by the media. Indeed, this high degree of complexity led the authors of the AEVS to conclude that:

> Most Americans are not fully aware of our current environmental challenges because such awareness requires a high level of knowledge about environmental issues, a strong understanding of how the environment relates to the economy, and a long-range perspective. Inability to comprehend the issues and visualize future benefits prevents people from acting." "Given this lack of understanding, to expect most Americans to change their standard of living today for environmental benefits tomorrow is not realistic. (Gunns, 2006, p. 10)

This particular finding is somewhat chilling in its implication because it implies that since the public is incapable of understanding and responding to environmental problems and issues that perhaps this responsibility should fall to those who *are* knowledgeable and motivated to act. In such a scenario individual freedom and autonomy may be at risk.

Predictably the perceived complexity of environmental issues is paralleled by priorities that compete with environmental concerns to include:

1.   Financial Woes (I have trouble making ends meet)
2.   Religious Values (I try to follow Jesus' model)
3.   Modernity (environmentalism is old solutions to old problems, repeating mistakes)
4.   Personal Safety (I worry about myself or a family becoming a victim of crime)
5.   No Good Taxes (I think taxes never solve any problems)
6.   Education Imperative (using tax dollars fund education will better the economy)
7.   Political Futility (why worry about political issues, I can't do anything anyway)
8.   Cynicism (politicians and 'the system' are controlled by special interest groups) (Gunns, 2006, p. 12)

These findings illustrate the value-pluralism with which the average citizen must cope. These multiple value concerns stand in stark contrast to the comparatively narrower and near monolithic values of academic environmentalists who have the luxury to focus upon environmental values virtually to the exclusion of all other concerns. The disparity between the array of values academics and citizens concern themselves with on a daily basis may explain to some extent why environmental philosophy has been more at home in the academy than in the public square. Similarly, it may explain why so many citizens choose to be "wallflowers" rather than dance with environmentalism and environmentalists.

Yet another reason academic environmentalists choose to stay clear of the public arena pertains to environmentalism and environmentalists "public-image problem." Noting that as of 2006 only 44% of Americans were willing to identify themselves as environmentalists, AEVS researchers observed that "many Americans view the environmental movement as traditional, dated, and somewhat out of touch with current society" (Gunns, 2006, p. 14), which in part they attribute to popular images of environmentalists as "eco-terrorists," "soy and granola" advocates, "partisan liberals," and "regulators" imposing high costs and taxes upon citizens. In short, the public does not find environmentalists or their movement particularly appealing. Results from the survey suggest that what was once a broad-based public environmental movement has been transformed into a personal agenda and concern. These findings, coupled with the fact that people are overwhelmed prioritizing "earth-oriented" issues, may explain why so "few American embrace personal responsibility for the environment" (Gunns, 2006, p. 13).

## National Surveys and Polls: More Environmental Tepidity

The picture portrayed in the AEVS is not encouraging for those committed to the environmental movement. Given AEVS findings public engagement regarding environmental issues seems tepid at best. Regrettably, the AEVS findings have been ratified by a series of reputable public polls conducted since 2006 that in aggregate portend a future policy environment in which the public's investment in environmentalists and environmentalism is at best equivocal. It would seem that when it comes to environmental issues – nobody wants to dance.

Consider these finding from recent public polls, beginning with results from a 2009 ABC News/Washington Post Poll (PollingReport.com, 2012) which asked *"How much do you trust the things that scientists say about the environment: completely, a lot, a moderate amount, a little, or not at all?"* In responding to this question, 59% of respondents indicated that they "generally trust" environmental scientists while 41% registered little to no trust. However, when responses are considered as a whole 71% of respondents register "moderate" to "no" trust while only 29% registered "complete" trust. Their findings imply that the public harbors reservations regarding the degree to which they trust the reports and opinions of so-called environmental experts.

Many polls ask adults how they feel about environmental issues, but one group whose values regarding the environment are often disregarded are America's school-aged youth. Their omission is somewhat surprising given the significant federally funded support annually allocated for environmental education in secondary schools – some $5.6 to $7.8 million appropriated annually through the National Environmental Education Act of 1990 alone (Bearden, 2002). According to an analysis of data derived from the Monitoring the Future survey (MTF) – a survey annually administered to high school students since 1976 – interest in the environment and conservation peaked in the 1990's and has been steadily declining since (Wray-Lake, Flannigan & Osgood, 2008). Penn State researchers sampled trend data between 1976 and 2005 drawing upon a sample size of almost 100,000 student responses. Their results confirmed a "precipitous decline in high school senior's reports of conservation behaviors across the three decades of 1976-2005." In analyzing a four-item conservation behavior scale incorporated into the MTF survey, they documented a decrease in average scores over the study period in excess of 3.5 standard deviations – suggesting that between 1976 and 2005 students had become increasingly unwilling to engage in even basic conservation habits like turning off lights, lowering the thermostat, recycling and the like (Wray-Lake, Flannigan & Osgood, 2008, p. 12).

These results suggest that young people have been gradually drifting away from engaging in basic environmental and conservation habits, implying their interest in environmental issues is also waning. Findings like these from among the nation's youth incline one to wonder whether adults are also turning their backs on environmentalism and conservation, "tuning out" to environmentalism and becoming less inclined to identify themselves as "environmentalists."

A series of questions included in an ABC/Planet Green/Stanford University poll between 1980 and 2008 (PollingReport.com, 2012) shed light on this speculation by asking respondents "Do you consider yourself be an environmentalist?" When this question was first posed 76% of respondents answered in the affirmative and 20% responded in the negative and 4% were undecided. In 1995 63% of respondents self-identified as environmentalists, 35% indicated they were not environmentalists and 2% were undecided. By 1999 respondents were almost equally likely to identify themselves as environmentalist or as not (50% environmentalists, 48% not environmentalists and 2% undecided). However, in 2000 the ratio of responses reversed and for the first time the majority of respondents identified themselves as not being environmentalists at 52% while 47% self-identified themselves as environmentalists (1% undecided). Finally by 2008 58% claimed to not be environmentalists, 41% claimed they were and 1% was unsure. The trends regarding this question are illustrated in Figure 1.

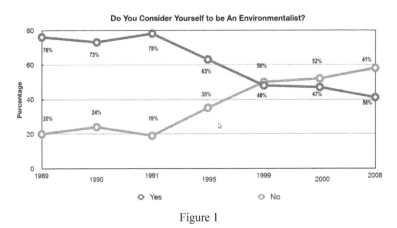

Figure 1

Obviously since 1989 there has been a steady decline in the percentage of people self-identifying as environmentalists. As illustrated, this is not a recent change of heart among the respondents but rather a steady trend that has been long in the making.

A 2010 Gallup poll (Dunlap, 2010) posed a similar question asking respondents "Thinking specifically about the environmental movement, do you think of yourself as -- an active participant in the environmental movement, sympathetic towards the movement, but not active, neutral, or unsympathetic towards the environmental movement?" This is likewise a question Gallup has been asking annually since April of 2000. Figure 2 reflects the patterns of response to this question over the decade.

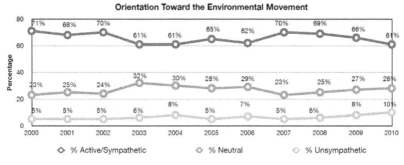

Figure 2

According to the poll's findings over the course of a decade there has been a 10% decrease in the percentage of respondents indicating they were active and sympathetic towards the environmental movement (71% in 2000 versus 61% in 2010). Comparatively there has been a smaller 5% increase in the number of persons identifying themselves as unsympathetic toward the environmental movement (5% in 2000 and 10% in 2010), and another 5% uptick among those who identify themselves as neutral on the issue (23% in 2000 and 28% in 2010). Respondents were also asked in the same poll the degree to which they believed the environmental movement by and large had done more good than harm or more harm than good. Figure 3 illustrates the response trend between 2000 and 2010.

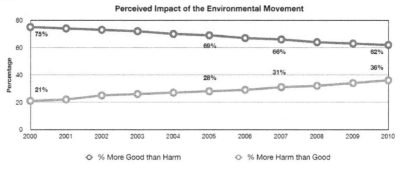

Figure 3

Once again over the period of a decade the percentage of respondents believing that the environmental movement has done more good than harm slipped by 13%

(from 75% to 62%) while the percentage who believe it has done more harm than good increased 15% (from 21% to 36%).

In reviewing the findings from the ABC and Gallup polls there is no denying that the currency of the environmental movement and the willingness of citizens to identify with that movement has declined over a decade or more. For all the reasons reflected in the 2006 AEVS poll and others yet unknown, the data inarguably suggest that Americans are generally ambivalent and disengaged from the environmental movement. Moreover, as if further proof were needed of the sad state of environmental issues and concerns among the general public, a 2012 CBS News provides more evidence yet. The 2012 CBS poll (PollReport.com, 2012) asked respondents what issues they believed were of the greatest priority and environmental issues didn't make the top-ten list. In point of fact environmental concerns have not made it to the top-10 priority issue list in CBS polls for at least the last 5 years.

So, if Americans are not principally interested in the environment, then what are they most concerned about? The answer to the question is "economics." Figure 4 Illustrates the findings of a Gallup poll conducted between 1984 and 2010 asking respondents to prioritize environmental protection versus economic growth.

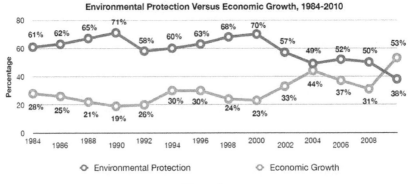

Figure 4

While there has been a great deal of fluctuation in the relationship between these two variables there is a clear pattern emerging that variability between environmental protection and economic development began to narrow around 2000, when 70% of respondents prioritized environmental protection over economic growth (23%) with 2% undecided. By 2009 this trend reversed itself for the first time with economic growth outstripping environmental protection 51% to 42% with 7% undecided, and by 2010 that gap had widened to 53% favoring economic growth versus 38% favoring environmental protection with 9% undecided. By 2011 that gap had widened still further with 54% prioritizing economic growth and 36% prioritizing environmental protection with no undecided respondents (Jones, 2011). Obviously Americans are increasingly prioritizing economics over environment and doing so with a progressively growing degree of confidence. One can only assume that if the current international economic malaise continues that the prioritization of economic considerations over environmental ones can only be expected to continue well into the future.

In considering the trends documented in the various polls and surveys conducted by a variety or reputable polling organizations a clear pattern emerges. As economic growth remains sluggish and uncertain, an increasing percentage of Americans indicate that economic concerns trump environmental ones. Meanwhile sympathy, confidence and activism in the environmental movement declined as has the willingness of citizens to self-identify as environmentalists. Confidence has also waned among citizens regarding the credibility of environmental scientists, even as public perception has grown that the environmental movement is doing more harm than good. Moreover, these trends are occurring against the backdrop of growing number of citizens who increasingly find environmental issues too complex to cope with and cite a plethora of competing issues more germane to their daily lives than environmental ones. This is the larger context within which the balkanization of environmental philosophy and ethics has occurred. All signs indicate that if environmentalism is the name of the dance, it is becoming increasingly difficult to find a dance partner.

## Dancing Together to a Tune of Our Own Making

The introduction to this book playfully began with lyrics to Waylon Jennings' tune "It's a World Gone Crazy (Cotillion)" which is his social commentary upon how as a society we can't seem to cooperate or get along together. Jennings illustrates our plight in his mirthful tune by imagining a gaggle of men and women trying to dance together in a complex step requiring cooperation, taking turns, learning new moves, holding hands and following directions. We subtitled the introduction "We Can't Dance Together…Or Even Agree on a Tune" partly in jest but principally to illustrate the reality of the world of citizens, environmentalists, environmental philosophers and ethicists who seemingly can't work together on shared environmental problems.

There's no denying the harsh reality we all find ourselves, namely that on the whole we just can't seem to dance together. We increasingly find ourselves Balkanized within our various environmental schools of thought while the public distrusts, misunderstands, dislikes and often wonders who we are and what we are about. As if that is not cause enough for concern, we additionally find ourselves and our philosophical work increasingly marginalized by a thorny and recalcitrant set of economic problems that neither go away nor get any better. Clearly, if we are going to move beyond our current malaise and be about the business of cooperatively addressing the myriad environmental, economic, political and social issues confronting us, we simply must "agree on a tune and learn to dance together" – regardless of whether we like it or not.

To that end we present for your consideration *Ecopragmatics*. The story behind the title of this book is a bit unusual but worth understanding. Those familiar with *Nested Ecology* author Terry Wimberley's work know he is also a clergyman practicing for almost 30 years. While in seminary it was a rite of passage for every student to study Karl Barth's *Church Dogmatics* – all 14 volumes. Wimberley did not read all 14 volumes but read enough to be as impressed with the story behind the *Dogmatics* as he was with its remarkable content.

Barth's *Dogmatics* began as a series of sermons in 1947 delivered in the ruins of Bonn University following the destruction of the German homeland during the totalitarian regime of the Nazis and Adolf Hitler. Barth gave these sermons without benefit of written notes, in part because following the war paper was scarce. In fact the Nazis purposefully destroyed millions of books while millions more burned under the rain of bombs and artillery shells thereby robbing Germans of much of their cultural and intellectual heritage. When Barth began his *Dogmatics* Germany was rebuilding and his intent was to help the German church reunite, reorganize and reorient in the wake of the holocaust by delivering sermons designed to reacquaint the church with its doctoral foundations – foundations lost during the war. In effect Barth's mission was to help the church reclaim its core values.

Reclamation, reunification, reorganization, reorientation and rediscovering core values: these are the themes Barth addressed in his *Dogmatics* and they are the very ones that environmentalists and conservationists must consider given the magnitude and the severity of the innumerable environmental challenges before us. At this juncture environmental philosophy needs to step out of the academy, into the world and sell its wares to the public. In many ways environmental philosophy and ethics needs to begin wholly anew both within and outside of the academy.

While difficult, this is not a completely unique conundrum for philosophers. In fact, when William James penned his first works he did so principally because other philosophical schools had become esoteric and isolated from the practice of philosophy and ethics in the world most people live and die in. His lectures on *Pragmatism* like Barth's sermons were purposefully delivered to a broad audience rather than narrowly directed toward his academic colleagues. Like Barth he held out the promise of regular people being empowered to creatively think through their own moral, philosophical and ethical dilemmas without resorting to a professional clergyman, philosopher or ethicist for guidance. Barth's message to the German church seeking to rebuild itself was – "you can do it." James' message to regular people who attended his lectures was – "you can do it," and the message we environmental philosophers, ethicists, academics, activists and conservationists need to be communicating to the public is that when it comes to the very thorniest of our environmental problems – "we can do it."

The answer to the question we have not wanted to ask is summed up in the verb "do." Rather than "writing," "lecturing," "judging," "advocating," "demonstrating," or "pontificating" about environmental philosophy, ethics and policy perhaps it's time we actually rolled up our sleeves to "do" environmental philosophy ethics in the public square and not just within the confines of the academy. The time is ripe for thoughtful academics and professionals from a wide range of disciplines to be about the business of articulating environmental philosophy and ethics within the context of real people struggling with real and very complex environmental policy and social issues.

## Ecopragmatics: Can-do and Compromise

*Ecopragmatics* is an action-oriented approach to *doing* environmental philosophy in the public arena founded upon the premise that everyone practices environmental philosophy in one form or another and that it is both possible and necessary to philosophically engage people in an honest mutual, tolerant and practical dialogue to preserve and promote the interests of people and the larger environment. Consequently, this is a "can-do" book designed to provide a reasoned and pluralistic approach to thinking about environmental issues from the philosophical perspective of William James (James, 1900, 1903, 1907, 1909, 1911 & 1912). In so doing, we present a framework that doesn't create new ideas and information as much as it draws upon proven approaches to pragmatic problem-solving and compromising that have been around for quite a while but which have been developed and implemented largely beyond the realm of the environmental philosopher and ethicist and well beyond the experience of most environmental policymakers, professionals, advocates and activists.

Our approach to ecological pragmatics begins with the psychological pragmatics of William James (James 1904, 1912), exploring his ideas regarding pragmatism as method versus philosophy. In so doing we present a conceptual framework adapted from James' work providing a practical and useful template for considering environmental problems and issues. We also discuss the importance of recognizing that ecopragmatics necessarily involves embracing pluralism in every form (particularly as it applies to competing values, ethics and philosophies that must be engaged rather than ignored, bypassed or defeated). Likewise, we emphasize the degree to which values are constantly changing and undergoing transformation.

Since ecopragmatics unavoidably assumes the perspective of human beings living within the world, we introduce the reader to the concept of "necessary anthropocentrism" which asserts that humans are biologically, psychologically, socially and ecologically constrained to ultimately perceive the world around them in terms of human perceptions, thoughts, values, and culture. In a similar vein, we discuss the pragmatic human imperative to make a place and home in the world – referring to this imperative as "householding" and describing how it serves as a driving economic and ecological value around which all others are forced to compete (Wimberley, 2009). These two concepts – "necessary anthropocentrism" and "householding" serve as foundational assumptions undergirding environmental pragmatism. Thereafter, we proceed to some obligatory dimensions of environmental pragmatism by incorporating the ideas of philosophical pragmatist Ken Wilber.

Wilber introduces the concepts of "interiority" and "exteriority" to the pragmatic analysis of environmental issues. Wilber has distinguished himself by developing an ecological approach called "integral theory" in which he differentiates between "exteriority" - the objective (external) characteristics of individuals (e.g. behavioral features) and collectives (e.g. social characteristics) – and "interiority" - subjective individual (e.g. intentionality) and collective (e.g. cultural) characteristics (Wilber, 1997). This distinction proves useful when considering what individuals do versus what they feel and believe in regarding environmental. It also contributes to an understanding of how society collectively manifests itself externally, socially and organizationally versus how it expresses its interiority in terms culture and philosophy.

Once the dimensions of ecopragmatics have been established and discussed we provide a perspective on the process known as "framing" inspired by the work of Amos Tversky and Daniel Kahneman (1981), Donald Schon and Marin Rein (1994), Siegwart Lindenberg (2001& 2008) and Kurt Lewin (1976). These policy analysts and theoreticians developed their pragmatic approaches to conceptualizing issues in an effort to deal with very complex public policy controversies, and we were drawn to their work precisely because they were dealing with issue complexity that frankly characterizes virtually every contemporary environmental challenge. Likewise we favored their work because of the ease with which it could be incorporated into William James' pragmatic method. We employ their ideas to create a conceptual matrix incorporating a framework for classifying policy options as well as incorporating the language style and approach used to articulate each option. In this way we provide a context for studying environmental issues and problems while recognizing that each policy issue can and probably should be considered from a variety of contexts and perspectives.

The process of providing context to an issue or problem is what constitutes "framing." Frames can serve both to describe the problem at hand and suggest solutions. Nevertheless, this approach is tentative and flexible such that policy issues and problems may be framed and reframed as necessary, especially when any given framing metaphor fails to capture the essence of the situation or fails to lend itself to identifying a solution or solutions. This approach to conceptualizing issues will be incorporated into a revised pragmatic method built upon the foundation of William James' ideas and approach.

At the heart of William James' pragmatic method (James, 1904) is decision making. According to James, people are constantly in the process of observing, reading, listening and considering ideas and values; thereafter comparing what they have read, heard or observed to what they know or reasonably know to be true. It's as if people accumulate this vast repository of knowledge and information within themselves ("old-stock") and when exposed to new ideas or information ("new-stock") they automatically compare what they see or hear to what they know and value, and on the basis of these constant comparisons either reject, accept or partially accept or reject the new "new-stock" information.

This process has been widely discussed over the years by a plethora of policy makers specializing in decision theory. Of the many decision theorists who have approached their scholarship in the spirit of pragmatism none has been more influential than renowned Nobel laureate Herbert Simon. Simon is best known for his "satisficing" approach to decision making in which he suggests that in most instances when a decision is to be made that an individual or a group will begin their deliberation by considering their current state of affairs and then imagining a superior state of affairs they would like to realize (Simon, 1957). Once stakeholders have identified their desired state they proceed to search for alternatives to help them achieve their anticipated end. They search for options and in each case compare the option in relationship to their current situation and desired outcome, continuing to do so in a stepwise fashion until they arrive at an option that satisfies the greatest majority of their ideal outcome's characteristics and at that point they adopt this alternative. This effort Simon calls "satisficing" – i.e. forgoing the perfect outcome to realize the most functional and achievable outcome available given projected needs, time, value and cost considerations.

This satisficing approach (forgoing the ideal to realize the achievable and satisfying) will be applied to the James pragmatic methodology and will be augmented to a degree by the "mixed-scanning" decision making model of Amitai Etzioni (1967), who additionally discriminates between decision making approaches used to address both routine and comparatively important issues. Simon and Etzioni's approaches will be included in a revised version of James' methodology as "satisficing" approaches to pragmatic environmental deliberation.

While employing Simon's "satisficing" approach to decision making has been incorporated into ecopragmatics, it has been done so with one very important caveat – most decision making is usually not a rational process. We make this assertion on the grounds that modern psychological research – particularly that of moral psychologist Jonothan Haidt (2013, 2006) – demonstrates that people don't usually make "rational" decisions (especially about really important matters) but instead make intuitive decisions based on a complex set of characteristics to include emotions and then use rationality to justify, explain or cajole others into sharing their values. This insight is central to understanding an ecopragmatic method, particularly when it comes to understanding Wilber's concepts of "interiority" and "exteriority" as they apply to individuals, groups, communities and interest groups.

Having developed a pragmatic decision making tool for considering environmental issues we consider a policy approach specifically designed to engage individuals and stakeholders at the community level – "communitarianism". Communitarianism is designed to bring policy disputes as close to the community as possible and create an environment where to the greatest extent possible policy problems are resolved locally, consensually, informally and without recourse to legislative, executive or judicial decisions or actions. This community-centered approach, most notably championed by another Nobel laureate, Elinor Ostrom (2001), is we think best illustrated again in the work of Amitai Etzion (a sociologist and decision theorist) who writes about "communitarian" approaches to public policy. According to Etzioni:

> Communitarianism is a social philosophy that maintains that society should articulate what is good–that such articulations are both needed and legitimate. Communitarianism is often contrasted with classical liberalism, a philosophical position that holds each individual should formulate the good on his or her own. Communitarians examine the ways shared conceptions of the good (values) are formed, transmitted, justified, and enforced. Hence their interest in communities (and moral dialogues within them), historically transmitted values and mores, and the societal units that transmit and enforce values such the family, schools, and voluntary associations (social clubs, churches, and so forth), which are all parts of communities. (2003, p. 224)

Based upon this definition Etzioni believes that to the greatest extent policy issues should be resolved locally and informally whenever possible and that the needs of the individual of necessity must be balanced by the needs of the community. Etzioni's model is grounded in what he refers to as the "new golden rule" which asserts "Respect and uphold society's moral order as you would have society respect and uphold your autonomy to live a full life" (Etzioni, 1997 p. xviii).

Etzioni's approach is consistent with Ostrom's work and is well grounded in the history of communitarian thought as exemplified by the work of its founder, Alasdair MacIntyre (1988). Likewise, Etzioni's values are consistent with the communitarian perspective of Avner DeShalit (1995) who regards "community" as a transgenerational phenomenon. These contributions of communitarianism to environmental philosophy and policy will be discussed in greater length later in the book.

We also address issues of bias, absolutism, receptivity and critical thinking into modeling ecopragmatics. Time spent considering these perennially thorny issue is essential to the process of achieving a worthwhile and effective outcome to environmental issue analysis. Fortunately for the authors, James devoted considerable thought to these issues (James, 1904, 1912) and many of those considerations will be integrated into the revised James method fully elucidated later in the book.

## Principles of Ecopragmatics

Before proceeding to an overview of the book chapters, however, we would like to briefly share some principles promoting pragmatic thought and analysis derived from James' work.

In *Pragmatism* James describes his method in the following manner:

> A pragmatist turns his back resolutely and once for all upon a lot of inveterate habits dear to professional philosophers. He turns away from abstraction and insufficiency, from verbal solutions, from bad *a priori* reasons, from fixed principles, closed systems, and pretended absolutes and origins. He turns towards concreteness and adequacy, towards facts, towards action, and towards power. That means the empiricist temper regnant, and the rationalist temper sincerely given up. It means the open air and possibilities of nature, as against dogma, artificiality and the pretense of finality in truth. (James, 1907, p. 36)

Consequently for James, pragmatism in a nutshell involves:

> The attitude of looking away from first things, principles, 'categories,' supposed necessities; and of looking towards last things, fruits, consequences, facts. (James, 1907, p. 32)

For James, pragmatic philosophy transpired in the public square among people representing pluralistic values and interests. Arguably the best metaphorical description of where pragmatic interaction occurred was provided by an admirer of his work, Giovanni Papini, who compared it to "a corridor in a hotel" from which "innumerable chambers open out of it. In one you may find a man writing an atheistic volume; in the next someone on his knees praying for faith; in a third a chemist investigating a body's properties. ... They all own the corridor, and must pass through it" (James, 1907, p. 32).

James continues to address the manner in which we formulate theories to explain what we know and learn as well as how we employ information. He observes that:

> Theories thus become instruments, not answers to enigmas, in which we can rest. We don't lie back upon them, we move forward, and, on occasion, make nature over again by their aid. Pragmatism unstiffens all our theories, limbers them up and sets each one at work.(James, 1907, p.37)

While theory-building – a task we approach through "framing" - is key to James' method, before we can develop theories to explain the world around us and to inform our subsequent thoughts and actions James reminds us that we must reconcile what we know or believe to be true with new ideas and information that comes our way. James provides a guide for how he conceives of this process of idea comparison, noting that:

> The process here is always the same. The individual has a stock of old opinions already, but he meets a new experience that puts them to a strain. Somebody contradicts them; or in a reflective moment he discovers that they contradict each other; or he hears of facts with which they are incompatible; or desires arise in him, which they cease to satisfy. The result is an inward trouble to which his mind till then had been a stranger, and from which he seeks to escape by modifying his previous mass of opinions. He saves as much of it as he can, for in this matter of belief we are all extreme conservatives. So he tries to change first this opinion, and then that (for they resist change very variously), until at last some new idea comes up which he can graft upon the ancient stock with a minimum of disturbance of the latter, some idea that mediates between the stock and the new experience and runs them into one another most felicitously and expediently. This new idea is then adopted as the true one. It preserves the older stock of truths with a minimum of modification, stretching them just enough to make them admit the novelty, but conceiving that in ways as familiar as the case leaves possible. (James, 1907, p. 27)

Based upon this template, human beings are constantly engaged in comparing new information and ideas with the stock of existing ideas and values they carry with them as if stuffed in a well-worn suitcase. Consequently, people are perennially in the business of packing and unpacking their interior suitcase as they consider new ideas and information and compare it to what they already have conveniently packed away. When hearing new information, their natural inclination is to reject it if it doesn't somehow coincide with the ideas and information they already have safely packed away as "old-stock."

However, depending upon the degree to which the new idea or information is deemed significant then old ideas and values may be discarded for newer ones ("new-stock"), or alternately some of the characteristics or components of newer ideas and information may be grafted upon what James calls "old stock" – a gardener's term for a new plant variety introduced into the body of an older plant variety. This metaphor is most useful to the degree that it suggests that new ideas are most easily incorporated into the values of individuals if the "genetic makeup" of the new information bears appreciable resemblance to the older existing stock of values and ideas.

Given this brief summary and illustration of James' essential approach we have identified five attitudinal principles of ecopragmatics, the first three of which I will introduce now. The term "attitudinal" is used purposefully to emphasize a set of attitudes that promote a thoughtful yet pragmatic response to new events and experiences.

1.  *First Principle*: *Be Outcome Oriented* - look away from first things and toward last things.
    For James "first things" include principles, categories, supposed necessities, absolutes, biases and abstractions, while "last things" include outcomes, consequences, fruits, products and facts. Adopting this principle entails, to the greatest degree possible, setting aside all barriers that stand in the way of being intellectually receptive to hearing a new idea, allowing yourself to fully understand what is being communicated before critiquing it and to be able to project what you hear into a tentative future where you might consider the outcomes, consequences and experiences that might flow from it. Being able to so understand what you hear, read or see enable you to later make a coherent comparison between this new idea, value or information and compare it to the storehouse of information and values you currently hold to be true – what James calls "old-stock."

2.  *Second Principle*: *Be Mindful* – be ever-present and available to novelty. Cognizant that the first principle entails focusing energy and attention upon the case or idea before you and emptying your mind of any other conversation, dialogue or issue that you may also be working on or ruminating about, allow yourself to fully attend to the issue at hand.

3.  *Third Principle*: *Be Discriminating* - engage in thoughtful discernment. As you attend to the issue at hand allow your intuition to also work and look for indicators of bias or nuance that might cast the information you are receiving into another light. Likewise be aware of the context within which the information you are receiving is occurring, and the context within which you are receiving it. Above all focus upon the degree to which the ideas and information you consider meet James' criteria of adequacy, concreteness, factual, action-oriented, and empowering. While I avoid using acronyms, these characteristics of ideas are so vital to James' method that they are worth memorizing: Adequate, Concrete, Factual, Action-Oriented, and Empowering (ACFA-OE).

4.  *Fourth Principle: Remain Grounded in Past Experience* - honor the integrity and utility of old-stock values. These are the ideas, beliefs and

values people incorporate within themselves that inform how they live are time-tested and the product of trial, error and experience. They are, therefore, by definition formative of who people are and how they relate to the world. Consequently recognize and appreciate why old-stock values are cherished and don't discard them unless and until better ideas, information or values present themselves in a way that is compelling to heart and mind.

5. *Fifth Principle: Remain Open to New Experiences* - always be willing to reevaluate old-stock experiences in the light of newer ones. While recognizing the worth of old-stock ideas and values, allow yourself to realize superior values and ideas whenever they present themselves preferring to celebrate the birth of a new idea or opportunity rather than grieve the death of an old-stock value or notion.

In summary the Jamesian approach to pragmatics involve being mindful, outcome-oriented, discriminating, while remaining grounded in past experiences and perpetually open to new ones.

## Ecopragmatics & Environmental Imagining

The term imagining is inspired from the term "imagineer" as principally employed by the Walt Disney Company. Their use of the term imagineer was principally intended to combine the ideas of imagination and engineering employed together. While we very much like the term it is copyrighted by Disney and is unavailable for use in this text. Consequently we have coined a term combining imagination and animation to describe the process of imagining an idea and then animating this mental construct into a hypothetical projection of how that idea might actually be experienced if acted upon and actualized. This concept - "imagining" – is derived from the basics of William James's pragmatic method which – based upon the preceding discussion of his ideas – can most succinctly be expressed in the following fashion:

1. Beliefs become habits serving as rules of action.
2. The meaning of a belief is expressed in the *conduct* that follows or results from adopting the belief.
3. The conduct derived from a adopting a belief is predicated upon the expected experiential consequences assuming the belief is true.
4. Beliefs are constantly tested, evaluated and updated with new beliefs.
5. New beliefs are only adopted when their anticipated benefit is deemed to be of greater value than those provided by existing beliefs.
6. The comparative valuation of beliefs entails imagining one's future condition if the beliefs were behaviorally realized.

The idea of imagining corresponds to James' assertion that we comparatively evaluate the consequences flowing from beliefs and ideas by effectively projecting anticipated outcomes into an intermediate future and judging their anticipated "cash-value." This is process depends upon using one's imagination prior to taking any action. This is what we call "imagining."

While imaginating is a term inspired by the concept of imagineering, it differs from the latter in that imagineering implies bringing an idea into full reality and fruition whereas imaginating only implies projecting out in a mental exercise how an ideal might be experienced in reality. To that end, an imagineer would be someone who engineers their imagination into a tangible reality whereas an imaginator (one who engages in imaginating) simply uses their imagination to test out hypothetical outcomes that they intuitively suspect may flow from the implementation or appropriation of an idea, value or action. Historically the term "Imagineering" was employed well before Disney copyrighted it. Most notably, the late Texas poet, romantic and Mayor of Luckenbach, Texas, Hondo Crouch, emblemized the term to proclaim his profession on his business cards – appropriating a term that had been in popular usage since the early 1940s first by Alcoa and later by the *National Carbon Company*, *Larsen and Toubro*, and Boston University's *Imaginating Academy* (Imaginating Academy, 2012; Kovak, 2007; Naik, 2007).

We utilize the term *environmental imaginator* to provide a structure and process to James' pragmatic method - doing so pragmatically yet distinct from the manner in which the term has been employed at Disney, Alcoa etc. We will also assert that imaginating occurs "intuitively" as a part of normal human cognition and decision making and "deliberatively" as when a formal process is employed to assure that a group of decision makers consider policy issues by way of a common decision rubric or framework. In the interest of summarizing this approach we will first present the "deliberative" environmental imaginating process in outline form as it pertains to policy analysis.

## First: Carefully Consider the Case

Begin by studying the case at hand carefully seeking an understanding of the issues, stakeholders, constraints, processes, bias and opportunities for resolution and compromise. Consider the case's interiority (values), exteriority (actions), spatiality (such as who else, where else and what else is impacted) and account for the timelines associated with the evolution of the problem at hand as well as time constraints relative to resolving and/or ameliorating the problem. Likewise consider any "old-stock" values or ideas that you bring to the study of the case as well as biases. Also look for "new-stock" opportunities that may influence what you think about the case. Finally seek to understand how each stakeholder conceptualizes the issue and the solutions each seek. Thereafter be prepared to begin the process of metaphorically framing the case.

## Second: Reconsider the Five Principles of Ecopragmatics

Before proceeding to framing the case, take a few moments to reconsider it in terms of five attitudinal principles of ecopragmatics derived from James' pragmatic method:

1.  *First Principle*: *Be Outcome Oriented*
    Don't let "first things" (principles, categories, supposed necessities, absolutes, biases and abstractions) distract from "last things" (outcomes, consequences, fruits, products and facts).
2.  *Second Principle*: *Be Mindful*
    Empty your mind of any other conversation, dialogue or issue that you may also be working on or ruminating about and give the issue at hand your full attention.
3.  *Third Principle*: *Be Discriminating*
    Focus upon the degree to which the quality of the ideas and information you consider conform to the criteria of adequacy, concreteness, factual, action-oriented, and empowering (ACFA-OE).
4.  *Fourth Principle: Remain Grounded in Past Experience*
    Recognize and appreciate old-stock values and don't discard them unless and until better ideas, information or values present themselves in a way that is compelling to heart and mind.
5.  *Fifth Principle: Remain Open to New Experience*
    While recognizing the worth of old-stock ideas and values commit to substituting them with new-stock values whenever superior values and ideas present themselves.

Finally review the case information anew in terms of each of these five principles *looking for the "last-things"* (outcomes, consequences, fruits, products and facts) of value in the case, *identifying the novel*, unique and different in the case (regardless of whether this novelty is generally positive or negative), *determining the quality of the ideas, values and information* contained in the case (adequacy, concreteness, factual, action-oriented, and empowering - ACFA-OE), *identifying your and the stakeholder's old-stock values*, and *comparing them to new-stock values, ideas and information* that may lead to a change of mind or heart for you and/or among the stakeholders in the case.

## Third: Frame and If Necessary Re-Frame the Case Employing an Ecological Metaphor

Now consider how you might frame this particular case – selecting an appropriate environmental metaphor (eco-centric, eco-feminist, eco-justice, bio-centric, conservationist, free-market / libertarian, socialist, anarchistic, preservationist, aesthetic, chaos-theory, utilitarian, globalist etc.). If you fail to find a metaphor that helps frame the case from those suggested above then create one of your own. Within your frame include the dimensions of interiority and exteriority. In so doing, remember that understanding an issue may require reconfiguring it to fit within several frames – each of which suggests different problem formulations, inquiry and outcomes.

## Fourth: Specify the Thematic Perspective on the Problem and Develop a Tentative Conclusion

Adopting a thematic perspective simply entails developing a brief description of only a few words of the particular frame of reference you have chosen to develop the case from within. Be sure to identify emerging elements, forces and possible outcomes suggested by the way the case has been framed.

After having framed the case identity and the theme or themes emerging from it pinpoint key players, stakeholders, and contributing factors. Then describe the forces that define and drive the case's theme and suggest possible options, actions or interventions available to solve or ameliorate the problems associated with the case. In short imagine how these options, actions and interventions might produce different outcomes. Judge what outcomes seem most likely, which should be avoided and what an ideal outcome might look like. As you proceed keep in mind that achieving the desired ends may require reconsidering the five principles of ecopragmatics and applying them anew to the case.

## Fifth: Develop a Strategy for Pursuing a Resolution to the Case Problem

Having worked your way through the imaginating process to tentatively arrive at a set of possible outcomes (perhaps a worst case scenario, a likely outcome and an ideal one) consider how you might go about implementing a strategy to achieve an acceptable outcome that lies somewhere along the continuum between your ideal and likely outcomes. Utilize a "satisficing" approach to develop your strategy (i.e. prioritizing the best possible outcome given circumstances but short of ideal) and develop your plan to insure a balance between individual and community needs consistent with the communitarian ethic to "Respect and uphold society's moral order as you would have society respect and uphold your autonomy to live a full life" (Etzioni, 1996 p. xviii).

## Sixth: Review Your Analysis and Conclusions

Finally upon completing your plan briefly review your work to insure you have completed each portion of the environmental imaginating exercise and assure yourself that in developing your strategic approach you have answered each of the following questions to your satisfaction:

1.  How will you and the stakeholders know whether "old-stock" ideas and values are superior or inferior to the "new-stock" ideas and values presenting themselves in the case study?
2.  How will you and the stakeholders identify bias (theirs and others) and account for it in their deliberations and those of others?
3.  How will you and the stakeholders go about addressing the policy issue at hand within the confines of local communities and regions (i.e. utilizing communitarian approaches)?
4.  How will you and the stakeholders know when they have arrived at an acceptable conclusion to the issue at hand?

Hopefully this brief introduction to the strategic principles of ecopragmatics and deliberative imagining will provide a bit more insight into how the themes of pragmatic inquiry and policymaking will be approached in the book.

## Book Outline

The text to follows is nine chapters in length and developed around a format where theoretical and philosophical ideas are presented in a chapter followed by an illustrative case study in the subsequent chapter.

*Chapter 1: Straight Talk— The Pragmatism of William James*

The chapter – named after the song "Straight Talk" by Dolly Parton – cuts to the heart of pragmatism by calling for simplicity and straightforwardness in thinking as compared to the complexity and needless intricacies of academic thought and philosophies. The chapter begins with the psychological pragmatics of William James (James 1904, 1912), exploring his ideas regarding pragmatism as method versus philosophy and illustrating the extent to which his ideas are grounded in the earlier work of Charles Sanders Pierce (1878). In so doing we present a conceptual framework – a process we call "imaginating" - adapted from James' work providing a practical and useful deliberative template for considering environmental problems and issues. We also discuss the importance of acknowledging that ecopragmatics necessarily involves embracing pluralism in every form (particularly as it applies to competing values, ethics and philosophies that must be engaged rather than ignored, bypassed or defeated). Likewise, the chapter underscores the degree to which values are constantly changing and undergoing transformation – what James refers to as "streams of consciousness." To that end the chapter employs the metaphor of Elton John's "Pinball Wizard" to illustrate how James perceived the internal mental process of "flitting" like a bird from one perspective and value to another as an individual considers new information and experiences and compares this new experiences to "old-stock," "tried and true" values and experiences. Thereafter, James's ideas are compared to those of Dewey, Rorty, and others to discern differences in their orientation to pragmatism. The chapter ends with a more complete presentation of a Jamesian consequentialist approach to environmental philosophy and policy analysis that is contrasted to a Dewey methodology.

*Chapter 2: The L&N Don't Stop Here Anymore—Coal and Craig, Colorado*

Chapter two derives its name from a Jeanie Ritchie song immortalized by Johnny Cash that employs the metaphor of the coal town that has gone bust – a suitable metaphor to describe what is going on in Craig, Colorado. Thanks to the efforts of the Colorado State Assembly coal-fired electric power generation has been outlawed and the economy and culture of this home to Colorado's largest coal-fired generator has been permanently altered. The case of coal and Craig, Colorado provides a scenario imbued with both current and future saliency – the transition away from using coal to power electrical generation and the migration toward natural gas power plants. We introduce the reader to the case of Craig,

Colorado and the impact that discontinuing the use of coal-fired power generation is having upon the municipality and the region. We employ this case study to illustrate how a Jamesian philosophical orientation can be applied to interpret and analyze complex environmental policy issues such as the one confronting Colorado and the nation as electric power generation migrates away from coal and moves toward natural gas and nuclear power.

*Chapter 3: Simplify—Interiority, Exteriority and Necessary Anthropocentrism*

The title for chapter three comes from a tune entitled "Simplify" popularized by John Rich of the country duo *Big & Rich*. The chapter title and the song lyrics are indicative of James's philosophical intent – namely to bring philosophy out of the academy and into the public sphere to aid people in dealing with even the most complex philosophical problems. Simplification of complex issues, however, does not necessarily imply transforming something inherently complex into something simple. Instead it serves as a vehicle for breaking complex issues down into their constituent parts – in a sense "unbundling" complexity. Chapter three approaches this need to "simplify" the complex by focusing upon the concepts of interiority (what people feel, think and believe) and exteriority (what people say and do - actions). In this regard we rely upon Ken Wilber's integral theory (1997) that approaches interiority and exteriority from an individual and collective perspective. We assert that discriminating between interiority and exteriority in policy analysis proves useful to the degree it contributes to an understanding of how individuals and communities collectively externally manifest themselves versus how they express their interiority in terms of values, culture and convention. We elaborate upon Wilber's work from an environmental perspective (Esbjörn-Hargens & Zimmerman, 2009) while asserting that humans will remain "necessarily anthropocentric" in their environmental perspective since they are biologically, psychologically, socially and ecologically constrained to ultimately perceive the world around them in terms of human perceptions, thoughts, values, and culture (Wimberley, 2009).

*Chapter 4: Cool Water—The Floridan Aquifer and Groundwater Resources*

The fourth chapter illustrates the concepts of interiority and exteriority as applied to the case of the depletion of the Floridan Aquifer in North Central Florida (SRWMD, 2011). It employs the metaphor of the public's desire for clean, cool water – employing a lyric from a Marty Robbins song – and its unwillingness to realize that this cool, clear water is not endlessly available. In this instance, the Floridan Aquifer, the principal source of drinking water in Florida, has been steadily diminished for decades by the dramatic growth of the state's population as well as by increased agricultural and industrial use. We will employ this case study to illustrate the process of stakeholder identification in environmental policy analysis and to tentatively explain how the actions of each stakeholder in the state's groundwater dispute (their exteriorities) are informed by their underlying values, biases and philosophies (their interiorities). As in the instance of the Craig, Colorado coal dispute, this groundwater case also illustrates how environmental issues so quickly reach an impasse that by all appearances defies rational resolution. Hopefully throughout the course of this book, the reader will learn approaches that may prove useful in moving beyond issue-Balkanization. None of those skills is more important than learning how to identify and thoroughly empathize with key environmental stakeholders.

### Chapter 5: Stand Inside My Shoes—Framing and Reframing Seemingly Intractable Environmental Issues

Chapter five is devoted to putting environmental issues and stakeholders within novel contexts that lend themselves to problem resolution and the realization of common ground and common cause. Using the metaphor provided by folk music lyricist Bob Dylan, this chapter introduces the reader to a means for overcoming exteriority and by seeking interiority by figuratively "standing in the shoes of another". To this end we utilize the framing approaches of Amos Tversky and Daniel Kahneman (1981; 1986), Donald Schon and Marin Rein (1994), and Siegwart Lindenberg (2001& 2008). These researchers employ an array of metaphorical framework perspectives around which issues and problems may be defined from a variety of perspectives. We also explore the psychological and gestalt foundations of framing as a cognitive and perceptual exercise and additionally consider framing as it has been conceptualized in the fields of economics and management (Simon, 1957). Framing as an analytic approach is tentative and flexible such that policy issues and problems may be framed and reframed as necessary, especially when any given framing metaphor fails to capture the essence of the situation or fails to lend itself to identifying a solution or solutions. Framing serves as the principal contribution to Ecopragmatics – the one most consistent with James's metaphorical approach – to the degree that it allows for participants to identify novel options for problem resolution as well as provide an opportunity for participants to change their minds on seemingly intractable issues where impasse dominates.

### Chapter Six: Gyppo Loggers and Spotted Owls

Chapter six provides yet another case study designed to exemplify how framing a policy issue from the perspective of several stakeholders can provide an opportunity to discover where impasses between competing parties exist and common ground or novel solutions may be forthcoming. The title of this case comes from a famous tune by folksinger Buzz Martin in which he lauds the grit and tenacity of the American logger. We use this title to introduce a case study involving the tension between the need to preserve logging and the timber industry in the Pacific Northwest as a way of life and livelihood while simultaneously protecting old-growth "ancient" forests and their endangered inhabitants – the Northern Spotted Owl.

This case study will look at the decline of the logging industry in the Washington and Oregon and sort out the environmental, regulatory and economic forces that have resulted in a dramatic loss of jobs over the last decade. It will particularly address the role that environmental groups and organizations have played in reducing the volume of logging within this region. This particular case is most useful not only because it addresses a long term issue – namely management of the nation's forest lands while protecting fragile ecosystems and habitats – it also provides a multifaceted issue that can be framed economically, politically, bureaucratically, environmentally, socially and culturally.

*Chapter 7: Let's Work Together—Individual Freedom and Community Need*

Chapter seven explores an approach, known as "communitarianism" that is designed to bring policy disputes as close to the community as possible and to create an environment where to the greatest extent possible policy problems are resolved locally, informally and without recourse to legislative, executive or judicial decisions or actions. The title of the chapter comes from a song by the group Canned Heat and underscores the utter necessity of individuals finding a way to solve mutual problems. This community-centered approach, most notably championed by the late Nobel laureate, Elinor Ostrom (2009), is we think best illustrated again in the work of Amitai Etzioni who articulates "communitarian" approaches to public policy. According to Etzioni:

> Communitarians examine the ways shared conceptions of the good (values) are formed, transmitted, justified, and enforced. Hence their interest in communities (and moral dialogues within them), historically transmitted values and mores, and the societal units that transmit and enforce values such the family, schools, and voluntary associations (social clubs, churches, and so forth), which are all parts of communities.. (2003, p. 224)

Based upon this definition Etzioni believes that to the greatest extent policy issues should be resolved locally and informally whenever possible and that the needs of the individual of necessity must be balanced by the needs of the community. Etzioni's model is grounded in what he refers to as the "new golden rule" which asserts "Respect and uphold society's moral order as you would have society respect and uphold your autonomy to live a full life" (Etzioni, 1997 p. xviii). Etzioni's approach is well grounded in the history of communitarian thought as exemplified by the work of its founder, Alasdair MacIntyre (1988) and is responsive to DeShalit's trans-generational concerns (2004; 1995).

*Chapter 8: Oil and Water—The Green Tea Coalition*

This chapter presents a truly unique case where very disparate interest groups find common cause and to achieve a common goal, though for very different reasons. This chapter is designed to illustrate how a communitarian approach to policy resolution can be achieved at the state and local level by reframing policy issues with an eye toward discovering common concerns, cause and ultimately solutions to what would otherwise be unsolvable problems. In this case the Sierra Club has found common cause with the Georgia Tea Party in the interest of making solar energy more available to consumers while simultaneously allowing consumers to sell excess energy back to the utility company. The Sierra Club finds itself motivated to pursue such goals in the interest of promoting alternative fuels to combat climate change while the Georgia Tea Party champions the development of home-based solar energy to allow consumers to become increasingly energy independent and sell power back to the electrical grid.

*Chapter 9: Going Home: From Olmsted to the Carolina Thread Trail*

In the final chapter of the book we present a case study embodying virtually all of the principles and attributes associated with ecopragmatics and imaginating. The case also illustrates that while many environmental issues and problems resist resolution because of Balkanization of values and attitudes among competing interest groups, there are any number of local and regional examples where collaboration and cooperation contributes to positive community and environmental outcome. The case chosen to conclude this book and illustrate how ecopragmatics can and should work involves efforts in the states of North and South Carolina to create an integrated network of tails and greenways traversing the Charlotte / Mecklenburg County region. This case study is presented in historical context and critiqued in terms of how principles of ecopragmatics and imaginating were unwittingly employed to produce salutary community and environmental outcomes.

## Dewey, Rorty, Minteer, and Other Pragmatic Thinkers

Before proceeding any further, however, we want to acknowledge at the outset the work of our colleague at Arizona State University, Ben Minteer, for his important contributions to the field of environmental philosophy and ethics with his books *The Landscape of Reform* (2009) and *Refounding Environmental Ethics* (2012). We share a concern and frustration with the decidedly undemocratic and misanthropic direction non-anthropocentric environmental ethics has taken over the years. Ben has chosen to create a pragmatic approach to environmental ethics by employing the ideas of John Dewey – particularly in regard to Dewey's ideas about pragmatism and democracy. We will build upon Minteer's work later in the book when we compare and contrast some of Dewey's ideas with those of James and other pragmatist thinkers.

We also owe a debt of gratitude to other philosophers and writers who have articulated a pragmatic approach to environmental issues to include Bryan G. Norton author of *Sustainability: A Philosophy of Adaptive Ecosystem Management* (2005), Andrew Light and Eric Katz authors of *Environmental Pragmatism* (1996), Daniel Farber author of *Eco-Pragmatism* (1999), Sandra B. Rosenthal and Rogene Buchholz authors of *Rethinking Business Ethics* (1999) as well as Kelly Parker (1990) and Keith Hirokawa (2002).

Although we have been influenced by the work of all these writers our particular approach to pragmatism is much more psychological and metaphorical than that used by Minteer and we don't operate within some of the constraints he addressed regarding criticism of his work by J. Baird Callicott (1999). However, we recognize that Dewey's influence on Minteers ideas is particularly important to the degree it emphasizes democratic processes and inclusion. We sincerely hope that the reader will appreciate that communitarianism is in part the means by which our own approach to pragmatism seeks to promote democratic process and value pluralism in addressing pressing environmental problems.

# Chapter 1: Straight Talk—The Pragmatism of William James

"Gimme some straight talk, straight talk -- and hold the sugar please
Straight talk, straight talk -- sounds plenty sweet to me
Don't talk to me in circles in some mumbo-jumbo jive
Gimme just straight talk, straight talk and we're gonna be alright."

*Straight Talk*
By Dolly Parton

## The Problem with Philosophers

Had singer/songwriter Dolly Parton been consulted in the writing of *Ecopragmatics* she would probably have advised us to do everything we could to engage the reader in some "straight talk" regarding the topic at hand, assuming that if we succeed in making that initial connection to our audience then we could reasonably expect the reader or listener to "hang in" and read the entire book. However if we were to lose the reader at the outset, then the chances of them reading beyond the first few sentences would be slight. This insight puts the onus on us to avoid drowning the reader in tedium and boredom either at the outset of the book or anywhere thereafter.

When writing a book involving philosophical discussions the principle challenge facing the author is to not produce a text that is tedious and boring. Typically when people are presented with the prospects of reading philosophical material they immediately expect to be bored and frustrated with the tedium of the writer. These expectations are seldom disappointed. We suspect that part of the problem lies in the very personality of the philosopher. While running the risk of overgeneralizing, we suspect that those who find philosophy interesting all too often exhibit traits and habits that segregate them from the very persons they would like to have read their work. In a nutshell, philosophers more than virtually any other academic group could be characterized as largely a group of "misfits," "weirdos," and perhaps "nerds" who just don't "get" the social and cultural conventions and habits that "normal" people who are not philosophically oriented tend to experience.

Gene Witmer, a philosopher from the University of Florida elegantly presents the case for this perspective noting that:

> It is a familiar observation that philosophers tend to be less than perfectly socialized. For lack of a more diplomatic description, we are, of course, a bunch of weirdos." "But—let's be more precise, if not more diplomatic. What I have in mind is that we—or, at least, a large portion of us—are not so quick to pick up on social cues or expectations. Often, conventions are flouted not out of deliberate rebellion but a kind of cluelessness that takes time and energy to overcome." "This is hardly unique to philosophers; nor is it universally true of them; but it is common enough. (Witmer, 2011, p. 7)

There is benefit in being able to consider the world from a unique or distinct perspective as compared to the worldviews of "most people" – whoever they may be. Such unique perspectives allows the philosopher to experience the world around them in "new ways" but in so doing creates the challenge of communicating this divergent perspective to those grounded in the day-to-day known and "ordinary" world.

We suspect that the problem the philosopher faces is that he or she tends to "over-think" their experiences rather than being able to also consider their surrounding naturally and intuitively as appears to be the case with most "regular" "normal" normal people who are not philosophers. In short the philosopher may be able to think rationally and analytically but may not be able to readily think and communicate intuitively and pragmatically. Philosophers may suffer from the tendency to "over-think" and "over-analyze" the world around them rather than intuitively experiencing the world. Again, Witmer has some interesting insights into this issue observing that:

> What others apparently find perfectly natural or intuitive, the misfit [philosopher] finds foreign, puzzling, alien. How others talk to each other, how they decide what to do next in a group setting, how they know what will strike others as "cool" or whatnot—all of it is rather strange." "Other people seemingly know just how to behave, how to talk, how to interact, but I don't; what is going on? For this sort of misfit, anyway, the social world is often just perplexing. It resists mastery, and this is maddening. (Witmer, 2011, p.7)

Assuming Witmer's observations are correct and accurately characterize many if not most philosophers, then the task of a philosopher who wants to "fit in" and interact with the non-philosophical world of "real people" is to simplify their ideas and couch them within the context of the day-to-day experiences of regular people. In short they must learn how to think and communicate intuitively – the way most "regular" people do – and replace complex and arcane language with "straight talk" along the lines championed by Dolly Parton in her song by the same name.

In writing this book, we have purposefully chosen to communicate our ideas about environmental philosophy and policy with words and ideas that are intuitive and illustrative rather than bury the reader under the weight of arcane terms and concepts derived from the philosopher's inherent need to be exact and literal – which too often translates into tedium and boredom.

The ideas of William James lend themselves admirably to the task we have set out for ourselves which is to communicate to a reading audience how to think about important environmental issues in common-sense, pragmatic ways. We like James' approach because frankly he never fit the mold of the boring, tedious philosopher isolated form the everyday world of real people. He disliked the elitism of the philosophers of his day and equally disliked their arcane and often meaningless gibberish. So he took matters in his own hands and in his speeches to citizens in communities around America as well as in his writing and teaching sought to use metaphor and illustrations to help people intuitively articulate their personal philosophical values. In so doing he replaced arcane "philosophy-speak" with "straight talk." That said we still have the challenge before us of helping the reader understand where James' ideas came from and how they relate to modern environmental problems and issues. So of necessity we must introduce this book on *Ecopragmatics* by explaining pragmatic philosophy in the most straightforward, intuitive and understandable manner possible.

## Consequences and Metaphor

This introductory chapter will stand out as distinct from all the others to follow in that it begins the discussion of ecopragmatics from a decidedly philosophical perspective. The chapters to follow will continue to develop many of the ideas first presented here, but the will increasingly do so within the context of contemporary case studies and examples designed to "flesh out" the otherwise "bare-bones" perspective of the philosopher. Our intent in proceeding in this way is to ground the concepts associated with ecopragmatics in the philosophical work of the pragmatists William James and John Dewey. It will further develop their ideas within the context of more contemporary thinkers such as Herbert Simon, Ken Wilber and Amati Etzioni. However, we will principally focus upon the ideas of William James in the belief that his metaphorical and intuitive approaches to decision making are uniquely suited to addressing environmental problems in our time.

William James' work, unlike that of John Dewey, is unique in terms of his use of metaphor. To date few have been successful in describing James's pragmatism without reverting to the use of metaphor (Mustain, 2006; Perley, 2006; Seigfried, 2006). In this regard we are no exception. The reader will note that throughout the text we have inserted lyrics from popular tunes that metaphorically capture the theme of each chapter. We do so out of a somewhat whimsical desire to honor James' metaphorical approach with a bit of metaphor of our own. For instance, at the outset of this chapter we introduced metaphor into the chapter title employing some lyrics from a famous Dolly Parton tune to underscore the notion that James would undoubtedly have resonated to – namely the need to replace philosophical "mumbo-jumbo" and tedium of traditional philosophical language with "straight talk" and plain language that people can readily understand and relate to. From James's perspective people should be fully capable of "doing" philosophy by considering options for action, comparing these options to internal values, biases, ideas and preferences and then proceeding to act and judge the worth of their ideas and actions in terms of the consequences that flow from this process.

The inspiration underlying James's consequentialism stems from the founder of pragmatism, Charles Sanders Peirce (1878). A mathematician, logician, and philosopher, Peirce was employed as a chemist most of his life. Frustrated by the prevailing rationalist and idealist methods of the 19th century, Peirce saw the need for a new concept of truth reflecting the empirical and social practice of science. How the scientific method is actually practiced – how the academic community self-organizes, interprets, and uses knowledge – were basic philosophical questions Peirce employed in constructing a novel theory of knowledge focusing upon outcomes and their meanings. Peirce's experimental work as a scientist was, therefore, a major experiential source of inspiration behind the term "pragmatism" as elucidated by James, Dewey and others.

For James, meaning is not derived from complex language, ideas and verbiage but from consequences flowing from daily decision-making and action. In a series of lectures conducted in 1898 at the University of California at Berkeley James addressed the centrality of consequences to thought and philosophy. His lectures, later published as "Philosophical Conceptions and Practical Results," asserted the following:

> If there were any part of a thought that made no difference in the thought's practical consequences, then that part would be no proper element of the thought's significance. The effective meaning of any philosophical proposition can always be brought down to some particular consequence in our future practical experience. (James, 1898, p. 328-329)

According to James, thoughts have consequences and it is the consequences of thoughts and ideas that give those thoughts and ideas meaning. Beyond experiencing actual consequences flowing from thoughts and ideas these mental machinations are meaningless. James states his point clearly in *Pragmatism* (1907) when he observes that:

> The pragmatic method is primarily a method of settling metaphysical disputes that otherwise might be interminable. Is the world one or many? – fated or free? – material or spiritual? – here are notions either of which may or may not hold good of the world; and disputes over such notions are unending. The pragmatic method in such cases is to try to interpret each notion by tracing its respective practical consequences. What difference would it practically make to any one if this notion rather than that notion were true? If no practical difference whatever can be traced, then the alternatives mean practically the same thing, and all dispute is idle. Whenever a dispute is serious, we ought to be able to show some practical difference that must follow from one side or the other's being right. (James, 1907, p. 128)

What James is emphasizing in this statement is that ideas produce practical consequences and that for these consequences to be of any value to a person they must answer the question "what difference would it practically make to any one if this notion rather than that notion were true?" The message James is communicating is that for ideas to be consequential they must make a difference in how a person might think or act or how others might react.

Consider if you will the lyrics to a tune by singer and songwriter Jerry Jeff Walker entitled *"The Wheel:"*

> If I took a rollin' wheel
> And rolled it ten times round,
> Would it travel far from here,
> Or would it just go round Round and Round?

Let's assume that the spinner of the wheel places the fingers of their left hand on the top of a wheel standing perpendicular to the ground and with their right hand they spun the wheel similar to the way a coin is spun on a tabletop. Ten times the wheel is spun suggesting that the wheel spins faster and faster. On the tenth spin the holder takes their left hand away from the top of the wheel and allows it to rotate on its own. Assuming the land surround the wheel is flat and level, the wheel is likely to spin around for a few moments and then – as it loses momentum – it should spin more slowly and fall harmlessly to the ground. However, if one assumed that the ground upon which it spun was sloped then releasing the spinning wheel might result in it traveling downhill. If it traveled spinning downhill and no obstacles stood in the way then the consequences of the action would be that you would have to ramble down the hill to retrieve the wheel. However, if the wheel encountered an obstacle, such as spinning on to a busy highway and collided with a vehicle then the consequence of spinning the wheel could be much more serious and costly. So, given James's pragmatic approach, you would have an opportunity to consider all likely outcomes of spinning the wheel prior to taking the initiative to actually do so and you would assess the potential consequences based upon observations (such as the slope of the land and the presence of streets and highways) as well as on the basis of what your stock of knowledge consisted of relative to spinning wheels, coins, etc. In a real way, James's approach allows humans to project anticipated outcomes into the future on the basis of past experience.

James's philosophy is consequentialist in nature, meaning one chooses to frame or contextualize one's principles,

> to effect the end you choose to pursue, the connexion between "choice" and "best" being supposedly such that choosing reflectively means that you choose how to act so as to produce the best consequences. (Anscombe, 1958, p. 9)

As noted before, James's consequentialism was derived from the philosophy of Pierce, particularly from his 1878 article "How to Make Our Ideas Clear." Therein, Peirce articulates what would later become known as the pragmatic maxim:

> Consider what effects, which might conceivably have practical bearings, we conceive the object of our conception to have. Then, our conception

of those effects is the whole of our conception of the object.(Peirce, 1878, p. 132)

What Peirce conveys in this maxim is that many seemingly unsolvable problems arise from confusion, indefiniteness, or misapplication in the use of language. James relied upon this maxim in formulating his interpretation of the pragmatic method. By emphasizing the need for practical consequences, Peirce and James employ the pragmatic method to slice through the context-removed abstractions of intellectual problems. Accordingly, if ideas do not make any difference in our relation to their effects, then the intellectual problem is just an empty thought experiment devoid of consequence in relation to daily experience and contemporary knowledge.

While William James's *Pragmatism* (1907) is regarded as his signature philosophical work, it's worth remembering however that James is also revered as one of the founders of modern psychology – acknowledged by many as the "Father of American Psychology" (Nevid, 2011; Murphy, 2008; Serafin & Bendixen, 2005; Zimmerman & Schunk, 2003; Collins et al., 2000; Scotten, Chinen & Battista, 1996; Fischer, 1994; Bjork, 1983). Indeed, it could be asserted that his pragmatism (which he referred to as principally a method of philosophical inquiry) essentially consisted of the application of his psychological approach to cognition, perception, intention, behavior, and response.

Arguably, William James was first and foremost a psychologist who practiced philosophy rather than a philosopher pure and simple. For James any action was always preceded by reflection upon experience followed by literally visualizing or imagining the action before it occurred, as well as gauging the consequences of that action in terms of potential responses and the meaning of those responses (Kerr, 2008). This process is at the heart of what we will refer to as "imagining" or quite literally cognitively projecting oneself into possible futures based upon past experience, current values and philosophies, and in anticipation of possible outcomes, responses, meanings and implications. This imagining process is, we believe, a reassertion of James's perspective on human cognition, behavior and response.

The importance of this insight can hardly be overstated. The genius of James's psychology is his ability to conceptualize the complex workings of the human psyche and his major contribution is his employment of metaphor as frankly the only means by which the complexity and fluidity of human cognition and action could be adequately explained. In short, we believe he was compelled to rely upon metaphor to communicate his ideas because no better means was available. This is hardly a novel insight. Poets, songwriters, novelists and storytellers have long since appreciated the power of metaphor to convey intricate and complex ideas. In fact, the degree to which empiricist thinkers went out of their way to avoid the use of such tools may in part have contributed to the intellectual stultification and arbitrariness that James felt compelled to rebel against. In essence, for James metaphor was the best possible tool for conveying and understanding complexity and the employment of anything less was simply inadequate and unacceptable.

James's psychology was preoccupied with the importance of consequences. He reiterated this emphasis throughout his landmark book *Principles of Psychology* (1890) observing that,

> Our psychology must therefore take account not only of the conditions antecedent to mental states, but of their results consequences as well. (James, 1890, p. 5)

With these words he contradicts the principle competing psychological approach of the time - "intuitivism" (Lossky, 1928) - with a functionalist approach that principally measures psychological phenomena in terms of consequences. The fact that James' ideas competed with those of Lossky is both historically interesting and of immediate concern to this text.

For Lossky's intuitivism "discloses and overcomes the false premise of the separation between the cognizing subject and the cognized object. Intuitivism with its thesis according to which knowledge is not a copy, a symbol or a manifestation of reality in the cognizing subject, *but reality itself*, life itself" and as such capable of overcoming "the dichotomy of knowing and being" (Slossky, 1924, p. 326). Historically James consequentialist philosophy rendered Lossky's ideas antiquated and incomplete. However, in recent years psychologists have reassessed the role of intuition in how people think and act and have concluded that in fact people approach problems and obstacles intuitively, reacting to how they perceive the external world as "a reality itself" and thereafter utilize reason to explain, justify and cajole others to their point of view (Haidt, 2013, 2006). More on this research will be discussed later in the text. For the present, however, what this suggests is that whereas in the era of James one philosophical idea tended to crowd out others in popularity, today we can embrace both philosophical approaches in terms of what they contribute to our understanding of decision making – which as psychological research has demonstrated is both rationally consequentialist and intuitive in form.

Yet in our time the ideas of James are widely studied and incorporated into any number of disciplines to include education, philosophy, psychology, political science and more while Lossky's work has been largely forgotten. Consequentialist oriented pragmatism has proved to be a durable idea that among other accomplishments has served to pave the way for the eventual emergence of behavioral psychology.

James's consequentialist psychology occurs within a pluralistic life experience where,

> the sundry parts of reality *may be externally related*. Everything you can think of, however vast or inclusive, has on the pluralistic view a genuinely "external" environment of some sort or amount. Things are "with" one another in many ways, but nothing includes everything, or dominates over everything. The word "and" trails along after every sentence. Something always escapes. "Ever not quite" has to be said of the best attempts made anywhere in the universe at attaining all-inclusiveness. The pluralistic world is thus more like a federal republic than like an empire or a kingdom. However much may be collected,

however much may report itself as present at any effective centre of consciousness or action, something else is self-governed and absent and unreduced to unity. (James 1909, p. 321-322)

The implication derived from this worldview is that all experiences are tentative, intertwined and contingent upon the consequences of each experience serially realized. What results is a tension between what is known, perceived, felt, valued and what is outwardly experienced – a tension between interiority and exteriority. This tension is resolved by constantly organizing and reorganizing what would otherwise be chaotic experience, filtering experience through a prism of internalized knowledge and beliefs to create order out of disarray. Even so, order often eludes even the best efforts to make sense of experience and regularly chaos rules. Yet, as James contends, people are nevertheless driven to interpret the seemingly senseless and will persist in doing so until at least some tentative resolution or conclusion is derived. In those moments, relief can be sweet and as James observes,

> our pleasure at finding that a chaos of facts is the expression of a single underlying fact is like the relief of the musician at resolving a confused mass of sound into melodic or harmonic order. (James 1879, p. 318)

People naturally find themselves drawn to the passion for distinguishing the particulars from the whole in all their individual completeness. They employ theories and hypotheses as tools to wrestle unity from disunity and from this struggle emerge with an assuredness that some might equate with faith, which in James's case implies a psychological faith in the empirical verifiability of our own beliefs or ideas. There is a sentiment of trust in the relative frame by which people tentatively intertwine experiences upon rational means and ends.

Ultimately the intent of James's philosophical method is the pursuit of truth that he refers to as a process rather than a mere outcome or artifact. Accordingly,

> The truth of an idea is not a stagnant property inherent in it. Truth happens to an idea. It becomes true, is made true by events. Its verity *is* in fact an event, a process, the process namely of its verifying itself, its verification. Its validity is the process of its validation. (James, 1908, p. 5)

Therefore, if truth can only be known via the process of discovering it then truth by nature is a dynamic entity that can never truly be transformed into a "thing" frozen in time or space. Instead it is constantly undergoing transformation and change and is only discernible to the knower through the process of pursuing it.

James's ideas presage the advent of chaos theory by acknowledging the essential fluidity and disunity of experience even as the psychological self seeks to create at least a preliminary and tentative unity and order. Accordingly,

> nothing real is absolutely simple, that every smallest bit of experience is a *multum in parvo* plurally related, that each relation is one aspect, character, or function, way of its being taken, or way of its taking

> something else; and that a bit of reality when actively engaged in one of these relations is not *by that very fact* engaged in all the other relations simultaneously. (James, 1911, p. 322)

In James's psychological approach to philosophical thought pluralistic experience becomes the mediating process from which truth ultimately emerges. James conceives of a theory of radical empiricism where experience is both subjective and objective all rolled into one. His unwillingness to categorize experience in either-or terms as subjective versus objective can prove frustrating to the mind looking for neat distinctions. However, his amalgamative approach to consciousness and content serves to explain his understanding of psychological perception and thought.

Accordingly James asserts that "consciousness" (subjectivity) and "content" (objectivity) cannot be narrowly characterized in terms of their heterogeneity as much as they can be conceived in unity and relationship to one another. James elucidates on this idea when he observes that,

> Experience, … and the separation of it into consciousness and content comes not by way of subtraction, but by way of addition-the addition, to a given concrete piece of it, of other sets of experiences, in connection with which severally its use or function may be of two different kinds. (James, 1912, p. 4)

As if realizing that this theoretical explanation of the relationship between consciousness and content may yet still be inadequate, James resorts to his favorite explanatory tool – metaphor – which in this case he presents as paint on a canvas.

> In a pot in a paint-shop, along with other paints, it serves in its entirety as so much saleable matter. Spread on a canvas, with other paints around it, it represents, on the contrary, a feature in a picture and performs a spiritual function. Just so, we maintain, does a given undivided portion of experience, taken in one context of associates, play the part of a knower, of a state of mind, of 'consciousness'; while in a different context the same undivided bit of experience plays the part of a thing known, of an objective 'content.' In a word, in one group it figures as a thought, in another group as a thing. And, since it can figure in both groups simultaneously we have every right to speak of it as subjective and objective, both at once. (James, 1912, p.4-5)

Viewed from this perspective dualism is both "preserved" *and* "reinterpreted"

> so that, instead of being mysterious and elusive, it becomes verifiable and concrete. It is an affair of relations, it falls outside, not inside, the single experience considered, and can always be particularized and defined. (James, 1912, p.5)

In more contemporary language, what James is referring to here is perception, understanding and consequences derived through experience – so-called "pure experience" a concept he initially introduced to readers in "Does Consciousness Exist? " (James, 1904). Therein he explains that the "instant field of the present is always experience in its 'pure' state" by which he meant "plain unqualified actuality, a simple *that*, as yet undifferentiated into thing and thought, and only virtually classifiable as objective fact or as some one's opinion about fact" (James, 1904, p.485). Such, pure experience is not a static phenomenon but is instead dynamic – a virtual stream of consciousness where,

> transitions and arrivals (or terminations) are the only events that happen, though they happen by so many sorts of path. The only experience that one experience can perform is to lead into another experience; and the only fulfillment we can speak of is the reaching of a certain experienced end. When one experience leads to (or can lead to) the same end as another, they agree in function. But the whole system of experiences as they are immediately given presents itself as a quasi-chaos through which one can pass out of an initial term in many directions and yet end in the same terminus, moving from next to next by a great many possible paths. (James, 1907, p. 30)

These are the words James used alluding to streams of consciousness in 1907. However, he first employed the stream metaphor in 1892 along whose tributaries a bird might traverse by way of a series of "flights" and "perching." Accordingly,

> resting-places are usually occupied by sensorial imaginations of some sort, whose peculiarity is that they can be held before the mind for an indefinite time, and contemplated without changing" and places of flight are filled with thoughts of relations, static or dynamic, that for the most part obtain between the matters contemplated in the periods of comparative rest. (James, 1892, p. 27).

Employing the metaphor of a bird working its way along a stream, James differentiates between the "resting places" (substantive parts of streams of thought) and the "places of flight" (transitive parts of such streams) and concludes that,

> our thinking tends at all times towards some other substantive part than the one from which it has just been dislodged. And we may say that the main use of the transitive parts is to lead us from one substantive conclusion to another. (James, 1892, p. 27)

### The Pinball Wizard Metaphor and Streams of Consciousness

As we observed when beginning this chapter, and as we have subsequently demonstrated, James principally employs metaphor to illustrate his ideas. Now we would like to illustrate "streams of consciousness" via the more contemporary metaphor of Pete Townshend's tune "*Pinball Wizard.*" For our purposes, consider the following verses: (Townshend, 1969).

> He stands like a statue,
> Becomes part of the machine.
> Feeling all the bumpers
> Always playing clean.
> plays by intuition,
> The digit counters fall
> That deaf, dumb and blind kid
> Sure plays a mean pinball!"

> "Ain't got no distractions
> Can't hear no buzzers and bells,
> Don't see no lights a flashin'
> Plays by sense of smell.
> Always gets the replay,
> Never seen him fall,
> That deaf, dumb and blind kid
> Sure plays a mean pinball."

> "Even on my favorite table
> He can beat my best.
> His disciples lead him in
> And he just does the rest.
> He's got crazy flipper fingers
> Never seen him fall.
> That deaf, dumb and blind kid
> Sure plays a mean pinball!

The storyline here is improbable but useful. A deaf, dumb and blind kid masters the pinball machine seemingly kinetically and intuitively. He begins by pulling back the long plunger that propels the silver ball down a narrow chute and into the heart of the machine where it will rattle, roll, bounce and spin across countless lights, collide with all variety of bumpers and under the sure hand of the *Pinball Wizard* be propelled repeatedly, again and again throughout the obstacle course inside the machine and in so doing rack up an every growing tally on the scoreboard. In this analogy the ball is consciousness and its movement throughout the internal maze of the pinball machine is James's stream of consciousness. Moving along through the machine, at the mercy of the *Pinball Wizard* who blindly propels the ball (perhaps kinetically and by way of sound) into one unseen obstacle after another. In so doing the ball alternately perches for a moment after colliding with a barrier or upon momentarily losing it momentum (in James' jargon, realizing a substantive moment of reflection and comparison and contemplation), only to be followed by "places of flight" where the ball moves in all directions at any number of speeds (again in James' nomenclature, transitive states where thoughts are directed toward the next substantive destination – one different from the last). Each pinball match begins with the release of the plunger and ends with the ball eventually coming to a complete rest in the ball slot, only to be reenergized and reintroduced again into a new match unique from the match that preceded it as well as to the ones that will subsequently occur.

This, we think, is a fitting analogy to describe what James conceptualizes when he talks about conscious experience. Human beings are constantly being exposed to external events and influences that enter their minds through all the senses. These externalities strike us with varying degrees of force and velocity – some being perceived as gradual and gentle and others perceived as violent, sudden and volatile. The moment these external events, forces, ideas and the like collide with our senses they are transformed into conscious experiences that rattle around within us, much like the pinball does, colliding with one idea, belief, emotion, memory, sensation etc. after another and – depending upon the nature of the obstacle they collide with – are propelled at varying velocities and angles into yet other structures within our psyches until at length their energy is dissipated. Moment to moment living, consequently, is an ongoing chain of pinball matches, each different from the last and unique from the next. However, as with the *Pinball Wizard*, with each match our experience in playing the game matures as we continually "perch" - reflect upon our performance in the game as if it were a "thing" – and "fly" - incorporating what we learned from the last match into the manner in which we propel the ball through the next match and every match thereafter. Ultimately, the *Pinball Wizard* concludes the game, and measures his successfulness not only against the consequences of his efforts – the pinball score – but additionally considers the consequences of his effort that day against past performances and anticipated future consequences.

## Truth through Consequences

According to James, "the true is the name of whatever proves itself to be good in the way of belief, and good, too, for definite assignable reasons" (James, 1907, p. 42). For James, truth is ultimately realized in consequences, suggesting that for him truth is fully consequential. Grounded as it is in a psychological functionalism where the veracity or truthfulness of ideas and propositions is reflected in consequential relationships James defines truth pragmatically as a relation capable of being experienced, described and named. Accordingly he claims that it is,

> The relation to its object that makes an idea true in any given instance, is, we say, embodied in intermediate details of reality which lead towards the object, which vary in every instance, and which in every instance can be concretely traced. The chain of workings which an opinion sets up IS the opinion's truth, falsehood, or irrelevancy, as the case may be. Every idea that a man has works some consequences in him, in the shape either of bodily actions or of other ideas. Through these consequences the man's relations to surrounding realities are modified. He is carried nearer to some of them and farther from others, and gets now the feeling that the idea has worked satisfactorily, now that it has not. The idea has put him into touch with something that fulfills its intent, or it has not. (James, 1911, p. 235)

In so addressing the issue of truth, James parts-company from philosophical absolutists of his time who regarded truth in normative terms possessing a legitimacy and authority independent of the consideration or action of individuals. Instead he spoke in strikingly psychological terms asserting

> Every idea that a man has works some consequences in him, in the shape either of bodily actions or of other ideas. (James 1911, p. 112)

So conceived James not only defines truth in terms of the consequences of ideas and values, but additionally implies physiological, behavioral and ideational change and transformation along the lines just discussed relative to conscious experience.

Accordingly the process by which truth is realized is brokered by what James refers to as "intermediate details of reality which lead towards the object" (James, 1911, p. 235). This "intermediate" reality has in more recent years been redefined as the "subtle dimension" to include spiritual dimensions, as well as emotional, mental and spiritual consciousness. Ken Wilber addressed this "intermediate" reality in his work on integral theory – something he refers to as the "subtle energies" of soul and spirit (Wilber, 2010). The subtle energies also refer to ideas and practices associated with a number of Eastern religious traditions and include such things as "vital forces," the energetic dynamics of human relationships, the energies of the earth, and planetary influences (Collinge, 1998).

However, when James refers to "intermediate details" he is referring to cognitive and behavioral characteristics associated with his functionalist psychological approach to include elements of perception, volition, emotion, and thought that was first presented in *Principles of Psychology* (James, 1890, p. 947) and later eluded to in *The Meaning of Truth* (James, 1911, p. 224). In fact, we think he most directly identifies these "intermediary details" when he observes that:

> The whole concrete course of an individual's thinking life is explicable by the cooperation of his interests and impulses, his sensational experiences, his associations, and his voluntary acts of choice. (James, 1900, p. 1484)

These are the mediating influences between experience and the consequences of those experiences from which James derives meaning. We use the term *mediating* rather than James's "intermediary" term because mediating reflects the degree to which experience is actively shaped, formed, and transformed by interests, impulses, associations and sensation experiences. In this regard, we think the term better captures the spirit of James's vision of what happens during the period of intermediacy.

A later neo-pragmatist, Hilary Putnam, also resonates to James's perspective on truth by arguing that it is counterproductive to assert that there is no normative sense of truth to which human beings relate. Putnam argues that, unlike the comparatively relativistic pragmatist Richard Rorty, "it doesn't follow that language and thought do not describe something outside themselves, even if that something can only be described by describing it (that is by employing language and thought)." Putnam also *argues* that normative values and beliefs play "an essential role *within* language and thought themselves and, more importantly, within our lives" (Putnam, 1995, p. 297).

Returning to the *Pinball Wizard* analogy, these intermediary or mediating influences are the figurative bumpers against which the pinball (consciousness) bounces setting of buzzers, whistles, bells and lights. Our consciousness is constantly being ricocheted against one influence or another and at each moment our consciousness crystalizes for at least a moment and we are able to perceive that conscious moment as a thing (idea, concept, insight, intuition etc.) that is tentatively held in place until the next experience comes along that will cause us to reframe and re-conceptualize our fount of knowledge to that point. In other words, while consciousness flows like a stream it also forms eddies and laps at the shoreline as it moves along and all of these influences impact the fluidity, rate and outcome of the stream of consciousness. Since values are constantly in the process of being shaped and reshaped by conscious experience, it is virtually impossible for a pragmatic approach to philosophy to produce absolute values and outcomes since values are constantly being subjected to the "truth-test" of experience. In rejecting value absolutism James has sometimes been erroneously accused of being a relativist – one who views all truth as contingent upon the values and consensus of any given period of time (Firebraugh, 1953).

Pragmatic methods can be employed to analyze psychological attitudes that characterize any given truth as being arbitrary or absolute in value. James acknowledges that individuals may regard any number truths to be absolute and normative upon their lives and behavior. However, since pragmatism for James is principally a method rather than a philosophy per se, he reinterprets truth as that which individuals consider in terms of the practical consequences such values have upon their lives and are free to incorporate those "truths" which functionally serve their living while rejecting truths that fail to contribute in a practical way to their way of life. Consequently truth which some have called "activated truth" can be perceived as "useful because it is "true" (cognitively) or it is true (pragmatically) because it is useful" (Thayer, 1975, p.xxix; James, 1911).

## Pragmatism, Utilitarianism, and Relativism

James's pragmatic method has also been criticized as being nothing more than preference utilitarianism that seeks to maximize satisfaction (Bromley, 2004). Robert Richardson in part concurs claiming "utilitarianism was stepfather to pragmatism with its concern with results, with "fruits not roots" (Richardson, 2006, p. 158). To the degree that individuals may, to use the hallway analogy employed by James in *Pragmatism* (1907), periodically open doors in the hallway and discover utilitarian options at their disposal, they may indeed in specific instances choose to act in utilitarian ways. However, depending upon circumstances and those mediating or intermediary influences that individuals embody within themselves, they may also choose at any given time to embrace deontological values, situational ethics, religious piety or any number of alternative philosophical approaches depending upon the degree to which doing so helps them makes sense of the world and their rightful or functional place within it. As James observed these philosophical alternatives serve as theoretical perspectives on the world and as such,

> theories become instruments, not answers to enigmas, in which we can rest. We don't lie back upon them, we move forward, and, on occasion, make nature over again by their aid. Pragmatism unstiffens all our theories, limbers them up and sets each one at work. Being nothing essentially new, it harmonizes with many ancient philosophic tendencies. It agrees with nominalism for instance, in always appealing to particulars; with utilitarianism in emphasizing practical aspects; with positivism in its disdain for verbal solutions, useless questions and metaphysical abstraction. (James, 1907, p. 30)

Based upon this assertion James finds himself in agreement with his fellow pragmatist of the era – John Dewey – who would have also affirmed the instrumentality of the pragmatic method (Dewey, 1907).

Others have associated pragmatism with relativism (Thayer-Bacon, 2002). While it is understandable how such a conclusion might be drawn for any particular decision or action arrived at in a pragmatic fashion, James interpretation of how "absolute" values can be incorporated into a pragmatic model does much to dispel concern in this regard. James asserts that

> All philosophies are hypotheses, to which all our faculties, emotional as well as logical, help us, and the truest of which will at the final integration of things be found in possession of the men whose faculties on the whole had the best divining power. (James, 1884, p. 286)

With these words James reassures those committed to lofty and shared values and beliefs that the "truest" of our philosophies will be retained by discerning people because they are experientially persuaded by their value and worth. This discernment process also applies to absolute values such as religious values but the process of discernment is required - applying the claims of absolute values to human purposes and experiences. In this regard, James suggests that when

> theological ideas prove to have a value for concrete life, they will be true for pragmatism in the sense of being good for so much. For how much more they are true will depend entirely on their relations to the other truths that also have to be acknowledged. (James, 1907, p. 29).

Truth for James is consequential and contextual since the meaning of truth depends on its perspective relative to the person experiencing it. Accordingly James counsels tolerance toward those who cling to "absolute truth" regardless of whether truth is embodied in a religious faith or a philosophy. James asserts that a belief in absolutes (for instance God) is an experience that can literally make a positive difference in a person's life thereby creating what James calls "cash value" or tangible worth. For James a belief in "absolutes" could be construed as a true experience for an individual if they have derived value from the belief. James recognized that the association of absolute values and experienced tangible benefit of worth or value could prove controversial in some circles such as among religious institutions – prompting him to make the following observation:

> I am well aware how odd it must seem to some of you to hear me say that an idea is 'true' so long as to believe it is profitable to our lives. That it is good for as much as it profits you [I] will gladly admit. If what we do by its aid is good, you will allow the idea itself to be good in so far forth, for we are the better for possessing it. (James, 1907, p. 30)

James also counsels tolerance and forgoing the need to challenge every claim to truth – even absolute truth. The rationale behind this, beyond an appreciation for the pluralistic values of people and the usefulness of religion and belief in absolutes is his conviction that "the true is the name of whatever proves itself to be good in the way of belief, and good, too, for definite assignable reasons" – such as tolerance (James, 1907, p. 30).

James goes out of his way to accommodate absolute values within a system that only imbues values with worth on the basis of their consequences. In this regard, if the consequences of so-called absolute values are positive, then their worth has been demonstrated. However, in doing so James runs the risk of having his ideas trivialized as contextually driven philosophical relativism that ultimately renders all values contingent to circumstances, consequences and outcomes.

Such a relativist assumption, however, ignores one of the guiding principles undergirding pragmatism as proffered by Peirce, James and Dewey – namely fallibilism - the propensity among humans to be wrong about their beliefs and actions (Margolis, 1998). These early pragmatists – as is the case with contemporary pragmatists such as Rorty (1982), Putnam (1995) and Fish (1980) – all recognize the imperfection of knowledge and the capacity of human beings to draw the wrong conclusions and make choices at odds with available knowledge and values. Likewise they recognize the fallibility of knowledge itself. Given this perspective all decisions and all actions are contingent – even when the best effort is made to exclude all bias and incorporate all pertinent information – and in this regard all actions are contingent upon the available information and the context within which the information was disseminated and received. These are the exterior characteristics of decision-making.

Equally important are the interior intermediary and mediating values and constructs that also serve to shape perceptions and thereby actions and consequences. Fallibility is also contingent upon psychological and emotional characteristics interior to the decision-maker and actor that can render ideas and actions contingent and "relativist." Such contingency appears to be endemic to the human experience. Thus, without exception, fallibilism qualifies the degree to which anyone can realize "absolute certainty" in any intellectual endeavor and necessarily introduces a degree of contingency or relativism into even the most well considered deliberation or action.

The inverse is similarly true. As a student of James at Harvard University, the conceptual pragmatist Clarence Irving Lewis was keenly aware of these relativist criticisms against pragmatism. Lewis observed in addressing this relativist charge that,

> There is no contradiction between the relativity of knowledge and the independence of its object. If the real object can be known at all, it can be known only in relation to a mind; and if the mind were different the nature of the object as known might well be different. Nevertheless the description of the object as known is true description of an independent reality. (Lewis, 1929, p. 154-155)

Accordingly, experience is constructed by thought from the data of sense (1929, p. 29), and it was upon this foundation that the sociologists Peter Berger and Thomas Luckman would later create their influential thesis *The Social Construction of Reality* (1966) that persuaded generations of social scientists since to recognize the unique nature of human perception grounded within the environmental contexts within which individuals experience reality. We will build upon this perspective later in the book by using a framing approach to public policy that necessitates understanding the worldview of individual environmental stakeholders by attempting to perceive the world from their individual vantage points.

## Comparing the Explicit Method of Dewey with the Metaphorical Method of James

The rationale behind William James's approach to philosophy can be summed up in a single sentence:

> The whole function of philosophy ought to be to find out what definite difference it will make to you and me, at definite instants of our life, if this world-formula or that world-formula be the true one (James, 1907, p. 20).

In a real sense, James's method involves the ongoing process of determining the value or worth of one "world-formula" after another. He proffers a stream of consciousness model to describe this continuous valuing effort preferring to conceptualize his ideas in metaphorical terms that we suspect he employed in his lectures and writing to engage and find common cause with his listening and reading audience. James's intuitive and metaphorical approach to pragmatism stands in stark contrast to the comparatively rigorous reasoned and structured methodology of John Dewey. Dewey's philosophy is principally socially oriented concerned with human experience in problem solving. By comparison, James introspectively focuses upon the inner experiences of people, particularly "the quiet domain, the relatively non-social, non-directed, and pre-descriptive aspects of sensory perception" (Stephens, 2009, p. 233). Moreover, he introduces an approach to empiricism based upon streams of consciousness "that seeks to undermine the divisions of subject and object, fact and value, mind and body" (Stephens, 2012, p. 31).

Dewey and James are the names most closely associated with American pragmatism. Philosopher Ben Minteer incorporated Dewey's approach to pragmatism into his environmental ethics even as we have incorporated the ideas of William James (Minteer, 2009; 2012). Dewey in *Logic: The Theory of Inquiry*

(1938) provides a six-step method of inquiry grounded in the scientific method that begins with *(1)* quandary and uncertainty (an indeterminate situation) proceeds to *(2)* address the quandary by subjecting it to systematic inquiry (institution of a problem or problem definition) which *(3)* ideally produces a problem statement suggestive of a solution (the determination of a problem solution) by means of *(4)* the application of reason (reasoning) involving *(5)* an analysis of pertinent facts and information to gauge their meaning (operational characteristics) to *(6)* ultimately produce conclusions that are compared to what is scientifically know as well as compared to so-called common sense (common sense and scientific inquiry) (Dewey, 1938, p. 101-119).

In Dewey's methodology knowledge is the natural byproduct of human experience rather than some *a priori* entity standing beyond the process of experiencing and knowing. He conceives of knowledge instrumentally - referring to the usefulness or functionality of knowledge for the production of more knowledge or other consequences human beings would value. Dewey conceived of this process as involving a reflective intelligence in which knowledge and experience are employed as tools to fulfill human needs and desires contingent to the setting within which experience occurs (Dewey, 1916).

In this regard Dewey's philosophical foundations begin with the concept of "instrumentalism" (denoting the functionality or usefulness of an idea, object or experience) that he conceptualizes in the following terms:

> A thing is more significantly what it makes possible than what it immediately is. The very conception of cognitive meaning, intellectual significance, is that things in their immediacy are subordinated to what they portend and give evidence of." ... "[A] thing is not taken immediately but is referred to something that may come in consequence of it. Intellectual meanings may be appropriated, enjoyed and appreciated; but the character of the intellectual meaning is instrumental. Fortunate for us is it that tools and their using can be directly enjoyed; otherwise all work would be drudgery. But this additive fact does not alter the definition of a tool; it remains a thing used as agency for some concluding event. (Dewey, 1904, p. 105)

Dewey's use of the word "thing" can be applied to both objective and subjective phenomenon such that for instance a wooden rail may be considered in terms of its function as either a part of a split-rail fence or, when used to dislodge a stone, as a lever. Similarly an idea, such as the notion of beauty could be construed as the end-state of an activity (a consequence) or as a tool or standard by which varieties of beauty could be judged and chosen. Regardless of how the tool is employed, Dewey asserts that it is the consequence of the use of a tool that gives the thing meaning rather than the "thing-like" nature of the tool itself. Meaning – that which is derived, "appropriated, enjoyed, and appreciated" – is itself instrumental and resides as a subjective experience that can be employed in an instrumental fashion (as agency) for yet another concluding or consequential event.

This is Dewey's philosophy of instrumentalism that can be metaphorically recognized in terms familiar to James as a stream, chain or thread of reflective thought:

> the successive portions of the reflective thought grow out of one another and support one another; they do not come and go in a medley. Each phase is a step from something to something – technically speaking; it is a term of thought. Each term leaves a deposit which is utilized in the next term. The stream or flow becomes a train, chain, or thread. (Dewey, 1910, p.2)

Taken as a whole – and setting aside for the moment Dewey's empirical method – the pragmatism of James and Dewey is instrumentalist and consequentialist since in both formulations meaning is derived from consequences and in turn becomes instrumental to the realization of yet other consequences which create additional new meaning and provide new tools for understanding and action.

Where the two approaches differ is in terms of the interiority of their methods. Dewey's model, while psychological to a degree, is principally concerned with "reflection" as a "consecutive ordering in such a way that each [idea] determines the next as its proper outcome, while each leans back on its predecessor" (Dewey, 1910, p. 2). James, on the other hand, is concerned with the ongoing perceptive gestalt of human identity and interaction with the world, (i.e. awareness of the essence, form and relationships among the elements of unfolding reality) and characterizes "the continuous identity of each personal consciousness as a name for the practical fact that new experiences come which look back on the old ones" ... "and greet and appropriate them as 'mine'" (James, 1912, p. 129). Admittedly, James approach to streams of consciousness also allows for reflection such as when the metaphorical bird "perches" on a branch for a moment along the course of the stream of consciousness to consider the world as if it were in a freeze-frame mode. That said, the gestalt of James approach is not so much involved with the moments of reflection as much as it is the continuous process and context within which the metaphorical bird is "perching" then "flying," where the bird chooses to perch and fly and the product that flows from this continuous process of considering, interpreting and pursuing consequences anew and again (James, 1892).

While Dewey was an admirer of James work, their methodologies differed in at least one other substantive fashion. For James, pragmatism was rather simply summed up as acquiring "[t]he attitude of looking away from first things, principles, 'categories,' supposed necessities; and of looking towards last things, fruits, consequences, facts" (James, 1907, p. 54-55). By comparison Dewey's pragmatism is more involved, methodological and structured. For instance in considering the consequences of scientific inquiry Dewey asserted that:

> Scientific distinctions are not meaningful by reference to something essential or 'real' in a world beyond our experience; rather, their meaning can only be determined by relating them to specific situations, histories, and future experimental and practical consequences. (Dewey, 1934, p. 18)

For Dewey pragmatism is personally experienced "In this world -- our *life* -- we confront obstacles, formulate problems, devise solutions, and act experimentally" and scientific inquiry aids human beings in acting "experimentally" by "explaining the natural roots of inquiry, and then by detailing how inquiry can work ... to make life better" (Dewey, 1934, p. 61). Both Dewey and James are consequentialist in orientation since for both thinkers meaning flows from consequences. Likewise both rely upon lived experience to produce meaning and learning. However, Dewey's pragmatism could be rightly characterized as instrumental and experimental in nature whereas James was more intuitive and metaphorical in his approach.

## Imaginating Cash-value: Deciphering the Jamesian Metaphorical Method

The unifying metaphor of James' pragmatism — i.e. the degree to which a person's beliefs can be analyzed or the reasons for a decision measured — is grounded in the notion that any experiential truth necessarily has "cash-value." James first employed the term "cash-value" in *Philosophical Conceptions and Practical Results* (1898) and reiterated the concept in *Pragmatism* (1907) with the intent of demonstrating how common substances or concepts could be narrowly construed in terms of their inherent value in the life experiences of individuals. For James, the cash-value of a concept or idea reflects its "experiential worth," recognizing that the value would be highly variable from one circumstance to another or from the perspective of different individuals.

This metaphorical reference to the monetary value of an entity allows James to speak to the true value of the consequences of ideas and actions but does so without committing him to any particular stringent methodology such as that which Dewey employs. However, the negative connotations arising from this metaphor can be problematic and require deciphering. It is critical to avoid the temptation of relegating pragmatism off as an intellectual expression of American capitalism. On the contrary, the power of the metaphor elucidates the cross-cultural universality transcending political, religious, or personal belief systems.

The commerce of cash - values reflects the universal psychological need to establish comparative worth in satisfying human needs and guiding human actions and choices. Trade and the exchange of goods or services are fundamental to all human societies, and in a general sense the commerce of ideas grants each stakeholder both a psychological and sociological vehicle for measuring evolving value across individuals and institutions. In *Pragmatism* James employed the metaphor "cash-value" to refer to the actual experiences of individuals and the worth they associate with those experiences.

James' usage of the term "cash-value" is designed to serve several purposes. For instance, the concept of an idea having cash-value structures worth in material terms. Value is not rationally abstracted from life but drawn from it and employed to comparatively value the ever-changing practical consequences of behavior by prescribing worth to choices and ideas. Likewise, the values assigned say as much or more about the nature of the values and experiences of the evaluator as it does about the inherent value of the idea, experience or thing itself. For instance, if someone is willing to pay three times more for a parcel of land than another person, nothing has changed concerning the objective worth of the land. What varies across prospective buyers is the individual perspective of the buyer as determined by their motivations, experiences and the stock of ideas driving the prospective buyer's choices. Finally, the concept of cash-value belies the relational character of conceptual worth. Value is not intrinsic to the thing-itself as some innate quality of an object but is measured against other ideas, experiences, values and objects. Through the give and take of this valuation process, the cash-value of ideas serves as a "rough and ready" heuristic metaphor for experienced worth (Gotkin, 1985).

## Policy Analytic Frameworks: James and Dewey

Since Dewey presents an empirical format for considering environmental issues that James does not provide, it could be argued that a Dewey approach to environmental ethics is easier to articulate given the six-step structure he provides. James, on the other hand, presents his ideas principally by way of metaphor and analogy requiring the development of a framework embodying his pragmatic values in the interest of introducing pragmatism into the rigor of policy analysis or decision-making.

We provide a six-step approach to deliberative pragmatic policy analysis and decision-making based upon the ideas of William James in the introduction to this book. We use the term "deliberative" to distinguish between the systematic policy analytic approach of imagining that we provide for policymakers and analysts versus the comparatively automatic and intuitive approach to imagining that is almost unconsciously employed by virtually everyone as they move from past, through present and into future experiences. More will be said of this form of imagining later in the text.

Briefly, here is a recap of a deliberative approach to imagining:

1.  *Carefully Consider the Case:* Consider the case's interiority and exteriority (based upon the ideas of Ken Wilber), tentatively define the problem, clarify issues, identify stakeholders, perspectives, note key process, opportunities, biases, compare new-stock and old-stock ideas, in preparation for framing.

2.  *Reconsider the Five Attitudinal Principles of Ecopragmatics Derived From James:*
    i.    *Be Outcome Oriented*
    ii.   *Be Mindful*
    iii.  *Be Discriminating*
    iv.   *Be Grounded in Past Experiences*
    v.    *Be Open to New Experiences*

3.  *Metaphorically Frame and If Necessary Re-Frame the Case:* Frame and reframe case – to include interior and exterior dimensions -in metaphorical terms that serves to help explain the case and suggest solutions to problems.

4.  *Specify the Thematic Perspective on the Problem and Develop Tentative Conclusions:* Adopting a theme involves assigning a descriptor to the particular frame of reference you have selected. In

selecting the theme make a point of identifying emerging elements, forces and possible outcomes suggested by the way the case has been framed. Consider reframing where necessary. Empathetically put yourself in the position of each stakeholder and consider the range of conclusions they might consider (or not) and project the worst, likely and ideal outcomes on the basis of your analysis.

5. ***Develop a Strategy for Pursuing a Resolution to the Case Problem:*** Identify an achievable and acceptable outcome supported by your analysis and develop a *satisficing* strategy of realizing this outcome in a fashion consistent with broad citizen participation and investment.

6. ***Review Your Analysis and Conclusion****s*: Review your efforts to insure that that all six steps have been addressed and answer the following questions:

    a. How will you and the stakeholders know whether "old-stock" ideas and values are superior or inferior to the "new-stock" ideas and values presenting themselves in the case study?

    b. How will you and the stakeholders identify bias (theirs and others) and account for it in their deliberations and those of others?

    c. How will you and the stakeholders go about addressing the policy issue at hand within the confines of local communities and regions (i.e. utilizing communitarian approaches)?

    d. How will you and the stakeholders know when they have arrived at an acceptable conclusion to the issue at hand?

In formulating this six-step methodology, we must emphasize that the paradigm is principally *derived* from James's works and is not a literal methodology attributable to him as is the case with Dewey's empirical methodology. Table 1 compares the two approaches. The paradigm which we attribute to James's ideas – what we call "imaginating" - incorporates scholarly and professional developments subsequent to James – particularly a hermeneutical approach called "framing" (Morgan, 2007; Schon & Rein, 1994) that roughly corresponds to James's instrumentalism where theoretical perspectives serve as instruments or tools to detect novelty and "unstiffen" philosophical and theoretical assumptions (James, 1907, p.37).

Table 1: Jamesian & Dewey's Pragmatic Methods

| Jamesian Approach | Dewey Approach |
|---|---|
| 1. Preliminary analysis and problem identification | 1. Acknowledging quandary and uncertainty |
| 2. Reconsider case via eco-pragmatic principles | 2. Subject quandary to systemic inquiry |
| 3. Frame and if necessary re-frame the case | 3. Produce problem statements suggesting solution |
| 4. Set thematic perspective and tentative conclusions | 4. Engage in Reasoned problem-solving effort |

| 5. Develop a strategy for pursuing a resolution | 5. Analyze pertinent facts and information |
|---|---|
| 6. Review your analysis and conclusions | 6. Produce reasoned common-sense conclusions |

## Imaginating's Brief Departure from James: Dewey and Communitarianism

In introducing the communitarian policy perspective to "imaginating", we made a brief departure from James and turned instead to John Dewey's democratic principles of citizen involvement and participation. In so doing, we are particularly reminded of these words from Dewey:

> The keynote of democracy as a way of life may be expressed; it seems to me, as the necessity for the participation of every mature human being in formation of the values that regulate the living of men together: which is necessary from the standpoint of both the general social welfare and the full development of human beings as individuals. Universal suffrage, recurring elections, responsibility of those who are in political power to the voters, and the other factors of democratic government are means that have been found expedient for realizing democracy as the truly human way of living. (Dewey, 1946, p. 57)

Dewey also concludes that:

> The strongest point to be made in behalf of even such rudimentary political forms as democracy has attained, popular voting, majority rule and so on, is that to some extent they involve a consultation and discussion which concerns social needs and troubles. (Dewey, 1916, p. 206)

Perhaps Dewey's clearest vision rendering his concept of democracy largely consistent with contemporary communitarian ideas is to be found in *The Public and its Problems* (1927) in which he espouses the values of pluralism, citizen participation, and communication. Said Dewey,

> Till the Great Society is converted in to a Great Community, the Public will remain in eclipse. Communication can alone create a great community. (Dewey, 1927, p. 142)

This concept of a "Good Community" within a "Great Society" (a term later employed to describe the political agenda of the administration of former President Lyndon B. Johnson) is at the heart of communitarian values (Dorrien, 1995, p. 337).

In formulating his *New Communitarian Thinking* (1995) Amitai Etzioni looked to Dewey's emphasis upon "voluntary groupings" through whose efforts the "Good Community and the "Great Society" are realized. Etzioni's communitarianism embraces the realization of "a good liberal (or social

democratic) state [that] enhances the possibilities for cooperative coping"
(Etzioni, 1995, p. 67). However, he fears excessive authority ceded to the state.
Consequently, Etzioni endorses Dewey's ideas of informal and formal association
realized through an array of "voluntary groupings" and broadly draws upon
Dewey's pluralistic ideas from *The Public and Its Problems* (1927) as well as
from Dewey's 1920 book *Reconstruction in Philosophy*.

It was within this latter text that Dewey spoke of "voluntary groupings"
which he argued should be considered to be of "coequal importance" and
essential for the realization of democracy (Dewey, 1920, p. 1888). From Dewey's
perspective

> the state remains highly important – but its importance consists more and
> more in its power to foster and coordinate the activities of voluntary
> groupings. Only nominally is it in any modern community the end for
> the sake of which all other societies and organizations exist. Groupings
> for promoting the diversity of goods that men share have become the
> real social units. They occupy the place which traditional theory has
> claimed for mere isolated individuals or for the supreme and single
> political organization. (Dewey, 1920, p. 203-204)

So construed "voluntary groupings" serve as buffers between the state and the
public and help curb the excesses of government principally because they
comprise "the real social units" upon which government is dependent.

Obviously one of the reasons Etzioni was attracted to Dewey's ideas was his
growing concern that an overemphasis upon individualism within the society
could very well threaten the social, political and economic stability of the state
(Etzioni, 2002). Rather than living in a society dominated by individual interests,
Etzioni styled communitarianism sought a balance between the interests of the
sovereign state and the public organized in voluntary groupings or associations –
a vision well stated by Dewey with the following words:

> Without strong and competent individuals, the bonds and ties that form a
> society have nothing to lay hold on. Apart from associations with one
> another, individuals are isolated from one another and fade and wither;
> or are opposed to one another and their conflicts injure individual
> development. Law, state, church, family, friendship, industrial
> associations, these and other institutions and arrangements are necessary
> in order that individuals may grow and find their specific capacities and
> functions. Without their aid and support human life is, as Hobbes said,
> brutish, solitary, nasty. (Dewey, 1920, p. 188)

According to Dewey, these "primary groupings" in local communities serve to
give "the individual members of valued associations greater liberty and security"
and contribute to interpersonal accountability (Dewey, 1927, p. 280).

Social groupings, informal social institutions, civic association and civic
communication are the characteristics of Dewey's approach that most strongly
correlate with the growing communitarian literature – particularly in terms of
Etzioni's work. Admittedly William James ideas could also be associated with

modern communitarian thought – particularly regarding his emphasis upon pluralism that he refers to as, "the doctrine that … the sundry parts of reality *may be externally related*" (Dewey, 1909, p. 129). Pluralism serves as the principal driver of communitarianism of the sort Etzioni describes, promoting a balance between authority and autonomy in the community (Crowder, 2006). In that regard Dewey and James have made historical contributions of our understanding of this phenomenon. However, Dewey's explanation of pluralism in community context makes the clearest connection between pragmatism, pluralism and communitarianism, and it is for that reason we have incorporated some of Dewey's ideas into what is otherwise a Jamesian approach.

## Jamesian Imaginating versus Dewey's Empirical Method

The six-step imaginating process that we associate with James incorporates many of Dewey's methodological steps. For instance preliminary problem identification occurs in the Jamesian model during step 1 and is refined through steps 2-4. Dewey formally makes a problem statement in step 3 after identifying a quandary or uncertainty in step one and investigating it in step 2. By comparison, the James approach assumes there is a quandary or uncertainty that contributes to a problem but does not necessarily do so in explicit terms. Similarly, Dewey makes an explicit appeal to the scientific method in step 2 of his model.

In the James approach a value assessment is conducted during step 2 and in steps 3 and 4 the driving methodology for the analysis involves varying the context within which the issue or case at hand is construed and reformulating a different set of problem statements and suggested alternatives that flow from reframing the issue. Step 5 assumes a satisficing perspective to problem solving and produces a strategy to employ in resolving the problem. Step 6 assumes that a resolution is actually implemented and reflects upon the process to determine if the outcome or outcomes of the strategy and the process that created it were more or less successful. By comparison the Dewey approach seeks to resolve the problem addressed during step 4, analyze the facts and outcomes related to the resolution and the resolution process during step 5 and in step 6 draw conclusions to the entire process of inquiry and action.

To a significant degree the objectives of steps 4 and 5 of the James approach are similar to the final three steps of the Dewey methodology. However, what principally differentiates the James approach from that of Dewey is that the Dewey method addresses issues within a particular frame of reference and generates options and resolutions in a serial fashion whereas the James approach develops numerous problem statements and possible resolutions by conceptualizing and re-conceptualizing the problem from a variety of perspectives and then reflexively reconsiders the entire deliberative process based upon a plurality of perspectives embodying a variety of problem statements and possible courses for resolution. While both James and Dewey essentially share a common stream of consciousness understanding of how human beings perceive and engage the world around them, they principally differ in that Dewey is rigorously methodological in probing and problem solving whereas James's approach is pluralistic, intuitive, metaphorical and construed within a variety of contexts.

Arguably, few of the pragmatist writers who follow Dewey are as rigorously methodologically (Kivinen and Piirolnen, 2006; David, 2007) and like James extensively rely upon the use of metaphor. This particularly applies to perhaps the most famous of the neo-pragmatist thinkers Richard Rorty. Rorty's approach essentially abandoned the pursuit of any form of absolute truth approaching experience in a much more contingent fashion, seeking to liberate thought from presuppositions based upon superstition or archaic religious ideas and replace these older metaphors with newer ones grounded in reason and experience (Rorty, 2003).

Metaphorically speaking, Rorty claims "Pragmatism is a philosophical therapy. It helps you stop asking the unhelpful questions"(Rorty, 2003). Accordingly if one's philosophical orientation is pragmatic "you can forget whether an ideal is authentic or legitimate or universal or deep, and just ask whether it's useful for solving the problems of the day" (Rorty, 2003). To this end Rorty employs metaphor to ask the question of whether any idea or approach is "useful for solving the problems of the day" and as a result he has sometimes been dismissed as being narrowly relativistic in his approach (Norris, 1998).

What Rorty does not provide, however, is a methodology that lends itself to interpreting reality along the lines that Dewey's methodology does. For this reason, those wishing to employ a pragmatic approach to understanding public policy issues and problems – particularly environmental ones – must look to Dewey or James for methodologies. Ben Minteer (2009; 2012) has developed a pragmatic approach to environmental problems grounded in Dewey. What follows in the next chapter is a brief look at how an environmental issue might look like if approached from an imagining approach derived from William James - particularly the first two steps of imagining.

# Chapter 2: The L&N Don't Stop Here Anymore—Coal and Craig, Colorado

> "I was born and raised in the mouth of the Hazard Hollow
> Coal cars rambled past my door
> Now they're standin' in a rusty row all-empty
> And the L & N Don't stop here anymore."

> *The L&N Don't Stop Here Anymore*
> Jeanie Ritchie

## When the L&N Don't Stop There Anymore: Clean Air and Coal in Colorado

This famous song set in Hazard County, Kentucky tells the all too familiar story of coal mines "playing-out" and coal towns disappearing. This is precisely the situation currently facing residents of Craig, Colorado. In this case its not a shortage of coal that is closing the town it's the interface of environmentalists, politics and economics that is crippling a community and costing scores of Coloradoans their jobs. This chapter will consider the case of Craig, Colorado first as an introductory example of imagining applied to policy analysis.

State and federal regulations designed to comply with the Clean Air Act are increasingly involved with more tightly regulating carbon emissions emanating from the nation's coal powered electrical generation plants. In so doing, these regulations impose additional costs upon the public since comparatively low-cost carbon fuels are incrementally eliminated and replaced with comparatively higher priced sustainable energy resources. However the people most directly impacted by efforts to reduce carbon emissions from coal powered plants are those located in communities whose local economies are most significantly dependent upon these electrical generation facilities.

A case in point is Craig, Colorado, home of Tri-State Generation and Transmission Association's Craig Station, Colorado's largest coal-powered generating plant. What follows is a case study based upon news articles and press releases that briefly describe the ecological-economic impasse emerging in Craig,

Colorado and across the West. These are the kinds of brief news and information sources that many citizens rely upon to brief themselves regarding emerging issues. We will utilize these information resources as the basis for an environmental issue analysis utilizing the first steps of the William James inspired imaginating exercise as they apply to issues associate with "coal" and "Craig, Colorado."

## Imaginating: The Case of Craig, Colorado—Case Summary

In this case we will discuss some of the early stages of imaginating as a deliberative process while recognizing that most people likely engage in many of the deliberative steps of imaginating as a virtually automatic intutitive process. The first task in imaginating is to understand the situation, issue or case at hand. In this instance the environmental, economic, political and social issues of concern center upon the municipality of Craig, Colorado – population 10,000. Craig is a community facing economic extinction thanks to ever-stricter EPA standards and a new energy bill passed by the Colorado legislature. The bill, the Clean Air, Clean Jobs Act of 2010, required Colorado investor-owned utilities (IOUs such as Xcel Energy and Black Hills Energy) to curtail carbon emissions in the state by shutting down coal powered electric plants and replacing them with electricity generated by natural gas principally purchased outside the state. It is anticipated that the legislation will result in an 88% reduction in nitrogen oxide and a 28% reduction in carbon dioxide, while "retiring 551 megawatts (MW) of coal- fired electric generation, controlling 742 MW of coal-fired generation with emission reducing retrofits, and fuel switching 443 MW of coal-fired generation to natural gas." The law also mandated that 30 percent of energy generated in the state come from renewable sources by 2020 (Futch, Flaherty & Gilbert, 2011).

The net effect of this legislation is that Tri-State Generation and Transmission Association – a power generating association who sells power to the state's IOUs (Xcel and Black Hills Power) - is being forced to close its Craig Unit that employs half of the residents of the municipality of Craig (Janowiak, 2012). The Craig Unit is the largest coal powered electrical power plant in Colorado generating an annual output of 655 megawatts of power that is comparably cheaper than that which could be produced by natural gas that is piped into Colorado from gas fields outside the state. Operated by Tri-State, the Craig Unit employs approximately 300 plant workers and indirectly supports the employment of another 445 persons at the company owned Trapper and Colowyo mines nearby (Tri-State, 2012). Beyond the direct loss of employment connected to the Craig Unit and surrounding mines, local industries and businesses dependent upon the plant and mines for their revenue are also threatened, having already weathered the nation's protracted economic recession principally due to the nation's demand for cheap energy resources (Janowiak, 2012).

The emerging economic catastrophe befalling the community is particularly tragic since beginning in 2002 the Craig Unit underwent significant reengineering to comply with federal Clean Air Act standards – a multi-year $121 million retrofit investment (Tri-State, 2010). These upgrades were prompted by a lawsuit filed by the Sierra Club in 1993. Tri-State settled with the Sierra Club in 2001 agreeing to limits on sulfur dioxide, nitrogen oxide, and particulate matter releases (True, 2011). According to that agreement, Tri-State was assured that no additional air pollution controls would be imposed upon them for 15 years once the achieved the new emission limits that were incorporated in the federally mandated State Implementation Plan (SIP) (True, 2011). Clearly the Colorado Clean Air, Clean Jobs Act violates the agreement Tri-State made with the Colorado SIP thus providing fodder for a lawsuit to seek relief from the act.

The Clean Air, Clean Jobs Act of 2010 was championed by a number of prominent environmental groups to include Environmental Colorado, The Sierra Club, Colorado Conservation Voters, and the Western Resource Advocates. Opponents of the legislation included the Colorado Mining Association, Black Hills Energy, Xcel Energy (initially), The Trapper, Twenty-Mile and Colowyo mines, the Craig Colorado Chamber of Commerce, the municipality of Craig, as well as out of state interests such as the American Energy Association (Smith, 2010). The Congressional Research Service observed that critics of EPA inspired regulations (such as those embodied in the Colorado legislation) claim that such rules will create a

> regulatory "train wreck" that would impose excessive costs and lead to plant retirements that could threaten the adequacy of electricity capacity (i.e., reliability of supply) across the country, especially from now through 2017. (McCarthy & Copeland, 2011)

Proponents of the legislation cited concerns regarding ozone levels (Colorado is out of compliance with EPA's 2008 ozone standard of 75 parts per billion (ppb)), and atmospheric haze (Futch, 2011). The Craig Unit has been the focus of an ongoing environmental controversy regarding air pollution in northwest Colorado's Mt. Zirkel Wilderness Area. Xcel energy, while initially opposed to the bill cooperated with the Colorado Public Utilities Commission and Colorado Governor Bill Ritter to support the legislation fearing more draconian intervention by the U.S. Environmental Protection Agency (Yeatman & Cooke, 2010). Opponents to the bill based their opposition on the dire economic impact of abandoning coal powered energy, increases the cost of energy to Colorado consumers and the comparatively higher initial cost of natural gas piped into Colorado from other states. They also challenged the degree to which coal-powered electric plants pollute the air noting that 98% of the air carbon dioxide emissions in the state came from mobile sources (Yeatman & Cooke, 2010).

What is transpiring in Colorado portends what is to become of coal powered electric plants nationwide. According to John W. Rowe, Chairman CEO, Exelon Corporation

> Neither new nuclear, coal with carbon capture and sequestration, wind nor solar are economic. They are not economic because of energy prices, an excess of generating capacity and very low load growth. Energy efficiency and uprates at existing nuclear plants are economic at today's prices. New gas plants and coal to gas switching are the next cheapest options at a cost of $69 per MWh and $82 per MWh respectively, and those sources of cleaner energy are only needed as demand returns or supply is tightened by EPA regulations. New wind,

new nuclear, solar and clean coal all cost over $100 per MWh when you take into account the capacity factors, supply back up and so forth. Federal subsidies shift a portion of the costs from electric ratepayers to taxpayers, but do not change the overall economics (Rowe, 2011).

What this implies is that coal-fired electricity generation that has historically been utilized for "base-load" (24hr/7day weeks, year-round) is being replaced with the only feasible cost/effective alternative at this time capable of fully meeting base-load requirements – namely natural gas (Yeatman & Cooke, 2010). Hopefully the viability of natural gas as a base-load alternative will persist, but its longevity as an energy source depends on whether its price remains low. Natural gas prices, however, depend upon the availability of natural gas resources and the ability to get these resources to market (supply) as well as upon consumer demand (Ziegler, 2010).

Regardless of the economic and environmental forces that have contributed to the immediate economic insult to the community of Craig, Colorado, their deleterious impacts upon the citizens have been experienced personally. According to the American Energy Association (AEA), what is transpiring in Craig is nothing short of a local economic disaster. Commenting upon the crisis emerging in Craig, AEA President Thomas Pyle observed that,

> Everybody in that town is tied to coal-fired energy. If those coal units shut down, and if the coal mines shut down, then Craig shuts down. Between EPA's plan to retire 10 percent of the nation's coal-fired generating capacity and onerous state renewable mandates, the Obama agenda is clear: bankrupt the people who are providing affordable coal-fired energy and turn places like Craig into a Ghost Town. Really what's happening in Colorado is a perfect storm of federal regulations hammering down on the energy industry and state regulations that are having a tremendous impact on the cost of electricity. (Pyle, 2012)

This economic and ecological "perfect storm" has left the people of Craig in the lurch as money and jobs leave the coal fields and move to the gas fields. Kirk Ziegler of KUNC Community Based Radio for Northern Colorado commented upon this trend noting "There's been a lot of natural gas drilling here, until recently when many of the rigs picked up and moved to new finds on the east coast" (Ziegler, 2010). The migration of these energy-related jobs represent a significant economic loss to the community and that includes the Moffat County, Colorado tax base. Local Peabody coal miner Doyle Mann laments "This is our way of life, this is what we came to Craig for, it's made us a good living. I hate to see any of that go away" (Ziegler, 2010). Fortunately for Mann and his fellow miners – at least over the short-run - the overall impact of the bill to the state's coal industry is likely to be negligible since most of Colorado's coal is exported (IER, 2010).

Generally speaking natural gas is arguably the energy source of choice for generating base-load levels of electricity. Even states like Colorado with a history of having resisted renewable energy mandates are discovering that natural gas is the most appealing energy alternative – in part because (unlike coal) it can be brought to market more quickly and unlike wind and solar, it is available in the evenings and when the wind abides. Moreover, utility companies can build natural gas powered plants and operate them for a fraction of what it costs to build and operate coal plants (Ziegler, 2010). However, these attributes of natural gas electric generation fail to account for the vast coal reserves to be found throughout the United States and likewise fail to address the potential for the gasification of coal for use in clean-coal power generation units (Wu et. al., 2010).

In light of the sea-change in energy markets throughout Colorado, many families in Craig are preparing for the worst, cashing in some of their coal stock investments, making extra house payments and paying off other debts in anticipation of being laid off from the coal company. Yet others are leaving Craig in the expectation that it will ultimately become a ghost town (Ziegler, 2010). However, while some may regard Craig's fate as inevitable, community leaders have decided to contest the state law.

Craig and a number of other communities across Northern Colorado whose economies are linked to coal have chosen to resist the state law and its supporters in the courts. In fact several Northern Colorado Counties (Mesa, Garfield, Rio Blanco, Moffat and Routt) joined forces to form the Association Governments of Northwest Colorado (AGNC) and have filed a lawsuit challenging the Clean Air, Clean Jobs Act. On April 23, 2012 the Colorado Supreme Court agreed to review the act and determine whether the legislation violated the constitutional rights of the residents of these Northern Colorado counties (Jaffe, 2012).

## Preliminary Analysis: Key Stakeholders

Having briefly summarized the case, the next task in imaginating involves analyzing the case to identify the key stakeholders. An oversimplified dichotomy could be proffered for this case consisting of those favoring the use of coal as an energy source and those opposed. It is important to realize, however, that in any policy dispute there are always those who take no direct part in the policy process (i.e. they don't have a "dog in the hunt") although they may ultimately be impacted by a policy shift. However among those favoring or opposing "big coal" in Colorado there are motivating factors at work. Stakeholders are not simply defined by their values or what they choose to do or refrain from doing they are also gauged in terms of their ability to influence the policy process. This is a central feature in identifying and understanding stakeholders.

Often numerically small groups of stakeholders can exert remarkable political and social influence if they can leverage their ideas rendering them visible and influential. Of course the success of their efforts is significantly enhanced when these stakeholders have access to significant funding. Colorado's power utilities to include Tri-State and its industry allies had access to considerable financial resources to utilize for political influence but lost their cause to a coalition of citizens, environmentalists and an eco-friendly legislature (Rascalli, 2010). Consequently one way to conceive of this case situation is to consider it as a contest between the industrially owned utilities (IOUs) and the environmentalists. Historically, the IOUs have won these contests due to their access to superior funding and legislative influence. However, as the composition of the electorate changed, climate change became a national issue, and more citizens became environmentally sensitive, the degree of coal influence diminished and the result of that process was the passage of the 2010 Colorado Clean Air – Clean Jobs Act (Adams, 2010).

Essentially, what emerged in Colorado was a pitched battle over energy and environment that included a number of influential stakeholders to include (1) *public utility companies* and their industry trade groups and allies, (2) well organized *environmental groups* to include Environmental Colorado, Colorado Conservation Voters, and the Sierra Club, coalesced to defeat the Colorado Miner's Association and Tri-State (Bowe, 2010; Singer, 2010) (3*) coal-powered plants and feeder mines* who were impacted by the new state law (to include the Craig Unit), (4) *affiliated business and industries* dependent upon these coal-generated plants (5) *specific municipalities* who will be significantly harmed by the demise of the coal related industries in Colorado, (6) *coal industry dependent citizens* residing in communities and areas impacted by the demise of "big-coal," and (7) *other citizens and utility payers* who will pay for the transition to natural gas. While each of these stakeholders played important roles in the outcome of this case, without doubt the player that exerted the principal influence that made the Clean Air, Clean Jobs Act possible was an eighth stakeholder residing beyond the state boundaries: namely (8) the *U.S. Environmental Protection Agency* whose rules (exteriorities) and values (interiorities) flowed seamlessly from the Whitehouse to the Colorado statehouse.

Among the stakeholders, however, none were as deeply or personally affected by the state ban on coal-powered electricity as the residents and municipal officials of Craig and Moffat County, Colorado. Interestingly enough, a certain paradox emerges when contrasting the expressed values of the municipality of Craig and Tri-State. According to the Craig Colorado Chamber of Commerce, their community is "the land of rugged adventure and rugged landscapes" whereas the Tri-State corporate slogan is "The Cooperative Spirit Builds Strong Communities and a Better World." These two value characterizations reflect the desires of a community seeking to figuratively 'have its cake and eat it too" as stakeholders simultaneously want coal-related jobs and value the outdoor life of the type afforded by their community.

As expected, many in and around Craig and across Northern Colorado are frustrated and angry that the interests of others living beyond the bounds of their community have had such a deleterious effect upon their way of life (Talamani, 2010; Yeatman & Cooke, 2010; Smith, 2010). By comparison the state's influential environmental organizations are ecstatic with the outcome of this energy/climate battle – perhaps none happier than John Nielsen, Energy Director of the of the Western Resources Association, who applauded the signing of the Clean Air, Clean Jobs Act saying:

> This new law creates a coordinated frame- work to reduce air pollution in an efficient and cost-effective way. It will result in cleaner air and healthier communities and will further strengthen Colorado's position as a clean energy leader. (Nielsen, 2010, p. 1)

## Exteriorities and Interiorities

Having identified and portrayed the stakeholders in this case, the imaginator identifies and contrasts the values and actions of the stakeholders – their so-called "interiorities" and "exteriorities." Although we are well ahead of a more complete explanation of what is meant by interiorities and exteriorities, we will proceed and demonstrate how these terms apply within the context of this case. The term exteriority refers to the observable exterior characteristics of an entity or phenomenon to include appearance, manner, behavior, consequences and products of behavior, action and volition. By comparison interiority refers to the inner characteristics of and entity or phenomenon to include temperament, values, perspective, motivation, orientation, temperment etc. From a Jamesian perspective exteriorities are more or less equivalent with "consequences" and interiorities are generally consistent with values, ideas and philosophies.

In speaking of each concept we can conceive of exterior or interior characteristics as constituting a set of "exteriorities" or "interiorities" pertinent to the case or issue at hand. Likewise, we will conclude that in any given situation a set of exteriorities and interiorities favoring one perspective on a policy issue may persevere or trump competing sets of exteriorities and interiorities. This implies that in aggregate one set of interiorities or exteriorities might prove to be more compelling or influential in either defining or resolving a case conundrum than is another. In the case of Craig, Colorado the measure of which exteriority/interiority set has triumphed at any point in time is measured by the consequences of their actions – a thoroughly Jamesian perspective.

The Craig, Colorado case involves a number of prominent exteriorities. From the perspective of Tri-State Generation and Transmission Association (Tri-State) the principal exteriority is coal and all that flows from it – i.e. payroll, economic stimulus, trade, electric power, and political and economic influence. All of these important exteriorities are at play and at risk due to economic forces and the actions of legislators, environmentalists, lobbyists, regulators and voters who have come together to agree upon clean air standards and enforcement. A complimentary set of exteriorities pertaining to Tri-State and all electric power providers in Colorado involves substituting natural gas for coal in base-load power production.

The exteriorities at play for the state legislature and the U.S. Congress by way of the Environmental Protection Agency and its regulations include clean air legislation and regulations, a demonstrable policy to reduce and ultimately eliminate the use of carbon fuels and in this case coal; an expressed preference for natural gas and renewable fuels such as wind and solar, as well as a demonstrated willingness to increase taxes on energy and the cost of living to achieve these environmental goals. Still other exteriorities associated include a readiness to tolerate increased unemployment in the coal fields and a similar will to impoverish particular energy-related communities to pursue an environmental agenda. However, balanced against these costs are the anticipated advantages of cleaner air, cheaper and more efficient natural gas energy production and compensating jobs and economic growth associated with the substitution of natural gas for coal.

Environmental groups, such as the Western Reserve Association, the Sierra Club, and Environmental Colorado exhibit exteriorities of their own such as publicizing their organization's values, demonstrating political and economic power, engaging in political and economic intimidation and threat directed toward energy producers, and educating the public on issues pertaining to energy development, use and conservation. Energy advocacy groups such as the American Energy Association and the California-based Electric Power Research Institute consider the Craig, Colorado case as emblematic of the larger national and international struggle to substitute carbon-based energy sources with non-carbon based fuels – considering natural gas use as a 'bridge-fuel' on the journey to a carbon free economy (Pickens, 2011). These energy advocacy organizations produce a number of pertinent exteriorities to include press and media coverage of the Craig situation, studies demonstrating economic and social disruption, access to "energy experts" touting the safety and utility of their energy products and significant political influence and leverage by way of industry-wide media and political funding

By comparison, the exteriorities exhibited by the residents of Craig, Colorado include unemployment, expressions of anger, frustration and desperation; efforts to forestall the closing of the Craig Unit; divestment of their economic resources to maintain their homes and livelihoods in Craig; appeals to legislative bodies, the courts and the media as well as decreased economic activity and relocation outside of Craig and Colorado to more promising economic markets. Likely exteriorities of the municipality of Craig include higher unemployment, municipal budget shortfalls, disruption of municipal services, higher taxes to accommodate the shrinking tax base and efforts to seek new economic options for their community.

Considered as a whole, it would appear the most influential exteriorities associated with this case fall on the side of those wanting to close the Craig Unit and as a result cripple the community of Craig. While energy advocates, local politicians, community residents and the news media (whose exteriorities principally revolve around viewership, listeners, readers and sales) are managing to introduce the rest of the nation to the community's plight, the overall power of national energy markets, environmental groups, legislatures and regulatory agencies appear to have the upper hand in this case. The question though is "why" does the coalition of interests championing the new Colorado law have the upper hand?

Answering the "why" of this case necessitates a review of the case's interiorities, particularly personal and institutional values and changing cultural mores and public beliefs. In this instance the most pertinent interiorities begin at the very highest level with the U.S. Environmental Protection Agency and its zealous policy of promoting the Clean Air Act by eliminating the nation's reliance on carbon-based fuels. Seemingly the genesis of the agency's values (as expressed in recent regulatory behavior) began in 2008 when then Senator Barack Obama in interview with a San Francisco Chronicle reporter claimed:

> I was the first to call for a 100% auction on the cap and trade system, which means that every unit of carbon or greenhouse gases emitted would be charged to the polluter. That will create a market in which whatever technologies are out there that are being presented, whatever power plants that are being built, that they would have to meet the rigors

of that market and the ratcheted down caps that are being placed, imposed every year. So if somebody wants to build a coal-powered plant, they can; it's just that it will bankrupt them because they're going to be charged a huge sum for all that greenhouse gas that's being emitted (Goss, 2009)

So the principal interiority driving this particular case is a commitment to a value on behalf of the now President of the United States Barack Obama and his leadership in the EPA to wean the nation off of carbon fuels beginning with coal. In short the EPA's interior motivations were predicated upon the belief that "coal is bad" for the environment and that it must be eliminated at all costs. Admittedly, then Senator Obama did not actively advocate for the outright banning of coal as an energy resource. Instead he told the reporter at the San Francisco Chronicle in 2008 "if somebody wants to build a coal-powered plant, they can. It's just that it will bankrupt them" (Goss, 2009). His intent, however, is clearly the elimination of coal as a significant energy resource in the U.S.

The EPA adopted this mandate and has vigorously regulated and threatened energy companies who fail to comply with their guidelines. It was undoubtedly for this reason that Xcel Energy came around to support the very Colorado clean air legislation that it had initially opposed. Their change of heart was in part was based upon their realization of yet another important interiority at EPA – a willingness to employ intimidation, or "the ends justify the means" (Berger, 2014; Bannister, 2013; Helman, 2012). Interestingly enough, intimidation is one of those characteristics that can be considered as both an exteriority – as when an intimidating act is committed – as well as an undergirding principle or value exemplified in the case of so-called "Theory X" approaches to policy that assume a dour perspective on human nature justifying the use of intimidation and force to implment executive rules and expectations (McGregor, 1969).

In 2010 EPA Region 6 Administrator Al Armendariz expressed such Theory-X values when he commented upon how he had metaphorically expressed his agency's general philosophy toward energy companies with the following anecdote:

> I was in a meeting once and I gave an analogy to my staff about my philosophy of enforcement, and I think it was probably a little crude and maybe not appropriate for the meeting but I'll go ahead and tell you what I said. It was kind of like how the Romans used to conquer little villages in the Mediterranean. They'd go into a little Turkish town somewhere, they'd find the first five guys they saw and they would crucify them. And then you know that town was really easy to manage for the next few years. And so you make examples out of people who are in this case not compliant with the law. Find people who are not compliant with the law, and you hit them as hard as you can and you make examples out of them, and there is a deterrent effect there. And, companies that are smart see that, they don't want to play that game, and they decide at that point that it's time to clean up. [...] So, that's our general philosophy. (*Inhofe, 2012*)

Armendariz's comments created a firestorm of criticism from many quarters forcing the EPA administrator to recant his metaphor (crucifixion) but not his intent (intimidation). Admittedly, Armendariz's responsibilities extend as far west as New Mexico while Colorado is part of EPA Region 8. It is not clear whether Region 8 employs the same philosophy as that evidenced in Region 6. Even so, this expression by Mr. Armendariz is an unusual and candid admission that crystalizes concerns that until now were no more than conjecture. Unfortunately these concerns have only been amplified by a trend dating back at least to 2008 involving the use of intimidation by the EPA, the Bureau of Land Management and other related agencies (Richardson, 2014; Barasch, 2013; Barraso, 2009; Raloff, 2008).

While no one can know with certainty whether the Region 8 EPA administrator shares Armendariz's values, given the frequency with which energy producers have complained about the heavy-handed tactics of the EPA (Holland, 2012; Miller, 2012; IBD, 2012; Denniston, 2012; ALF, 2012), it remains an open question whether or not some of the state's energy producers *may* have entered into a dialogue with the state assembly and the governor for fear of being singled out in the fashion the Region 6 EPA administrator describes. In other words this may be an instance in which it is "better to deal with the devil you know than it is to deal with the one you don't."

Well before Armendariz's views were publicized many prominent energy industry leaders had vociferously asserted that the EPA assumes a needlessly adversarial relationship with energy providers. Exemplary among these critics is John Hofmeister, CEO and founder of Citizens for Affordable Energy who calls the EPA "the political poodle of the president" while referring to the energy industry as:

> The only industry in the world which has allowed itself to create an extraordinarily adversarial relationship between companies, government, and consumers is the energy industry. (Hoffmeister, 2011)

Regarding the citizens of the State of Colorado, it would appear that by virtue of who they elected to the state legislature and the strong carbon-based environmental legislation that these representatives passed (Colorado Clean Air-Clean Jobs Act, 2010) the voters have undergone a change of heart and have reformulated their interior values regarding the environment such that they now value clean air more than they value the benefits to be derived from using cheap and abundant coal energy. Admittedly, part of their motivation is derived from the promise of preventing climate change and enjoying clearer vistas while realizing cheaper energy fueled by natural gas – an outcome that may or may not prove to be true (Walsh, 2011; Denning, 2012). What is demonstrable, however, is that switching to natural gas will save utility companies millions of dollars in retrofitting costs that they could have anticipated with coal fired plants (Associated Press, 2010).

So, having experienced a change of heart, Colorado's institutional and citizen advocates have agreed to suffer the likely short term cost increases associated with a nationwide spike in demand for natural gas (Begos, 2012). These anticipated cost increases are fueled by the wholesale transition of the nation's power plants from coal to natural gas thereby driving up competition of this new fuel source (Trembath et al., 2013). However, armed with the foreknowledge that over time natural gas costs should stabilize and the costs of maintaining these newly fueled power plants should decline a decided majority of Coloradoans seem prepared to pay more for electricity in the short run in the interest of reaping a host of environmental and economic benefits over the long term.

Even so, the environmental values of those convinced of the need to abandon coal as a power source don't necessarily apply to all state citizens, since not everyone supported either the candidates for legislature or endorsed the majority of members of the General Assembly who passed the Colorado Clean Air – Clean Jobs Act (2010). The interiorities expressed by these dissenting citizens reflect a variety of values among which is the belief that clean air can be achieved with clean coal technology (Eves, 2011) and that economic hardship doesn't necessary have to compliment clean-air initiatives (Podesta, 2011). These sentiments are well reflected in the statement of Steve Miller, CEO of the American Coalition for Clean Coal energy before the Colorado general assembly who asserted that

> Replacing coal with natural gas will not accomplish Colorado's economic or environmental goals. Not only is natural gas three times more expensive than coal nationally, but readily available, advanced clean coal technologies represent a lower cost alternative to meeting environmental regulations that were the impetus for the bill's consideration (ACCCE, 2010)

Similar sentiments have been expressed by the Association Governments of Northwest Colorado (AGNC) whose lawsuit against the State of Colorado over the Clean Air, Clean Jobs Act is now before the Colorado Supreme Court. In articulating their statement of purpose as an organization AGNC focus in part upon energy development and assert that:

> It is the stated policy of The Associated Governments of Northwest Colorado that energy development in Colorado, in all its forms, is beneficial for the economic sustainability of the state, the region and the local governments that make up the Association. Development of these resources, renewable or non-renewable, should always be done in a fashion that promotes the greatest efficiency and exhibit the least amount of environmental impact on the land. (AGNC, 2009)

AGNC's perspective and that expressed by ACCCE CEO Steve Miller are completely at odds with the interiorities of the various environmental groups associated with this legislation, to include Environmental Colorado, the Western Resource Association and the Sierra Club. For those involved in the coal and coal-powered electric generation business, or for those dependent upon these industries, their principal focus is upon human beings and their communities. They are in a word unabashedly anthropocentric in their orientation. By comparison, the various environmental groups are comparatively eco-centric in their perspectives. As we will discuss in a later chapter, these two stakeholder groups perceive issues of economy and ecology from very different paradigmatic perspectives – i.e. from different frame references – and the consequence of this "frame-misfit" is intractable controversy that is not readily amendable to rational discussion and problem solving. Among environmentalists, eco-centric values of necessity trump human interests and economics. Conversely, for the economic and consumer stakeholders in this case, anthropocentric concerns regarding community, economy and social role trump the environmental costs that may or may not occur if the current state of energy, economic and environmental affairs were to remain constant in the state of Colorado. Moreover, these deeply held values are reinforced by the exteriorities associated with coal production. Less obvious but still evident is a sense of accomplishment and satisfaction on behalf of the various environmental groups to have realized environmental justice enforced by governmental agencies. Business people and those who serve to directly benefit from coal production and coal powered energy reflect – on the other hand - a different set of interiorities valuing comparative independence from government involvement, maximal individual liberty and discretion, unfettered trade and personal autonomy.

Interiorities associated with social units and organizations usually assume the form of cultural values and mores. For instance, the culture of the energy companies encourages a faith in technological innovation, market decision-making, and confidence in their product's safety and long-term utility. These companies also embrace a philosophical belief that what they do and the products they provide are good for their companies and the community such as was earlier noted regarding their corporate slogan "The Cooperative Spirit Builds Strong Communities and a Better World" (Tri-State, 2012). The community of Craig, by comparison reflects it interiorities in terms of its Chamber of Commerce slogan - "the land of rugged adventure and rugged landscapes" (Craig Chamber of Commerce, 2012) - as well as through its community values, political philosophies, lifestyle preferences, and cultural characteristics and mores. Residents of Craig and its environs would like the opportunity to enjoy their natural surroundings based upon their ongoing employment in mining and electrical power generation. The Tri-State Association desires to realize the fruits of its multi-million dollar investment in clean coal technology by continuing to operate and provide electric power throughout the region, the state and beyond.

As was the case with the exteriorities, it would appear that the influence of the interiorities supporting the closing of the Craig Unit have democratically trumped those opposing the Clean Air, Clean Jobs Act. Simply stated, one set of individual and institutional values have dominated other competing sets. Those who cling to the belief that coal is bad for people and the environment have out-maneuvered and overpowered those who either believe that coal can be used safely for people and the environment, or are alternately indifferent to the issue of how or whether coal is used in the community, state or nation. Furthermore, the demonstrably heavy handed tactics of the EPA regarding coal usage nationwide along with their obvious ill-will regarding coal-based energy producers (Harder, 2012; Malewitz, 2012; News New Mexico Staff, 2012; Tremoglie, 2012; Slaughter, 2012; Mica, 2011) has created an environment in which local utilities find it in their interest to parley with their State General Assembly and Governor rather than exclusively deal with the proclivities of the EPA.

While the case of the City of Craig may serve to caution other states and communities from pursuing the environmental agenda adopted in Colorado, it seems certain that for the immediate future the influence of coal nationwide and in Colorado will wane (Davidson, 2014) – pending a shift in the interiorities of those individuals, groups and organizations in the state and nation who continually grapple for advantage in this environmental conflict. Likewise, the consequences of this episode of the ongoing Colorado energy debate may yet shift if, for instance, sufficient clean energy resources are not forthcoming resulting in unbearably high-energy costs to accompany increased energy taxation of all fuels. If these events were to unfold and the State of Colorado experienced an economic downturn, such as might result from business relocating to less regulated more energy-rich states or prospective industries and business choosing not to relocate to Colorado because of their energy policies, then the interior values of protecting the environment generally held by the public could be expected to give way to economic consideration thereby ushering coal energy back into Colorado again. Such prospects, however, dim over time as the infrastructure of coal-fired plants are refitted to burn natural gas or are left to deteriorate from neglect. Likewise, the workforce trained to work in such coal-fired facilities will also disperse and find new jobs and ultimately the expertise needed to run such plants will also be lost.

What this means is that in a democratic environment where stakeholders can influence the public policy process sometimes the outcomes of those processes may prove to be virtually irreversible, meaning that in all likelihood the chances of coal-fired electrical plants being re-opened once closed is pretty slim. Nevertheless, in a democratic and pluralistic process all outcomes and all consequences are contingent and temporary since outcomes are inevitably driven by beliefs and values. From a pragmatic perspective values do not derive their worth in any absolute sense that is not validated by human action and consequences.

## Processes and Perspectives

Imaginating also requires consideration of the dominant processes and perspectives involved. Two principal macro-processes are driving the events the municipality of Craig and across Colorado – and frankly the U.S. – one economic and the other ecological. Of these two the most significant process is the economic transformation of U.S. energy markets – particularly the electrical grid – as it moves away from an historical reliance upon coal generation and adopts cleaner natural gas. However, having arrived at this market decision, coal remains abundant across the U.S. and is not going away as an energy source. However, it is, with increasing frequency, beginning to leave the nation and travel overseas to foreign markets – especially China.

According to the U.S. Energy Information Agency (2011), coal use internationally has steadily risen over the last 30 years rising from 3,752,183 short tons in 1980 to 7,994,703 in 2010. By far the largest coal consumer is China who used 3,695,377 short tons in 2010 and the United States who used 1,048,295 short tons (followed by India and Russia who used 721,986 and 256,795 respectively). The U.S. – the world's fourth largest coal exporter – has been steadily increasing coal exports – rising from 49,942 short tons in 2005 to 81,716 in 2010 and 106,468 in 2011. The bulk of these exports are destined for China (EIA, 2011). What this means for Colorado's coal is that instead of this energy resource being consumed in the U.S. it will increasingly be exported with 2012 coal exports to China alone double over previous levels perhaps exceeding 12 million short tons (Thrasher, 2012).

These economic processes have been paralleled by the emergence of a U.S. Presidential administration and EPA supported by a Democrat majority in the U.S. Senate that has promulgated and enforced increasingly stringent environmental regulations since 2008. These political processes have been joyously received by the nation's leading environmental groups who have been particularly adroit in winning legislative victories promoting environmental health in several of the various states even when a stalemate in environmental policy has become the norm in the U.S. Congress (Safer States, 2014). However, while these political and complimentary economic processes have been playing out in terms of energy and environmental policies, the economic prospects of the nation's citizenry and the business sector has remained sluggish and uncertain – with expectations for a continuation of these persistent trends (Rugaber & Wiseman, 2012).

These divergent processes inevitably drive divergent perspectives - serving as an early introduction to what we will later be discussing in terms of issue framing. However, for the moment we will associate perspectives with paradigms along the lines of the work of Thomas Kuhn (1962). Kuhn spoke of "paradigm shifts" by which he referred to changes in perspectives on issues and problems that allowed problems and issues to be reconceived in a new light, thereby allowing for reformulations of what constitutes the problems or issues that need addressing, what factors contributed to them and what solutions might be forthcoming. This paradigmatic approach applies to the processes at hand in this case. From an economic perspective, the rationale for switching from coal to natural gas production entails improving air quality and maintaining base load capacity while utilizing a relatively abundant coal substitute in natural gas. From this perspective a set of environmental problems are solved (haze, climate change, particulate matter, nitrogen and sulfur oxides) while opportunity for another energy resource expands in terms of the natural gas market.

While the economic paradigm emerging from the energy economic processes solves problems, creates new problems and provides new opportunities, it also allows for reformulating the larger problem of eliminating carbon fuels in favor of renewables by using natural gas as a "bridge fuel." By comparison the environmental paradigm or perspective considers the events in Colorado and those emerging nationwide as the demise of domestic use of "big coal" – a perennially criticized industrial polluter. In this regard the problem – coal – is being replaced with a less problematic fuel in natural gas but still one that activists would like to also see completely eliminated and replaced with some form of yet to be developed abundant renewal fuel resource. Thus the environmentalist paradigm is not as rosy a scenario as that viewed from a purely economic perspective. This scenario, becomes less appealing when environmentalists consider that given increase exports of coal overseas and particularly to China, all they have really accomplished from a clean air perspective is the exportation of coal-generated pollution to an overseas site where it will continue to wreak havoc regionally and ultimately internationally.

However, for the consumer and small businesses, the switch to natural gas from coal will not be an inexpensive transition and in all likelihood will on the aggregate be a more expensive (though cleaner) alternative to coal since increased demand for natural gas, especially from oversea markets, is expected to drive up costs (DeAngelis, 2014; Hurdle, 2014). Of particular concern is the degree to which the shift from coal to natural gas powered electricity will destabilize the nation's electrical power grid, especially as coal generation plants are retired faster in some markets than natural gas power plants are brought on line. The result could be a pattern of "brownouts" and "blackouts" as well as a spike in the cost of electricity (U.S. Department of Energy, 2014). Such higher energy costs thwart job creation and business expansion although these "costs" do contribute to improved air quality. Thus from the paradigm / perspective of the consumer and entrepreneur, a switch to natural gas provides them with a marginal benefit (clean air) but, with higher energy costs, extracts a potentially significant personal and economic cost (Hemphill & Perry, 2012).

When these paradigms are considered together they produce additional paradigm-specific processes – outcomes emanating from each paradigmatic position – that are ultimately at odds with each other. The economic forces – largely driven by regulatory requirements for lower carbon emissions – drive down domestic coal use and increasing exports of coal to Asia. This pleases western environmental groups and state and federal regulators but in effect all that happens is coal related air pollution is simply exported overseas where foreign workers realize economic benefits (and experience deleterious health effects) while American small businesses and consumers see their already strained economic resources only further intensified.

From a political economic perspective (i.e. regarding those areas where political and economic incentives coincide) the Clean Air, Clean Jobs Act produces positive outcomes for regulators and environmentally concerned citizens, assists the federal government in achieving its clean-air goals and does so by only marginally imposing costs on IOUs while leaving coal mines free to export their product overseas. Since all economic benefits are realized at a cost, domestically the bulk of the cost of this Act falls upon energy consumers, coal-related workers, small businesses and local governments – particularly those businesses and governments economically dependent upon coal-powered electrical generation facilities. However, the remainder of the costs – and these are considerable – are borne by citizens residing overseas – particularly in Asia – and (air pollution circles the globe in the upper air currents) other nations and states whose air will become more polluted and who will experience other coal related environmental hazards such as acid rain (MacIntosh & Spengler, 2011).

Yet another way to metaphorically consider these paradigmatic-driven processes are in terms of conduits (Shanahan, 2008; Chen, 2005) or avenues designed to realize desired outcomes. Environmentalists utilize *regulatory conduits* that produce cleaner air, greater governmental control over energy production, and enhanced political power and influence. Needless to say, government regulators also utilized regulatory conduits. However their versions of these conduits are principally concerned with translating legislative language into regulatory directives whereas the environmentalists approach the regulatory conduit by translating community organization, fund raising and civic influence to prod legislators into enacting legislation that regulators will later embody in rules and guidelines. Energy companies favor *production conduits* allowing them to readily respond to demand for their products – whether coal, natural gas or electric power. From their corporate perspectives it makes little difference to them which product they sell or who or where their consumers reside as long as they are able to pursue the best economic return available for the least cost, while maintaining and expanding their market shares and spheres of influence.

Legislators pursue their efforts through *political conduits* that serve the interests of those who elected them and which serves their own career interests in remaining employed as politicians by influencing the voters and the political elite who contribute to their elections and keep them in power. Citizens also utilize political conduits but typically do so to elect government representation, to amend charters and constitutions and to influence governments at all levels to pay attention to their concerns. By comparison citizens utilize *civic conduits* designed to promote benefits for themselves and their communities that may or may not include political organizations and interest groups. The typically favor employing voluntary associations and informal community groups over more formal governmental options. In so doing they create necessary community checks and balances to formal governmental authority.

## Opportunities, Costs, Biases, and Potential Pitfalls

While it may be an overly simplistic observation, different conduits or paradigms suggest different sets of opportunities and costs, varying sources of bias, differing pitfalls and outcome shortcomings. Imaginators need to be prepared to expect variety when considering different conduits, perspectives, paradigms and frames. Consider the paradigms just discussed that readily illustrate this assertion.

Energy providers who have historically relied upon coal to fuel their generators must now transition to natural gas. While there will be unavoidable costs associated with this transition for them corporately as well as for their employees and consumers, this transition process holds out the promise of being able to operate their facilities with much less recurrent investment in clean air technology and allows them to present a much cleaner and more wholesome public image to their customers, regulators and legislators. Similarly coal companies, while surrendering domestic markets for coal, have the opportunity to expand their international market share. Likewise, if they are willing to invest in new technology, they may even be able to convince the Congress and state legislatures that gasified coal could prove to be as useful a "bridge fuel" as natural gas.

Environmentalist groups, by comparison, have been presented with an opportunity to consolidate their control and influence within the Office of the Governor of the State of Colorado, as well as within the General Assembly and among state regulatory agencies. Moreover, they may even have an opportunity to elect additional environmentally friendly legislators during upcoming elections, thereby further consolidating their influence in the Colorado General Assembly and the Governor's office.

While it may appear that communities such as Craig have not been afforded any opportunities throughout this process, in fact they too have been afforded a number of opportunities to include economizing in the scope and size of local government, courting new industries into their community, touting the benefits of a cleaner environment derived from natural gas generated electric power and reconfiguring their local school district to prepare students and residents for new jobs and new careers. In fact, while the economic displacement resulting from shutting down the Craig Unit will result in the costs of relocation and unemployment for many, even here the events which have unfolded in Craig and across Colorado provide citizens and workers the opportunity of starting anew in another setting – hopefully one that is more economically stable than Craig and Moffatt County, Colorado. Moreover, since electric power generation is switching from coal to natural gas, changes in electricity generation technology may provide an opportunity for some workers to transition from coal based electricity production to natural gas based production.

Imaginators must be particularly aware of the presence of bias – which is ever-present in each and every policy issue or controversy – when considering environmental issues, controversies and policies. Indeed, opportunities and the paradigms that generate them are built upon biases. While the term "bias" is often considered to be pejorative, in effect it serves as a necessary tool for simplifying situations that otherwise might prove to be overly complex and complicated. Biases are "old-stock" ideas and information that are acquired during repeated trial and error learning and experience. They are if you will "tentative hypotheses" about reality that are employed until they are either debunked or replaced with more useful bias. What this means is that the imaginator must abandon the idea of approaching any issue "*bias-free*" since such is not possible. Rather, the imaginator approaches issues and problems "*bias-aware*."

Consider, if you will, some of the prominent biases to be found in the Craig, Colorado case. One blatant bias comes from the variety of environmental groups supporting the Clean Air, Clean Jobs Act – namely the bias of "big coal." Typically the term "big coal" implies exploitation of land, air and people; excessive profiteering, iron-clad legislative and administrative influence, indifference to the values of clean air and water or healthy employees (Goodell, 2007; Black, 2012). In the Craig case, the principal target of environmental activists and advocacy groups was eliminating the power of "Big Coal" throughout Colorado and the nation. What this bias implies is that so steadfast is the animus toward the coal industry that among environmentalists and other coal critics, it is very difficult for protagonists to see anything of true value associated with the coal industry. What results is a metaphor in which a coal-free world is idealized while any situation in which coal might conceivably be employed – to include the gasification of coal in clean-coal technology processing plants – is considered categorically wrong.

On the other hand, those dedicated to the use of coal – particularly clean coal technology – look to the vast abundance of this fuel resource and the world's huge energy appetite and they are biased in favor of coal use – sometimes even to the exclusion of considering pertinent environmental impacts. Coal miners and workers in coal-fired electric plants share these pro-coal biases, since their livelihoods, culture and personal identities have been shaped by coal – sometimes over many generations. For those whose principal interests are politically fueled, bias may take other forms. For instance, if one's politics is progressive in form then supporting legislation, regulation and candidates that would increase regulations and reign in the power of the coal companies and IOUs might be an attractive bias to maintain. On the other hand, if one's political philosophy is more libertarian than progressive then government regulation of energy industries might be seen as an interference in the democratic operation of free markets and might be opposed regardless of what the environmental issues or realities were.

Regardless of where they originate, biases must be accounted for in imaginating and that especially applies to the biases of the imaginator. When considering any issue, controversy or case, the imaginator simply must identify their own biases and then consider these biases when looking toward stakeholders, paradigms, processes and issues that tend to support their biases or contradict them. Once again, the purpose of this exercise is not to arrive at bias free decisions but rather to arrive at "bias-aware" or "bias-informed" decisions – namely those decisions and conclusions that are arrived at after full consideration of one's own biases and those implicit and explicit within the controversy, case or issue at hand. The goal of bias awareness is to determine the degree to which past biases have been either confirmed, eliminated or modified – rendered all or in part valid and useful.

Finally, the imaginator must consider pitfalls that may befall advocates of any of a number of possible responses to the controversy or controversies at hand. One such pitfall has already been identified in terms of selling coal internationally. Mining coal and selling it in foreign markets spares the U.S. the immediate impact of coal-related air pollution and health effects, but it insures that others in other environs will suffer such consequences. Armed with this foreknowledge, it becomes extremely difficult to seriously argue for contributing to environmental and human health by eliminating the burning of coal in the U.S. when one knows full well that these deleterious environmental and health effects are being produced overseas as a consequence of international coal trade.

Yet another example of a pitfall has to do with the need for base-load fuel sources. Right now coal is meeting that need in the U.S. However, what if problems involved in cost, availability, transportation and use of natural gas were to render it less available than is currently believed. Already as the nation's electrical grid transitions from coal to natural gas concerns are being raised over potential energy blackout's along the northeastern U.S. since natural gas-fired plants are not coming online as quickly as coal-fired facilities are being phased out (Colman, 2014). Once coal-generated electric plants like Craig are mothballed then there will be no recourse to coal fired electricity if natural gas proves too difficult or expensive to get. Consequently a pitfall (i.e. a foregone opportunity) worth considerations is "what if we need coal and clean coal technology in the future but we have eliminated the capacity to readily transform this energy source into electric power? We present these as two illustrative pitfalls associated with this case, recognizing that there are numerous others that could also be cited.

## Novel Ideas and Approaches versus Tried and True

A Jamesian approach to imaginating requires the imaginator to compare what they know or believe to be true – "old-stock ideas" – with novel, newer approaches and ideas and to weigh the two against one another to the end of choosing to either maintain, eliminate or modify (change) "old-stock" ideas in whole or part. The net effect of this process is creating what James called "new-stock" ideas. Achieving this end entails first being aware of what one believes, knows or generally holds to be true and of worth followed by the capacity to identify new and "novel" ideas and approaches where novel means "different than what you typically do or think."

There were a number of components of the Craig, Colorado case that were novel depending upon the paradigm or perspective one brought to the case. If one were a hidebound coal advocate then considering powering the same plants in your region that had always provided electricity with natural gas would have been novel and noteworthy but antagonistic to the desire to use coal resources in as efficient a manner as possible. If one were involved in one of the major environmental organizations promoting the Clean Air, Clean Jobs Act, it would have been a novel idea to consider gasifying coal to use in a way comparable to the way natural gas would be employed for electric power generation. Coal mines who have historically sold their coal within the U.S. might find it novel to consider using a slurry process to transport their product by pipeline to ports for shipment overseas or if the price of oil gets high enough to make it profitable to engage in "coal to liquid" conversion to produce fuels that could be used in airplanes, trucks and automobiles (Webber, 2009; Cox, 1983). Likewise, employees of coal powered electric plants might find it novel to see themselves working in natural gas powered plants.

However, from a Jamesian perspective, it is not enough that an idea be novel, it must also be compelling – compelling enough in fact that it leads an individual to revise their old-stock ideas to accommodate new-stock values and information. For instance, those familiar with the potential for the gasification of coal for electric power might choose to discount the "novelty" of natural gas powered electric plants in light of the prodigious deposits of coal to be found across the U.S. After all, U.S. coal reserves account for 29% of the known coal reserves on the planet (Leeb, 2011). Consequently while reliable renewable fuels are currently being developed but not yet fully available, a thoughtful imaginator might look at the huge U.S. coal reserve and consider it in light of the nation's natural gas reserves (4% of the world's total) (Long, 2010) and conclude that on the way to developing reliable alternative fuels it might be prudent to gasify as much of the nation's coal reserves as possible before permanently depleting the nation's natural gas reserves. From this perspective, substituting natural gas for coal might not be as functional as substituting gasified carbon fuel (natural gas or coal) for granular carbon fuel.

While new-stock or novel ideas and issues must be compelling enough to change opinions and replace or revise old-stock ideas the manner in which they may be perceived as being compelling may be multifold. From a narrowly rational perspective, we might expect old-stock values and ideas to be transformed by rationally compelling arguments and ideas. However, human beings seldom operate on rationality alone and may also change their minds on the basis of other compelling influences to include intuition, emotion, passion, prejudice (bias), aesthetics and more (a.k.a. James's intermediate processes). James's stream of consciousness metaphor for human logic actually accounts for these various forces and influences by referring to one might refer to as the "perching-points" for his metaphorical flitting "bird" of consciousness, as "objects of thought" or "subjective objects" that might consist of reason, bias, passion, faith, patriotism, aesthetics or any number of other "objects" of logic – which is to say that for James logic is not fully synonymous with rationality (James, 1890). From such a perspective human thought consists of five characteristics:

1.  Every thought tends to be part of a personal consciousness.
2.  Within each personal consciousness thought is always changing.
3.  Within each personal consciousness thought is sensibly continuous.
4.  It always appears to deal with objects independent of itself.
5.  It is interested in some parts of these objects to the exclusion of others, and welcomes or rejects - *chooses* from among them, in a word - all the while. (James, 1890, p. 225)

The human stream of consciousness is ultimately in pursuit of that which is perceived to be experientially and consequentially "true" and useful regardless of whether that truth is perceived rationally, philosophically, spiritually, emotionally, aesthetically or on the basis of prejudice or bias. According to James:

> We live in a world of realities that can be infinitely useful or infinitely harmful. Ideas that tell us which of them to expect count as the true ideas in all this primary sphere of verification, and the pursuit of such ideas is a primary human duty. The possession of truth, so far from being here an end in itself, is only a preliminary means towards other vital satisfactions. If I am lost in the woods and starved, and find what looks like a cow-path, it is of the utmost importance that I should think of a human habitation at the end of it, for if I do so and follow it, I save myself. The true thought is useful here because the house which is its object is useful. The practical value of true ideas is thus primarily derived from the practical importance of their objects to us. (James, 1907, 1923)

So stated these objects of thought become compelling and even true on the basis of their inherent utility to the thinker. In some cases ideas or objects of thought may not lend themselves to truth or utility in one set of circumstances while in other contexts these same objects may prove to be compellingly useful. For instance, returning to James's metaphor of following a cow path:

> I may on another occasion have no use for the house [at the end of the cow path]; and then my idea of it, however verifiable, will be practically irrelevant, and had better remain latent. Yet since almost any object may someday become temporarily important, the advantage of having a general stock of extra truths, of ideas that shall be true of merely

> possible situations, is obvious. We store such extra truths away in our memories, and with the overflow we fill our books of reference. Whenever such an extra truth becomes practically relevant to one of our emergencies, it passes from cold-storage to do work in the world, and our belief in it grows active. You can say of it then either that "it is useful because it is true" or that "it is true because it is useful." Both these phrases mean exactly the same thing, namely that here is an idea that gets fulfilled and can be verified (James, 1907, p. 140)

So utility and truth (two components of what we might want to call compellability) are not just based upon rational and non-rational factors, they are also contextual. Moreover, these contextual moments of thought exist in a fluid relationship to one another as one moment of consciousness slips into the next. Accordingly,

> From this simple cue pragmatism gets her general notion of truth as something essentially bound up with the way in which one moment in our experience may lead us towards other moments which it will be worthwhile to have been led to. Primarily, and on the common-sense level, the truth of a state of mind means this function of a leading that is worthwhile. When a moment in our experience, of any kind whatever, inspires us with a thought that is true, that means that sooner or later we dip by that thought's guidance into the particulars of experience again and make advantageous connexion with them. This is a vague enough statement, but I beg you to retain it, for it is essential. (James, 1907, p. 124)

Ultimately these threads of human experience are generally accepted as credible at their face value and become part of the "currency of truth" we exchange with one another. As James wisely observed:

> Truth lives, in fact, for the most part on a credit system. Our thoughts and beliefs "pass," so long as nothing challenges them, just as bank-notes pass so long as nobody refuses them. But this all points to direct face-to-face verifications somewhere, without which the fabric of truth collapses like a financial system with no cash-basis whatever. You accept my verification of one thing, I yours of another. We trade on each other's truth. But beliefs verified concretely by somebody are the posts of the whole superstructure. (James, 1907, p. 125)

In the case of coal and Craig, Colorado what is demonstrably clear is that those who "traded" on one another's truths were those of like-mind who shared a gestalt of the issue in which rationality, bias, aesthetics, spirituality and more are amalgamated together into a totality in which it is very difficult to logically or rationally dislodge any one set of ideas or values. Truths shared, therefore principally occur within a common paradigm or frame while truths falling beyond these shared gestalts are generally discounted or ignored. This is what we will later refer to as paradigm or frame conflict (Schon & Rein, 1984). Such conflicts are not readily amenable to logical or rational resolution and instead appeal to a plethora of other values, emotions and ideas that promote conflict across frames or paradigms and which thwart rational resolution of problems. Consequently, environmental advocates in Colorado can't envision themselves empathizing with or engaging "big coal" to problem-solve and vice versa. The product of such frame conflict – as we shall soon see – is perennial conflict and stalemate.

## Tentative Problem Identification and the Five Attitudinal Principles of Ecopragmatics

Having employed the tools and perspectives of the imaginator we can tentatively identify the principal problem of this case as being one of "frame conflict" in which pro-environmental groups, regulators, legislators and citizens find themselves in a paradigmatic impasse with pro-coal, pro-coal power, libertarians, free marketers, local officials and a coal-dependent business economy that relies upon coal-fueled power for their livelihoods. Resolution of this conflict is most difficult because the conflict is based upon emotion, ideology and belief as much as much or more than it is upon reason and negotiation. In such instances a "winner-takes-all" mentality emerges in which there are those who benefit from policy changes or comparably suffer until such time as the economic and political valence of the community changes again and the tables are turned – rendering former winners losers and vice versa.

Of course this is not an ideal resolution to issues as important as those emerging around clean air in Colorado or nationwide. It is, however the current state of affairs (i.e. the Balkanization referred to in the Introduction) and is only improved upon when shared paradigms are found and employed by all, at least to the greatest degree possible. We would argue that ecopragmatics provides an opportunity for at least some degree of congruence on common problems and issues precisely because it ultimately prioritizes options that are most useful and meaningful to a community. The inclusion of a communitarian approach that furthers democratic processes along the lines of those advocated by Dewey is not an academic exercise but is instead a key component of ecopragmatics.

We argue that as much as possible environmental problems and issues should be addressed and resolved locally – and frankly as locally as possible. The rationale for this is to appeal to the community mindedness of all stakeholders – since community is what all share in common – and to work on this commonality as a shared value around which other values may be revalued or negotiated. Moreover the problem should be identified in such a way that all the stakeholders can relate to it, regard it as an authentic representation of the issue and feel as though the problem definition lends itself to finding possible solutions.

For instance if the stakeholders define the problem of burning coal in Craig as a climate change issue then the problem is framed so broadly that it can't be adequately addressed in the local community. Similarly if it is defined as a clean air problem for Colorado and the nation then it once again has been defined too broadly. However, if the problem were defined economically and socially in terms of how abandoning coal would impact the local community then perhaps the conversation might focus upon transitioning the energy economy of Craig from coal to natural gas so as to insure an ongoing economic base for the community. What is required is a democratic process that values community and state and community leaders willing to aid the community in making what appears to be an unavoidable transition.

Applying James's five principles of pragmatics to ecological issues is pointless outside of a larger democratic paradigm in which members of communities are provided a variety of ways to express and realize community values and processes that promote their freedom and well-being. We will delve into this communitarian portion of the ecopragmatic approach and imagining a bit later. However, in the interest of realizing some preliminary closure to the Craig, Colorado case, we would like to briefly comment upon how the five principles of ecopragmatics might be applied to this policy dispute.

## Principle One: Be Outcome Oriented

One of the factors most frequently contributing to policy resolution impasses is the penchant to become ensnared in the minutiae of policy issues and lose sight of possible outcomes worth pursuing and realizing (Mederova-Bergstom et al., 2011; Marton, 2011). As entrepreneur and CEO of Virgin Airlines Richard Branson says, "never let facts get in the way of a good idea" (DeWitt & Meyer, 2005, p. 150). In short the policy debate is sometimes compromised by allowing the supposed facts and beliefs associated with an issue interfere with keeping an eye upon what James called "last things."

In the case of Craig, Colorado it is conceivable that all parties involved in the policy dispute regarding coal might come together to identify areas where they can agree upon a set of shared outcomes – "last things" – that maximize community benefits and minimize disproportionate imposition of costs upon any one group. Transitioning the local economy is an obvious example of a shared concern around which possible outcomes could be developed. However this is a theoretical proposition only realized when the community embraces an ethic such as that expressed in the communitarian vision of a "new golden rule" to "respect and uphold society's (*the community's*) moral order as you would have society (*the community*) respect and uphold your autonomy" (Etzioni, 1997, p. xviii).

For the City of Craig moving forward means valuing individual interests but doing so in such a way that vouchsafes the interests of the community to remain socially and economically sustainable. Assuming that such a commitment is forthcoming from state and local leaders then participants have an opportunity to creatively "imagine-through" the issues and possible solutions relating to Craig's social and economic viability and begin to envision a range of acceptable community outcomes around which action plans can be developed for the community to realize a new sense of community based upon a new economic foundation. One of the most significant risks associated with considering alternative economic paradigms for the community is paralysis born of feeling overwhelmed by too many options and too many outcomes – so called "paralysis by analysis" (Langley, 1995).

However, as a practical manner – and as James himself observed – the process of thoughtful consideration is a fluid affair and most people are intuitively able to work their way through the complexities of processes and outcomes to find options they perceive as being "true" to their needs and values while also meeting to the greatest degree possible the needs of the community. Of course the caveat to this entire process of imagining and planning for a better community future is the expectation that the participants will actually want to remain a part of the newly transformed community. If that commitment is absent then the deliberative process has failed before it ever began.

## Principle Two: Be Mindful

The productive imaginator remains ever-present (Taylor, 2011). Such imaginators remain available to novelty meaning that they make a concerted effort to not allow their current old-stock knowledge, values and biases to impair recognizing new ideas that they may choose to adopt and apply to their own situations. The Craig, Colorado case is replete with novelty, most of which was not seriously entertained by many of the principle stakeholders due to their unreflective commitment to conceptual paradigms and frames that disallowed reflecting upon new and available options.

One of the best examples of such novelty was the foregone consideration by the Colorado legislature and environmental groups regarding the gasification of coal to power electric plants. In this instance environmental groups preferred the importation of natural gas beyond the state borders to considering the gasification of coal in the State of Colorado. The net effect upon air quality would be virtually identical. The only difference involved is that instead of structurally un-employing coal miners and workers at the Craig Unit and disrupting the economic interests connected to coal in the region, coal gasification would have only changed how coal was to be used not whether it would be used and would have guaranteed the economic security of Northern Colorado while simultaneously improving the state's air quality. Of course, the reason this option was not considered involved the degree to which "big coal" as an industry had become vilified in the minds of the state's environmentalists (Sweet, 2010). So-called "frame" or "paradigm" conflicts preclude discovering novelty let alone discovering novel solutions that turn 'lose-lose' scenarios into 'win-win' ones.

## Principle Three: Thoughtfully Discriminate

The operant word here of course is "thoughtful" and while necessary it is in point of fact frequently missing in policy determinations – having been substituted with a reflexive and pre-cognitive penchant for operating upon predisposed bias. As noted in an earlier chapter and reiterated throughout the text, modern decision science research has concluded that human beings don't make rational decisions per se, but instead make intuitive decision and use reason as a way of justifying, explaining or winning others over to our opinions. That said, bias is a given in any policy deliberation which is why the process must be "bias-aware."

Unfortunately bias has become a derogatory word most frequently associated with "prejudice." While the two terms are related, bias reflects "old-stock" knowledge or values based upon lived experience and it is always the starting point around which new ideas and experiences are interpreted. Prejudice on the other had is a term describing someone who doesn't openly think and rethink what they know or believe or what they think they know or believe. It is if you will a "hardening of the categories" and when found in an individual, group, organization or community it becomes prima facie grounds for excluding that entity from the deliberative process. Prejudicial stakeholders involved in an issue are unwilling to be aware of their biases and account for them when engaging in deliberation. By comparison those who are bias-aware engage in a thoughtful discrimination that entails dispassionately and critically reflecting upon the issues at hand – doing so in full recognition that all people approach this task with predispositions and biases.

In regard to the Craig, Colorado case, thoughtful discrimination would have allowed for the identification of possible 'win-win' policy options such as exploring coal gasification. Similarly it might have led state legislators, environmentalists, coal-producers, IOUs and others to consider the reorientation of the coal industry away from domestic consumption and toward international markets – perhaps looking toward investments in coal slurry technology that might have made it possible to readily export Colorado coal to foreign markets (Papachristodoulou & Trass, 2009).

Likewise, had thoughtful discrimination at the community level been applied in the Craig, Colorado case environmentalists might have been able to suspend their frames of reference regarding "big-coal' allowing these pro-environmental interests to discover that 'big-coal' was not exclusively an environmental foe that needed to be defeated, but was also a vital energy provider who makes significant contributions to the communities and environment of Colorado. However, such insight is impossible when 'bias' and 'bigotry' preclude thoughtful deliberation and discrimination between action options.

## Principle Four: Be Grounded in Past Experiences

As James has observed:

> since almost any object may someday become temporarily important, the advantage of having a general stock of extra truths, of ideas that shall be true of merely possible situations, is obvious. We store such extra truths away in our memories, and with the overflow we fill our books of reference. Whenever such an extra truth becomes practically relevant to one of our emergencies, it passes from cold-storage to do work in the world, and our belief in it grows active. (James, 1907, p. 140)

This "general stock of extra truths" – that which we know from experience to be true and potentially useful - is in great part what old-stock values consist of. We accumulate these truths, values, ideas and principles and employ them when the circumstances suggest they may be useful and even true for us. This old-stock reserve is the product of countless encounters and interactions. They are maintained because we recognize them as useful and in conformity with what we know to be true and useful in the world. It is for these reasons that James suggests that these old-stock ideas and values deserve our respect and attention. However, when old-stock equates with uncritical bias and bigotry then these values become an obstacle for experiencing the novel rather than serving as a catalyst for the next creative moment and outcome. Likewise, if preconceived notions and experience stand in the way of what James calls the acquisition of those "extra-truths" (things we are aware of but haven't yet tested to determine their truth or utility) then imaginators may find themselves wanting of a broad and inclusive set of ideas and options to apply to specific problems and issues.

Again, in the Craig, Colorado situation, fixed attitudes on the part of the environmentalist groups precluded conceptualizing opportunities of working with the state's coal mines and IOUs in creative ways to improve air quality and protect jobs. Likewise similar biases against the state environmentalists precluded the IOUs and coal mines from finding common cause with them. Consequently, while the inherent value of old-stock values should be respected, equal consideration should be given to biases and prejudices that preclude discovering novel and useful options to problems.

## Principle Five: Be Open to New Experiences

According to James, the default option for most people when confronted with novelty is to renew old-stock values and ideas only when superior new stock options become available. What this implies is a commitment to maintaining continuity of experience while remaining flexible and open to change. Moreover it requires striking a balance between the tried and true and other options that may prove to be more useful and truthful.

Sticking to one's values and beliefs, and acting upon what one has learned to be true is an admirable characteristic and, as noted above, these hard-won values and truths should not be thoughtlessly surrendered until better values and ideas are forthcoming. However, the definition of prejudice is to cling to ideas and values that are demonstrably untrue, inaccurate or dysfunctional even in the light of evidence illustrating such. Unfortunately, in some of the most divisive and protracted controversies and debates, neither side is seemingly willingly or able to renew old-stock with new-stock ideas when a prejudicial paradigm or frame of reference is embraced.

Craig, Colorado is exemplary of this "frame-freeze" to the degree that novel ideas and approaches have not been broadly considered and explored. Indeed it would seem as the decision to close the Craig coal facility was made with virtually no input or forethought of how this decision would impact the local community. From all accounts, the people in the area were completely left out of the decision loop. This is the essence of the Balkanization of values and ideas that this book began with and left unchecked such intransigence leads to perpetual stalemate. As we noted above, the only true antidote to this outcome is to broaden the conversation from individual or group good and well-being to the broader community and common good and well-being as is embraced within the tenets of communitarianism.

## Imaginating as Stream of Consciousness

William James first addressed what he perceived to be "streams of consciousness" in 1890 with this observation:

The first and foremost concrete fact which everyone will affirm to belong to his inner experience is the fact that consciousness of some sort goes on. 'States of mind' succeed each other..." "Consciousness, then, does not appear to itself chopped up in bits." It is nothing jointed; it flows. A 'river' or a 'stream' are the metaphors by which it is most naturally described. *In talking of it hereafter, let us call it the stream of thought, of consciousness, or of subjective life.* (James, 1890, p. 19)

Streams of consciousness are how we universally perceive the world around us and constitutes the inherent psychological process through which we engage problems, issues and ideas. The Craig, Colorado case study that introduced this chapter was perceived by the reader through a stream of consciousness to include visual images of the town, its stakeholders and processes. Associations were instantly made within this stream of thought and image and new associations were formed at least tentatively on the fly. Interesting and cogent facts and information were noted and figuratively filed away. Impressions were formed, facts and information were sorted and resorted and conclusions formatted and reformatted as new information was forthcoming in the case.

The readers familiarized themselves with the particulars of the case study but were not engaged in policy analysis as a formal process – a structured process fully developed throughout the entirety of this book. Instead they engaged in the simple yet profound process of intuitive perception and reflection. These are the processes that people routinely engage in on a daily basis. This process, though proceeding seemingly autonomically, is also purposeful and learned. As such it is possible for individuals to school themselves in techniques and tactics for addressing new ideas and information. In essence, human perception and reflection can be progressively disciplined and refined to incorporate decision-making values and priorities. Metaphorically speaking, perception and reflection can be channeled or directed through interpretive or hermeneutical lenses or prisms that serve to provide a value context for what is perceived and considered.

This is precisely what occurs when James's five principles of pragmatics are routinely, even habitually applied to considering new ideas, information and experiences. These five principles logically flow together and can be acquired as a mental perceptual discipline, namely being outcome oriented, mindful, discriminating, grounded in past experiences, yet open to new experiences. These principles are the very heart of a Jamesian approach to pragmatics and when applied to environmental problems and issues create the foundations of an ecopragmatic way of thinking that dedicated imaginators can learn to acquire and incorporate into the way they think about each and every environmentally-oriented issue and problem.

# Chapter 3: Simplify—Interiority, Exteriority, and Necessary Anthropocentrism

Oh the complicated nature in the way this world revolves
Can trick us into thinkin' we've got problems we can't solve
We gotta get back to the basics, break it down to black and white
Take a little time to rewind and simplify.

*Simplify*
John Rich

## Simplification: Unbundling Interiority and Exteriority

The title for this chapter comes from a tune entitled "Simplify" popularized by John Rich of the country duo *Big & Rich*. The chapter title and the song lyrics are indicative of James's philosophical intent – namely to bring philosophy out of the academy and into the public sphere to aid people in dealing with even the most complex philosophical problems. Simplification of complex issues, however, does not necessarily imply transforming something inherently complex into something simple. Instead it serves as a vehicle for breaking complex issues down into their constituent parts – in a sense "unbundling" complexity.

One of the best ways to begin grasping and unraveling complex issues is to discriminate between issues of interiority (what people feel, think and believe - intentions) from issues of exteriority (what people say and do - actions). A dedication to such an effort on the part of participants in complex policy disputes is essential if new options and solutions are to be discovered and employed. Unfortunately, people do not always act in a fashion that is fully congruent with their stated values.

For instance, politicians will often battle one another during primaries saying the worst possible things about one another only to coalesce during general elections to support one another as if they had never uttered a critical word or harbored a critical thought against the opposing candidate. For seemingly inexplicable reasons they will express one value about a person at one time and turn right around weeks or months later and utter a seemingly contradictory value

– what psychologists call "cognitive dissonance" (Festinger, 1957). Cognitive dissonance refers to situations in which individuals appear to embrace a set of conflicting attitudes producing feelings of discomfort that are only relieved by either changing their beliefs or actions to regain a sense of congruity and harmony. In many instances, this describes the process James alluded to when he spoke of replacing old-stock ideas with new-stock ones. However, regardless of which paradigm one considers this phenomenon – that of James or Festinger - what this implies is that to fully understand what people do or what they value it is necessary to study their exteriorities (actions) as well as the interiorities (values, feelings, perceptions) that ideally work together to produce a harmonic outcome.

Ken Wilber has been most instrumental in recent years in introducing this basic insight into policy analysis and particularly in regard to understanding environmental issues. His approach to understanding human interaction is popularly referred to as "integral theory" which Wilber describes with the acronym AQAL (all quadrants, levels, lines, states and types). In many circles, Wilber's acronym has been replaced with the term "integral operating system (IOS)" which describes how humans interact with one another and with the world by way of individual and collective interior and exterior perspectives. Wilber conceptualizes this integral operating system as analogous to a computer operating system that integrates the various mental states human beings experience (i.e. waking, sleeping, dreaming) and relates these to various stages of consciousness (roughly equivalent to stages of human development, maturity, etc.) and levels of action, organization or complexity accompanying these developmental stages. He provides the following example to illustrate his perspective:

> If we look at moral development, for example, we find that an infant at birth has not yet been socialized into the culture's ethics and conventions; this is called the *preconventional* stage. It is also called egocentric, in that the infant's awareness is largely self-absorbed. But as the young child begins to learn its culture's rules and norms, it grows into the conventional stage of morals. This stage is also called *ethnocentric*, in that it centers on the child's particular group, tribe, clan, or nation, and it therefore tends to exclude care for those not of one's group. But at the next major stage of moral development, the *postconventional* stage, the individual's identity expands once again, this time to include a care and concern for all peoples, regardless of race, color, sex, or creed, which is why this stage is also called *worldcentric*. Thus, moral development tends to move from "me" (egocentric) to "us" (ethnocentric) to "all of us" (worldcentric)—a good example of the unfolding stages of consciousness. (Wilber, 2012)

What Wilber describes is the ever-expansive growth of the human self over time and in relationship to the people, community, culture and world in which they are embedded. This is the process by which the individual emerges from a narrow self-preoccupation and transcends self, becoming reoriented toward the social milieu around which their social self is defined and redefined. This "social self" is what psychologist George Herbert Mead referred to as: "The self which consciously stands over against other selves thus becomes an object, an other to himself" (Mead, 1913). As such the realization of the "social self" embodies a state of being in which the person perceives themselves simultaneously in the first-person as an "I" and also in the third-person as an "other" to himself and all others.

## Nested Ecology and Integral Theory

This conceptual and developmental model – moving from the narrow "I" to the social "we" - is consistent with Wimberley's nested ecological approach (Wimberley, 2009) in which human beings relate to the world as individual selves dwelling within personal ecologies and progressively extend their perceptions and behaviors to include family, friends and community – the sphere of social ecology – which also includes organizations, institutions, government, culture, art and more. The driving force for this human extension from the personal and individual to the familial, community and cultural level is survival, satisfaction and meaning as derived from Abraham Maslow's hierarchy of needs paradigm (Maslow, 1934, p. 374). Sustainability, therefore, is a measure of the degree to which needs, desires, values and aspirations are met and sustained over time, with the understanding that ecological wholeness and health is defined by the degree to which requisite needs are met at each level (personal or self-ecology and social ecology). These two levels within the nested ecology model constitute what is otherwise referred to as human ecology.  Assuming that basic needs are adequately met at both ecological levels then humans are prepared to successfully engage the world of nature and the natural (environmental ecology) as well as consider the broader sets of worldly and other-worldly systems that constitute the universe as well that extending beyond the known and potentially known (i.e. cosmic ecology) (Wimberley, 2009).

At the heart of a nested ecology approach is the recognition that human beings are necessarily anthropocentric in their worldviews and are inevitably going to construe the world around them – to include the environment – within the context of their own particular individual, community and cultural needs, namely, from the perspective of their personal, social and cultural interiority. Rather than apologize for this orientation – reflecting the perspective of the deep ecologists – a nested ecological approach calls for individuals to accept and embrace *necessary anthropocentrism* as a means for self-preservation, self-enhancement and a value contributing to the perseverance of the human species. In this regard humans can be expected to do no more or less than any other species to insure their ongoing existence on the planet (Wimberley, 2009).

Wilber's integral theory likewise implies an appreciation of necessary anthropocentrism by developing a perspective on human behavior and culture incorporating aspects of interiority (internal psychological, mental, social and cultural processes) and exteriority (outwardly conveyed behavior, laws, mores, systems and consequences) pertaining to policy issues - to include environmental policy issues. Wilber's emphasis upon the evolution of the self from a "preconventional" to a "worldcentric" state roughly parallels our own notion of interactive, nested ecological spheres. Likewise it reflects the transition from narrow anthropocentrism to eco-sensibility and sustainability.

Table 2: The Four Modern Value Spheres

|  | Interior | Exterior |
|---|---|---|
| Individual | "I" Psychology/Art | "IT" Natural Science |
| Collective | "WE" Religion/Morality | "THEY" Social/System Science |

Source: McFarlane, 2000

Utilizing his integral operating system paradigm with its underlying theory of human development and interaction, Wilber creates what has come to be known as his "Four Quadrant Model" that succinctly illustrates how he views human beings interacting with one another (individually and collectively) by way of their behaviors and actions (exteriorities) as well as on the basis of their inward perceptions, values, philosophies etc. (interiorities) (McFarlane, 2000). This simple four-way perceptual schema translates an individual's interiorities in the realm of "I" "" and "mine" while exteriorities (i.e. that lying beyond the bounds of the self) are perceived as "it" and "that." This is the perceptual set of the individual, first-person, singular. By comparison, the perspective of the plural, second- and third-person collective substitutes "I" with "we" and "us" and replaces "it" with "they" and "them" (Table 2).

Table 3: Ontological / Epistemological Spectrums

|  | Subjective Knowing (Epistemology/Psyche) | Objective Being (Ontology/Cosmos) |
|---|---|---|
| Transcendent | Soul | God |
| Subtle | Mind | Archetypes/Ideas |
| Gross (Physical) | Body | Matter |

Source: McFarlane, 2000

Within the bounds of this typology subjective knowing (epistemology) is experienced as a spectrum of experiences beginning with the gross reality of the physical body, progressing to the subtle dimension of "mind" and "thought" and eventually experiencing a state transcendence typically associated with the soul. According to Wilber, these are the range of states of consciousness human beings experience in the first-person singular "I." Third-person states (objective being) span a similar spectrum, with gross or physical reality perceived as consisting of "matter," subtle states being associated with "archetypes," "ideas," "values," "philosophies," "theories" and the like, while transcendental reality is typically characterized in terms such as "God" or ultimate "Being" (Table 3). These are the various "quadrants" of reality that Wilber proffers from the perspective of the individual person, which can also be construed as the perceptual set of the "Interior "I"" and the "External "It"" (Table 4) (McFarlane, 2000).

Table 4: Ontological/Epistemological Integration into the Perceptual First-Person Singular

|                      | Interior "I" | Exterior "It"    |
|----------------------|--------------|------------------|
| **Transcendent**     | Soul         | God              |
| **Subtle**           | Mind         | Archetypes/Ideas |
| **Gross (Physical)** | Body         | Matter           |

*Source: McFarlane, 2000*

When the collective perspective is added to Wilber's Quadrant typology a subtler understanding of interiority and exteriority emerges. The upper-left quadrant of Wilber's model reflects the experience of the "I" (the interior-individual) whose orientation toward all things is "intentional" – namely pre-behavioral and pre-responsorial. This is the state of being that considers action immediately before initiating action and behavior. By comparison the lower-left quadrant reflects the experience of the "We" (the interior-collective) whose state of experience is principally "cultural" or what William James likes to refer to as the "old-stock" of values, knowledge and ideas that have been handed down and become a shared interior reality among the collective. The upper-right quadrant of Wilber's conceptual mode is the experienced "It" (the exterior-individual) that is construed behaviorally and existentially (i.e. shape, color, texture etc.). These are what the individual perceives as the individual bits of concrete reality existing beyond the bounds of the self. This quadrant is complemented by the lower-right quadrant in which the "Its" (exterior-collective) are encountered and experienced principally in terms of the "social" and the "systemic" (Table 5).

Table 5: Wilber's Four-Quadrant Summary

| Upper-Left Quadrant: I<br>Interior-Individual<br>Intentionality | Upper-Right Quadrant: IT<br>Exterior-Individual<br>Behavioral |
|---|---|
| Lower-Left Quadrant We<br>Interior-Collective<br>Cultural | Lower-Right Quadrant ITS<br>Exterior-Collective<br>Social (Systems) |

*Source: Kaslev, (2005)*

When this paradigm is applied to understanding issues or to complex policy analysis what it implies is that interiority expressed as intent (what James would refer to as values and philosophies) produces exteriority as expressed in behavior (consequences) and that meaning is derived from these consequences and internalized within the individual as values and philosophies. As Wimberley observes in *Nested Ecology* (2009) this process occurs within the context of personal or "social-ecology" as individuals affiliate together, achieve consensus regarding community values, refashion and reform cultural values and behaviorally translate these cultural reforms systemically within society and within and among systems. So what we have here is a feedback loop in which interiority (intent) produces exteriorities (behavior) whose consequences shape future interiority through individual values and philosophies, which ultimately shapes cultural values that transforms society and social systems that in turn influence individual interioirty. And "so it goes and so on" (Vonnegut, 1969).

## Order from Chaos

James alludes to the same process Wilber considers though using a different metaphorical vehicle for illustration: Accordingly, he notes that:

> The mind is at every stage a theatre of simultaneous possibilities. Consciousness consists in the comparison of these with each other, the selection of some, and the suppression of the rest by the reinforcing and inhibiting agency of attention. The highest and most elaborated mental products are filtered from the data chosen by the faculty next beneath, out of the mass offered by the faculty below that, which mass in turn was sifted from a still larger amount of yet simpler material, and so on. The mind, in short, works on the data it receives very much as a sculptor works on his block of stone. In a sense the statue stood there from eternity. But there were a thousand different ones beside it, and the sculptor alone is to thank for having extricated this one from the rest. (James, 1892, p. 288)

This process – while rendered somewhat orderly in James's metaphorical description – is essentially chaotic. Fredrick Ruf (1991) examines James and the persistence of chaos in his work and comments upon how James typically related to the world in pessimistic terms such as when comparing reality to a "black and jointless continuity of space." In his own words, James spoke eloquently regarding chaos:

> Just so the world of each of us, how so ever different our several views of it may be, all lay embedded in the primordial chaos of sensations, which gave the mere *matter* to the thought of all of us indifferently. We may, if we like, by our reasonings unwind things back to that black and jointless continuity of space and moving clouds of swarming atoms which science calls the only real world. But all the while the world *we* feel and live in will be that which our ancestors and we, by slowly cumulative strokes of choice, have extricated out of this, like sculptors, by simply removing portions of the given stuff. Other sculptors, other statues from the same stone! Other minds, other worlds from the same monotonous and inexpressive chaos! The world is but one in a million alike embedded, alike real to those who may abstract them. How different must be the worlds in the consciousness of ant, cuttlefish, or crab! (James, 1892, p. 288)

For James the streams of consciousness through which we make sense of the world along the lines of the bird that flits from one branch along the winding tributary to another – at each point making tentative sense of what lies beyond the bird's senses and drawing first tentative then lasting conclusions before endlessly moving on to other branches – is nothing less than the unique and persistent effort of humans to wrest order and meaning out of what otherwise appears to be chaos and disorder. In this particular regard James uses the metaphor of the sculptor who will find the image buried in the stone and bring it to life and purpose. When James's ideas are compared to those of Wilber what emerges is a more gradated paradigm for understanding the processes through which intentions are transformed into actions with meaningful consequences. Wilber's quadrant model serves the same purpose as James's metaphorical streams of consciousness and constitutes not so much a means for negating chaos as it does a template for making sense of what would otherwise be nonsensical and meaningless.

Wilber, like James, perceives that ultimately order emerges from the midst of chaos when he suggests that:

> Whenever material processes become very chaotic and "far from equilibrium," they tend under their own power to escape chaos by transforming it into higher and more structured order – commonly called "order out of chaos (Wilber, 2011, p. 13).

His understanding of the world is one in which chaos is constantly in the process of being re-ordered toward an end. Accordingly,

> Evolution has a direction, yes a principle of order out of chaos" … "in other words, a drive toward greater depth. Chance is defeated, depth emerges – the intrinsic value of the Kosmos increases with each unfolding. (Wilber, 2011, p. 58)

Wilber's quadrant model serves to provide a sense of perspective on what would otherwise be chaotic conditions by linking individual and collective interiority and exteriority. His is but a more in-depth and contextualized articulation of what James refers to when he speaks of intermediary factors such as values, biases, philosophies, etc. (interiority) and consequential actions – namely actions that translate intermediary or mediating factors into meaningful consequences - that in turn further shape intermediary factors and functions (old-stock values and ideas), ultimately influencing behavior and producing additional consequences. However, what Wilber contributes beyond the Jamesian perspective is the concept of interiority that produces intentionality upon which action (exteriority) and consequences are predicated.

Therefore the principal quality of Wilber's integral theory – "an all-inclusive framework that draws on the key insights of the world's greatest knowledge traditions" (Integral Institute, 2009), beyond dramatically expanding the value and philosophical palate for shaping the individual's realm of possible intentionality, is the methodology it offers for linking interior processes with exterior reality, action and consequences. By considering the degree to which interior factors such as values, experiences, biases, and philosophies shape individual intentions, behaviors and the consequences that accrue to these behaviors, the policymaker and the individual decision maker is provided a more inclusive perspective on the factors that may contribute to and thwart change within and among individuals and within and among communities and societies.

## The Relationship between Interiority and Exteriority: Big Coal

The Craig, Colorado case illustrates this point nicely. For instance, understanding the actions of the various environmental groups who sought to close the Craig Unit necessitates understanding their underlying intentionality's which in turn requires a clearer understanding of what their inherent values, philosophies and worldviews consist of. Without engaging in an in-depth analysis of the values underscoring each group, it is easy to glean from public comments that these groups bore significant animosity toward the coal companies, viewing them as essentially heartless corporate entities that do not care about their employees, people or the environment. For instance, Richard Meyers in his book *Slaughter in Serene* – the story of the 1927 Columbine coal miner strike in Colorado - asserts that coal mine owners and operators (to include the John D. Rockefeller family) were uncaring relative to the health and safety of miners and were indifferent to the "spilling of their blood" in the mines and along the International Workers of the World (a.k.a. "Wobblies") union picket lines (Meyers, 2005). This famous strike in Colorado coal country, where the striking miner faced bloody reprisals from owners and operators, has become part of the folklore of the environmental movement in the state and nationwide – laying an historical foundation upon which modern stereotypes of the exploitation of workers and the planet look for justification of contemporary attitudes and actions.

The stereotypical animus against "Big Coal," however is also reinforced by the visible damage it does to the landscape. For instance Tom Egan of the New York Times commenting upon the coal industry while reviewing Michael Shaynerson's book *Coal River* (2008) harshly criticized West Virginia's coal industry by noting that,

> If it is possible for one industry to destroy both land and culture, the coal companies clawing at West Virginia have found a way to do it. Used to be, coal mining was done deep underground, employing legions of miners. It was dangerous, but at least a little coal town could coexist down the road from the mine, and there was always a river nearby for fishing on Sunday afternoon. Now the industry employs far fewer people by simply blowing up entire hillsides - mountain-ectomies. Towns, farms, forests, schools, rivers - anything near the blast zone is a casualty. (Egan, 2008)

Egan's angst toward coal companies is even more poetically expressed by Shaynerson himself as he describes the "Coal River Valley" that is at the heart of his book:

> This is what lies behind the picturesque backdrop of roadside hills in the Coal River valley: mountains reduced to rubble by the practice the industry calls mountaintop mining and its critics call mountaintop removal. The landscape from Gibson's place is so much lower than his

mountaintop compound that it's hard to imagine the forested ridges that rose here before. It's like a man-made Grand Canyon, except that the Grand Canyon teems with life, and this panorama has none — none except the men who work the distant dozers and huge-wheeled dump trucks, their motors a constant, hornet-like hum. An underground mine needs hundreds of miners, but a skeleton crew can handle a miles-wide mountaintop site, setting the blasts and operating the heavy machinery to push rubble into valley streams below. That's one reason Whitesville looks as desperate as it does. The coal industry is making a killing. The Coal River valley is just getting killed. (Shaynerson, 2008, p. 6)

Returning to the discussion of the factors that shape interiorities and ultimately produce cultural values, it is easy to understand how – in the case of coal and coal mining –a history of violent labor relationships, ill-treatment of coal miners (as exemplified by black lung disease which is on the rise again (Maher, 2009), and catastrophic despoliation of landscapes can interact to create a powerful revulsion to coal and the companies who mine it. Events such as the ones just provided illustrate how deep and unyielding opinions among environmentalists regarding the evils of coal and coal mining can be formed and reinforced. Likewise, to the degree these perceptions are widely shared by individuals, they eventually form the cultural value base of groups, organizations and communities. From Wilber's perspective interiorities create and shape intentions that in turn influence behavioral exteriorities and consequences. Similarly from a Jamesian perspective, events and information shape values and beliefs that in turn inform actions and influence consequences. What we have here are two different ways of depicting a common process.

## Integral Ecology

When it comes to environmental policy issues, inadequate attention has often been directed toward their interiorities. Policy outcomes and goals are frequently discussed, proposed and articulated and interiorities identified in terms of the biases of the opposing interest in the policy debate (i.e. big coal is in the pockets of the financiers or manipulate and control the legislature or state executive). However, a serious and dispassionate analysis of the interiorities reflected in philosophies and values producing intentions and actions is seldom undertaken – particularly analyses directed toward the person engaged in doing the analysis. One of the real strengths of applying integral theory to environmental policy issues is its patently pluralistic worldview that admits *all* perspectives into consideration.

Sean Esbjörn-Hargens and Michael E. Zimmerman (2009) have applied Wilber's integral theory to the practice of environmental philosophy and policy analysis and have coined what they call "Integral Ecology," by which they mean,

the study of the subjective and objective aspects of organisms in relationship to their intersubjective and interobjective environments at all levels of depth and complexity. (Esbjörn-Hargens & Zimmerman, 2009, p. 478)

Accordingly Esbjörn-Hargens and Zimmerman assert that "integral ecologists" are, among other things:

- Committed to increasing their capacity to take and hold additional perspectives in order to dismantle self-other dynamics that arise in the course of addressing most environmental issues.

- Engaged in long-term personal transformational practices which develop their somatic, psychological, interpersonal, moral and spiritual dimensions. (Esbjörn-Hargens & Zimmerman, 2009, p. 486)

These are very ambitious goals for anyone interested in solving environmental problems and may likely be more ambitious than most people can reasonably expect to accomplish. Even so, what we have here is a blatantly pluralistic and integrative philosophy that is so very refreshing in an era characterized by ideological balkanization and policy framing stalemates. Yet here it is, a philosophical orientation that is as expansive as it is trend-setting – an approach committed to providing,

> a framework capable of organizing and integrating the riad perspectives and their multiple fields into a complex, multidimensional, post-disciplinary approach that defines and provides solutions for environmental problems. (Esbjörn-Hargens & Zimmerman, 2009, p. 478)

Accordingly, such an ecological approach demands of the adherent that they acquire an "integral ecological identity" (i.e. develop an inclusive sense of self that includes all aspects of the world), engage in "integral ecological action" (i.e. minimize one's ecological footprint), enter into an "integral ecological communion" with all beings (i.e. learn to resonate with the demands of human and non-human life) and acknowledge personal human membership in the "integral web of life" (namely, contributing at many levels and stages to positive systems of change and development) (Esbjörn-Hargens & Zimmerman, 2009, p. 312). Integral ecology, therefore, is not simply a philosophy it is a comprehensive way of life in the most complete sense of the word. It is at once philosophy, action, faith, and life itself. In fact Integral Theory is an ideological approach to framing policy issues that organizes "principles that are socially shared and persistent over time, that work symbolically to meaningfully structure the world" (Resse, et al., 2001) thereby providing "the lens through which people interpret issues" (Lyengar, 2009).

Arguably, William James's philosophical orientation also serves to frame issues in pursuit of pluralism. James's approach calls for the broadest possible inclusion of people and their ideas to inform action. For James pluralism implies acknowledging that

> nothing real is absolutely simple, that every smallest bit of experience is a *multum in parvo* plurally related, that each relation is one aspect, character, or function, way of its being taken, or way of its taking something else; and that a bit of reality when actively engaged in one of

> these relations is not *by that very fact* engaged in all the other relations simultaneously. The relations are not *all* what the French call *solidaires* with one another. (James, 1909, p. 321)

Therefore, pluralism implies that each and every person can be expected to experience the world around them in unique ways and that this plurality of expression and perception guarantees diversity of not only perception but response. As James observes, pluralism

> means only that the sundry parts of reality *may be externally related.* Everything you can think of, however vast or inclusive, has on the pluralistic view a genuinely "external" environment of some sort or amount. Things are "with" one another in many ways, but nothing includes everything, or dominates over everything. The word "and" trails along after every sentence. Something always escapes. "Ever not quite" has to be said of the best attempts made anywhere in the universe at attaining all-inclusiveness. The pluralistic world is thus more like a federal republic than like an empire or a kingdom. However much may be collected, however much may report itself as present at any effective centre of consciousness or action, something else is self-governed and absent and unreduced to unity. (James, 1909, p. 321)

The key concept James asserts in this narrative is the notion that no pluralistic worldview can be so inclusive as to include everything. Even so, integral ecology would appear to be interested in striving for the maximum degree of pluralistic inclusion possible as it calls for a total self-transformation and indeed takes on the aura of religious faith and piety. In fact this may be its most significant drawback to many who would consider approaching environmental issues from this point of view. Because it is a totalizing worldview it may prove to be unpalatable to those – particularly the religious – for whom many aspects of this approach is already ensconced in scripture, polity and faith.

## Re-framing: Walking in Another's Shoes

As we shall discuss in chapters to come, framing a policy issue is central to understanding the interiorities and exteriorities associated with it. Framing as a policy tool is particularly appropriate to the current culture in that most people derive their information on policy issues through the media and are constantly in the business of formulating and re-formulating their opinions based upon the information they receive. According to Stanford University professor Shanto Lyengard framing is most useful in understanding complex issues since:

- People use mental shortcuts to make sense of the world.
- Incoming information provides cues about where to "file" it mentally.
- People get most information about public affairs from the news media which, over time, creates a framework of expectation, or a dominant frame.

- Over time, we develop habits of thought and expectation and configure incoming. (Lyengard, 2009, p. 1)

Karen Umemoto of the University of Hawaii agrees and asserts "Culture, history and collective memory shape the interpretive frames through which meaning is made" (Umemoto, 2001, p. 20).

So if people tend to constantly frame the information they receive – yet another way of expressing William James's conceptualization of old-stock ideas being reshaped by values, philosophies, information and experiences into new-stock ideas – then there must be some intrinsic value in making an effort to experience the world through the lenses of the "frames" of others. In point of fact this is but a reassertion of the older adage about the value of "walking a mile in another's shoes."

Since we have been employing song lyrics throughout this text to illustrate metaphorical ways of thinking about complex issues, consider this take on "walking in another's shoes" by the songwriter Joe South:

> If I could be you, if you could be me
> For just one hour, if we could find a way
> To get inside each other's mind
> If you could see you through my eyes
> Instead your own ego I believe you'd be
> I believe you'd be surprised to see
> That you've been blind
> *Walk a mile in my shoes*
> *just walk a mile in my shoes*
> *Before you abuse, criticize and accuse*
> *Then walk a mile in my shoes*
> Now if we spend the day
> Throwin' stones at one another
> 'Cause I don't think, 'cause I don't think
> Or wear my hair the same way you do
> Well, I may be common people
> But I'm your brother
> And when you strike out
> You're tryin' to hurt me
> It's hurtin' you, Lord have mercy
> *Walk a mile in my shoes*
> *just walk a mile in my shoes*
> *Before you abuse, criticize and accuse*
> *Then walk a mile in my shoes.*

South captures the heart of the matter when he points out that our predetermined suppositions about one another serve to blind and alienate us and guarantee we relate to one another as adversaries rather than partners. Ideally we would prefer for differing factions engaged environmental policy disputes to discipline themselves to the point of attempting to walk in another's shoes and see the world through the eyes of others. This is the pluralist pursuit in public policy and is very much consistent with the goals of integral ecology and Jamesian pragmatics. However, the harsh reality is that unless people are somehow compelled to do so, most will resist projecting themselves into the situations of others and bothering to learn how reality looks through the eyes of others.

Certainly the environmental advocates seeking to shut down coal-powered electric production didn't seem interested in understanding the policy issues associated with coal from the worldview of the coal companies, nor did the converse occur. Sadly the product of that unwillingness to develop a sense of empathy for others involved in policy disputes has produced stalemate and impasse – an all too common outcome in environmental debates. However, had the environmental interests opposing coal production and use in Colorado bothered to make this effort, perhaps they would have come to appreciate the following perspective.

## Walking in Another's Shoes: Approaching Coal from the Perspective of the Coal Industry

For a moment, consider the perspective that might be realized if environmentalists opposing the use of coal in Colorado made a concerted effort to "walk in the shoes" of coal producers and coal-fired power companies as well as tread in the shoes of workers and communities dependent upon the coal-fired utility for jobs, tax bases and livelihoods. Doing so would expose them to a much different social, economic and environmental narrative than the one they currently embrace. However, doing so runs the risk of becoming empathetic of "Big Coal's" policy perspective.

For instance, what if they were to seriously consider the World Energy Council's report *Sustainable Global Energy Development: The Case of Coal* (2004) that asserts,

> Coal is the most abundant and widely distributed fossil fuel, and it can provide an affordable, reliable and safe supply of energy for hundreds of years. However, today coal is often dismissed as a part of the sustainable energy future due to its "poor" environmental credentials. Advanced clean coal technologies, which significantly reduce emissions from coal-fired power generation plants can help address this issue. Their costs are high though, and therefore make the wider deployment of these technologies in regions and countries where the use of coal is expected to grow most, practically unfeasible. (World Energy Council, 2004, p. 2)

The good news according to this international report is that coal is inexpensive, extremely abundant and can be utilized with minimal impact upon the atmosphere. However, the technologies required to utilize coal in an environmentally friendly fashion are very expensive and beyond the economic means of emerging nations. However, for affluent countries like the United States, these technological innovations – while expensive – are not beyond the realm of possibility, assuming that consumers are willing to pay the additional costs.

From the perspective of this international body, demand for coal will increase across the 21$^{st}$ century and must be considered as one of the planet's major energy resources, regardless of resistance from environmental groups. In fact the World Energy Council projects the following outcomes from now through the year 2030:

1.  Coal demand will increase from 2000-2030 from about 50 to 100%.
2.  The major alternative for of coal is natural gas – a fuel no better in terms of life cycle greenhouse gas emissions than oil or coal.
3.  Coal-powered electrical generation will remain dominant providing 37% of total electric generation in 2000 and 45% in 2030.
4.  Cumulative investments in coal mining, shipping and power generation will remain strong during the era 2001-2030 totaling US$1900 billion.
5.  Advanced coal combustion technologies (a.k.a. clean coal technologies) will fuel 33% of world power generation in 2030, and 72% of coal-based power generation.
6.  Advanced clean coal-based technologies could noticeably displace gas-fired combined cycle plants.
7.  Over the next two decades clean-coal technologies may well be the most effective single technology option to combat climate change, bridging the time for coal sequestration to gain maturity. (Philibert & Podkanski, 2005, p. 15; World Energy Council, 2004, p. 131)

These assertions suggest that coal may indeed be legitimately utilized as an energy resource through the year 2030. However it does not deal with the concerns regarding the despoliation that underground and surface mining has upon landscapes and the atmosphere.

An issue often lost in the environmental furor surround coal mining is the reality that in the U.S. reclamation is required for all coal mine operators (surface and underground) under the Surface Mining Control and Reclamation Act of 1977. Accordingly,

> Comprehensive and effective reclamation is a standard and integral part of coal mining operations. An estimated 2.5 million acres of coal mined lands have been restored to productive use. In addition, more than 100,000 acres of abandoned mines, remnants of neglect from a long-gone mining era, have also been reclaimed through money paid by today's coal producers into a national trust fund. (Mineral Information Institute, 2012).

Moreover, the World Coal Association goes even further to spell out the responsibilities coal operators have in regard to restoring the land following mining activities. They acknowledge that:

> Coal mining is only a temporary use of land, so it is vital that rehabilitation of land takes place once mining operations have stopped. In best practice a detailed rehabilitation or reclamation plan is designed and approved for each coal mine, covering the period from the start of operations until well after mining has finished. ... The cost of the

rehabilitation of the mined land is factored into the mine's operating costs. (World Coal Association, 2012)

Mine acid is also a major environmental problem associated with underground coal mining. However, even with this most troublesome of coal-related pollution, technologies and techniques exist which can dramatically mitigate water pollution. For instance, the World Coal Association suggests that,

> There are mine management methods that can minimize the problem of Acid Mine Drainage (AMD), and effective mine design can keep water away from acid generating materials and help prevent AMD occurring. AMD can be treated actively or passively.
>
> • Active treatment involves installing a water treatment plant, where the AMD is first dosed with lime to neutralize the acid and then passed through settling tanks to remove the sediment and particulate metals.
> • Passive treatment aims to develop a self-operating system that can treat the effluent without constant human intervention. (World Coal Association, 2012)

Limestone diversion wells - wells employing limestone bases to neutralize mine acidification - have also been employed which provide a comparatively inexpensive mechanism for relieving the problem of mine acid following underground mining operations (Arnold, 1991). Of course the most cost-effective approach to controlling mine acid drainage is to prevent its formation at the outset. This can be accomplished by chemically inhibiting acid generating reactions, inhibiting the microbes catalyzing acid generating reactions, and the employment of physical or geotechnical treatment technologies designed to minimize water contact and leaching (Skousen, 2011).

Critics of the coal industry have also been motivated by the legacy of mistreatment of miners and mine related safety and illness issues. While this history is both long and grim, generally speaking progress has been made in a number of areas. According to the U.S. National Mining Association, fatalities in coal mining have dropped 68% between 1990 and 2011 (from a rate of .04 per 200,000 work hours in 1990 to a rate of .02 per 200,000 work hours in 2011 (National Mining Association, 2012). However, "Black Lung" disease – while once on the downturn – is on the rise once again. According to the Centers for Disease Control and Prevention (CDC),

> While the prevalence of black lung disease had decreased by about 90% from 1969 to 1995 following the enactment of the Coal Mine Health and Safety Act, the downward trend of this disease in coal miners has stopped. Since 1995, the prevalence of black lung cases has more than doubled. Many current underground miners (some as young as in their 30s) are developing severe and advanced cases. Identification of advanced cases among miners under age 50 is of particular concern, as they were exposed to coal-mine dust in the years after implementation of

the disease prevention measures mandated by the 1969 federal legislation. An increased risk of pneumoconiosis has also been associated with work in certain mining jobs, in smaller mines, in several geographic areas, and among contract miners. (CDC, 2012)

So while mine fatalities are down, one of the oldest occupational illnesses associated with coal mining is once again on the rise, threatening the health of a growing number of coal miners. However, given advances in coal mining technology, fewer miners are required to mine coal which means that overall a smaller number of workers overall are impacted by mine-related illnesses and conditions.

Finally, animus toward the coal industry has also been fueled by the perception that coal industry employees are treated poorly. According to the National Mine Association (NMA) total employment in all coal-related fields has declined since 1985 from 184,373 to 89,209 in 2010. To a great extent this change reflects the shift in the industry from underground to surface mining and the utilization of new and improved technology (NMA, 2011). However, while the number of coal-field jobs has decreased dramatically since 1985, the annual wage base has increased (annually adjusted after 1981) from $3000 between 1937-1950 to $106,800 in 2011 (U.S. Department of Labor, 2012).

When all this information is factored into considering turning to clean coal technologies rather than abandoning coal all together then it becomes difficult to persist in relating to coal related industries within the parameters of old biases and stereotypes. Considering this new information allows all parties to the Craig Colorado case to dramatically expand the range of options to be considered when pursuing cleaner climates and economic sustainability. Ultimately, however, what stands in the way of such broader horizons is the reality that these old biases and stereotypes are driven by intuitive and emotional responses that must be purposefully recognized and acknowledged in the interest of considering new information and effectively "walking in the shoes of another."

## Ecopratmatics, Interiority, and Exteriority

This is the perspective a policy analyst or a person interested in appreciating the perspectives of other stakeholders in the environmental debate might take in attempting to resolve tough environmental issues. Consequently, the first step associated with an ecopragmatic approach to policy analysis involves *"carefully considering the case from the perspective of every other major stakeholder"* to arrive at an appreciation of their values, biases and perspectives. This process is difficult to achieve because it requires one to temporarily suspend (to the greatest degree possible) one's own perspective and biases in the interest of getting into the mind – the interiority – of another so as to come to some understanding regarding how that person's interior perspective produces intentionality, action and ultimately consequences.

In truth this process is seldom conducted in earnest and rarer still is it methodically employed in considering multiple stakeholders. Even so, this effort is indispensable when dealing with truly intractable policy problems of the sort that are commonplace when considering environmental issues. Yet even when this process is undertaken in earnest it is often narrowly conducted across the singular and plural exteriorities ("I" "We" and "They") focusing upon issues of politics, economics, science, social science or systems theory rather than dealing with the equally important interiorities of psychology, aesthetics, morality, spirituality, philosophy and religion. Tragically, when individual interiorities are not accounted for in this first step of ecopragmatics then any understanding of intentionality is forgone and when collective interiorities are omitted then the influence of group and community culture is completely lost.

The inclusion and integration of interiorities and exteriorities at the individual and collective level is of paramount importance that frankly renders the initial step in ecopragmatics - *carefully considering the case* – one of the most essential steps of them all. Granted that exteriorities associated with the policy perspectives of most stakeholders can be observed objectively and independent of taking a trek in the others shoes. However, the true meaning of those exteriorities and the consequences that are likely to flow from them can only be appreciated by seeking to inhabit the worldview of other stakeholders and learn how these exteriorities are influenced and made meaningful by the stakeholder's interiorities - philosophy, psychology, religion, aesthetics and culture.

## A Second Case Illustration: The Floridan Aquifer

In the interest of illustrating how this process might fruitfully be approached, we will subsequently turn to another case study – in this instance one involving a controversy pertaining to groundwater resources in the State of Florida. This case is somewhat different from the coal case provided earlier in that the Florida groundwater issue is one that has not yet moved to the forefront of citizen and legislative concern. This is an issue that many environmentalists, public officials, legislators and researchers are aware of but one that has not yet reached the level of crisis sufficient to motivate the public to demand a solution.

In the parlance of policymakers, this issue is not quite "ripe" enough for resolution. However, like the climate change issue, this one is of such overwhelming importance that waiting for it to ripen entails allowing Florida's potable groundwater reserves to virtually disappear before sounding the alarm. This is a classic example of the "boiled frog syndrome" (Quinn, 1996) in which a theoretical frog would make no effort to escape a beaker of water that is gradually heated to the boiling point, whereas if the water temperature were to precipitously increase then the theoretical frog would be expected to immediately extricate itself from the cauldron. Like the frog, Floridians bask in the illusion of living in a land of endless water when in fact water resources are steadily declining to the point of widespread drought. Metaphorically, it reminds one of the verses from Samuel Taylor Coleridge's "The Rime of the Ancient Mariner" (1798).

> Water, water everywhere
> and how the boards did shrink.
> Water, water everywhere
> nor any drop to drink.

In the case of Florida and its progressive groundwater crisis, the visible presence of so much water in the seas around Florida and on the surface of the land serves to mesmerize the public into a sense of well-being that measurements within the aquifer belie.

# Chapter 4: Cool Water—The Floridan Aquifer and Groundwater Resources

All day I've faced a barren waste
Without the taste of water, cool water
Old Dan and I with throats burned dry
And souls that cry for water
Cool, clear, water

*Cool Water*
Marty Robbins

## Water, Water, Everywhere…

One of Florida's hidden jewels are the series of freshwater springs found across the expanse of North and Central Florida – all gushing forth from deep in the underlying Floridan Aquifer. The Floridan Aquifer is one of the most productive aquifer systems in the world lying beneath a 100,000 square mile region in southern Alabama, southeastern Georgia, southern South Carolina, and virtually the entirety of Florida (Miller, 1990). The region works as a giant underground cistern that is charged with water that seeps through the overlying soil and permeable limestone karst formation into the caves and underground rivers of the aquifer. Where the karst limestone foundation comes to the surface, freshwater spring can be found pumping millions of gallons of potable, crystal clear – "cool, clear water" – to the surface.

Natives of North and Central Florida largely take these bounteous gifts of nature for granted and spend endless hours during the heat and humidity of the summer swimming or lounging in the springs or floating along one of Florida's crystal clear, spring-fed rivers such as the Weeki Wachee, Crystal, Chassahowitzka, Homossassa, Ichetucknee, Rainbow and Silver Springs rivers. Yet two of Florida's most famous springs – both of which reside in North Central Florida's Marion County, are in significant decline and have been for a at least 50 years. Over this period the magnitude of groundwater discharge from Rainbow Springs and Silver Springs Silver remained comparable. However, as groundwater use increased over the watersheds of both springs, there has been a marked decrease in the flow of Silver Springs relative to Rainbow Springs. The net effect of this change is that the magnitude of the spring flow of Rainbow Springs increased above that of Silver Springs in 1988 and this disproportionate flow has only increased over the intervening years (Knight, 2012).

The data indicate that there is something seriously wrong in the watersheds that feed these two first magnitude artesian springs. The most likely explanation for this shift in flows is that the groundwater basin feeding Silver Springs has diminished in volume relative to the watershed that feeds Rainbow Springs due to a combination of excessive groundwater pumping in west Marion County and reduced aquifer recharge. Since Rainbow Springs' water surface is about 12 feet lower than the water surface at Silver Springs, it was suggested that Rainbow Springs might be "pirating" flow from Silver Springs during dry periods (Knight, 2012).

Tourists by the thousands visit these springs to swim, float, fish and dive. Considered together, along with Florida's numerous freshwater streams, creeks, rivers and waterways, as well as the Atlantic Ocean and the Gulf of Mexico, these aquatic resources serve to give the "Sunshine State" its deserved reputation as one of the nation's foremost destinations for water sports. Moreover, Florida is situated in a subtropical zone characterized by hurricanes, tropical storms, regular thunderstorms and daily summer showers that serve to keep plant life green, lakes full, the aquifer charged, and virtually every ditch and canal brimming with water.

However, looks can be deceiving. Lying hidden underground, the Floridan Aquifer is not visible to the eyes of Florida's residents or tourists. Unfortunately, what lies beneath the feet of the state's citizens and visitors is an underground aquifer – a huge groundwater reserve – that has been undergoing steady depletion since the 1940's. For many years engineers with Florida's various water management districts have been monitoring groundwater levels in terms of feet above sea level and have done so since around for more than 50 years. These monitoring sites extend from South Georgia into central Florida. Today some 20 sites are monitored on a monthly basis by water management staff with five of those sites dating back to 1940. When 1940 water levels at the five oldest sites are compared to today's groundwater levels an average decrease of approximately 19 feet can be observed. Data dating back to as recently as 1976 indicates in the intervening period to 2012 the aquifer has fallen an average of 9 feet. When comparisons are made between all-time groundwater high levels with contemporary 2012 levels, an average decline in the Floridan Aquifer of approximately 20 feet can be observed (Wetherington, 2012).

This dramatic loss in groundwater potential over the last 40-50 years or more cannot be laid at the feet of climate change or prolonged drought. In these intervening years Florida has experienced numerous cycles of drought and plentiful rainfall. Consequently the only explanation for this dramatic decline in groundwater resources is increased human utilization driven by increased population, industry, industrialized agriculture which heavily relies upon groundwater irrigation of crops, urban sprawl, the inexorable growth in the number of golf clubs and landscaped communities that have sprung up across the state, more watered and manicured home lawns and inadequate water conservation and use. These are the culprits and they have long been known to be central to Florida's groundwater crisis – a crisis also shared by the rest of

America (Wurth et al., 2009). As the title of this chapter drawn from a famous Marty Robbins tune suggests, what is at stake in Florida and nationwide is sustainable access to "Cool Water."

## The Floridan Aquifer

The Floridan Aquifer consists of a carbonate rock formation (limestone and dolomite) that is in part eroded when rainwater containing diluted nitrogen and sulfur compounds permeates through the rocks – dissolving them through the action of weak sulfuric and nitric acidification - creating fissures, caverns and channels through which water flows and is absorbed. This eroded and dissolved limestone is referred to as "karst formations" meaning they have the appearance of a sponge and like a sponge are capable of containing vast amounts of groundwater (Andrews, 1990)

The Floridan Aquifer is shallowest along the Florida-Alabama border at around 100 feet and is deepest in west central Florida extending as deep as 3,500 feet (Katz, 1992). It is separated into the Upper Floridan Aquifer (a.k.a. the intermediate confining unit) and the deeper Lower Floridan Aquifer – an aquifer separated by a layer of less porous rock. The Upper Floridan Aquifer is very permeable and is the principle source of groundwater for the State of Florida. The Upper Floridan Aquifer is also characterized by a high degree of transmissivity – meaning that the water readily flows from higher elevations to lower ones, which usually means that the water flows from the higher elevations of the center of the state toward the coastal areas (Andrews, 1990).

The Lower Floridan Aquifer, while separated by intermediate layers of rock and sand in some parts of the state, often merges seamlessly with the Upper Floridan in parts of northern Florida. Typically the Lower Floridan Aquifer is separated from the Upper Floridan by what is called the "middle confining unit" consisting of sands, clays and less permeable stone. Although some portions of the Lower Floridan Aquifer contain freshwater, throughout much of its expanse it principally consists of brackish and salt water dating back to the era when the area of what is now Florida was once an ancient ocean during the Miocene and Pleistocene epochs. The Lower Floridan Aquifer typically ranges from 700 to 3,500 feet in depth (GDEP, 2000; Katz, 1992).

The area lying atop of the Upper Floridan (atop the Suwannee Limestone in northern Florida) is known as the surfical aquifer – typically 10 to 80 feet thick - and is the immediate source of surface and shallow groundwater (Grubbs & Christy, 2007, p. 19). This area consists of clastic material (sands, clay and some rocks) and is generally less permeable than the underlying Floridan Aquifer. Consequently this layer serves to confine the Upper Floridan Aquifer (Johnston & Bush, 1988). The permeability of the limestone rock formation is the principle reason why it is such a productive source of groundwater and the region of highest permeability for rainwater is that region roughly corresponding to the area of north central Florida and southernmost Georgia and extending southwest to the coast into the Hillsborough County area. The presence of this highly permeable aquifer is evidenced in the array of springs and crystal clear rivers that can be found across the state of Florida from the mouth of the Suwannee river, Southeast through the expanse of Marion County (Ocala and Dunnellon, FL) and over to the

St. Johns River in Volusia county to include Blue Springs. It can also be found along the "Big-Bend" region of Florida north of Tampa and extending north throughout the Suwannee and Santa Fe River basins.

## The Depletion of Groundwater Resources

In Florida, the ongoing depletion of the Floridan Aquifer essentially involves withdrawing water in greater volume than the historic recharge rate at which the aquifer replenishes groundwater supplies. Public water withdrawal has Increased 242% between 1960 and 1987 (from 530 to 1,811 million gallons per day) and since 1975 public water withdrawal levels have increased from around 1.2 million gallons per day in 1975 to 2.5 million gallons per day in 2005 (Marella, 1992; USGS, 2010). As noted above, over the period of 1976 to 2012 these increased withdrawal rates have been accompanied by at least an average 9-foot loss in groundwater levels across the range of sites being measured in the upper Floridan Aquifer. In some places the depletion of groundwater is much greater (Wetherington, 2012).

Given available information from the Florida Department of Environmental Protections Florida's water utilization pattern in 2005 can be characterized in the following terms:

- Groundwater withdrawals totaled 4,242 million gallons daily (mgd) providing drinking water for 16.1 million people or 90% of Florida's population.
- Surface-water withdrawals totaled 2,626 mgd providing drinking water for 1.8 million people or 10% of Florida's population.
- Almost 60% of groundwater or 2,526 mgd was drawn from the Floridan aquifer system.
- The Floridan Aquifer is the principal source of drinking water for Daytona Beach, Flagler Beach, Gainesville, Tampa, Jacksonville, Ocala, Orlando, St. Petersburg, and Tallahassee, as well as for a number of other South Florida municipalities and countless rural communities.
- Some 1,140 mgd of surface water was drawn from Lake Okeechobee and associated canals providing 43% of surface water used for potable purposes.
- Almost a quarter (24%) of the freshwater withdrawn in occurred in April and May.
- Approximately 11,486 mgd of saline water was used as cooling water associated with providing nearly 60% of the Florida's total electric power (mostly nuclear power).
- The largest withdrawal of freshwater occurred in Palm Beach County and the largest withdrawal of saline water occurred in Pasco County. (Marella, 2008)

The greatest proportion of fresh water resources – groundwater and surface water - was utilized for agricultural irrigation (40%) followed by the public's supply (domestic and industrial) at 37%. The largest consumers of groundwater included the general public (52%) and agricultural irrigation (31%). Commercial and industrial mining utilized 8.5% of groundwater resources, domestic wells (4%), recreational irrigation (4%) and electric power generation (.5%). Agricultural irrigation (56%) utilized the largest volume of surface water in 2005, followed by power generation (20.5 %) public water systems (13%), recreational irrigation (6%), and commercial-industrial-mining self-supplied (4.5%) (Marella, 2008).

Most significantly, per capita water use in Florida dramatically increased since the 1950's. In 1950 gross per capita water usage for the public supply – i.e. "water withdrawn for public use and distributed by a publicly- or privately-owned community water system" - averaged 100 gallons daily. By the early eighties that amount had increased to 180 gallons daily. Thereafter it dropped to a 2005 daily level of 160 gallons. Interestingly enough, prior to 1980 surface water was the principal source of freshwater in Florida. However after 1980 groundwater became Florida's principal freshwater source (FDEP, 2010). This in part explains the current state of Florida's dwindling groundwater resources.

Meanwhile domestic per capita usage – namely "water withdrawn in Florida by individual domestic or private wells for the purpose of providing drinking water" - dropped from 125 gallons daily in 1985 to approximately 92 gallons daily in 2005 (Marella, 2008). Undoubtedly the imposition of water restrictions throughout the state since 1980 have in part resulted in these marginal decreases in per capita water usage. However, even though per capita usage has declined slightly over the period, the state's population has almost doubled, increasing from 9,746,961 in 1980 to 17,516,732 in 2004 (Smith, 2005). Population pressures ultimately drive Florida's water crisis.

State population pressure – as illustrated by the elevation of total public daily water use from approximately 1,000 mgd use in 1975 to 2,500 mgd in 2005 – serves as the principal drain upon groundwater resources. However, agricultural water use is the single largest contributor to water consumption in the state. Average daily water consumption for agricultural purposes increased from 3,000 mgd in 1975 to 4,000 mgd in 1980 before state water conservation pressures and the adoption of better irrigation approaches such as drip irrigation reduced agricultural water utilization to 2,500 mgd. As noted earlier, 31% of groundwater resources go to agricultural use meaning that the remaining 69% comes from surface waters, principally from the system of canals in and around the Lake Okeechobee area (USGS, 2010).

By 2010 distinct changes could be seen in the state's use of surface water and groundwater even though the state's population continued to increase. Accordingly total water withdrawal in Florida increased over 2005 levels to 14,988 million gallons daily with saline water accounting for 57% of the water utilized and freshwater 43%. Of the freshwater resources utilized, groundwater accounted for 4,166 mgd or 65% of all freshwater withdrawals. Surface water accounted for the remaining 35%. Freshwater withdrawals were greatest in Palm Beach County (707 mgd) (Marella, 2014).

Florida's fresh groundwater reserves provided drinking water for 17.33 million people or 92% of Florida's population, whereas freshwater derived from surface sources provided drinking water for the remaining 8% of the population. Clearly, Florida continues to rely upon its groundwater resources as the principal source of fresh drinking water in the state. In 2010 the gross per capita use of freshwater in Florida amounted to 134 gallons daily and of this amount 85 gallons per day was used domestically. Of the groundwater used in Florida in 2010, approximately 62% was withdrawn from the Floridan Aquifer. These withdrawals principally occurred in North and Central Florida. Comparatively 56% of the freshwater resources used in South Florida came from surface sources associated with the Lake Okeechobee watershed (Marella, 2014).

Agricultural irrigation employed 40% of the total freshwater withdrawals (involving ground and surface freshwater resources), whereas public usage accounted for 35%. Of the freshwater resources used municipally and by other public users some 48% came from groundwater resources. Comparatively, agricultural users used 34% of the groundwater resources followed by mining (7%), recreational and landscaping (5%) and power generation (1%). Surface freshwater resources, by comparison, were principally utilized for agriculture (51%), power generation (25%), public freshwater usage (11%), recreational-landscaping (9%) and mining (4%). Saline surface water usage was almost entirely employed by public utilities for electrical power generation (99%) (Marella, 2014).

During the 2010 period Florida boasted some 18.8 million residents of which 41% resided within the bounds of the South Florida Water Management District headquartered which includes the entirety of the southern portion of Florida from the Kissimmee River watershed south to Key West. Another 25% resided in the Southwest Florida Water Management District extending along the west coast of Florida from Sarasota County in the south to Sumter County in the north. The St. Johns River Water Management District also served 25% of the state's residents, extending along the Atlantic Coast of Florida from Nassau County in the north to Indian River County to the south, extending inland to a portion of Okeechobee County, and north into Osceola, Orange, Seminole, Lake, Volusia, Marion, Alachua, Clay, Putnam, Flagler, Baker, Clay, St. Johns, Union, Duval and Nassau Counties. By comparison only 7% of the state's population resides in the Florida Panhandle served by the Northwest Florida Water Management District and only 2% of the population reside on top of the largest reservoir in the Florida Aquifer served by North Florida's Suwannee River Water Management District (Marella, 2014).

Between 1950 and 2010 Florida's population of Florida increased by 16.03 million (580 percent), and the total water withdrawal from both freshwater and saline sources increased by 12,334 mgd - translating into a 465% increase. That said, more recent trends indicate that total freshwater withdrawals decreased 22% between 2000 and 2010 (a decrease of 1,792 mgd) even as the population of the state increased by more than 8%. These trends reflect an increase in rainfall levels over the period as well as the development and utilization of alternate water sources and the employment of water conservation strategies. Increasingly stringent conservation regulations and mandates, and changes in economic conditions also contributed to this decrease (Marella, 2014).

In all freshwater utilization by public entities, agriculture and commercial mining all decreased over the decade of 2000-2010. By comparison, freshwater usage for recreational-landscape, irrigation and power generation remained at stable levels or marginally increased over the same period. Two principal contributors to decreases in freshwater usage is the practice of capturing and reusing partially treated sewage water – so called gray water – for irrigation as well as the use of highly mineralized, nonpotable groundwater as a source of drinking water. Such nonpotable water use for public consumption has dramatically increased from approximately 2 mgd in 1970 to 165 mgd in 2010 (Marella, 2014).

While the majority of the factors driving Florida's water usage are internal to the state, the nationwide demand for Florida's agricultural output also contributed. In 2010 Florida's top 5 agricultural exports were: (FASS, 2012)

1. Greenhouse and nursery products ($1.7 billion value and 22.4% of total farm receipts)
2. Oranges ($1.2 billion value and 16% of total farm receipts)
3. Tomatoes ($.6 billion value and 8.1% of total farm receipts)
4. Sugarcane ($.54 billion value and 7% of total farm receipts)
5. Beef cattle ($.5 billion value and 6.4% of total farm receipts)

Sixty-percent of Florida's agricultural production is destined for out of state markets and 40% is driven by state demand, which in part is driven by the growth in the state's resident population plus tourism. Consequently, in regard to groundwater resources employed for agriculture purposes, resident and visitor driven in-state demand accounts for approximately 12.4% of total groundwater utilization while agricultural exports (population demand beyond the state lines) account for 18.6% (FASS, 2012).

Next to tourism, agriculture is Florida's largest economic product. As of the year 2010 Florida agriculture encompassed some 47,500 commercial farms utilizing a total of 9.25 million acres, with an average farm size of 195 acres. The Florida Agricultural Statistics Service reports the addition of 3,500 new farms between 2001 and 2010. However, while the number of farms has increased, the total acreage under production decreased from 10,300,000 acres in 2001 to 9,250,000 acres in 2010 (FASS, 2012). This decrease in land utilization, when combined with the increased use of water-wise irrigation practices and regulatory watering restrictions likely explains the reduction in agricultural water use between 1980 and 2010.

## Florida Groundwater Regulators: State Water Management Districts

Given these dramatic statistics one might expect that leadership would have long since emerged in Florida to address these freshwater and groundwater issues. Unfortunately definitive action to deal with this looming environmental crisis seriously lags behind the extensive use of groundwater and the progressive depletion of the Floridan Aquifer. Currently, the state legislature has delegated the authority to deal with Florida's water issues to the Florida Department of Environmental Protection (FDEP) who is charged with producing an annual report projecting water demand needs into a twenty-year future and articulate plans being made at the level of each water management district to address future needs. As of t 2011 FDEP opened its report with this brief statement:

By 2030, Florida's demand for fresh water is estimated to increase by about 1.9 billion gallons per day (bgd) for a total of 8.2 bgd, and traditional sources of fresh groundwater will not be able to meet all of the additional demand. (FDEP, 2011)

So it would seem that the FDEP is fully aware of the gravity of the situation. At issue is how they propose addressing it.

Each water management district throughout the state is charged with creating regional water supply plans to address the looming shortage of water. These plans address the development of new water resources and identify how water district funds are being used as incentives for resource development. District water supply plans are predicated upon the assumption that Florida's population will steadily increase from a level of around 17 million in 2005 to an estimated 25 million in 2030. As of the year 2011 Florida's population already exceeds 19 million people (U.S. Census Bureau, 2012). As population increases, freshwater resources for the public supply are expected to proportionally increase. However, the FDEP projects that water use for agricultural use, domestic use, recreational irrigation, power generation and industrial / institutional / commercial use will remain at or around 2005 levels. In fact, the same assumption holds to the public supply in that the FDEP assumptions annually inflate 2005 water usage levels proportionally to account for steady increases in population growth (FDEP, 2011). What this means is that the water supply plans under development across the state are principally oriented toward meeting population driven public supply demand.

To the credit of Florida households, residential water use in homes has fallen 19% over the decade. Likewise the gross per capita water use has on the average has fallen 17%. Continued and ongoing reductions in water use are a central part of the strategies being proposed by all five of the state's water management districts – with a total reduction in annual demand over the period of 2005-2030 projected at 1,863 mgd statewide. Likewise, some 1,112 projects are underway statewide to eventually generate an additional 2,493 mgd of additional freshwater resources via aquifer storage projects (storing surface water during wet periods to use during drought), sewage and storm water reclamation, desalination of brackish water, development of surface water reservoirs and resources, and seawater desalination (FDEP, 2011).

The allocation of funds for these efforts is population-based meaning that the bulk of the funding goes to the most populous regions in the southern portion of the state. Among the state's five water management districts, the South Florida Water Management District (SFWMD) in West Palm Beach receives the largest portion of state funds from 2005-2009 ($65.85 million), followed by Southwest Florida Water Management District (SWFWMD) in Brooksville with ($53.75 million), St. Johns River Water Management District (SJRWMD) in Palatka ($53 million), and finally the Suwannee River Water Management District (SRWMD) in Live Oak and the Northwest Florida Water Management District in Havana, each of which received ($21.47 million) (FDEP, 2011).

Figure 5: Florida's Water Management Disctrict's

While this funding system is justifiable in terms of expected population growth and the need to increase water resources in those regions where the greatest growth is expected, it fails to recognize that the bulk of the fresh groundwater resources are situated in the Northern part of the state (particularly in the Suwannee River Water Management District) where state funding to address water problems is most meager. What makes this most problematic is that these groundwater resources are not static – they don't reside passively beneath the earth. Floridan Aquifer groundwater flows in swift streams southward to be consumed from wells situated well beyond the bounds of their Northern Florida water management districts.

## Suwannee River Water Management District (SRWMD)

Groundwater in the Upper Floridan aquifer tends to generally flow from higher elevations near the center of the state towards the coastal lowlands. Consequently the expanse of water contained in this aquifer extends from southern Jefferson and Wakulla counties on the west to Suwannee, Hamilton and Columbia counties near the northern Florida-Georgia line and extend southwest to Hillsborough County and Tampa Bay and southeast to Lakeland and just outside Orlando. Almost 60% of the state's groundwater reserves are contained in this one aquifer of which a very significant portion resides within the bounds of the Suwannee River Water Management District (see Figure 6). Moreover, the primary recharge region for the Floridan Aquifer's springs, lakes, rivers, and streams is situated in the Northwest, North Central, and Central areas of Florida. Even so, SRWMD has received the lowest funding for developing alternative resources and curtailing groundwater use of any of the other districts, with the exception of the Northwest Florida Water Management District that also shares the Floridan Aquifer in

Jackson and Holmes Counties along the Florida-Georgia border (Carriker, 2012; FDEP, 2011).

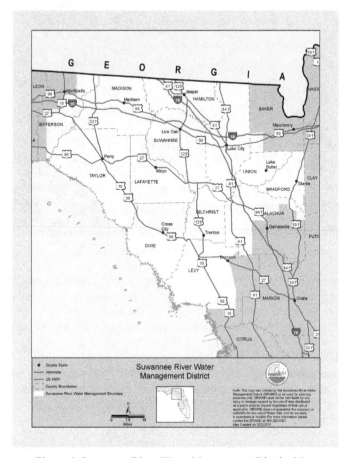

Figure 6: Suwannee River Water Management District Map

The Suwannee River Water Management District recognizes the serious groundwater reserve problem confronting them. According to their 2010 annual report:

> The 2010 Water Supply Assessment concluded that Upper Floridan Aquifer groundwater levels in the northeastern portion of the District are in decline. This area includes parts of Alachua, Baker, Bradford, Columbia, Hamilton, Suwannee and Union counties. According to actual District water level data and several professional publications, the aquifer level (i.e., potentiometric surface) has declined as much as 40 feet in northeast Florida and up to 20 feet in the northeastern section of the District. The Assessment concluded that these declines are predicted to impact District river and spring flows in certain areas during the 2010 to 2030 planning period. (SRWMD, 2010)

This summary report also concluded that:

> there has been a westward shift in the position of the no-flow
> groundwater boundary in northeast Florida. This no-flow boundary is
> also referred to as the groundwater divide. The shift has resulted in a loss
> of the groundwater contributing area to the District; therefore, further
> supporting predicted impacts to river and spring flows during the 2010 to
> 2030 planning period. (SRWMD, 2010).=

What this finding implies is that these southwestward groundwater flows are
depleting the Floridan Aquifer groundwater resources, while also contributing to
decreased surface water resources that might be used for recreation, irrigation and
for watering livestock. So severe is this problem that as of June 2012 springs such
as White Springs along the Suwannee reduced their flow while other springs –
such as Convict Springs in Lafayette County and Poe Springs in Alachua County
– virtually ceased flowing. Moreover, the upper reaches of the Santa Fe River
completely dried up and the lower reaches experienced periods where algae
blooms turned the river into a soupy slime (TheLedger.com, 2012).

The district's response to these exigencies involved collaborating in
analyzing the problem with the St. Johns River Water Management District to the
east that shares the Floridan Aquifer resources as well as coordinating efforts with
the Florida and Georgia Departments of Environmental Protection. According to
the district's water planning summary these plans entailed "working closely
together to share data and resources" and,

> developing a scope of work to study trends and potential impacts to the
> Upper Floridan aquifer, including but not limited to, evaluating the
> effects of migration of the groundwater divide and regional lowering of
> the potentiometric surface. This information will be used to predict
> future impacts to river and spring flows in the District and to formulate
> prevention and recovery strategies for impacted water resources.
> (SRWMD, 2010)

Central to the conclusions of this report is that regional groundwater withdrawals
have resulted in at least a 10 feet decline in the aquifer in the northeastern portion
of the district, along the upper Suwannee and Santa Fe Rivers. As a result of this
decline in northeastern aquifer levels the groundwater flow divide – the boundary
around which water flows principally south and west – has steadily shifted
westward, further depriving the upper northeastern reaches of the aquifer recharge
zone of needed water flow resulting in a 12.5% decline in recharge area in 1980,
13.7% in 1990 and a 19.7% decline in 2005 ultimately resulting in a decreased
groundwater recharge zone of 2,000 acres by 2010 (SRWMD, 2010). Decreases
in this recharge zone means less rainwater finding its way into the aquifer and
additional depletion of springs and groundwater resources.

In response to these trends SRWMD redrew the district's water supply
planning regional boundaries to focus upon the critical groundwater losses in the
northeastern upper Santa Fe River and Upper Suwannee River regions, the
northern Alapaha River drainage as well as their impact upon the lower Santa Fe

River and its confluence to the Suwannee River. Since part of the recharge area for the Floridan Aquifer lies in the adjacent St. Johns River Water Management District the SRWMD staff are working cooperatively with their neighboring district to develop a unified response. In developing alternative water supply plans the SRWMD's abiding philosophy supporting all proposed efforts is to develop alternative water strategies that offset current groundwater use.

One option under consideration involves capturing surface waters along the Suwannee during periods of flooding and storing these excess resources in surface and underground reservoirs. Another involves developing water reclamation projects for storm water, wastewater, brackish water and surface water in Live Oak, Lake City, Monticello, Fanning Springs and Cedar Key. It is anticipated that the district could be conserving 5 mgd through water reclamation by 2030. Particular consideration involves using brackish water from the Lower Floridan Aquifer to cool power plants. Aquifer storage of storm water runoff and gray water in the aquifer as well as developing surface reservoir resources is also being studied – although developing reservoir resources will entail lining lake-beds with plastic liners to prevent the stored water leaking into the aquifer below. The district's goal is to realize annual cumulative groundwater offsets of 574,498 million gallons by 2034 (SRWMD, 2012).

Of course the other option available to the district is to increase water conservation efforts so as to realize another annual cumulative groundwater offset of 87,250 million gallons and a cumulative decrement of 174,000 million gallons by 2014. It is anticipated that these goals can be achieved by implementing a conservation retrofit program for all water users in the district dedicated to assisting users in employing technologies and techniques that most efficiently utilize scarce water resources, as well as switching users to surface water resources when available. These efforts are particularly aimed at agricultural consumers who have the opportunity of using more water-efficient approaches to crop irrigation. Local governments are also being incorporated into the conservation plan in an effort to develop and enforce effective water use standards for citizens. Particular attention is being directed toward homeowner lawn care and stringent irrigation guidelines and technologies (SRWMD, 2012).

While these proposed activities and efforts appear to be positive responses to the groundwater issues of the region the only option that has been employed to any significant degree is water conservation. Likewise, it is worth noting that SRWMD is poorly funded to implement its goals and only began spending to assist in water reclamation in 2011 (SRWMD, 2011). Consequently, it may be a number of years before the groundwater resource savings outlined in their 2012 annual report can be realized. As is the case with federal budgeting, promises for savings must be ultimately measured against actual groundwater resource utilization reductions rather than from projected savings. Meanwhile the groundwater resources in the Floridan Aquifer and statewide continues to dwindle.

## Buckeye, PCS Phosphate, and the Jacksonville Electric Authority (JEA)

In considering groundwater conservation efforts for SRWMD, two industrial consumers users within the district and a public utility in adjacent Jacksonville stand out on the basis of the vast amount of groundwater resources they draw from the Upper Floridan Aquifer. These companies are Buckeye Technologies (formerly Buckeye Cellulose) of Foley, Florida in Taylor County, PCS Phosphate of White Springs in Hamilton County and the Jacksonville Electric Authority (JEA) in nearby Jacksonville (Duval County). The water usage of these industries and the public utility company hold the key to not only understanding the draw-down of the Floridan Aquifer in north Florida, they also hold the key to curtailing that draw-down and restoring the aquifer to health.

Buckeye Technologies is located in Foley, Florida situated near the Gulf coast in Taylor County. Their plant produces chemical cellulose, and non-woven materials such as personal hygiene care products, cleaning supplies, baby wipes, napkins, towels and tissues, and disposable tablecloths (Buckeye Technologies, 2011). Buckeye is the single largest consumer of groundwater in the region, pumping anywhere from 40 to 45 mgd from the aquifer. In fact in 2010 Buckeye utilized approximately 52% of the reported groundwater consumed on a daily basis in the SRWMD. Over the period 1995-2011 Buckeye has annually consumed 47% of the reported groundwater resources used in the SRWMD. By any measure, Buckeye is a prodigious water user and any conservation strategy to protect the aquifer from being depleted has to include Buckeye (SRWMD, 2011).

SRWMD authorized Buckeye to pump billions of gallons of water annually from the aquifer for use in their pulpwood mill on the Fenholloway River. Buckeye Technologies – a Proctor and Gamble subsidiary - has long been embroiled in environmental conflicts with the USEPA and the Florida Department of Environmental Protection (FDEP) as well as with local environmental groups such as Friends of the Fenholloway, Help Our Polluted Environment (HOPE), and the Legal Environmental Assistance Foundation (LEAF). To date most of the environmental controversies surrounding Buckeye Technologies have involved issues associated with water pollution along the Fenholloway River basin in Taylor County (Perry, FL). This shallow river sits atop the western portion of the Floridan Aquifer and drains what is locally known as San Pedro Bay, a swampy expanse bordering Taylor, Lafayette and Madison counties. In 2000 an EPA funded study noted that

> The river typically has no flow in the vicinity of the mill as a result of the production well water withdrawal, with the paper mill discharge accounting for up to 90 percent of the flow in the river. From the paper mill effluent discharge point to the confluence of Spring Creek with Fenholloway River, 17.7 km (11 mi), there is little fresh water input to the system. (Sousa et al., 2000, p. 1)

"Buckeye," as the locals refer to it, is one of the most notorious polluters in the state, most notably described by Diane Roberts of the *Tampa Bay Times* (2007) as, "the state's most shameless polluter." Accordingly,

> Buckeye Cellulose, which spews pulp mill effluent into the Fenholloway River and the Gulf of Mexico, has been blamed for a host of environmental nightmares, including contaminated ground water, poisoned sediments and that rank odor (fainter now than it used to be but still present) announcing that you are nearing the river. The dioxins and endocrine disruptors Buckeye spits out kill marine life and even cause female fish to grow male genitals. Then there's that 10-square-mile dead zone in the gulf - all this along what is supposed to be Florida's "Nature Coast". (Roberts, 2007)

In point of fact Buckeye was destined from the outset to destroy the Fenholloway River even before it began building its plant in Foley. In the interest of attracting an industrial employer to rural Taylor County Florida, the county commission petitioned the Florida legislature to reclassify the Fenholloway River into an "industrial" stream, thereby making it possible for the river to be used for industrial waste discharge. In April 1947 the legislature passed and the governor signed a bill pertaining to the Fenholloway (Horning, 2005). This new law,

> empowered [industries} to discharge and deposit sewage, industrial and chemical wastes and effluents, or any of them, into the waters of the Fenholloway River and the waters of the Gulf of Mexico into which said river flows. (Florida State Statutes, Chapter 24952-No. 1338, 1947).

Then State Senator Leroy Collins (and later Florida's Governor) sponsored this legislation – an act that seems to be environmentally callous given today's environmental sensibilities. However, taken from the perspective of an economically depressed North Florida economy, this decision takes on a different perspective. As former Buckeye Public Relations Manager Dan Simmons observed,

> The company came in and took advantage of the situation and back then the people weren't as conscious of the need to improve the environment. Senator Leroy Collins voted for the plant. It is hard to go back and vilify him for doing what they thought was right. It was after World War II, people needed jobs, the economy had to be rebuilt. Well here is–a good industry and high paying jobs. They knew it was going to impact the river and that is why they passed the law, so they could legally impact the river (Simmons, 1999)

Sadly despite the original rationale for destroying the Fenholloway, the river quickly became Florida's most polluted tributary and the 30th most polluted river in the U.S dumping tons of the deadly toxin Dioxin into the stream and the Gulf of Mexico annually (Environmental Law Reporter, 1989).

The Buckeye plant began producing pulp in 1954 (Horning, 2005). Pulp production is a water-intensive enterprise employing the plant's resources day in and day out. In fact around the time the Buckeye plant began to process wood chips into pulp, pulpwood production in the U.S. consumed 4% of the total industrial water use in the nation (Mussey, 1955). Since then demand for pulpwood products has only grown, as have the number of pulpwood plants nationwide. Despite the ongoing and serious environmental problems attributable to Buckeye over the years, the Florida Pulpwood and Paper Association (FPPA) depicts their industry as a "green" industry promoting environmental protection and sustainability. In their own words:

> The industry is Florida's leading manufacturer in sustainability and providing green jobs. The industry employs over 30,000 Floridians in high-paying jobs, leads the way on recycling and renewable energy generation, and sustainably manages Florida's forests. (FPPA, 2012)

FPPA also claims that despite criticism to the contrary, the industry is sustainable to the degree that its forestlands serve as recharge zones for the underlying aquifer. Accordingly,

> The impact of FPPAEA members on water usage is sometimes misunderstood. The industry's consumptive water usage from groundwater is generally viewed by the public as extraordinarily high. However, this usage is offset many times, a ratio estimated at more than 30 to 1, by providing significant recharge to both groundwater and surface water from its forests. (FPPA, 2012)

In the case of the Buckeye facility, however, this claim that forest-land offsets water use with recharge fails to account for the fact that the bulk of the water used in industrial production is diverted into the Gulf of Mexico and is not cleaned and redistributed on the land to recharge the aquifer. In fact given the steady decline in the Floridan Aquifer groundwater levels, it is obvious that water consumption is outstripping aquifer recharge rates on Buckeye owned or managed forestlands.

It is worth reiterating that pulpwood plants consume prodigious amounts of tree and water resources. Trees – slash pine – are plentiful throughout the Taylor, Dixie, Lafayette and Madison County area. Water, while available is less so and of necessity must be drawn from the aquifer. Upon delivery to the plant slash pine logs are reduced to chips and soaked in a strong chemical mixture to separate the cellulose from the surrounding plant matter. Thereafter the cellulose is bleached and processed into any number of products from cardboard and paper to plastics and resins (Horning, 2005).

Since 1954 the Buckeye plant has been voraciously consuming tree and water resources from the region, producing cellulose products and dumping the waste effluent directly into the Fenholloway River and in so doing dramatically drawing-down groundwater reserves while dumping poisonous toxic waste into a heretofore clean natural stream, the Gulf of Mexico and into the aquifer. To this day the Fenholloway serves as the principal release point for the vast amount of effluent produced by the plant daily. It will continue to serve this function until the 15.3-mile pipeline to the Gulf for transporting treated effluent is completed. Once the effluent flow ceases to make its way down the Fenholloway channel the river will return to its prior state as a shallow stream depleted by 90% of its former water volume. However it will take generations for the toxins found on the river bottom to be safely encased in clays and other sediments, sealing them from the aquatic life of the river.

Fortunately, thanks to the concerted of local environmentalists the USEPA reclassified the Fenholloway again in 1997 into a freshwater stream protected under the aegis of the Clean Water Act. When the reclassification occurred the plant filed a permit with FDEP requesting to pipe the effluent from the plant some 15 miles directly into the Gulf of Mexico. FDEP ultimately authorized a plan for treating the plant's wastewater and allowed for the treated effluent to be piped to the Gulf of Mexico. This ruling continues to be contested by environmental groups to include the Sierra Club (Bennett, 2007).

While attention has historically been devoted to wastewater discharges at the Foley plant, an equally important issue concerning Buckeye pertains to the tremendous volume of water it pumps from the aquifer to process the chipped pulpwood into marketable products. According to Jill Tao of the University of Oklahoma in her analysis of the Buckeye situation:

> In order to process cellulose, the plant had to pump an astronomical amount of groundwater up to the processing facility, and then release the water as effluent after processing. (Tao, 2002)

Buckeye's water usage is enormous averaging 15331 million gallons annually (mga) between 1995 and 2011 (SRWMD, 2012).

A rule of thumb applied by all the state's water management districts is that industrial users should use water of the least acceptable quality, which in the case of users like Buckeye, would require them to use surface water or brackish water if available and cost efficient (FAC, 2005). For instance, the other major pulpwood plant in North Florida is the Georgia-Pacific facility in Palatka, Florida – located in the adjacent St. Johns River Water Management District (SJRWMD). This plant also sits atop the Floridan Aquifer and throughout most of its history used groundwater resources in a fashion comparable to the Buckeye plant. However, working with SJRWMD, they have transitioned almost entirely to using surface water drawn from Rice Creek, a tributary of the St. Johns River. They draw off excess storm water runoff from the creek during rainy periods and store this water in a set of huge reservoirs reserved for industrial use. Moreover the company has spent millions of dollars building water treatment plants that allow them to reuse vast sums of water daily. The Palatka mill uses 500-700 million gallons of water daily but thanks to their water treatment facilities only 4% of that water is discharged daily, resulting in a 40% decrease in total water consumption since 1998 and a 90% reduction of groundwater use over the same period (McGhee, 2007, p. 3).

Theoretically Buckeye could also make the transition away from groundwater to surface water resources. However, the volume of flow from the Fenholloway River is inadequate to meet their daily water requirements, leaving only the brackish water on the Taylor County coast and the salt water reserves in the Lower Floridan aquifer as alternatives. Needless to say, the operational costs for Buckeye to produce these water resources via desalination would be very steep, and undoubtedly higher than what the surface water costs have been for Georgia-Pacific in Palatka.

For instance, Texas has been involved in desalination by way of reverse-osmosis water treatment for many years now. As of 2009, it cost those using desalinated brackish water - those generating a volume of 50-100 mgd – somewhere between $3.59-$3.89 per 1000 gallon (Arroyo & Shirazi, 2009) to produce freshwater. Since Buckeye uses somewhere around 50 mgd, the daily cost to the plant for water (incorporating capitalization and operational costs for a desalination facility) would conservatively range between $180,000 to $195,000 daily. These additional costs to the company could prove to be cost-prohibitive and may render them economically uncompetitive. Consequently requiring Buckeye to use this alternative source may in fact force them to relocate their operation to a site where water is less costly.

Buckeye is not however the only significant water user in the SRWMD region. Another industrial user – PCS Phosphate in White Springs, Florida – consumes almost as much water on a daily basis averaging 11004 mga between 1995 and 2011 (SRWMD, 2012). PCS Phosphate is a Florida subsidiary of PotashCorp an international company producing by capacity the largest volume of fertilizer products in the world – 20% of the world's potash, phosphate and nitrogen (PotashCorp, 2012). The White Springs plant produces phosphate, phosphoric acid, and phosphate feed for cattle. This plant, formerly known as Occidental Agricultural Chemical Company (a subsidiary of Occidental Petroleum Company), has been operating in White Springs for more than 40 years (Rabchevsky, 1997) and produces 3.6 million tons of phosphate rock, 0.97 million tons phosphoric acid, and 0.28 million tons of phosphate feed annually (PotashCorps, 2012).

Phosphate is a significant economic driver for the State of Florida. Since the turn of the 20th century, phosphate mining has been extensive in North Florida and statewide. To date Florida phosphate reserves account for approximately 20% of all reserves on the planet and meets 65% of the U.S. phosphate fertilizers demand and 10% of the total global demand (FDACS, 2012). Likewise a significant proportion of the nation's fluorosilicic acid used in water fluoridation comes from Florida (Glasser, 1998). In 2010 Florida phosphate products generated $2 billion total revenues for the state (Mosaic, 2012).

The Dorr-Oliver Occidental Phosphate Complex opened in White Springs in the late sixties. This plant has also been associated with its share of environmental issues – principally the release of phosphoric acid fumes into the atmosphere. Processing phosphate rock into phosphoric acid involves processing sand and rock dug from a phosphate mine (so-called overburden) and separating out the phosphate content (approximately 7%). Thereafter the phosphate is degraded in a 93% solution of sulfuric acid to produce silica tetra fluoride gas – which when brought into contact with water creates flurosilicic acid and gypsum – which is radioactive. The byproducts of the phosphoric acid production process are most harmful to those inhaling the flurosilicic acid, since when the acid comes into contact with the moisture in lung tissue it produces hydrofluoric acid – an extremely corrosive agent. The radioactive byproducts associated with gypsum include uranium hexafluoride and radon hexafluoride (Williams, 2003; Glasser, 1998).

By 2010 PCS Phosphate acquired the White Springs plant and like its predecessor dealt with disposing of a variety of waste products to include spent overburden material (stored in piles thousands of feet in width and a hundred feet high) which PCS plans to eventually re-vegetate, as well as excess clays and sand which are piped into settling pits where the heavier particulates are allowed to settle. At PCS Phosphate's White Springs facility these pits become covered with algae slime given the high phosphate content of the water. It is unclear how long the refuse from the phosphate processing will have to settle before the water becomes clean enough to discharge (Williams, 2003).

Understandably, working in a phosphate plant can be hazardous to employee health as Douglas Glasser reflects in his experiences working at the Occidental (now PCS Phosphate) plant in the mid seventies. According to Glasser:

> The work environment was very bad at the Dorr-Oliver complex. OSHA had not been formed when the facility was built. We worked in thick acidic fumes and vapors: Silica tetra fluoride, hydrogen fluoride, sulfur dioxide, fumes and defoamers, and gypsum and phosphate rock dusts on a daily basis. Occidental's safety program was basically nonexistent at that time. Wearing of safety glasses was not enforced, respirators were available on a limited basis and self-contained breathing apparatus was not available. I would frequently cough up blood when the fumes were bad. I began to miss work frequently because of terrible chest colds. Some of the old-timers said I had "chemical pneumonia." Radionuclides were also present as Uranium-328, Radium-226, Radon-222, Polonium-210, etc." We would develop acid sores and rashes on our arms, hands and feet. (Glasser, 1998)

Beyond air pollution, the acidic byproducts could be problematic when flushed as effluent into the adjacent Suwannee River. Of greater concern, however, is the degree of phosphate pollution in the Suwannee River. As of 2004 phosphate levels in the Suwannee River exceeded EPA standards 80% of the time. Sources of this pollution could logically be credited to fertilizer runoff from surrounding ranches, and dairy farms and / or from the PCS Phosphate plant in White Springs (Dutzik & Baliga, 2004). The contamination of Florida's streams, rivers, bays, estuaries and the aquifer from phosphate mining, processing and fertilizer use has long been a point of controversy. More specifically, some critics have been adamant that phosphate-processing plants lying near the state's rivers are significant contributors to the increased phosphate deposits found in streams and rivers statewide – to include the Suwannee River (Cunningham, 1980).

The Save Our Suwannee (SOS) environmental group likewise asserts that phosphate mining and processing in and along the Suwannee has contributed to phosphate water pollution (SOS, 2012). Earthjustice concurs with SOS and weighed in on the issue of Suwannee River phosphate pollution observing that:

> The Corps and EPA created a significant new threat to the health of the Suwannee watershed in March 2003 when they released a Final Supplemental Environmental Impact Statement approving the Potash Corporation of Saskatchewan's (PCS) proposed Hamilton County Mine expansion, which eliminated 3,997 acres of forested wetlands as "waters of the United States."[20] With this decision, the agencies dramatically

reduced their calculation of federally protected wetlands — from 5,768 to 1,671 acres — associated with expanding the massive phosphate mining operation in the deep bend of the Suwannee River as it snakes through Hamilton County. (Earthjustice, 2004, p. 10)

Despite these allegations, a conclusive link between the PCS Phosphate plant and Suwannee River phosphate levels has yet to be demonstrated.

In fact, in 2005 PCS Phosphate's White Springs plant was designated as the state's leader in best practices and the company was recognized with a "Sustainable Florida Award" sponsored by The Council for Sustainable Florida (Suwannee Democrat, 2005). Even so, according to a 2003 USEPA determination, the industry related destruction of wetlands in and around the big bend area of the river in Hamilton County raises questions regarding the long-term water quality viability of the river once the filtering capacity of these wetlands is eliminated. Admittedly, Florida requires phosphate operations like the one at White Springs to mitigate any damage they do to wetlands in mining phosphate. Such reclaimed land following mining has been recognized as promoting natural species diversity – particular regarding birdlife in and around mining ponds (Maehr, 1981). Unfortunately mitigated land beyond the bounds of the river basin fails to provide the filtering function of wetlands in and along the river, so while mitigation occurs, arguably something is lost in terms of the water filtering contributions of riparian wetlands.

## Two Industries Consume 80% of Daily Reported Groundwater

Together, Buckeye and PCS Phosphate account for more than 80% of the groundwater usage reported to the SRWMD between 1995 and 2011. Tables 6 through 9 illustrate this use. However to really appreciate the extent of the Buckeye and PCS Phosphate water use it is useful to compare the total reported water use of the two small rural counties where these plants operate (Taylor and Hamilton counties respectively) with reported water use in much more populous counties in the water management district. For instance Alachua County is the home the University of Florida in Gainesville, Florida. The population of Gainesville in 2005 (not the county, just the city) was 100,879 and Alachua County encompassed 210,323 inhabitants (U.S. Census Bureau, 2005). Meanwhile the population of Hamilton County Florida was 13,983 (McGovern, 2008). Despite this huge population differential in 2005 rural Hamilton County – home of PCS Phosphate – used 54.86 mgd while more populous Alachua County averaged 60.56 mgd. Similarly, in 2005 Taylor County (home of Buckeye Technologies with a population of 19,622) used 49.25 mgd. (USGS, 2007). When these figures are translated into per capita water usage Alachua County used 280 gallons per citizen daily whereas Hamilton County residents used 4,000 gallons daily and Taylor County residents used 2,500 gallons daily. The per capita disparity in water is use is impressive.

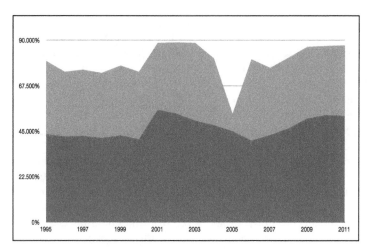

Table 6: Annual Percentage of Groundwater Utilized by Buckeye (blue) and PCS
Phosphate (green)

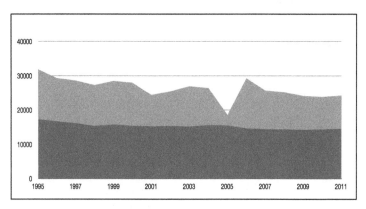

Table 7: Annual Groundwater Usage (mga) by Buckeye (blue) and PCS Phosphate (green)

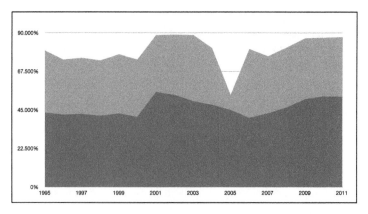

Table 8: Daily Percentage of Groundwater Usage by Buckeye (blue) and PCS Phosphate
(green)

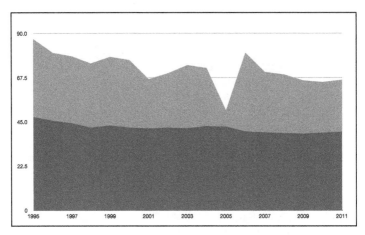

Table 9: Daily Groundwater Usage (mgd) by Buckeye (blue) and PCS Phosphate (green)

Despite these dramatic differences, the data provided by SRWMD from which these figures were derived remains exceedingly incomplete – meaning that their reports reflect minimalist estimates of groundwater use. SRWMD data is based upon reported usage not actual usage. Consequently in considering actual groundwater use within this water management district one should recognize the district is underestimating groundwater usage by some significant unknown factor. Unlike other water management districts throughout the state, SRWMD has been wholly dependent upon the voluntary reporting of users. Consequently in some years municipalities report what they use and in others they don't. Likewise some businesses go through cycles, often for several years, of failing to report water usage. More importantly, a whole series of commercial enterprises throughout the region – principally quarries and mines – consistently fail to report water usage as do agricultural users.

A significant factor in the degree of missing water use data in this district is that unlike other water management districts statewide SRWMD has not acted to mandate annual reports from all water users. The reasons for this omission are unclear, but probably reflects the degree to which the bulk of water users are agricultural concerns for whom monitoring daily water use may be technologically unachievable or economically infeasible. Alternately, the water management district leadership and staff may be accommodating political and economic influences from the members of their governing board. Even so, regardless of SRWMD's reasoning in this matter all the other water management districts in Florida also serve large agricultural interests and they manage to collect agricultural water use data as required. So more than likely the missing data for the SRWMD may have more to do with the historical organizational culture of the district than involving any inherent inability / unwillingness of users to measure annual water usage.

It is of particular importance to gather information on agricultural water use since the district reserves 75% of groundwater reserves for agricultural use. Based upon reported data, they would appear to be failing at meeting this goal. Yet when one takes into account that the district has little information on agricultural use, it becomes clear that despite the tremendous amount of water being used by

Buckeye and PCS Phosphate, perhaps an equal or even greater amount of water may be used by an assortment of agricultural operators.

For instance, in 2005 – a year when a concerted effort was made to gauge agricultural use statewide - the various counties comprising the SRWMD were estimated to have used approximately 111 mgd for agriculture purposes. Meanwhile in that same year total water use for the district was reported at around 95 mgd. (USGS, 2007). If these figures are any indication of the degree of under-reporting of water use throughout the region, it may be a safe assumption that reported water use over the years by SRWMD may represent half of the actual water consumption. Water management district staff are working on ways to alleviate this problem by requiring all users to report use or risk financial consequences and by monitoring electric usage at pump sites (domestic, agricultural, public and commercial) to estimate water usage (Phillips, 2012).

Returning to the two biggest SRWMD users, however, water district staff report being well aware of the disproportionate use of groundwater by Buckeye and PCS Phosphate and are looking to alternative sources – though budget restrictions are hampering them from aggressively pursuing this agenda. In 15 years or so, PCS Phosphate will have effectively depleted Hamilton County Florida and its environs of available phosphate, meaning the plant will virtually close and no longer use water at the current rate. Indeed, for 2012 PCS Phosphate has requested a 10% reduction in its pumping permit from the district (Phillips, 2012). By comparison, the Foley pulpwood plant appears to be committed to ongoing operation rendering it an excellent candidate for switching to desalinated water.

Pressure on the Floridan Aquifer within the bounds of the SRWMD also comes from the adjacent St. Johns River Water Management District (SJRWMD) – particularly from the City of Jacksonville on the Atlantic coast who recently opened a huge power facility – the Jacksonville Electric Authority (JEA). This new facility has a permit from SJRWMD to pump as much as 155 million gallons of groundwater per day through the year 2031 (Curry, 2011). The JEA plant employs clean-coal technology that entails crushing coal, adding water and cooking the brew until the coal is fully gasified. This effort requires a daily supply of some 162 million gallons (NCFRPC, 2012). Groundwater use by JEA is alleged to have drastically reduced groundwater levels in Columbia County (Lake City, FL) and county commissioners have taken steps to file a lawsuit against the utility to protect ground water resources. According to Columbia County Commissioner Jody DuPree

> Our water in Columbia County is our lifeblood. The permit they (SJRWMD) issued was not a standard three-to-five year permit, it was a 20-year permit. We aren't going to have any water in our rivers in 20 years. (Lake City Journal, 2011)

Arguably the county leaders in Lafayette and Dixie counties – the counties lying immediately east of the Buckeye plant in Foley – could be making a similar argument against Buckeye claiming that their tremendous groundwater usage reduces the water table in the aquifer and is in part responsible for virtually all of the ponds and lakes in these two counties drying up throughout the last two decades. However these rural people are not particularly disposed to protesting and filing law suits against Buckeye or any other entity. Besides, Buckeye is one of the largest employers – directly and indirectly through the harvesting of pulpwood – in Lafayette and Taylor, and Dixie Counties. Protesting Buckeye's water use runs perilously close to biting the veritable hand that feeds them so reluctance to complain may dominate the personal and economic loss suffered in these counties by the depletion of the aquifer.

Moreover, historically challenging Buckeye on environmental grounds resulted in personal retaliation and threatened loss of jobs in the area (Horning, 2005). For instance when the local environmental group Help Our Polluted Environment (HOPE) emerged in Taylor County, many employees at the Foley plant volunteered to share information with environmental leaders but typically did so by insuring their own identities remained secret. As one such worker expressed,

> I can't get involved in this because my husband [or brother] works at the mill. I don't know what could happen to me, they might burn down my house if I get involved with your group, but I'm on your side. (Horning, 2005, p. 48)

As Joy Towles, co-founder of HOPE observed:

> The community didn't want us investigating anything. For us (HOPE) to say anything, the economic value for the community would be lost. The only thing they're thinking about is the dollar bill. What they (the community) don't (sic) realize is that sure this mill provides jobs, benefits such as retirement, partial health benefits and so on and so forth. It's also their money that's paying for their insurance to treat a disease or an ailment that the company's effluent causes. The only thing they can see is the physical dollar. (Horning, 2005, p.48)

## Environmental Advocacy Stakeholders

To this point in the narrative, much as been written regarding the groundwater regulators and the largest consumers of groundwater. Yet there are other very significant stakeholders in the Floridan Aquifer case – principally a number of environmental and nonprofit organizations that organized to insure Florida's groundwater resources remain clean and sustainable. Of those, none is more visible than Help Our Polluted Environment (HOPE). This environmental organization was founded by Joy Towles Ezell, a Taylor County resident who returned to her home county after working beyond its bounds for some years only to discover the extent to which Buckeye was destroying the Fenholloway River. Ms. Ezell is also co-founder of a number of environmental groups to include Taylor Residents United for the Environment (TRUE), and the Environmental Alliance for North Florida. These organizations constitute the major stakeholders in protecting surface and groundwater resources in western region of the SRWMD (Strickler, 2011). They have been instrumental in forcing Buckeye to clean up discharged wastewater and they are central to protecting the region's groundwater from industrial depletion.

Save our Suwannee (SOS) is another important environmental group involved with protecting groundwater resources in the aquifer – and in fact is the best organized and most visible of the state environmental groups seeking to protect the Floridan Aquifer in North Central Florida. It does so by pursuing an ambitious agenda to include participating in water management district meetings and workshops, participating in county commission and municipal council meetings throughout the region, cooperating with other environmental and advocacy groups, promoting community education regarding groundwater issues, communicating with stakeholders in the community regarding groundwater concerns and conservation and pursuing legal action as necessary (SOS, 2012).

Our Santa Fe (2012) is dedicated to addressing the algae pollution in the Santa Fe River and the Suwannee River basins. Over recent years numerous springs have ceased flowing throughout this riparian system with the upper reaches of the Santa Fe River having gone completely dry due to the over use of groundwater resources by farmers, JEA and PCS Phosphate throughout the northeastern portion of the SRWMD. This group, along with SOS, is involved in an intensive water sampling, public relations and political advocacy effort at the county and state level.

Yet another significant stakeholder in the Floridan Aquifer debate in North Central Florida is the Florida Springs Institute (FSI) located in Gainesville, Florida whose stated mission is:

> to provide a focal point for improving the understanding of springs ecology and to foster the development of science-based education and management actions needed to restore and protect springs throughout Florida. (FSI, 2012)

To achieve this mission the institute is pursuing a number of goals to include developing baseline data indicative of current groundwater capacity, disseminating information on groundwater resources and environmental threats, promoting water conservation, advocating on behalf of environmentally sustainable economic activity and promoting an extensive public education campaign regarding Florida's water needs and challenges (FSI, 2012). FSI promotes a holistic perspective in which the personal lifestyle of individuals and communities, economic development and ecological sustainability achieve balance with the understanding that such balance must protect and sustain the region's springs, streams and aquifer resources.

By comparison, the Florida Groundwater Association assumes a more pecuniary perspective. Unlike other groups and associations interested in promoting the health of the Floridan Aquifer the Florida Groundwater Association (FGA) is an organization that principally represents the interests of well contractors and includes contractors within and beyond the bounds of the State of Florida (FGA, 2012). The FGA also includes officials with the state's various water management districts since they are the state's regulatory authority in these matters. The mission statement of the FGA clearly delineates its scope of concern regarding the state's groundwater resources:

The mission of the Florida Ground Water Association is to provide professional and technical leadership in the advancement of the ground water industry and in the protection, the promotion, and the responsible development and use of ground water resources in the State of Florida. In support of this mission, we are committed to: Serving as a Statewide education and information resource; serving as a communication link for our diverse membership to allow them to address their unique needs and the issues facing the ground water industry; and serving the people and the organizations who produce, study, utilize, remediate, market protect or manage ground water or related products and services in the State of Florida. (FGA, 2012)

Although their mission statement includes protecting groundwater resources, it does so within the context of maintaining their commercial interests in drilling more wells, and obviously drilling more wells results in ever more water being depleted from the aquifer.

## Earthjustice and Federal Litigation against USEPA Over Water Nutrient Limits

The most significant environmental organization in this debate however is the environmental advocacy group Earthjustice who in 2008 filed a federal lawsuit against the USEPA under the auspices of the Clean Water Act in the Northern District of Florida. The lawsuit filed on behalf of the Florida Wildlife Federation, the Conservancy of Southwest Florida, the Environmental Confederation of Southwest Florida, St. John's Riverkeeper, and the Sierra Club was prompted by the extensive degree to which the state's rivers and waterways had become polluted with manure, nutrients and sewage runoff.

At first glance it may appear that the Earthjustice lawsuit, directed as it is toward the enforcement of surface waters under the Clean Water Act, is not germane to Florida's groundwater issue. However, as exemplified in the instance of the upper Santa Fe River basin, when groundwater is depleted springs stop flowing and river flow slows resulting in increased algae growth. Likewise, phosphate and nitrogen pollution of surface waters often begins when fertilizers percolate through the karst formation of the aquifer, into the groundwater reserve and ultimately boils up in springs situated in and along riverbeds throughout North Central Florida. While federal legislation appears to distinguish between laws governing surface water and groundwater, in reality the two are inextricably linked such that depletion of groundwater resources in the aquifer contributes to sluggish streams and springs thereby contributing to algae growth and the destruction of aquatic organisms in surface waters.

In 2009 the USEPA issued guidelines regarding numeric limits for the phosphorus and nitrogen associated with waterborne sewage, fertilizer and manure. These limits were designed to be the threshold point beyond which increased levels would result in immediate action by the state's water management districts. As such they were compared to "speed limit signs" that when exceeded resulted in fines and regulatory action to reduce nitrogen and phosphorous levels.

To date water management districts have found themselves hamstrung in exercising this regulatory authority in part because of limitations in available funding and technology such as the funding needed by the SRWMD to accurately monitor groundwater use or create the alternatives to relying upon the Upper Floridan Aquifer. For instance, had the district actually acquired the funds and the technology (e.g. water monitoring technology) to prevent the depletion of groundwater resources in the Floridan Aquifer they may have been able to avoid the current state of affairs that has produced stagnant and dry springs, parched streambeds, dry lakebeds and rivers covered in algae slime. Moreover, had they been about the business over many years of developing surface reservoirs, deep aquifer water reserves (such as treated wastewater and storm water injection), and desalination plants in addition to aggressively pursued water conservation – especially among industrial and utility users like Buckeye, PCS Phosphate and JEA – then the district might have been able to utilize alternative water resources during times of drought and provide an alternative to water use "as-usual" within their region.

Even so, the bulk of the water management district's inability to adequately respond to the state's water crisis lies with FDEP rulemaking process following the issuance in 2009 of USEPA nitrogen / phosphorous limits. In effect the response of FDEP has been to "study the issue." Accordingly, FDEP

> plans to develop numeric criteria for causal variables (phosphorus and nitrogen) and/or response variables (potentially chlorophyll a and transparency), recognizing the hydrologic variability (waterbody type) and spatial variability (location within Florida) of the nutrient levels of the state's waters, and the variability in ecosystem response to nutrient concentrations. FDEP's preferred approach is to develop cause/effect relationships between nutrients and valued ecological attributes, and to establish nutrient criteria that ensure that the designated uses of Florida's waters are maintained. (FDEP, 2009)

FDEP construed the process of regulating water nutrient levels as being inherently more complicated than managing toxin levels. They noted that:

> It must be recognized that nutrients should not be regulated at levels that are artificially lower than those concentrations required for normal ecosystem functioning. If humans were to reduce nutrients below the levels that natural aquatic systems are accustomed to, adverse biological effects (disruption of trophic dynamics, loss of representative taxa) would occur. (FDEP, 2009, p. 1).

Consequently, FDEP chose to develop nutrient limits by establishing criteria to "protect against scientifically determined adverse biological responses" (FDEP, 2009, p. 17), which is to say their actual imposition of additional nutrient limits mandated additional study and research. While these studies proceeded FDEP continued to enforce the Clean Water Act standards by utilizing a nutrient standard employing the principle that, "in no case shall nutrient concentrations of a body of water be altered so as to cause an imbalance in natural populations of flora or fauna" and which additionally asserts "the discharge of nutrients shall continue to be limited as needed to prevent violations of other standards contained in this chapter," (FAC, Chapter 62-302, 2010).

Critics, such as the Florida Water Coalition, have taken issue with FDEP asserting that their approach "does not trigger enforcement or corrective actions" and

> instead of preventing algae blooms and other manifestations of biologically unhealthy conditions, the DEP rule actually requires the system to become very unhealthy and polluted before requiring any water improvements. (Chamlee, 2011)

From the perspective of critics, the FDEP approach renders it unable to proactively respond to the state's declining water health – a perspective that unfortunately is reinforced by FDEP's anemic response to a whole series of surface and groundwater issues statewide over a number of years. As Manley Fuller, President of the Florida Wildlife Federation has observed, "

> Under the state DEP rule, by the time the state takes action, a waterway is already slimed. The whole point is to clean it up before it gets that bad. (Earthjustice, 2011)

In 2010 USEPA issued new nutrient limits for Florida. Earthjustice and the groups it represents responded observing that EPA has not "successfully regulated away nutrient pollution," reminding the agency that:

> Many members of the organizations Earthjustice represented are personally and economically adversely affected by the eutrophication of Florida's waters caused by nitrogen and phosphorus pollution. The pollution has resulted in the greening of Florida's waters to the detriment of Florida's public drinking water sources, its tourism industry, and its waterfront based property values. (USEPA, 2010)

Earthjustice and its plaintiff's continued observing that:

> Florida's current narrative standard for nutrients allows pristine river systems and lakes to be virtually destroyed by nutrient pollution because there is nothing to alert the public to a fertilization problem until toxic algae mats and green slime indisputably evidence the fact that an "imbalance in flora and fauna" has occurred. For example, the Santa Fe River and Orange Lake have both been designated as Outstanding Florida Waters under Florida law, and therefore were supposedly specially protected from degradation. Yet both are impaired due to nutrient pollution, and both suffer from serious algae outbreaks. As succinctly stated by scientists in the Soil and Water Science Department at the University of Florida, use of a narrative nutrient standard "often results in a water body becoming impaired". (Earthjustice, 2010)

Earthjustice filed a second lawsuit against USEPA in 2011 claiming the agency had failed to require the State of Florida to protect residents and tourists from health-threatening toxic algae outbreaks. According to David Guest, the Earthjustice attorney who filed the lawsuit in Federal Court in Tallahassee, EPA's failure to require Florida to adopt a more effective nutrient limit rule was principally motivated by political and economic considerations. Accordingly he asserts that:

> The state DEP rule was basically written by lobbyists for corporate polluters." Polluters know it is cheaper for them to use our public waters as their private sewers, and the state is giving them the green light to keep doing it. (Earthjustice, 2011)

These are strident charges implying that business and economic interests are trumping environmental concerns. Yet when one considers the tensions in the SRWMD between protecting the interests of several large regional industries (a large municipal utility company, a phosphate fertilizer producer, a wood cellulose plant and a sprawling agricultural industry consisting of farmers, ranchers and dairymen), it is hard not to conclude that to some significant degree water policy is in fact being driven by economics and jobs.

As the state's water crisis continued to grow and manifest itself in ever new ways, the patience of the presiding Federal Judge ruling on the Earthjustice lawsuit (Florida Wildlife Federation, Inc. et al v. Johnson et al., 2008) finally wore thin and on June 3, 2012 Judge Robert Hinkle ordered USEPA to establish new water pollution limits for Florida within the next six months or face legal sanctions. According to the judge

> The defendants should take note. The effort that began in 1998 to establish numeric nutrient criteria for Florida waters must be completed. The defendants should not expect a further extension".(Gainesville Sun, 2012)

### Actions and Intentions: Exteriorities and Interiorities

This case study exemplifies how intentions, philosophies, values, and culture informs policies, actions, outputs, products and ultimately consequences – what Ken Wilber respectively referred to as "interiorities" and "exteriorities" (Wilber, 1995). An ecopragmatic approach to policymaking and decision analysis consistent with the values of William James assumes a paradigm in which the individual's ideas and values shape the community even as the values and actions of the community shape the individual. Thus it is essential to understand the interplay between these key individual and collective interior and exterior forces. As James suggests,

> social evolution is a resultant of the interaction of two wholly distinct factors, - the individual, deriving his peculiar gifts from the play of physiological and infra-social forces, but bearing all the power of initiative and origination in his hands; and, second, the social

environment, with its power of adopting or rejecting both him and his gifts. Both factors are essential to change. The community stagnates without the impulse of the individual. The impulse dies away without the sympathy of the community. (James, 1880)

Applying this insight into the ongoing interplay between the interiorities and exteriorities of individuals and the community requires the policy analyst to undertake a detailed stakeholder analysis to include an understanding of each stakeholder's interiorities and exteriorities and to consider the functioning of both individual and collective values, actions and consequences. The intent of this necessary effort is to unbundle complex issues and allow participants in environmental policy debates to come to an informed understanding of the perspectives of as many of the participants as possible. In short, employing Wilber's notion of interiority (those internal factors that produce intentions leading to actions and consequences) and exteriority (the products of values, philosophies, cultural mores, biases and intentions that derive meaning by producing consequences) encapsulate those factors which link the actions of stakeholders with their underlying values, beliefs and intentions.

As noted from the outset, Florida's groundwater resources problem is not a "ripe" policy issue meaning that its significance has yet uniformly impressed itself upon the consciences of voters, consumers and lawmakers. It is, in part thwarted from being moved to resolution by the mere fact of changes in rain patterns from year to year. For instance the 2012 drought was replaced by a wet season in 2014 that left much of the once parched region flooded. Nevertheless, the underlying pressures on the Floridan Aquifer remain and the diminishment of groundwater reserve persists even in the face of additional rainfall in 2013 and 2014 (Spear, 2014; Allaben, 2013; Pittman, 2013). Sadly it will probably require renewed drought (a periodic feature of Florida's climate), additional depletion of groundwater reserves across the expanse of the Floridan Aquifer, a further deepening of the crisis and a loss of access to clean groundwater to ultimately propel this issue to the forefront of Florida politics. Regretably, a groundwater crisis must likely come to full fruition before a policy response can be expected to occur.

Unfortunately this is one of those now classic environmental issues where stalemate and gridlock rule and reasoned problem solving has taken a holiday. We know that one of the major reasons this occurs is because interested parties seldom make "reasoned" responses as much as they intuitively and emotionally react to hardships and concerns. Yet, even in these situations, it is possible to discover functional policy options if one is willing to temporarily suspend one's own emotions, values and agendas and make a concerted effort to consider the issues at hand through the perceptual lenses of each of the major stakeholders. Successfully entering into this effort requires considering the values, philosophies and biases that motivate individuals, groups and communities and that ultimate promote intent to act (i.e. interiorities) as well as the array of actions, products and objective outcomes that individuals and collectives produce (exteriorities) that reflect their underlying values, philosophies and culture.

In this case there are a plethora of stakeholders who are contesting groundwater rights, quantity and quality. Indeed, regardless of whether anyone wants to publicly acknowledge it, the state of Florida is perilously close to finding itself embroiled in a war over groundwater, with the opening salvo of that war having occurred when JEA began pumping millions of gallons of groundwater out of the Floridan Aquifer. Whenever such conflicts emerge one expects to find politicians intimately involved. Admittedly, in the narrative presented so far the role of politicians has been inferred rather than fully explained and has principally involved county and regulatory officials. In considering interiorities (inwardly held values) and exteriorities (outwardly expressed action), one must consider the politician's perspective at the local, state and national level.

This case has a lot to say about the actions (exteriorities) of local county commissioners, beginning with the decision in 1947 of county commissioners in Taylor County to sacrifice the county's environmental health and resources to attract industry and employment to their rural area. Their actions (petitioning the legislature, recruiting Buckeye, enabling Buckeye to do what it desired to further economic ends at the expense of the local environment) are clear as is their underling motivation (interiorities) – namely to bring jobs and prosperity to their community - valuing jobs over the environment. These interior values are frankly shared to a great degree by the county commissioners in Dixie, Lafayette, Hamilton, Suwannee and Madison Counties in that these elected officials, while concerned about the impact local industries are imposing upon their land, lakes and groundwater resources, county officials choose to largely remain silent since their overriding philosophical value also prioritizes jobs and economics.

In truth, these local politicians have probably long since convinced themselves that they could have economic prosperity *and* abundant groundwater and surface water resources. From a psychological perspective, they have arguably been in denial regarding the inevitable toll some industrial activities have upon fragile environmental resources. Now that the crisis is upon them, I imagine they find themselves devoid of policy options since to advocate for protecting the aquifer may entail arguing against maintaining their current economic relationships with several major agricultural and industrial employers. In a "jobs-versus-environment" situation, they may likely find themselves acting upon values and philosophies that are economic in orientation - even doing so in the full knowledge that their penchant for jobs over the environment may ultimately lead to an environmental crisis.

This denial is in part a manifestation of Gerald Hardin's "the tragedy of the commons" (what everyone owns nobody takes care of) in which the erroneous assumption is made (at least at the psychological level) that natural resources are limitless (Hardin, 1988). Once this assumption is made (an interior value) it is likely not to be reassessed until circumstances (exteriorities) force the person to reconcile what they believe (resources are plentiful) versus what they experience (resources are scarce).

Of course the perennial interiority value motivating politicians is reelection. This need to remain in elected office creates incentives for politicians to appeal to the immediate interests of the public which sometimes means that they have a penchant for ultimately contradicting themselves such as when county commissioners accommodate the desires of agricultural and industrial interests to bring jobs to their communities and at a later date, when environmental protection becomes the public's principle interest, reverse themselves and more aggressively regulate those same industries they once courted and obliged. The history of the Taylor County commission regarding the Fenholloway River is exemplary of this fickle political behavior.

A related interiority associated with the tragedy of the commons is the mistaken belief that what "I" do or what "my" community does from an environmental perspective has no impact upon anyone else or any other community. This kind of thinking undoubtedly serves to comfort leaders in White Springs and Perry Florida that their excessive use of groundwater to support their local industrial economies has absolutely no impact whatsoever on other communities, precisely because they also assume, groundwater resources are plentiful – even when they are not. Thus the tragedy of the commons theme serves to explain in part the interiorities of at least some local politicians.

Within the counties where Buckeye and PCS Phosphate exert economic influence, it is also important to account for the range of decisions, actions and products (exteriorities) produced within the counties recognizing that the values of government officials and community leaders delimit the range of permissible exteriorities. Such considerations might include the decision of an employer to relocate to or away from a county, the actions of voters to elect more fiscally conservative or liberal officials, and decisions influencing the nature and volume of goods and services produced within a county or the county's GDP. However, it is highly likely that the citizens, businesses, and industries associated with the pulp and phosphate industries as well as the plant managers and supervisors who administer those facilities experience a significant degree of cognitive dissonance in rationalizing what they do.

Undoubtedly there must be some considerable degree of dissonance between what these individuals and groups sanction within their communities in the interest of promoting jobs and economic interests versus how they actually feel regarding the costs these jobs are having upon the land and water resources in their communities. As the psychologist Leon Festinger (1962) concluded, when actions (exteriorities) are at odds with values and beliefs (interiorities) then some form of rationalization must occur to reconcile the disparity. In regard to these communities, their economies and their impact upon water resources, it's a good bet that rationalizations include outright denial of how serious the groundwater / surface water issues are as well as employing the illusory belief that groundwater resources are ultimately infinite. After all, this is Florida is it not?

Among politicians, county commissioners make decisions and enact environmental and economic policies at the local level. Sometimes, as in the case of large cities, city councils play this role also. Their principal exteriorities – statutory and regulatory - predominantly include policies and controls facilitating economic support for their principal employers while simultaneously protecting the rights of citizens and the natural resources of their local areas. Of course achieving a balance between these often opposing goals is tricky and, in regard to the counties in question that balance predictably tends to favor local economic needs.

The predominant economic output from this region of Florida includes phosphate products, pulpwood, processed pulpwood products and a variety of agricultural products (e.g. dairy, beef, chickens, eggs, feed crops, watermelons, tobacco, etc.) and ornamental crops (domestic and native landscape plants). These products and their cash value are the principal economic exteriorities directly produced in the region. These products in turn drive a broad range of secondary products and services which in conjunction with the primary products define the economy of this region. The value of these products, goods and services in great part defines what citizens in North Central Florida value most and it is against this valuation that concerns regarding sustainable groundwater resources compete. At present, that stark comparison of the value of the current economy in the region versus the value of sustainable groundwater resources has not quite piqued the public's attention, again in great part because the "tragedy of the commons" mentality erroneously assumes groundwater resources are limitless when in fact they are finite and shrinking.

Of course, the underlying issue here is that groundwater is seriously undervalued in economic terms. If the water management districts could find the courage to begin charging consumers for at least a part of the value of the water resources used then consumption would decline and the rate of groundwater depletion would be reduced. That said, the North Florida community as a collective body embraces a wide range of cultural and community values (interiorities). More than likely the bulk of these values – such as promoting the good life for local citizens, enjoying outdoor sports and activities, living on the land and raising one's own crops and livestock – are not readily perceived as being in conflict with having ongoing access to seemingly abundant clean groundwater. There is a "have one's cake and eat it too" assumption at work that will only dissipate when groundwater resources become painfully, obviously and permanently scarce. Thereafter the community response is likely to be sudden, strident and punitive, but the options in the grip of actual groundwater depletion will be few and costly. So stated, it is not as if the larger communities in all of the counties encompassed by SRWMD are indifferent to maintaining the springs, rivers, creeks and lakes that make their part of Florida so special and unique. Undoubtedly they do value these water resources, it is just that until a true crisis emerges in which the springs quit running, the rivers dry up or become fetid, the illusion of sitting on top of virtually limitless water reserves will persist.

The environmental groups and organizations and the water management districts are all invested in seeing the problems of groundwater in the Floridan Aquifer addressed before the water is largely or fully depleted. The interiorities of their advocacy for groundwater protection include a sense of aesthetics and appreciation for the beauty and refreshment to be derived from boating, fishing, swimming and diving within the truly unique springs and rivers of North Central Florida. They are also motivated in terms of deep concern for the aquatic life of these rivers and streams as well as their impact upon the complex ecosystems that depend upon the aquifer, its springs and rivers for sustenance. While consumers and perhaps average citizens tend to prioritize human needs over environmental ones, these environmentalists and to a significant degree the staff of the SRWMD tend to adopt a more eco-centric approach if for no other reason to provide an advocacy for nature that may be missing when more narrow human utilitarian concerns dominate – as they do at the current time regarding this slowly developing water crisis.

Moreover, most of the environmental groups and organizations associated with the groundwater issue are less accommodating to the needs and interests of

Buckeye, PCS Phosphate JEA or regional agriculturalists. In fact they ask a very basic and important question – namely, is it justifiable to tolerate industrial activities that consistently foul the waterways, pollute the air, and drain the region of its groundwater resources. In short they ask the question "economic development at what cost?" Given current trends, the economic activities of these large industries and the Jacksonville electric utility appears to be unsustainable if they continue to rely in such large measure upon Floridan Aquifer groundwater.

## Florida's Governor's Response

The farmer, sportsman, business man or woman whose lifestyles and livelihoods across the region are compromised because too much water is used by too few has the right to assert their own values and demand justice – assuming the current trends in groundwater usage persist. In times like this such citizens look to the state and federal governments for help. In Tallahassee Federal Judge Robert Hinkle has made such an appeal and his mandate may prove to be one of the critical acts to have unfolded in this case to date. Hinkle is requiring the USEPA (and by extension the FDEP) to affirmatively act to deal with a surface water issue (nutrient overload) that in great part is being driven by groundwater depletion (at least in North Central Florida). This should force the state and federal governments to act – but will they.

Currently the state and federal governments are financially broke. The federal government spends more than it brings in in taxes and makes up the difference by printing money and borrowing from banks and other countries (Peter G. Peterson Foundation, 2010). Likewise, the State of Florida has been hard hit by the ongoing economic recession (Glassman, 2012). Long-term revenues are down and a fiscally conservative electorate has elected a spendthrift governor (Governor Rick Scott) who has been slashing the state budget right and left – to include cutting funding to the FDEP and the water management districts. Scott and his supporters operate on the principles of spending what you have, refraining from borrowing, and maximizing economic development and job creation in the state. Given these interiorities it is not realistic to expect that the Governor and the state's fiscally conservative legislature to devote much in the way of finances to the state's groundwater issue.

In 2011, Governor Scott cut funding to the state's water management districts by $700 million (Scott, 2011) in the interest of focusing the districts upon their core mission of "water supply, flood protection, water quality and natural systems protection." FDEP Secretary Herschel Vinyard responded to these budget deductions and the additional $2.4 billion in reductions that the Governor indicated would also be forthcoming by observing,

> These budget reductions are an important first step in ensuring that the water management districts focus on their core environmental missions and the reductions reflect a significant savings for Florida taxpayers. (Vinyard, 2011)

The water management districts' budget cuts send the clear message that at least for the present the state's fiscal crisis trumps its groundwater crisis. The water management districts are to do whatever is required to meet their core mission but to do so with fewer staff and smaller budgets.

This budget directive from Florida's governor reflects an all-important action and decision in this case – the principal exteriority overall – communicating that immediate economic concerns must of necessity be prioritized over the immanent threat to Florida's groundwater resources. Issues relating to Florida's water will have to wait. Those familiar with Florida's housing crisis and the deep economic downturn that followed it can't help but appreciate the governor's motivation to restore his state to fiscal health. It is also unfortunate that Florida is now experiencing a groundwater resource problem that may prove to be at least as economically damaging to the state over the long run as the housing crisis has been over the last four years. Nevertheless, when considering the degree to which just one water management district – SRWMD – is struggling to avert a groundwater crisis within budgetary restrictions wholly inadequate to the challenges they face, one can't help but wonder whether any of these districts truly have the budget, staff and technology needed for a truly proactive response to the looming water crisis.

All indications suggest they do not and they will ultimately fail to prevent the depletion of the aquifer and sadly be blamed for the failure. Given current Florida budget restrictions, the state's water management districts could be compared to a military unit deployed to the field to engage in combat but charged to do so without adequate arms, leadership, tactics and support. To send a military unit into the field unprepared and unsupported is unconscionable. Asking Florida's water management districts to tackle the state's water issues without first appreciating the proportions of the issues they face is no less unconscionable.

While some among the environmental community may want to characterize the conservative Governor Scott as callous regarding the environment (Rab, 2011) it is more charitable to conclude that the Governor simply has not come to a full and deep appreciation of the enormity of the current groundwater crisis and the ongoing threat to the Floridan Aquifer. Perhaps a decision against USEPA and FDEP from the federal bench will force him to move the state's water issues to center stage. Likewise as water resources become more visibly scarce in the capital of Tallahassee he may come to personally recognize the enormity of the issue facing the state. Likewise, one can only hope that water management district staff and the Secretary of the Florida Department of Environmental Protection can finally focus his attention and effort upon this burgeoning crisis.

However, chances are good that Florida's governor will in the near term continue to run the water management districts on a very restricted budget believing in part that the crisis for Florida's groundwater is something that is going to happen somewhere in the future – maybe even beyond his term in office. This is a sizeable gamble and it is reasonable to surmise that Governor Scott may find himself forced into prioritizing this issue – regardless of the fiscal vicissitudes – when enough of the state's springs cease to flow, when statewide wells go dry, and when rivers and lakes uniformly shrink, dry up or turn into slime and the water that attracts tourists by the millions evaporates along with millions and millions of tourist-related dollars.

# Chapter 5: Stand inside My Shoes—Framing and Reframing Seemingly Intractable Environmental Issues

I wish that for just one time
You could stand inside my shoes
And just for that one moment
I could be you

> *Positively Fourth Street*
> Bob Dylan

## If I Could Be You (And You Me)

Bob Dylan's lyrics express a sentiment that more than likely most people have experienced at least once in their lives - namely the desire for others to see the world as they see it, even as they learn how to see the world through the eyes of others. However, as is so clearly illustrated in *Nested Ecology* (Wimberley, 2009), the reality of human existence is that people live out their lives within their own skins and only get to experience reality in the first-person from within the bounded reality of their own existence. Nevertheless, they are capable of developing a sense of empathy and learn how to figuratively put themselves in the place of others – if you will "walk a mile in another's shoes." Empathy and the ability to imagine what the world looks like through others' eyes – even as one wishes others could appreciate one's own perspective – is a vital skill to acquire if one is to develop the capacity for creatively problem solving and negotiating with others. Even so empathy itself is "bounded" to the degree that one can never fully transcend the inherent physical, perceptual and cultural characteristics of self nor fully understand the bounded reality of others.

The lived reality of human existence and human rationality are necessarily interwoven and people make use of the boundaries between what they think and what they experience to literally construct a social representation of themselves (Klein & Goethals, 2010). Also known as the "social construction of reality" (Berger & Luckman, 1967) this process occurs during every waking moment of life as human beings necessarily proceed down one stream of consciousness after another, and throughout each twist and turn of these endless streams of experience they are compelled to constantly compare new information to old information and experience and on the basis of this comparison decide and act. Constrained as they are within the confines of their own bodies, personalities, cultures and experiences, the human capacity for choice and decision-making is for all practical purposes "bounded" or delimited. This means that despite the fact they can conceive of a seemingly endless array of choices and options, in truth most of these options are more theoretical and imaginary than immediately possible and only a comparatively small number of options and choices for decision and action are practically available. Consequently, decision-making necessarily entails forgoing the "ideal" or "imagined" option or outcome in favor of those ideas, experiences and actions that are possible and available. In this way life within the context of nested ecological systems – as perceived from the perspective of the human actor – must employ a "bounded rationality" in the interest of moving beyond consideration to action.

## Satisficing and Bounded Rationality

At the outset of the text we presented the ideas of Nobel laureate economist Herbert Simon regarding decision-making theory. We introduced the reader to Simon's concept of "satisficing"– also known as the "stop rule"- which calls for the decision maker engaged in the search for suitable alternatives to the decision at hand to "Stop searching as soon as you have found an alternative that meets your aspiration level" (Simon, 1979, p. 173). Satisficing provides a set of boundaries within which a decision maker looks for alternatives by defining a set of expectations within which all available options are compared. This is Simon's approach to "bounded rationality" which quite literally means making decisions upon the basis of a finite set of needs, expectations or values. Accordingly,

> Bounded rationality begins to emerge when we examine situations involving decision-making under uncertainty and imperfect competition." "Rationality is bounded when it falls short of omniscience. And the failures of omniscience are largely failures of knowing all the alternatives, uncertainty about relevant exogenous events, and inability to calculate consequences. (Simon, 1978, p. 349; 356)

Two concepts are central to the concept of bounded rationality, namely search and satisficing. Searching involves seeking alternative explanations or meanings associated with ideas, issues or problems that are bounded by a set of expectations, values or needs. Accordingly, "If the alternatives for choice are not given initially to the decision maker, then he must search for them" (Simon, 1978, p. 356). Searching necessarily involves looking for alternatives by comparing each option against its potential to provide meaning, insight, solutions or context for whatever idea, issue, problem or opportunity that prompted the decision maker to look for alternatives in the first place. For instance,

> As an alternative, one could postulate that the decision maker had formed some aspiration as to how good an alternative he should find. As soon as he discovered an alternative for choice meeting his level of aspiration, he would terminate the search and choose that alternative. I called this mode of selection satisficing. (Simon, 1978, p. 356)

Once the first alternative - satisfying (the decision criteria or normative expectations of the decision maker) - is found then the search is immediately halted and the alternative that best conforms to the expectations of the decision maker is selected. Unrealized "ideal" or theoretically "best" alternatives are forgone (given the time and expense involved in finding such a solution) in the interest of accepting that option which serves to optimize the majority of the decision maker's search criteria and promote action. This approach, as noted earlier, corresponds to William James' stream of consciousness model in which new ideas are examined and compared to "old stock knowledge" and thereafter accepted or rejected in whole or part (James, 1948). Simon builds upon James' analogy and creates a satisficing approach that incrementally examines ideas relating to yet differing from those a person currently holds and by comparing each idea to some mental template or standard (even if done intuitively tentatively and experimentally), subsequently selecting an alternative that maximizes more of their personal needs, values or expectations than any other option currently available.

## The Limits of Rational Decision-making and Decision Frames

If, as Simon asserts, "rationality is bounded when it falls short of omniscience" it could also be argued that rationality is compromised when decisions are deliberated on the basis of factors other than the exercise of reason. In an ideal or theoretical world, human beings customarily engage in "rational" decision-making - implying they weigh their choices on the basis of carefully calculating the potential ramifications of any and every significant thought and action. However, in the world of experience, everyone is aware of the degree to which many decisions – sometimes even consequential ones – are made on the basis of intuition, emotion, bias, reflex or conditioning.

In these situations a person's stated values and actual behaviors don't match – such as in the case of the television evangelist who denounces adultery to his viewers but engages in an extra-marital relationship himself. This phenomenon is known as "cognitive dissonance" (Festinger, 1957, 1959). "Cognitive dissonance" is in turn predicated upon a theory of "cognitive consistency" that assumes people seek behavioral consistency in terms of their attitudes and beliefs and avoid situations or circumstances in which actions and values are at odds. Thus, when individuals inevitably find themselves in predicaments where there is an inconsistency between beliefs and actions they fashion a rationalization to justify or explain their disjointed belief/ behavioral conundrum and then proceed to adjust either their values or behavior so that the two come into some form of congruity.

Amos Tversky's and Daniel Kahneman's developed what they called "prospect theory" in an effort to respond to seemingly irrational and contradictory tendencies in human decision-making. According to the theory's authors,

> Prospect theory distinguishes two phases in the choice process: an early phase of editing and a subsequent phase of evaluation. The editing phase consists of a preliminary analysis of the offered prospects, which often yields a simpler representation of these prospects. In the second phase, the edited prospects are evaluated and the prospect of highest value is chosen. (Kahneman & Tversky, 1979, p. 274)

In empirically testing their theory Kahneman and Tversky demonstrated that people's attitudes toward risk perceived "gains" differs significantly from their attitudes toward perceived "losses" (Tversky & Kahneman, 1981). Their research put the then popular and accepted "expected utility model" of individual decision-making to the test, defining "expected utility" in terms of

> a set of axioms, for example, transitivity of preferences, which provide criteria for the rationality of choices. The choices of an individual who conforms to the axioms can be described in terms of the utilities of various outcomes for that individual. The utility of a risky prospect is equal to the expected utility of its outcomes, obtained by weighting the utility of each possible outcome by its probability. When faced with a choice, a rational decision-maker will prefer the prospect that offers the highest expected utility. (Tversky & Kahneman, 1981, p. 453)

In so doing the authors introduced the concept of "decision frame" or "the decision-maker's conception of the acts, outcomes, and contingencies associated with a particular choice"(Tversky & Kahneman, 1981, p. 453). The particular decision frame adopted is in turn influenced by how the problem is formulated and the "norms, habits, and personal characteristics of the decision-maker" (Tversky & Kahneman, 1981, p. 453). Decision frames serve to place boundaries around decisions in a fashion consistent with the satisficing approach of Herbert Simon. Moreover, decision frames serve to elaborate upon the process William James described in his metaphorical "streams of consciousness" (James, 1948).

Decision frames are also consistent with the extensive research of social theorists and scientists who have developed nuanced and contextually grounded perspectives on human behavior and culture based upon the work of Kurt Lewin's "field theory" (1976). Lewin approached human behavior as a "gestalt" (Köhler, 1947) where the context for decision-making and action is conceived socio-culturally and topographically. According to field theory decision-making and behavior occur in "a topographical region encircled by other regions that are not accessible" to the decider and actor. Consequently all thinking and action are for Lewin ultimately defined in terms of spaces for individual "free movement" or "(Lewin, 1976, p. 309).

Field theory principally concerns itself with the psychological and social spaces individuals operate within and particularly the nature of the boundaries separating one social space from another. In short, theorists who employ field theory consider human behavior within the context of the nature of the boundaries separating one person and group from another in terms of the rigidity of the field boundaries, their permeability, flexibility, resilience, consistency and more. In so doing field theorists literally serve to "flesh-out" the boundaries that frame decisions formulated by individuals and groups in interacting with one another (Emery & Trist, 1965; Eng, 1978; Bordieu, 1985; Mohr, 2005).

Framing and reframing decisions and problem solving inevitably incorporates a field theory perspective but does so within the additional context of "uncertainty." Tversky and Kahenman's research considers common decision situations in which conclusions are drawn on the basis of significant uncertainty – meaning in the absence of quantifiable standards. To illustrate their point they employ the following analogy:

> If while traveling in a mountain range you notice that the apparent relative height of mountain peaks varies with your vantage point, you will conclude that some impressions of relative height must be erroneous, even when you have no access to the correct answer. Similarly, one may discover that the relative attractiveness of options varies when the same decision problem is framed in different ways. (Tversky & Kahneman, 1981, p. 457)

James would have appreciated this metaphorical approach in that it illustrates how most people automatically and often unconsciously adjust their perceptions to organize and make sense of the world they perceive around them. In the case of the trip through the mountain range, the perceiver selectively focuses upon the relative height of objects surrounding them to achieve a sense of relative proportion. The salient feature of this example is they "selectively" focus upon one aspect of their mountainous surrounding while allowing perspectives to go unviewed or to be considered only peripherally. Tversky and Kahneman spent 30 years studying how people typically framed their decisions and arrived at the following general conclusions: (Levy, 1992)

- *Risk Aversion:* Most people are averse to loss when the perceived pain of loss is greater than an equal expectation of gain. (e.g. the experience of losing a $20 bill in the grocery store is more painful than the pleasure of finding a $20 bill in the grocery store parking lot).
- *Reference Points:* Most people require context for making decisions and employ "reference points" to gauge change. These reference points are fluid not static and are typically relative not absolute (e.g. most people would prefer purchasing their gas at a local filling station rather than traveling 25 miles down the road to save a penny a gallon on fuel).
- *Breaking Even:* People are typically willing to engage in risky behavior if they perceive a reasonable opportunity to "break even" (e.g. the "in for a dollar, in for a dime" analogy in which people making an investment in a commodity that falls in price will invest more into that commodity in hopes it will rise in value and they will be able to recoup their losses).
- *Over Emphasize Small Probabilities:* Because people tend to selectively consider decision choices they tend to outweigh comparatively small

potential or expected effects (e.g. purchasing a year's supply of food in anticipation of the imminent crash of the stock market).

- *Minimize or Ignore Large Probabilities:* People tend to underestimate the likelihood of highly probable events from occurring (e.g. the most recent U.S. real estate bubble in which home prices skyrocketed fueled by the large volume of purchase lacking the assets to underwrite the value of these homes.

Kahneman and Tversky's prospect theory later influenced Lindenberg's "goal framing theory" (GFT) (Lindenberg, 2001; 2008) that is still widely employed to explain how people choose to comply with laws, rules and regulations. According to Lindenberg's theory,

> actors anticipate and evaluate the consequences of the options available to achieve a goal, and choose the one that is likely to best satisfy their purpose. GFT also assumes that one's goals and the way one defines the situation are interrelated: perception and motivation tend to harmonize in a to-and-fro process. (Etienne, 2010, p.3)

Consequently goals become tentative and situation-dependent rather than stable and uniform as preferences are quite literally constructed out of experience rather than being entirely preconceived or revealed. Moreover GFT assumes that most decision-makers formulate options in regard to several very different goals (Etienne, 2010, p.3-4).

Goal framing theory has been applied to many compliance issues and problems. It has been particularly useful to the degree that it identifies three principal or "master" motivations that inform most environmental decisions and actions, namely: hedonic, economic and normative considerations (Lindenberg & Steg, 2007). According to GFT most people comport themselves around one or more of these three frames of reference in an effort to improve their condition. However they tend to do so in a distinctly modal fashion by principally relying on one of the three frames of reference or master motivations. If, for instance, their principal motivation is to improve how they feel in the here and now they will choose to interpret reality and act within a hedonic frame that is self-centered and self-concerned. Alternately, if their prime motivation is to "guard and improve one's resources" they will realize this utilitarian outcome by pursuing a frame emphasizing economic gain. However, assuming that their principal motivation involves acting appropriately or consistent with social norms then they may choose a "normative" modality (van Trijp, 2013, p. 40)

At the heart of GFT is the realization that individuals tend to be principally oriented toward one of three modalities - hedonic, economic, and normative - and in some cases must force themselves (or be compelled) to regard their decision-making and behavior from another perspective. Alternately stated, GFT asserts that people tend to approach issues with one of these three modalities in the forefront of their consciousness, such that changing behavior and values requires "reframing" their master motivations from one modality to another or others. This insight has proved useful in applying GFT to issues of environmental sustainability and compliance to regulatory requirements (van Trijp, 2013; Birkenshaw et al., 2013; Wallen, 2012; Avineri & Waygood, 2011).

## Decision Framing and Hardening of the Categories

Modern decision framing has developed around the work of researchers such as Kahneman, Tversky, Lindenberg and Lewin. Certainly one of its most useful attributes has been its utility as a tool for exploring the interiorities of others involved in policy analysis and debates regarding potential issues and options (Wilber, 1987). The contemporary utilization of the concept of framing and reframing has been widely adapted to a host of professional and academic disciplines to include mental health (Wang, 2004), medicine (McElroy & Seta, 2003), education (Fine, 1991), public administration (Waitzkin, Yager & Santos, 2012), economics (Tversky & Kahneman, 1986), anthropology (Scheiring, 2007), sociology (Benford & Snow, 2000), political science (Chong & Druckman, 2007) and more. Regardless of where the concept is employed its central purpose remains consistent: to provide a variety of vantage points to issues and behavior that may hopefully contribute to collaboration, tolerance, acceptance, compromise and problem solving. In this regard frame theory has become one of the principal tools employed by those seeking to deal with the world's most intractable problems because it captures the relational nature of ideas and their contexts.

Arguably, some of the most intractable controversies of our modern times involve environmental issues, whether they entail climate change, water resources, clean air or environmental justice. The ongoing resistance of these issues to compromise and planning undoubtedly centers around the "Balkanization" of issues by a variety of interest groups – creating an effect which we refer to as "hardening of the categories." Each interest group surrounds itself with its own imagery, resources, values, supporters, and rhetoric and employs these tools to wage ideological warfare against those with whom they disagree – regardless of whether or not those who disagree with them are similarly "Balkanized." In this way each Balkanized interest group or faction enters into conflict with one another but seldom dialogue, and the underlying reason for this ongoing friction is that neither fortified group cares to acknowledge, explore, understand nor appreciate the "issue frame" of the other. Consequently, important issues remain unaddressed, unexplored, unresolved and unresponsive to either philosophical or political discourse.

Simon's work helps us understand how people create boundaries around knowledge in the interest of problem-solving and acting, while Festinger, Tversky, Kahneman, Lindenberg and others provide insight to the seeming irrationality that so often accompanies human behavior and communication. However, in most instances decision-making is considered at the group and organizational level and not so much at the individual or personal level. Yet, if one assumes the perspective of William James whose psychologically-infused philosophy begins with the functioning of the human psyche and personality, then opportunities may yet exist to develop an individually oriented philosophical approach to considering some of life's most difficult issues by allowing individuals to literally "imagine" themselves seeing the world through the "frames" (perspectives, experiences, values) of others. This process of appreciating how others frame issues and allowing that understanding to engender empathy, appreciation, adaptation and compromise is one that may hold great promise for enabling ordinary individuals to grapple with confounding, disagreeable, and controversial issues. That said, one might inquire as to how one might achieve such a nuanced perspective.

## Framing and the Limits of Rationality: Moral Psychology Research

At the heart of the framing approach is a belief that by enabling individuals to figuratively "walk in the shoes of another" they come to appreciate another's perspective and employ reasoning to change their beliefs and attitudes. However, this assumption of reasoned rationality underlying a variety of framing approaches has undergone significant challenges emanating from a growing body of psychological and social science research. Arguably Lindenberg's work is one of the first to seriously challenge the stereotype of the rational decision-maker with his identification of the master motivational frames most people employ and can frankly find themselves stuck within (hedonistic, utilitarian gain and normative) (Lindenberg & Steg, 2007). Yet despite the considerable influence goal framing theory has exerted over what we know or think we know about decision-making, even more significant is the work of psychologist Jonathan Haidt – to include his widely read text *The Righteous Mind: Why Good People are Divided by Politics and Religion* (Haidt, 2013).

Haidt, like so many other behavioral and social scientists began his professional career assuming that ultimately - despite the predictable interfering influences of passion, bias and emotion - human beings made decisions on the basis of rationality. Indeed, when rational decision-making fails to occur in interpersonal relationships it is commonplace to blame this failed rationality on the interference of emotion (Bermúdez, 2009; Kacelnik, 2006). In this regard, researchers have often assumed that ultimately people sought rational solutions to difficult problems in such a way that reason ruled emotion. This has been the traditional assumption of a host of significant thinkers from Kant (1900) to Kohlberg (1969). Indeed, the field of cognitive psychology emerged in response to the desire to learn about and improve upon the human capacity for rational thought and action.

Haidt, began his research in moral psychology – the study of the psychological processes that produce moral thought and action – by accepting the Platonic perspective of the primacy of reason over emotion. Yet experience seemed to suggest otherwise, compelling him to seriously consider the views of philosopher David Hume who asserted that "reason is and ought to be the slave of the passions" such that it never pretends "to any other office than serving and obeying them" (Hume, 1896). Reflecting upon Hume's words, Haidt began to question whether reason in fact rules over emotion or whether the relationship was inverse and reason serves human passions and emotion.

Haidt's suspicion that the accepted wisdom of the relationship between reason and emotion was reversed became even more accentuated when he reviewed the research of Howard Margolis a social theorist at the University of Chicago. In his book *Patterns, Thinking, and Cognition: A Theory of Judgment* (1987), Margolis argued that the brain is a device that usually gets things right, and there is no reason to suppose that the means by which it does so look at all like the manipulations of propositions in logic or like the algorithms that run contemporary computers. (p. 68).

Given this perspective and on the basis of extended research Margolis developed a two-step model of deliberation which begins with the search for patterns of activity, objects, relationships or behavior – "seeing-that" – that can be quickly and be readily associated with a set of behavioral responses for the purpose of arriving at a judgment. "Seeing that" occurs intuitively at virtually a synaptic or autonomic level. These quick associations made by identifying patterns and matching patterns to familiar behaviors allows the deliberator to quickly process vast amounts of complex information and respond appropriately. "Seeing-that" is a method by which the brain becomes hard-wired for learned responses on the basis of repetition and experience. The second part of the deliberative process involves "reasoning-why." Unlike "seeing that" – which is virtually an autonomic process, "reasoning-why" is a conscious and deliberative process that seeks to explain how we arrive at a judgment or how others could reach their judgments. (Margolis, 1987, p. 76).

Margolis's perspective of how humans process information and utilize decision-making is fully compatible with William James's ideas about streams of consciousness and the seemingly autonomic fashion with which perceptions are rationally and emotionally integrated and translated into responses and cognitions. Margolis's findings have been confirmed by a growing body of research conducted by Haidt and others who have concluded that rationality – rather than ruling emotions - is in fact the servant of these intuitive responses (Lazarus, 1996; Kahneman, 2003; Gazzanigia, 2005; Damasio, 2005). In so doing this corpus of research serves to explain how the "gut" reactions of individuals are legitimized, explained and defended.

Haidt ultimately concluded that the stream of consciousness phenomenon first described by James was in fact not an essentially rational process but was rather an intuitive one which he described as "the dozens or hundreds of rapid, effortless moral judgments and decisions we all make every day" of which "only a few come to us in full-blown emotions" (Haidt, 2013, p. 45). Like James, Haidt employs metaphor to explain the relationship between intuition – which he characterizes as an elephant ("seeing-that" or automatic responses and process leading to judgment to include, emotion and intuition) - and a rider known as reason ("reasoning-why" or language-based reasoning involving controlled, explanatory and ultimately argumentative processes that serve to justify judgments) (Haidt, 2006).

The rider in this metaphor plays several important roles for the elephant it serves to include anticipating the future, making better decisions in the present, avoiding disasters, learning new skills, mastering new technologies, helping the elephant to achieve its goals and most importantly serving as a spokesman for the elephant. In this regard, Haidt asserts that the "rider is skilled at fabricating post hoc explanations for whatever the elephant has just done" as well as "finding reasons to justify whatever the elephant will do next" (Haidt, 2013, p. 46).

   This partnership of rider and elephant serves to describe the fashion in which people engage in pattern recognition that in turns produces rationalization, explanation or argument principally employed to explain and defend not only individual values and norms but more importantly the values and perspectives of groups with whom the individual most clearly identifies. Accordingly, reason typically serves to argue intuitive insights and perspectives shared by individuals and the groups they most strongly identify with in the hopes of winning over the opponent to one's side or in this case to one's reference group. If Haidt and other social and psychological researchers are correct then the principle use of reason is to win arguments on behalf of cherished individual and group interests. Even so, one wonders if there is not also an important case to be made for the virtues of compromise and accommodation.

## Accommodation and Compromise

Turn of the century industrialist Henry Ford clearly understood the importance of accommodation and compromise when he observed that "If there is any one secret to success it lies in the ability to get the other person's point of view and see things from their angle as well as yours" (Carnegie, 1936, p. 35). Haidt resonates to Ford's observations and notes that,

> It's such an obvious point, yet few of us apply it in moral and political arguments because our righteous minds so readily shift into combat mode. The rider and the elephant work together smoothly to fend off attacks and lob rhetorical grenades of their own. The performance may impress our friends and show allies we are committed members of the team, but no matter how good our logic, its not going to change the minds of our opponents if they are in combat mode too. If you really want to change someone's mind on a moral or political matter, you'll need to see things from that person's angle as well as your own. And if you do truly see it the other person's way – deeply and intuitively – you might even find your own mind opening in response. Empathy is an antidote to righteousness, although it's very difficult to empathize over a moral divide. (Haidt, 2013, p. 49)

Although Haidt's work acknowledges and explains the difficulties involved in so-called "rational" dialogue, he underscores the importance of thoughtful dialogue and compromise, noting

> If you want to change someone's mind about a moral or political issue, *talk to the elephant first*. If you ask people to believe something that violates their intuitions, they will devote their efforts to finding an escape hatch – a reason to doubt your argument of conclusion. They will almost always succeed. (Haidt, 2013, p. 50)

In other words opinions are typically not changed outside of the process of interpersonal interaction and communication. While Balkanization is always a possibility in the midst of these interpersonal communications so is persuasion and the reformulation of opinions. If this were not self-evidently true then human beings would not so regularly engage in argumentative behavior designed to win others over to their side. Haidt's research suggests that persuasion occurs by virtue of social interaction (social persuasion), reasoned argument (reasoned persuasion), and under circumstances where individuals experience a set of conflicting intuitions demanding resolution. He explains this phenomenon by once again relying upon metaphor (self-persuasion).

> The elephant may not often change its direction in response to objections from its own rider, but it is easily steered by the presence of friendly elephants (that's the social persuasion link in the social intuitionist model) or by good arguments given to it by the riders of those friendly elephants (that's the reason persuasion link). There are even times when we change our minds on our own, with no help from other people. Sometimes we have conflicting intuitions about something, as many people do about abortion and controversial issues. (Haidt, 2013, p. 64)

Haidt stands in the tradition of William James who consistently argued for a functionalist perspective on the nature and workings of the human mind. James was one of the first psychologists to encourage his peers to principally come to understand the mind in terms of what it actually did rather than as an abstract or theoretically derived process. When James's perspective is applied to Haidt's work it is hard to escape Haidt's own conclusion that

> moral reasoning has been shaped, tuned and crafted to help us pursue socially strategic goals, such as guarding our reputations and convincing other people to support us or our team in disputes. (Haidt, 2013, p. 65)

Ultimately Haidt's research demonstrates that most humans function on the basis of intuition and not reason, asserting that "the worship of reason is itself an illustration of one of the most long-lived delusions in Western history: the rationalist delusion" in which reason is held to be the most noble human attribute (Haidt, 2013, p. 103). Given this insight, it is vital that those engaged in the business of policy-making and problem solving perceive the world as it is and adopt the functionalist perspective of William James. If rational approaches to brokering our differences fail to produce sustainable and acceptable solutions then the question becomes how to employ intuitive methods in a mutually productive fashion.

## Framing and Reframing 101: A Survival Scenario

Framing serves to create the very empathetic interaction that Haidt espouses. The basics of framing and reframing must first be conceived of as a virtually intuitive response of humans – often unreflectively experienced – on a moment-by-moment basis. They perceive, compare, evaluate and act again, and again, and again and each experience and action adjusts the "frame" within which the next perception, thought and action will occur. In other words, at its base, "framing" is simply another world for "perception" and "re-framing" is but another way to conceive of adjusting one's perceptions or motivational frame.

In this text we are interested in engaging the reader to think about framing and reframing personally and informally (as is the case with everyday perception, cognition and action) as well as beginning to think of framing and reframing in a more systematic and planned sense. At the heart of our approach to framing is the concept of "imaginating." Imaginating, as noted earlier, is a term that incorporates two ideas: imagination and animation. So conceived, imaginating implies consideration of potential and possible actions, options and outcomes (imagination) followed by a concerted effort to cognitively construct a hypothetical future in which one can consider how these ideas might be employed (animation). What this implies is that "imaginating" allows the individual to consider and even visualize a different state of affairs than the one they are currently experiencing. "Imaginating" manifests imagination in terms of concerted and reasoned action.

For instance, consider someone residing in a large metropolitan area in the U.S. who takes a hiking trip along the Appalachian Trail. Along the way they become thirsty and discover they have depleted their last bottle of drinking water. Experiencing thirst, they start looking for a stream or creek to drink from. At length they find a sluggish, muddy stream in which algae is blooming. Since they are thirsty, they consider drinking from the stream. However, they hesitate because the stream water they visualize and smell looks so very much at odds with previous experiences of consuming fresh water obtained either through a municipal water systems back home or in comparison to the last container of bottled water they consumed on the trail. So they see, feel, smell and consider the quality and safety of this water source - weighing the perceived risks of drinking this water against the benefit of assuaging their thirst and at length proceeding to look for water that more nearly complies with their mental image of safe clean water.

Later they encounter another stream of crystal clear water that smells fresh, is swiftly flowing, free of surface algae, supportive of animal life and cool to touch. They compare their sensorium's report on this stream with past experiences with safe and clean water and at length decide to fill the canteen with water (while of course dropping a purification pill into the canteen). In this instance the individual's perception of the quality of the water encountered more nearly complies with "old-stock" experiences and hiker chooses to drink the water.

In both of these instances the individual imagined, projected a possible outcome (animated their imaginings) and ultimately acted – thus fulfilling the basic criteria for imaginating. Likewise, in both instances intuition and pattern recognition led to judgments and actions while reason likely served to justify the judgments and actions in the mind of the hiker. However, what might have happened had not this hiker encountered a fresh water source?

For instance, let's assume the hiker is now on a day jaunt in the Sonoran Desert of Arizona and strays off of the hiking trail and becomes lost. Finding themselves lost in the heat of the desert over a longer duration than anticipated they soon run out of water and become dehydrated. There are no streams to be found in this environment. The only liquid available to the hiker is the liquid they produce – namely urine. So they are faced with a dilemma – dehydrate and die or drink their urine and live. At first the prospect of drinking their urine makes the hiker nauseated – principally because the mental comparison they make of imagining the actual ingestion of urine (with its urine smell, taste and appearance) is so completely at odds with their experiences of drinking clean, pure water. However, as the sun continues to bear down and the reality sets in that they might die out in the desert unless they can find a way to begin rehydrating, they eventually move beyond "imagining" drinking urine to actually doing so and in so doing survive to be subsequently rescued.

In this latter instance the hiker was forced to experience a new and frankly unsavory reality – drinking urine. In the process of experiencing this reality, however, they re-shuffled their cache of "old-stock" experiences and knowledge making room for a possible alternative that more than likely had heretofore not been a part of their experiential repertoire. Moreover, they created an option for themselves that they would have probably never contemplated or felt to be justifiable under "normal" circumstances.

Yet his desert situation was a completely different "frame" of reference than anything that had occurred before. Within a "normal" frame of reference, drinking urine would have been considered deviant and reprehensible. However within a "survival" frame of reference, drinking urine was absolutely necessary. This reframing of his situation forced the hiker to update their experiential databases, redefine (reframed) what was possible and adjusted their behavioral and attitudinal repertoire to reflect this new learning. In this regard they moved beyond simply imagining a new reality and proceeded to the next steps of animating their imaginings and finally actively creating new reality and new experiences. They engaged in "imaginating" – i.e. transforming considered experience into actual experience and new memories.

So far these examples of imaginating have involved a single individual experiencing problems and challenges to be solved and worked through alone. Things become much more complex when another individual is added to the scenario. Consider again the conundrum involving becoming lost in the Sonoran Desert without drinking water. Now let's assume we have a couple of hikers – perhaps a husband and wife – who are faced with the situation of having to consume their own urine to survive.

After considering the alternatives, the wife goes ahead and drinks her urine and is witnessed doing so by her husband. Her husband, however, is completely disgusted by the prospects of drinking his urine and is further put-off having witnessed his wife doing so. He recognizes that he and his wife are operating within a drastically altered frame of reference that requires them both doing something quite unsavory. But he needs to survive, so he imagines what it must have been like for his wife to ingest urine. He observes her actions and imagines how it must have felt, tasted, smelled for her to have done so and he speculates as to what must have been going through her mind and what mental associations she was making – associations like "what must my husband think of me?" and "what would others think of me if they knew?" Moreover, they might also reflect upon the fact that since ingesting urine had become a literal reality, what else might they be capable of?" The husband is quite literally trying to stand in his wife's shoes and imagine what it must have been like for her to do something he knows she would have been loath to do under normal circumstances. To employ

Margolis's nomenclature, the hiker has first engaged in "seeing-that" as it applies to his wife's behavior and has arrived at a judgment that he will justify by "reasoning-why" she did what she did and why he is going to do what he will do.

The husband's thoughts and musings reflect his effort to be empathetic to his wife's actions, and he does so – in part - to reconsider and if you will reframe his relationship with his wife as well as in regard to his own situation in the desert. He is compelled to engage in this mental exercise for quite literally his own life depends upon it. At issue is whether he will follow suit and drink his own urine and potentially survive, or succumb to his disgust and disdain and choose to die in the desert rather than saving himself by performing what he considers to be a repulsive act. Ultimately he will act but not before he mentally animates his imaginings about what it means to drink urine and quite literally projects a mental scenario to help him anticipate what might happen if he either chooses not to drink the urine versus what will happen if he follows his wife suit and drinks it.

## Intuitive Versus Deliberative Imagining

While these scenarios portray framing and reframing in extreme and unusual situations, they amply demonstrate the basic characteristics of what we will call "intuitive imagining" or imagining that happens at virtually an automatic, autonomic and seemingly pre-reflective level. While it took several paragraphs to describe the Sonoran Desert survival scenario, the relative time it would have taken for each of the hiker's to consider their situation and act would have likely taken only minutes upon realizing they were without water and rapidly dehydrating – especially if the hikers had been privy to desert survival instruction which most experienced desert hikers would have been familiar with. Intuitive imagining is the sort James describes when describing streams of consciousness. It is a type that almost viscerally recognizes changes in frames and contexts and proceeds to adjust and justify expectations and behavior on the basis of these intuitive changes in framing. Moreover, intuitive imagining involving relationships with others entails constantly imagining what the current and potential frames of reference may mean and feel like to others and how they might influence another's actions and attitudes.

When we talk about using imagining and reframing as tools in problem-solving seemingly intractable environmental issues, we in part rely upon the process of intuitive imagining as a psychological metaphor and tool to aid the individual in becoming reflective and eventually deliberative in terms of understanding how they and others think and respond to problems, opportunities and issues. In so doing they employ this information to adjust their frames of references allowing collaboration and compromise with others.

Intuitive imagining is a psychologically grounded skill that can be reflected upon, understood and employed to increase the range of opportunities for action and problem resolution. The process of reflecting upon one's action is the "reasoning-why" step that inevitably follows judgments and actions emanating from "seeing-that." Being able to understand how intuitive imagining works and reflecting upon this process empowers the individual to frame and reframe their situations (again reasoning-why or rationalizing their prior judgments and actions) to allow for a greater array of behavioral and attitudinal options to address future issues of concern. This is the psychological representation of framing – namely "seeing-that" and "reasoning-why."

When framing becomes more than an individual exercise it takes on its social persona and becomes "deliberative imagining." Deliberative imagining is not pre-reflective or automatic in nature. In fact it is just the opposite. As the name implies, deliberative imagining is thoroughly reasoned, planned, systematic and of course "deliberative" meaning it is purposeful, calculated, planned, organized and intentional in form. Moreover, deliberative imagining is designed to justify one's actions and to cajole or convince others into sharing one's views. Likewise, deliberative imagining helps the decision-maker understand and predict the behavior and attitudes of individuals, as well as anticipate the responses and values of groups and organizations – thus making it the social corollary to the essential psychological process of intuitive imagining.

Most of the models used to frame social issues have employed deliberative imagining approaches. Illustrative of this approach is the work of Erick Knight (2012). Knight uses a magnifying glass metaphor to illustrate how so many individuals and groups go about considering important issues and problems. He claims that it is a natural tendency for people to look at social issues and problems and try to "zoom in" as if they were looking at the problems through the lens of a magnifying glass and focus upon one portion of the problem (that which can be framed in the lens of the magnifying glass) while ignoring all the surrounding areas just beyond the frame of the magnifying glass. In this way they tend to partition problems into their constituent pieces, often focusing upon the "shiniest" and most obvious features of the problem rather than considering the problem in context – as a whole. This penchant becomes particularly problematic when a number of interest groups involved in an issue each narrowly focus upon an aspect of an issue.

For instance, consider the issue of oil and gas exploration and development. Energy exploration companies tend to focus upon the geology, technology and economics associated with finding and identifying these resources. While they also recognize and put some effort into understanding the environmental ramifications of their industry, this concern necessarily plays a smaller part in their overall orientation toward finding and exploiting energy sources.

On the other hand labor unions and workforce participants involved in oil and gas exploration tend to principally think of the industry in terms of what energy resources can do for members, their families and their communities and for them work in this field is construed as a necessary foundation for acquiring and maintaining a level of economic and social stability and affluence. They too consider environmental issues when thinking of their work, but their principle concern is their jobs and their lifestyles. Municipalities, local businesses and financial institutions think similarly to the industry employees and consider the businesses involved in the oil and gas industry to be desirable partners in community and economic development. They too want clean environments but they prioritize employment and economic development followed in priority by clean environments.

Environmental groups and activists, on the other hand, tend to principally see the industry as polluters and exploiters: polluters of air, land and water and exploiters of natural resources. While they recognize the contributions energy companies make to the economy, employment and the nation's energy needs, they tend to principally focus upon the environmental ramifications of the industry and only peripherally concern themselves with other portions of this framed industry mosaic beyond the "shiny green" environmental parts (Rogers, 2010; McKibben, 2008).

Employing Knight's analogy, each group tends to focus upon the part of energy production that most nearly corresponds to their values and concerns and by narrowly focusing on this aspect of oil and gas production, tend to ignore, minimize or misconstrue the interests of others. That which is focused upon is that which is most highly valued by individuals as members of their particular constituent reference groups. Consequently, when they advocate or argue for a particular issue, they do so in the interest of defending what they intuitively value and seek to convince, cajole or coerce others to abandon their particular perspective on the issue to joining theirs. Once again, we see a process at work consistent with the research of Margolis and Haidt in which policy perspectives serve as rationales for deeply held intuitive values shared by interest groups.

Despite the fact that reason will be employed to defend and advocate for intuitively held individual and group values Knight, and other social theorists tend to conceive of reframing as an essentially rational deliberative process through which diverse issue interests might be brought together for the purpose of (1) understanding the perspectives and concerns of others (2) seeking common cause with other groups wherever possible and (3) searching for compromise and accommodation of otherwise seemingly intractable issues. While the deliberative process clearly utilizes rational argument it is nevertheless an argumentative process principally designed to win one another over to the other's perspective or at a minimum, a process in which the participants justify their intuitive values and resultant actions to the members of their key constituencies. What the deliberative process is not is one of reasoned inquiry in the pursuit of the most "rational" outcome possible.

Instead it is a give-and-take between adversaries who at best can only achieve a compromise that they can intuitively justify to themselves and to those whose opinions they most value. This is not to say that the process of give and take inherent in framing can't shape and even change intuitive values of any of the participants for it can and inevitably will to the extent that compromises must be rationalized against individual and shared values. However, on the main, these changes are marginal and incremental and are seldom dramatic and sweeping.

That said it is unavoidable for human beings to *not* employ magnifying glasses to understand issues and problems for the magnifying glass is nothing more than a metaphor for framing. The issue at-hand argues Knight is not *that* we frame issues but rather *how narrowly and incompletely we tend to do so*. Because the framing process is so narrowly conceived even the most attentive policy framer will inevitably ignore or underestimate the importance of other perspectives that, upon further reflection, they may also come to value.

J. Davidson Frame has also considered the issue of framing social issues and concluded that

> We must go beyond the traditional perspective that decision-making can be handled mechanically, with a view to promoting rationality, logic,

optimal results. The reality is that when dealing with poorly defined, nontrivial decisions, which characterize decisions of consequence, we must roll up our sleeves and prepare to get dirty. (Frame, 2013, p. 1)

Frame's assertion underscores an important but frankly troubling characteristic of deliberative imagining – namely that most non-trivial decisions are not simply defined by the force of reason and logic. They are also emotionally charged, ill-defined and frankly "messy." Perforce a deliberative approach to framing must necessarily account for intuition, irrationality and emotion and in many cases must eschew simple, neat and "organized" answers for complex, involved, seemingly irrational and ill-defined solutions and options. Moreover, rather than conceiving of framing as an "in-and-out" "over-and-done" process of inquiry and action, one must bear the discomfort of remaining in dialogue and engagement with others with whom one is competing to define the terms and conditions in which the issue is "framed."

## Competing Frames: A Frame-logic Paradigm

For every important issue there is an array of interest groups seeking to define and control how the issue will be framed in the policy context. Successfully reframing issues entails recognizing this implicit competition for control and actively engaging in a series of deliberative imagining exercises designed to help the imaginator begin to fathom the Frame-logic of those with whom they compete for control over framing the issue at hand (McAdam & Scott, 2005). Frame-logic is shorthand for understanding the intentionality and values that motivates another to assume a particular frame of reference on the issue at hand. The goal of deliberative imagining is to interact with others with whom one competes for control of the frame to allow for collaboration and compromise so that one may participate in "co-constituting" the fame – meaning to provide input and influence into how the issue at hand will be ultimately framed at least for the present.

It is important to recognize that framing and reframing policy issues is not about domination or destroying an ideological opponent. To the contrary, framing and reframing policy issues and employing a deliberative imagining approach to doing so involves identifying congruencies across value systems and needs and fashioning compromises on the basis of those shared values, concerns and needs. Similarly, framing and reframing issues is not a one-time endeavor with a distinct beginning and end. Rather it is an ongoing process requiring individuals and groups to respectfully remain in contact and communication with one another. In short, it is the establishment of a long-term, mutually respectful empathetic bond between people and groups. It is a process that from the outset must involve people who can and will communicate and compromise while necessarily excluding those whose radical (meaning uncompromising) values only permit winning or losing in an all-or-none fashion.

The first step in successfully engaging in framing and reframing issues – beyond understanding that one is inherently in competition with others to successfully define the nature of the frame – is to recognize that while frame competitors may disagree on some components of the frame and the issue it encompasses, there are other areas of concern around which frame competitors may likely agree. Consequently they should expect to remain in contact (and perhaps conflict) with one another and engage one another around each framing encounter in such a way that insures they can sustainably remain on good terms with one another so that each party is willing to be mutually available to address future issues and conflicts. Again, while frame competitors may play the role of antagonists around any particular issue, all competitors must be related to in a mutually respectful manner so that they can continue to deliberate with one another regarding issues over the foreseeable issues. This of course means resisting treating frame competitors as "enemies" but rather relating to them as temporary adversaries and ongoing civic partners.

Phenomenologist Max Scheler (1980) provides a perspective for finding common cause with those one might disagree with on any particular issue by commenting upon what he calls irreducible "spheres of objects" that that all people participate in to include:

> (a) the *absolute* sphere of reality and value, of the Holy, (b) the sphere of the *with-world*, including its past and future, i.e. the world of society and history, or the world of what is the 'other'; (c) the sphere of the *outer and inner worlds*, as well as the sphere of one's own *lived body and its environment*; (d) the sphere of what is 'alive'; and (e) the sphere of what is *inanimate* and of what appears to be 'dead' in the *corporeal world*. (Scheler, 1980, p. 71).

These spheres of objects are places where human interests conjoin. Some of these spheres, such as the "lived body and its environment" can be only experienced subjectively as arguably would be the case for the experience of death. However human beings can and do interact with one in the "absolute" sphere and the "with world" and within these share common types of knowledge to include:

1. *myth and legend*, as undifferentiated preliminary forms of religious, metaphysical, natural and historical knowledge;
2. the knowledge implicit in everyday *natural language* (in contrast to learned, poetic, or technical language)" ..
3. the *religious knowledge* in its various levels of fixation ranging from pious, emotive and vague intuition up to the fixated dogmas of priestly church;
4. the basic forms of *mystical knowledge*; *philoophica-meta physical knowledge*;
5. the *positive knowledge* of mathematics and the natural sciences and the humanities and
6. *technological knowledge* (Scheler, 1980, p. 76)

Donald Schön and Martin Rein have incorporated Scheler's worldview into their approach to dealing with intractable policy issues by proposing several strategies that can be employed to potentially identify areas of common cause and concern across policy deliberators. These include:

- *Expand Shared Spheres of Interest*: Moving beyond a narrow sphere's of concern to larger spheres of knowledge, values and information, seeking areas of agreement around which dialogue might be established: i.e. to seek common perceptions and values,
- *Verify Frame Criteria*: Consensually seek verifiable and identifiable criteria for evaluating frame options and choosing options within this sub-set,
- *Employing Frame "Mapping"*: Visually translate information, data and concepts from one frame paradigm into another. (Schön & Rein, 1994, p. 43)

This process is in part what the authors call "frame reflection" or what we refer to as "Frame-logic." The shared purpose in engaging in this process is to "stand in one another's shoes" to understand how issues and ideas are experienced by others and to use that information to fashion agreements and compromises.

For Schön and Rein such reflection is conceptualized within a set of frameworks proffered by a protégé of Herbert Simon – economist James March of Carnegie Mellon University. March argued that policy issue propositions should be considered in terms of their "truth," "beauty" and "justice" (March, 2003). Schön and Rein employed these tenets and added additional frameworks to arrive at a typology to evaluate frames to include (a) truth, (b) beauty, (c) justice, (d) coherence, (e) inclusiveness and (f) utility or fruitfulness (Schön & Rein, 1994, p. 44). By making these normative distinctions regarding the nature, value and worth of frames Schön and Rein contributed to "Frame-logic" or an understanding of the values and rationale supporting the frame perspective of any particular participant in a frame conflict.

We assert in *Ecopragmatics* that any effort to legitimately understand how others perceive and relate to any particular issue must at least tentatively employ a Frame-logic paradigm that serves to organize and simplify the logic employed by others – be it a person, group, organization or aggregate of others. Schön and Rein employ Marsh's values, which could fruitfully be applied to most any policy issue. However, different issues demand different Frame-logic paradigms. No single paradigm works for all issues nor captures the concerns and perspectives of the people and groups concerned with the issue. Indeed, we argue that individuals and groups committed to issue/policy resolution should experiment and develop an array of Frame-logic paradigms to assist them in conceptualizing and re-conceptualizing issues from a variety of perspectives. Doing so, of course, requires acknowledging that intuitive-derived reasoning will be applied to rationalize how the individual has come to their judgment and how to win their opponents over to their seemingly "correct" perspective. Truly coming to learn how others employ their reasoning requires the deliberator to at least temporarily suspend their own self-serving use of reason.

Our rationale for fostering frame reflection among participants was best articulated by Schön and Rein who observed that,

> When scientists or policy makers are caught up in frame conflict, their ability to reach agreement depends on their learning to understand one another's point of view. In order to do this, however, each party would

have to be able to put in terms of his or her own frame the meaning of the situation as seen by the other in terms of the other's frame. The antagonists might then create a reciprocal, frame-reflective discourse. Reflecting on the frames of their adversaries, as well as on their own frames, they would try to reason their way to conflict resolution. (Schön & Rein, 1994, p. 45)

## Framing and Reframing Seemingly Intractable Environmental Issues

Since we are principally concerned with seemingly intractable environmental issues we sought to develop a basic Frame-logic paradigm that captured some of the most salient features of contemporary environmental controversies. We were principally concerned regarding the extent to which environmental policy conflicts involve assigning blame (Figueres, 2012; Lercher, 2004), proffering simplistic solutions to complex problems (Kemp, 2004; Drew, 1985), and developing propaganda to motivate the public and policy makers to support one position or another (Knickerbocker, 1997; Mayo, 1978). The literature in this regard illustrates how "the-blame-game," the misdiagnosis of the causes of and the contributors to environmental problems, and the confusion between propaganda and objective science can serve to needlessly complicate deliberations over environmental issues and in some cases stymie positive action to resolve issues.

One notable exception to the dearth of literature seeking to successfully engage adversaries in environmental issues is *Making Sense of Environmental Conflicts: Frames and Cases* (2003) by Roy Lewicki, Barbara Gray and Michael Elliott. These authors rely upon an extensive research base to present a number of frame perspectives – all of which we would characterize as "deliberative" – that can be readily applied in seeking to understand the complex motivations and values that characterize adversaries in seemingly intractable environmental issues. A summary of the frame perspectives these authors apply includes:

- *Identity Frames* – Perspectives based upon self/group identity,
- *Characterization Frames* - Frames asserting how people or groups explain the behavior and nature of other individuals and groups,
- *Conflict Management Frames* – Frames addressing the manner in which conflict should be managed (e.g. avoidance/passivity, fact-finding, joint problem solving, authority based upon expertise, adjudication, appeal to political action, appeal to market economy, struggle, sabotage and violence, other conflict management models),
- *Whole Story Frames*  - Encapsulated stories, narratives or vignettes explaining what the dispute was about,
- *Social Control Frames* – Similar to conflict management frames, social control frames represent individual and group perspectives regarding how decisions on social issues should be resolved,
- *Power Frames* - Frames explaining how power is exercised in conflicts to include:
  - Authority/Positional: Ability to make decisions on the basis of role, job description or rank in the organization,

o Resources: Power attributable to access to resources,
o Expertise: Power based upon unique knowledge or expertise,
o Personal: Power based upon persona and interpersonal skills,
o Coalitional/Relational: Power based upon who you know or are associated with,
o Sympathy/Vulnerability: Power based upon real or perceived victimhood,
o Force/Threat: Coercive power,
o Moral/Righteous Power: Power based upon moral certitude:
o Voice: Power based upon one's ability to effectively make, shape and disseminate the message.

• *Risk Frames* - Frames based upon real and perceived risks associated with the policy dispute to include perceptions of potential or real gains and losses associated with issue resolution (Lewicki, Gray & Elliott, 2003, p. 21-34).

Of these frame perspectives, one in particular stands out to the degree to which it has been applied to environmental policy; namely identity frames. Notable among the advocates of this framing approach is Lianne Lefsrud and Renate Meyer who employed identity frames to study the climate change issue and, on the basis of survey research directed toward 1077 professional engineers and geoscientists, succeeded in identifying five frames peculiar to that issue to include those advocating for:

1. *Compliance with the Kyoto Protocol*: Asserting that "climate change is happening, that it is not a normal cycle of nature, and humans are the main or central cause" (Lefsrud & Meyer, 2012, p. 1492).
2. *Nature is Overwhelming:* Suggesting "changes to the climate are natural, normal cycles of the Earth. Their focus is on the past: 'If you think about it, global warming is what brought us out of the Ice Age.' Humans are too insignificant to have an impact on nature" (Lefsrud & Meyer, 2012, p. 1492-1493).
3. *Economic Responsibility:* Construing "climate change as being natural or human caused. More than any other group, they underscore that the 'real' cause of climate change is unknown as nature is forever changing and uncontrollable. Similar to the 'nature is overwhelming' adherents, they disagree that climate change poses any significant public risk and see no impact on their personal life. They are also less likely to believe that the scientific debate is settled and that the IPCC modeling is accurate. In their prognostic framing, they point to the harm the Kyoto Protocol and all regulation will do to the economy" (Lefsrud & Meyer, 2012, p.1493).
4. *Fatalists:* Diagnosing "climate change as both human- and naturally caused. 'Fatalists consider climate change to be a smaller public risk with little impact on their personal life. They are sceptical that the scientific debate is settled regarding the IPCC modeling" (Lefsrud & Meyer, 2012, p.1494).

5.  *Regulation Activists:* Considering "climate change as being both human-
    and naturally caused, posing a moderate public risk, with only slight
    impact on their personal life. Advocates do not significantly vary from
    the mean in how they consider the magnitude, extent, or time scale of
    climate change. They are also sceptical with regard to the scientific
    debate being settled and are the most indecisive whether IPCC modeling
    is accurate" (Lefsrud & Meyer, 2012, p.1494).

This particular approach to identity framing is research-based and seeks to
identify consensually held characteristics among groups of professionals
thereafter employing these shared identities to better understand areas of
agreement and disagreement among adherents. This same empirical approach can
be applied to participants involved in any number of environmental issues and
can produce frame perceptions that are unique to those issues and their
constituents.

These frame perspectives provide an array of "lenses" through which options
for resolving environmental issues can be construed. Each participant in a policy
dispute will utilize a definitive frame that may include some of the characteristics
previously described or include other frame perspectives. Regardless of which
frame perspective is chosen, moving beyond the stalemate that most adversaries
find themselves in relative to environmental issues requires that participants be
willing to "reframe" their perspectives. There are a number of ways in which this
can occur to include:

1.  Shifting from specific interests to more general ones,
2.  Narrowing the issues or breaking them into smaller parts,
3.  Translating disputes over values into interests,
4.  Identifying superordinate (or overarching) goals;
5.  Agreeing to disagree. (Lewicki, Gray & Elliott, 2003)

While any of these reframing approaches may be employed, they do not capture
the importance of intuition in decision-making since Lewicki, Gray and Elliott's
work predated the research in moral psychology published by Jonathan Haidt and
others. Recognizing the importance of intuition in decision-framing and decision-
making, we believe that utilizing a framing and reframing perspective based upon
frame perspectives *and* communication styles might add yet another valuable
perspective to addressing some of the most intractable issues.

We do so out of concern that how people and groups communicate their
values is ultimately as important as the content of their communications (Amit,
Wakslak & Trope, 2013). We emphasize communication (language) style to
reflect contemporary research underscoring the importance of non-rational and
intuitive factors in decision-making and the relationship between intuition and
communication style. We do so recognizing that the form in which information is
presented to decision-makers appears to influence the degree to which intuition is
employed in the decision process. Consequently,

> different decision outcomes might be the result of people processing
> information more intuitively or more rationally based only on the

manner in which information is presented to them. (Sinclair, 2011, p. 102)

Given these concerns, we have concluded that our Frame-logic paradigm should focus upon:

1. Three Conceptual Frame Perspectives: (Benford & Snow, 2000)
   a. Diagnostic Frames - serving to define problems and assign responsibility,
   b. Prognostic Frames - providing solutions to identified problems and issues;
   c. Motivational Frames - serving to convince key groups of actors why and how they should respond.
2. Four Frame Communication/Language Perspectives: ((Hulme, 2009; Bennet & Bennet, 2008; Peacock, 2006; Mehan, 1981).
   a. Language of Lament and Nostalgia - lamenting the loss of an ideal or much better state of affairs,
   b. Language of Fear and Apocalypse - articulating a fear of total destruction and human annihilation,
   c. Language of Pride and Control   - reflecting the sometimes exaggerated belief the human ingenuity can overcome all obstacles,
   d. Language of Justice and Equity - which interprets all framed issues in terms of fairness, rights, obligations and opportunities.

We employed these particular language groupings believing that they served to capture much of the rhetoric of the contemporary environmental policy debate.

We were principally motivated to do so on the basis of Jimmie Killingsworth and Jacqueline Palmer's book *Ecospeak* (1992) in which the authors grapple with the manner in which the term "environmentalist" has been employed. They conclude that:

> The popular and the scientific meanings of environmentalist were originally used not as self-designations by proponents of environmental protection or evolutionary environmentalism but were applied by opponents or observers of these proponents. The terms began in both instances as a designation for outsiders. Whereas in scientific usage environmentalism denotes an opposition to the accepted dogma of geneticism in the popular usage the term exists without a clear opposite suggesting an ideological content, a distinction between the environmentalists and the rest of us. (Killingsworth & Palmer, 1992, p. 42)

Their conclusions emphasize the degree to which labels like "environmentalist" or "environmentalism" can be used as weapons in rhetorical debates within and among environmental groups and opponents and can serve to needlessly obfuscate the consideration of important environmental issues. In recognition of this seemingly indelible feature of the contemporary environmental debate we chose to employ the language classification developed by Mike Hulme (2009) believing that this relatively straightforward taxonomy would prove useful when coupled with Benford and Snow's (2000) tri-part frame scheme. Table 10 illustrates how conceptual and language styles might be framed in relationship to one another.

Table 10: Frame-logic Paradigm: Frame Perspectives and Language Orientation

|  | *Diagnostic Perspective* | *Prognostic Perspective* | *Motivational Perspective* |
|---|---|---|---|
| *Lament/Nostalgia Language* | Current problems reflect the breakdown of established norms of a bygone era. | What worked in the past can once again work to solve current problems. | By returning values that worked in the past we will be able to have a better future. |
| *Fear/Apocalyptic Language* | Human beings are destroying the entire planet and everything on it, including themselves. | Human culture must be dramatically curtailed to save the world and to save humanity. | By cooperating to restrain human excesses you guarantee a future for all. |
| *Pride/Control Language* | There are no problems that human ingenuity cannot eventually solve | Human technology and science will eventually overcome the worst ills to be found in the world. | By investing in science and technology you guarantee a better life for you and your family. |
| *Justice/Equality Language* | Human injustice is paralleled by ecological injustice and taken together this produces inequality among people and species. | Only when all people and all species are treated equally will there be lasting justice and peace on the planet. | Promoting justice and equality among people and across species creates a more peaceful and sustainable world. |

The convergence of frame perspectives and language approaches reflected above provides a useful illustration of how frame competitors might not only characterize their own positions on an issue, but additionally may be useful in understanding the Frame-logic of others. This is but a starting point for each participant to begin the process of deliberatively imaginating how their competitors formulate and articulate their values and perspectives. Each cell in the matrix above would need to be considered and explored in detail. For instance, one might consider the diagnostic cell for the pride/control language style and inquire to determine the extent to which the assertion "there are no problems that human ingenuity cannot eventually solve" is sincerely believed and acted upon. Alternatively, for the prognostic cell pertaining to fearful and apocalyptic language one might want to consider the risks and benefits associated with the assertion "Human culture must be dramatically curtailed to save the world and to save humanity." Considering such an assertion and the ramifications related to it allows one to enter into the Frame-logic of other frame competitors and in so doing not only learn about their values and perspectives but additionally begin the process of considering the degree to which the values and perspective of others might be worth incorporating at least in part into one's own value system.

## Identifying Stakeholders and Developing Framing Themes

The frame logic paradigm presented above is to be applied to the various "players" or "stakeholders" with an interest or investment in a particular environmental problem or issue. Consequently the next steps involved in framing entails identifying as many of the pertinent participants involved in a policy issue or problem as possible, and using the frame logic matrix above tentatively assign each player to one of the matrix cells. Having so characterized each participant, player or stakeholder, one then goes about the process of developing some thematic categories for each player, even those who may share a particular cell in the matrix. Each constituent group will – despite their overall agreement with others sharing their matrix cell – possess characteristics unique to their group, cause or organization. It is important to develop as many of these thematic categorizations as possible and to assign a name to each that accurately reflects their concerns.

For instance, a wide array of constituencies might share a passion for clean freshwater resources but may do so from a variety of perspectives. Representatives of Ducks Unlimited might value the fresh water in as habitat for ducks and places where hunters can hunt ducks. Comparably Bassmasters might value the water as habitat for large and small-mouth bass and the American Canoe Association values fresh water resources for paddling and camping. Utilizing the Frame-logic paradigm above, arguably all of these organizations would fall within either the "pride/control" and "justice/equality" language cells – depending upon the degree to which the organization's philosophical orientation prioritized conservationist versus environmentalist values – with organizations principally embracing a conservationist perspective falling within the "pride/control" panels and those distrusting conservationist principles falling within the "justice/equality" cells.

However, what if the Frame-logic matrix was revised around the degree of anthropocentrism the participant in the environmental issue or problem embrace. Table 11 illustrates this configuration.

Table 11: Frame-logic Paradigm: Frame Perspectives and Anthropocentrism

|  | Diagnostic Perspective | Prognostic Perspective | Motivational Perspective |
|---|---|---|---|
| **Exclusively Anthropocentric** | Humans have an unqualified right to use natural resources as they see fit although they *may* make environmental demands that are unsustainable. | Innovation and technology can be employed to achieve homeostasis between human demands and environmental sustainability. | Human innovation, technology and restraint can be employed to restore and maintain environmental sustainability. |
| **Somewhat Anthropocentric** | Humans have a qualified right to use natural resources but sometimes fail to recognize that other species have a right to exist also. | Innovation and technology can be employed to achieve environmental sustainability but only to the extent such use also fosters the sustainability of other species. | Environmental and human sustainability is best pursued through the wise use of innovation and technology coupled with human restraint in resource use. |
| **Somewhat Anti-anthropocentric** | Humans are entitled to minimally use natural resources but such use must only minimally encroach upon the existence of other species and ecosystems. | Human innovation and technology, while useful, must not be substituted for the exercise of human behavioral and cultural restraint in their interaction with the environment. | Significant human restraint in natural resource use is the best way to insure a sustainable environment and sustainable human culture. |
| **Exclusively Anti-anthropocentric** | Humans have no inherent right to environmental resources and are not entitled to threaten the existence of other species through their utilization of natural resources. | Un-checked humans will exploit the environment to the point of utter human and eco-devastation and technological innovation alone won't prevent this outcome. | Minimizing human use of natural resources and generally curtailing their environmental access is the best way to insure environmental sustainability. |

In this second paradigm values regarding anthropocentrism are substituted for the language of framing. Given this altered framework and based upon the public statements and actions of our three stakeholders we might well find them interested in promoting the sustainability of freshwater resources in any three of the four cells of paradigm two (with the exception of the anti-anthropocentric cell), whereas in the first paradigm we are probably more likely to find them in the "justice/equality" and "pride/control" cells than in the "fear/apocalypse" and "lament/nostalgia" cells. However, if we were to construct a number of such Frame-logic matrices along the lines of these two we could likely be able to tease out any number of other nuances regarding the themes they pursue.

For the sake of illustration let's look at three other proponents of freshwater conservation who approach the issue from noticeably different perspectives – the World Health Organization (WHO), the Sierra Club and the American Sportfishing Association (ASA). In 2008 ASA – the nation's largest sportfishing organization- asserted in their annual report that:

> While many people recognize the recreational and economic benefits of fishing, its significant conservation benefits often go unnoticed. For each fishing-tackle purchase and each gallon of boating fuel consumed, a portion of the money is returned to state fish and wildlife agencies for conservation efforts. America's success in restoring many species of fish and wildlife and protecting natural habitat can largely be credited to the billions of dollars generated by sportsmen and women. Sportfishing companies are proud of their role in advancing a portion of their proceeds to fund one of the world's greatest conservation assets—the Sport Fish. Through the Federal Aid in Sport Fish Restoration Act, passed in 1950 at the request of the fishing industry, special excise taxes on fishing gear and boating fuel have contributed billions of dollars for fish and wildlife conservation. Added each year to this are nearly $650 million in annual fishing license sales plus approximately $200 million in private donations by anglers for conservation efforts. Sportfishing is truly a major economic driver and America's conservation powerhouse. (ASA, 2008, p. 2-3)

Given this perspective we would have to conclude that the association is very anthropocentric in its orientation and uses language that is most nearly congruent to the "pride/control" language grouping.

By comparison, here is how the WHO approached the issue of freshwater conservation.

> Freshwater is essential to maintain human health. It is also essential for maintaining many of the ecosystems which provide our food and other essential goods and services. Of all the water available on Earth, about 2.5% is fresh, and a good part is inaccessible to us. The availability of this small fraction of freshwater found in rivers, lakes and underground is increasingly threatened by land-use, deforestation, climate change and increased consumption of freshwater by growing populations and industry. Additionally, the quality of this water is threatened by increasing pollution, particularly in urban areas and in relation to intensified agriculture. By protecting freshwater ecosystems we are also

protecting our health. Over 1 billion people lack access to safe water supplies, while 2.6 billion people lack adequate sanitation. Lack of sanitation leads to widespread microbial contamination of drinking water. (Corvalan, Hales & McMichael, 2005, p.2)

This statement is quite clearly one that embraces a somewhat anthropocentric perspective coupled with a "pride/control" and "justice/equality" language set. Comparing the public statements of ASA and WHO one would have to conclude that they appear to differ only perhaps in the degree of their anthropocentrism. This implies that around the issue of conservation of freshwater resources that there should be a great deal of room for agreement between these two organizations.

However a different pattern emerges if one considers an organization like Earth First. This radical environmental organization takes a decidedly less compromising position when its leaders assert that:

> Revolt is not a military operation but a social affair. However, this does not negate the very real necessity that space plays. We need social spaces, places for us to get organized, places that can sustain life, places worth calling home." "We need material structures and thread to weave them together. The material structures will, at first, be social centers, radical neighborhoods, appropriated land, but will transform into autonomous rebel communities, archipelagos of revolt, and experiments in food and water acquisition that develop beyond organic farms and water conservation." "We must recognize ourselves as a part of those who will be impacted by the social consequences of global ecological crisis and who already are impacted by capitalism. Only then can we imagine what it would look like to be a part of a social force that is not an expression of a moral impulse, but a need for survival and desire for utopia. What if "climate justice" meant seizing the means of distributing clean water and producing clean water systems in autonomous zones?" "Whether we call it "climate justice" or whether we relate our notion of we to a philosophy of biocentricism, we are still failing to draw lines that are based in reality. Reality: We will die without clean water, and we will go to prison if we get caught breaking the laws that we are going to break—laws we must break if we are going to survive. Reality: Extinction of most life on the planet includes the ecosystems that we rely on and are intimately attached to. Reality: We are components of capitalist society, which transforms everything into capital including our relationships, desires and self. (Sionnach, 2009)

So described, Earth First principally uses the language of "justice/equality" and "fear/apocalypse" while assuming an aggressively anti-anthropocentric orientation. Consequently, it would seem that there is little common ground to be found between Earth First, ASA or the World Health Organization.

If we were to develop theme categories for these three organizations based upon these limited sets of statements and assertions we might develop Earth First under the theme "Revolution and Redistribution" based upon their public statements about revolutionary change and the redistribution of natural resources away from capitalist models and in the direction of socialist ones. For the ASA we might assign the theme "Fish and Finance" given their desire to be allowed to fish freshwater resources at will and promote conservation through user fees and fishing-oriented consumption taxes. Finally in regard to the WHO we would probably adopt the theme "Clean Water and Health" given their commitment to clean water not so much for ecological reasons but rather to promote public health and wellness. While these themes don't tell one everything they need to know to understand how these three organizations frame their policy issues, they do provide a handy template for anticipating how they might be expected to respond to environmental problems and issues and they also suggest ways in which they might find common cause with other groups and organizations. We will develop this process of theme assignment in the following chapter with an in depth case study.

In developing the case we will describe the forces that define and drive the environmental theme and suggest possible alternatives for addressing the environmental issues of concern. We will employ the thematic metaphor to aid in analyzing and reflecting upon how the various stakeholders might act and interact with other stakeholders. The case analysis will conclude with the positing of a set of possible outcomes – worst, likely and ideal – for implementing a strategy to achieve an acceptable resolution to the problem or issue at hand. In so doing we will employ "satisficing" approach that insures a balance between individual and community needs consistent with the communitarian ethic to "Respect and uphold society's moral order as you would have society respect and uphold your autonomy to live a full life" (Etzioni, 1996 p. xviii). We will apply this Frame-logic paradigm in the following to begin the process of trying to understand what it is like to "stand in the shoes" on another and in so doing, begin to understand how the world looks through their eyes. Hopefully by undertaking this analysis we will begin to develop some skills in working with and appreciating the sensibilities of others, as well as allowing their experiences and values to influence our own.

# Chapter 6: Gyppo Loggers and Spotted Owls

I'm just a poor old gyppo logger,
Trying to make ends meet.
Got equipment I've got to pay for,
And a family that's got to eat.
But these guys from the Forest Service,
Every time they come around,
All they do is look for something wrong
So they can close you down.

*Fire Danger*
Buzz Martin

## Gyppo Loggers, the Northern Spotted Owl, and the End of a Way of Life

The opening lines to Buzz Martin's well known logging tune "Fire Danger" captures the frustration of the so-called "gyppo logger" – a colloquial term for a logger who either independently operates a small logging company working with a local sawmill, or is in the employ of one of these independent sawmill or lumber operations. These small independent operators do what they can to eke out a living cutting and transporting timber to the sawmill but do so under significant economic, environmental and regulatory duress. Indeed the gyppo logger is but one of a much larger cast of characters who converge in a seemingly endless controversy between those who make a living in the timber industry and those who would curtail or eliminate timbering in the interest of protecting the forests, their ecosystems and their fragile and sometimes endangered inhabitants. Nowhere has this conflict out played out longer or with more controversy than in the Pacific Northwest. Among the extensive cast of characters vying for a role in the timber versus environment controversy none stands larger than the diminutive northern spotted owl.

The northern spotted owl - referred to hereafter as simply the "spotted owl" - was first identified in Oregon's Willamette National Forest in 1968 and by 1990 it was added to the list of protected species under the federal Endangered Species

Act (ESA). As a consequence, the owl's habitat – mostly old-growth timber – came under the protection of the U.S. Forest Service in the interest of preserving the species. It is worth noting that the bulk of the spotted owl's habitat is situated virtually entirely on federal lands with 74% of that habitat managed by the U.S. Forest service, 12% administered by the Bureau of Land Management, 8% residing the nation's national parks and the remaining portion situated on lands subject to management by the Bureau of Indian Affairs. Virtually none of the northern or California spotted owl's habitat remains on privately held land since virtually all old-growth on these lands has been logged (Myers, 1991, p. 626). Consequently, the spotted owl controversy has led to comparatively intensive logging on state and locally owned land where regulatory impediments to logging are not as intensive.

Federal protection of the spotted owl did much to curtail timber harvesting within the bounds of national forests and other public lands. Consequently, for many the owl became emblematic of the decline of forest related industries and those who would protect the owl and its habitat came to be seen as immanent threats to a way of life that loggers, truckers, lumberjacks and others whose livelihoods had centered upon timber and timber products over many generations. However, as is the case with so many environmental controversies, the reality of the demise of the timber industry is much more involved and nuanced than might first appear to be the case. While undoubtedly the spotted owl contributed to a decline in timber harvests, it was not the principle driver for the decline of timber-related employment, since that decline began well before the northern spotted owl controversy emerged in 1990.

## The Steady Decline of the Timber Industry in the Pacific Northwest

During World War II U.S. demand for timber dramatically increased as the nation built battleships requiring wood planking and later embarked on a protracted building boom following the war as veterans returned home and sought to build homes and establish families. Vast amounts of timber were required to feed the seemingly insatiable demand for lumber and nowhere were larger timber reserves to be found than among the various states of the Pacific Northwest.

Northwestern timber-related industries have historically defined the culture of many small and middle-sized communities in northern California, Washington and Oregon (Six, 1995). Beginning in the mid-nineties the local culture of these Pacific Northwest communities came under considerable external pressure as a consequence of technological innovations in timber harvesting, new approaches to forest management and environmental pressures – in part driven by the Endangered Species Act (ESA) - that principally emanated from urban areas geographically distant from the forests, forest-related industries and the communities who depended upon forest products for their livelihoods. These pressures continue to this day.

During the late 1980's timber production increased as the industry responded to a baby-boomer driven increase in housing demand. This increased demand for timber –produced with fewer workers due to technological innovations in timber harvesting - created incentives for public and private forestland to be maximally utilized for timber production, though sometimes detrimental to the natural environment. During this era, forestland was principally treated as an economic resource that required scientific management to produce a "sustained yield" as mandated by the 1944 Sustained-Yield Act, which was developed to insure a virtually endless source of timber products (Clary, 1987). However with the advent of a renewed environmental consciousness nationwide during the late twentieth and early twenty-first century, concern shifted from economic productivity to environmental preservation and protection – particularly in regard to protecting the environment of the California and the northern spotted owl and the old-growth forests that these species inhabited (Marcot & Thomas, 1997).

Concern over the habitat for the owls emerged as an environmental concern during the early nineties which prompted a number of economic analyses to determine the impact upon timber-dependent communities and their industries that would result from restricting logging on public lands to protect this endangered species. The results of the various economic impact studies were contradictory in their findings ranging from the loss of thousands to tens of thousands of jobs. So while a significant economic impact could be anticipated, the magnitude of that impact remained uncertain (Marcot & Thomas, 1997, p. 2).

Beyond the direct influence of environmental concerns, historically the region's timber industry had experienced a boom period following WWII, went into a slump during the 1980 recession and then increased in volume in the late eighties and beyond as a consequence of the housing boom of that era. By 1983 national timber demand was projected to increase from 12 billion board feet in 1976 to more than 23 feet board feet billion in (2030) (USTA, 1983, p. 91). In fact, U.S. timber production outpaced the 1983 estimates and by 2009 22.9 billion board feet was produced, with some 10.9 billion board feet produced in the Western states of Washington, Oregon, California, Montana and Idaho (Warren, 2010, p. 1-2). Nevertheless, while total U.S. timber production grew since the 1980's, production levels fell among the three largest timber producing Pacific Northwest states. In Washington, total timber production fell from 4,224 million board feet in 1999 to 3,885 million board feet in 2008. In Oregon, timber production levels declined from 6,056 million board feet to 4,724 million board feet while in California production levels plummeted from 3,216 to 1,920 million board feet over the 1999-2008 period (Warren, 2010, p. 7).

In the two largest timber-producing states in the Pacific Northwest – Washington and Oregon – the bulk of timber production came from private lands. However, in Washington timber production on privately held lands decreased from 3,131 to 2,067 million board feet between 2000 and 2008. Likewise, in Oregon production on these lands fell from 3,167 to 2,739 million board feet over the same period. State lands were the next largest sources of timber, though much less productive than production on private lands. In Washington timber production on state lands actually increased marginally from 559 million board feet to 693 million board feet between 2000 and 2008 while in Oregon production increased from 255 to 278 million board feet over the same period (Warren, 2010, p. 21). Meanwhile, timber production on federal lands increased from 441 million board feet in 2000 to 552 million board feet in 2006 (2008 data was unavailable). By comparison, Oregon's timber production on federal land remained essentially stable over the same period decreasing from 497 million board feet in 1999 to 424 million board feet in 2008 (Warren, 2010, p. 21).

Predictably decreases in timber production across the Pacific Northwest diminished the timber-related workforce as a result of decreased timber yield and technological innovations in timber harvesting. In Washington and Oregon, total timber related employment fell from 1.07 million workers to 730,000 workers between 2000 and 2008 (Warren, 2010, p. 25). Total timber related employment declined 55% between 1989 and 2009 in California, and declined 30% in Oregon and 51% in Washington over the same period (ICE, 2012, p. 3-11, 3-12, 3-13).

When these employment rates are translated into payroll figures the economic impact of the declining industry becomes apparent. Between 1989 and 2009 timber payrolls dropped from $4,696,686 to $1,985,147 for a 58% decrease in payroll (ICE, 2012, p. 3-10). In Oregon payrolls decreased from $3,656,829 to $1,397,301 (62%) and in Washington they decreased from $2,630,498 to $1,356,597 (48%) over the same period (ICE, 2012, p. 3-11, 3-12; 3-13). Clearly, changes in forest management practices and reductions in timber harvests from protected lands produced a significant economic loss for the region.

## Regulatory Impacts upon Timber Production in Washington and Oregon

In considering the impact of the spotted owl regulation under the ESA, it is important to recognize the percentage of forested area that falls under federal, state and private ownership and the extent of timber production internationally, nationally and within northern spotted owl habitat. As of 2010 The United States, Russia, Canada, Japan, Sweden, Germany, Poland, France, Finland, and Brazil were the principal producers of lumber worldwide (Campbell Group, 2013) with some 30,402,200 hectares of land in the United States covered with forestland. Some 13,033,000 hectares of U.S. forestland was publicly owned and 17,177,500 hectares held in private hands (FAO, 2010, p. 10 & 15).

According to a 2012 economic impact report provided on behalf of the U.S. Fish and Wildlife Service 12,021,123 acres of forestland within the spotted owl habitat in the Pacific Northwest is owned by the federal government (or 86% of the land in the habitat). The remaining 670,671 acres is owned by the various states and 1,269,890 acres is held privately (IEC, 2012, p. ES-4). Within this habitat region the U.S. Forest Service identifies the following factors as principally impacting the northern spotted owl:

- Timber Management: Timber harvest has contributed to Northern Spotted Owl (NSO) habitat loss, degradation, and fragmentation and was the main basis for the original listing of the NSO in 1990. Timber management activities represent the primary land use within proposed critical habitat..

- Wildfire Management: NSO habitat is particularly vulnerable to wildfire in drier forest systems, which have experienced recent wildfire losses that have exceeded the range of historical variability. Some habitat losses resulting from increased wildfire frequency, intensity, and size can be attributed to excessive fuel buildup resulting from many decades of fire suppression. Fire management activities that benefit the NSO may include modified fuel reduction and fire suppression practices.

- Road Construction and other Linear Projects: Construction and maintenance of linear projects such as roads, natural gas pipelines, and electric power transmission lines can negatively impact the NSO and its critical habitat through direct habitat loss related to removal of hazard trees and noise disturbance related to blasting actions.
- Other Forest and Species Management: The presence of the barred owl in NSO habitat is considered one of the most significant threats currently facing the NSO. In areas where these species co-exist, the NSO faces competition for habitat, nest sites and prey; the two species may hybridize; and the barred owl may occasionally prey on the NSO. Management programs to control the barred owl may possibly include direct removal of the species. Forest management activities recommended to benefit the NSO may include minimization of blow-downs and wind-throw events through maintenance of large, contiguous blocks of older forest. (ICE, 2012, p. 1-7)

Of these obstacles timber management is the principal economic activity threatening the spotted owl. Obviously curtailing timber production is considered essential to owl habitat protection. Accordingly, timber production throughout the spotted owl's California habitat has decreased by 66% between 1990 and 2010. Similarly, timber yields in the spotted owl habitat have decreased by 42% in Oregon and 54% in Washington over the same period (ICE, 2012, p. 3-5). What this means is that timber production on private lands throughout the three-state region has decreased form approximately 8 million board feet in 1990 to less than 7 million board feet in 2000 to less than 5 million board feet in 2010. Similarly, timber production on public lands has decreased from 4 million board feet in 1990 to 1 million board feet in 2000 and then marginally increased to 1.5 million board feet in 2010 (ICE, 2012, p. 3-8). These changes have produced an 11% timber-related unemployment rate in 2010 in the spotted owl habitat area in California, and an 11% and 10% unemployment rate within the spotted owl's habitat in Oregon and Washington respectively (ICE, 2012, p. 3-10).

While it is tempting to attribute the decline in the timber industry in the Pacific Northwest to regulatory activities to protect the spotted owl, the reality of the situation is much more complicated. The Industrial Economics Incorporated (ICE) economic analysis provided for the U.S. Forest Service clearly delineates factors chiefly responsible for the economic decline of the timber industry to include:

- *Industry / Market Characteristics*: "The timber industry is characterized as being highly competitive; there is a relatively low degree of concentration of production among the largest producers and there is essentially a single national price for commodity grades of lumber."
- *Competitive Factors*: "In recent decades, competition has intensified with increased harvesting in the U.S. South and interior Canadian Provinces."
- *Technological Innovations*: "New technologies and increased mechanization have led to mill closures; generally, less efficient mills located near Federal forests have been closed in favor of larger more

advanced facilities closer to major transportation corridors or private timberlands."

- *Federal Regulations*: Refers to restrictions on timber harvesting related to the ESA and in particular protection of the habitat of the northern spotted owl.

- *International Trade and Timber Ownership*: "Shifts in international trade, and changes in timberland ownership, have contributed to changes in the Pacific Northwest timber industry."

- *Changes in Demand for Timber Products*: "Fluctuations in domestic consumption, [demand for timber] is driven by demand for the final products into which wood is a material input. End uses for harvested wood have evolved over the years, moving from solid wood outputs to composite products such as particleboard and paper. In addition, increasing wood-use efficiency, use of recycled fiber, and product substitutes have contributed to a reduction in timber demand. In recent years, demand for softwood lumber and structural panels has been increasingly unstable due to the downturn in housing construction" (ICE, 2012, p. 3-16; 3-17).

The story of timber decline in the Pacific Northwest is complicated, and certainly much more complicated than the songster Buzz Martin's lyrics suggest – pitting the interests of the gyppo logger against the regulatory authority of the U.S. Forest Service.

Timbering in the Pacific Northwest has always been a unique and complicated affair dating back to the earliest European settlement of the area. At the time of European settlement old-growth forest dominated some two-thirds of the available landmass in the region or some 16,672,976 hectares. (Stritholt, Dellsala & Jiang, 2005, p. 364). The size and scale of the trees settlers encountered was unprecedented, to the point where the density of the trees and the degree to which their tops completely blocked sunlight created a dark, damp and virtually impenetrable barrier for settlement (Jones, 1894, p. 365).

So dense was the forest cover that in 1826 Hudson Bay Company representative George Simpson dismissed the utility of settling in the forests north of the Columbia River, noting that the area is "covered with almost impenetrable forests" (Ficken, 1987, p. 16). At the time living this part of the world entailed living in darkness since the tree canopy virtually blocked out all sunlight. Consequently, establishing communities entailed clearing out spaces where the sunlight could beam down and around which subsistence crops could be grown. These spaces are now known as "clear-cuts" since all trees are removed.

While these open spaces provide habitats for humans and some land for growing crops, the process of clearing a patch of old-growth forest exposed the trees facing the clearing to winds that could topple them upon other trees or upon the clearing itself. Despite this risk, setters cleared open spaces for towns and farms as they turned their energies to making a living by timbering. Once again, however, the density of tree-growth presented a problem. Without open spaces for the tree to fall into and to be cut and trimmed for transport to the sawmill it was impossible to engage in logging. So seemingly out of necessity, additional clear-cuts were provided where trees could be safely felled, cut, stored and transported.

In modern times these clear-cut areas are considered the epitome of environmental destructiveness and excess. Moreover these unsightly swaths of devastated forest have served to motivate many to end the practice. Arguably, however, the very nature of the northwest old-growth forests require clear-cutting. Dietrich (1992) makes this point eloquently when he observes that,

> The sheer volume of wood in Pacific Northwest old-growth forests is an obstacle to harvesting it. Unlike tropical forests, trees in temperate climates decay slowly, thus making the ground a crisscrossed obstacle course of fallen logs. Trees also grow tall and have narrow branch structures, allowing the forest to pack a lot of stems into a small area. As a result, the biomass, or total weight of living matter in these temperate forests is typically four times that of the densest tropical forest. (Dietrich, 1992, p. 122)

Critics of the method have argued that selective logging should be employed. However this process is not as easily achieved as one might imagine. Again Dietrich observes that

> This astonishing volume [of timber biomass] makes harvesting the forests lucrative, but the trees and downed logs are so dense that it is difficult to log selectively by cutting only some of the trees. Those cut can damage the survivors when they fall, and can damage them again and again when dragged across the ground to be loaded onto trucks. It is expensive to work around standing trees and those left may topple of shed branches that could injure loggers. Even if they survive logging, critics contend the trees left behind may blow down in high winds. (Dietrich, 1992, p. 122)

The irony of the controversy over old-growth forests involving species such as the ponderosa pine and the redwood is that while the wood from these trees is very valuable – particularly for making furniture, flooring and cabinets – it is extremely difficult to harvest and because it is slow growing requires a long growth period in order for timber companies to experience a return on investment by replanting the native species. For that reason, the more quickly growing Douglas Fir is often planted in clear-cuts in part because the interval from planting to harvest is shorter, it is very popular particular for housing uses, and because it is not as large as its native cousins and easier to cut, transport and mill. Moreover, if the Douglas Fir is not allowed to age into old-growth, then these tree plantations don't provide habitat for the spotted owl which means landowners are free to harvest timber without interference from the state and federal governments.

From an economic perspective, timber interests who plant Douglas Fir following clear-cuts of old-growth forests can look forward to more future cuts with less hassle than if they were replanting native stock. Moreover, since the spotted owl favors the slower growing Lodgepole and Ponderosa pine stock, younger stands of Douglas Fir don't appear to attract spotted owls to the same degree that native species do. While this fact serves to reduce the spotted owl's habitat, from an economic perspective it simplifies the work of timber interests in terms of planting and harvesting timber with minimal governmental interference.

As complicated as the whole issue is, it is additionally complicated by the regulatory stance of the federal government, particularly regarding the Northwest Forest Plan (1994) introduced by President Bill Clinton and revised (Western Oregon Plan Revisions or WOPR) under the administration of George W. Bush. Arguably it is the intensity of the political dispute over logging on federal lands in this region that drives the central theme of the dispute centering upon the loggers (in this case the gyppo loggers) and the enforcement activities of the U.S. Forest Service and the U.S. Fish and Wildlife Service.

## The Northwest Forest Plan and WOPR

The Northwest Forest Plan (NWFP), adopted by Congress in 1994, regulates and controls federal public forests in Washington, Oregon, and northern California. NWFP was forged to improve upon historically unsustainable forest management and logging practices on federal land in the interest of protecting old-growth forest resources. The plan creates a number of special land-use designations to achieve its goals to include: (Thomas et al, 2006; US Forest Service, 1993)

- *Late Successional Reserves (LSR)*: The plan reserves 30%, or 7.4 million acres, of federal land as LSR to protect existing old-growth forests and wildlife habitat, and to promote future old-growth habitat.
- *Riparian Reserves (RR)*: The plan sets aside 10% of federal forestland, or 2.6 million acres, for the protection of sensitive buffer land adjacent to streams, marshes, lakes, ponds and wetlands. So called "RRs" serve to maintain clean water reserves for spawning fish, wildlife human beings.
- *Matrix*: NWFP calls for more than 4 million acres to be designated as "matrix" land to be allocated for multiple uses to include timber harvesting to include 1 million acres of old-growth forest.
- *Adaptive Management Areas (AMA)*: The plan calls for 1.5 million acres of land falling within the LSR, RR and Matrix designations to be used as experimental areas for the purposed of developing alternative strategies to address the region's burgeoning economic, social and environmental needs.

These designated areas serve to promote the forest resource goals of the U.S. Bureau of Land Management (BLM) whose staff administer the plan. Among the four land use designations, however, timber harvesting is only permitted on Matrix and AMA designated lands.

The NWFP plan was subsequently revised in two ways. In 1995 the Congress enacted Timber Salvage Rider to the NWFP grandfathering BLM initiated timber sales (Blum & Wigington, 2013) and allowing forest land to continue to be harvested for timber. In 2008 the administration of George W. Bush sought to revise the NWFP in regard to some 2.6 million acres of BLM lands in Oregon. This revision became known as the Western Oregon Plan Revisions or WOPR (Center for Effective Government, 2008). The Western Oregon Plan Revisions, sought to quadruple old-growth forest logging and eliminate or reduce logging's impact upon wildlife reserves, streamside buffers as well as to support the region's salmon and steelhead fisheries and guarantee clean water resources.

What made WOPR controversial were the provisions permitting logging on Matrix and AMA designated lands. Logging activities threatened old-growth forest resources, which was a point of particular environmental concern on its own merit. However, these ancient old-growth forests also provided habitat to the endangered spotted owl and any logging activities occurring within old-growth forests threatened the very existence of this endangered species. During the early nineties the U.S. Fish and Wildlife Service (USFWS) drafted but did not implement a recovery plan to protect the spotted owl under the aegis of the ESA. By 1994, the Clinton administration employed NWFP as their principle recovery plan for the owl (Center for Effective Government, 2007).

By 2003, the USFWS was sued by the Center for Biological Diversity and three other plaintiffs (The Center For Sierra Nevada Conservation, Natural Resources Defense Council, and Sierra Nevada Forest Protection Campaign) represented by Earthjustice for failing to provide protection for the spotted owl under the ESA (Center for Biological Diversity et al. versus Gale A. Norton and Marshall P. Jones, 2003). The suit challenged a February 2003 decision denying the petition to extend protection under the ESA for the spotted owl. The USFWS rationale asserted the owl's habitat fell under the protection of the Sierra Nevada Framework restricting logging in old growth forests (USFS, 2001).

In 2009 the Obama administration withdrew WOPR, again preventing logging among ancient-growth tree stands. In 2011 the Western Environmental Law Center (WELC) involved itself in the WOPR controversy but failed to have the WOPR provisions reversed (Carollo, 2011). WELC judicial efforts were stymied by the American Forest Resource Council (AFRC), the Carpenter's Industrial Council, and Douglas Timber Operators (DTO) (AFRC, 2012). However, by 2012 WELC finally succeeded in obtaining an injunction enforcing WOPR in an Oregon federal court (Brown, 2012) and timber production in these Northwest forests was subrogated to protecting old-growth forests and saving the spotted owl.

This chain of events portrays a story in which priorities for forest use changed with Presidential administrations – with use having been restricted under the presidency of Bill Clinton, relaxed under the George W. Bush administration, and then restricted anew within the presidency of Barack Obama. Consequently, unraveling the policy conundrum of the timber and environmental issue in the Pacific Northwest requires one to minimally understand the perspectives of at least four of the major players in this debate – namely the loggers, the timber industry, the environmentalists and the regulators (in the form of Forest Service and Fish and Wildlife Service officials). In seeking to frame and re-frame this particular controversy, we will not endeavor to present the perspective of all of the participants in this policy issue – for there are many. Instead we will focus upon the central four stakeholders.

## Loggers, Environmentalists, Regulators, and Timberland Industry

Since 1990 and the implementation of the ESA restrictions on logging in spotted owl habitat, the ultimate demise of the Pacific Northwest timber industry has been predicted. Not surprisingly, despite persuasive economic and industry data to the contrary, the decline of timbering has been principally blamed upon the inability of environmentalists and folks involved in the timber industry to meaningfully communicate with one another relative to spotted owl habitat. As a 1990 investigative report published in *The Seattle Times* observed "environmentalists and timber people often use the same vocabulary when talking about forests, as if they agree on what words mean" (McDermott & Nagoki, 1990) when in fact the two groups use the same words in very different contexts. For instance,

> Most loggers insist there's still plenty of forest to go around and snort at suggestions that the resource is running out. Many resist even contemplation of the idea. Most environmentalists insist that too much has already disappeared. (McDermott & Nagoki, 1990)

Nor do the two groups agree upon a shared understanding of what constitutes a forest.

> Environmentalists say a forest has in it many other things, the trees being just one class of perhaps thousands. By emerging social and increasingly legal definitions, these other things - northern spotted owls, for example - are in the forest expressly not to be removed. The timber industry's conception of the modern, managed forest is nearly the opposite. Most crudely put, a managed forest has in it only the trees and they are put there solely for the purpose of being removed. It is a fiber farm, closer in conception to a factory than a forest. (McDermott & Nagoki, 1990)

The net effect of this miscommunication between two powerful interest groups is stalemate and balkanization – observed in this case more than a decade ago and an impasse that has only strengthened in intensity over the intervening years.

One particular observation from this 1990 Seattle Times article undoubtedly remains as true today as it did more than a decade ago and that regards the still widely touted concept of "the multiple-use forest" – meaning a place for natural environmental habitat and species, recreation, and commercial industry. Namely,

> There has yet to be found a "multiple-use forest," to use the contemporary vernacular, expansive enough to contain the definitions both the environmental community and the timber industry would seek to apply to it. (McDermott & Nagoki, 1990)

As was the case in 1990, the battlefield between timber interests and environmentalists lies on the forest floor – a so-called "multi-use" forest that contestants cannot seem to negotiate in terms of who will use what, when, where and how. This region is the territory around which any effort to frame policy issues lies and the key participants in this debate involve those individuals and the groups they are affiliated with that trod this littered troubled ground.

Resolving this conflict entails coming to an intuitive appreciation of the identity of these contestants, how they relate to the forest, what it means to them, what they value, need, and fear. The approach to framing policy issues presented in this text is inherently intuitive and is based upon a pragmatic approach calling for deliberators to be aware that their reasoning and actions are driven by instinctive responses to the world around them with reasoning serving to explain, justify or convince others of the worth and correctness of their intuitive responses. This intuitive process is consistent with William James' "stream of consciousness" metaphor in which patterns of experience elicit intuitive responses that in turn are followed by rationality born to serve intuition and feelings. The process of framing policy issues is intended to make the cast of policy deliberators sensitive to this intuitive process in the interest of doing the unintuitive – namely understanding and empathizing with the emotions, values and reasoning of their opponents to seek a means by which the policy issue can be reframed for some degree of mutual benefit.

The first part of this process is often the toughest and involves bringing some of the antagonists in the policy dispute to the figurative bargaining table. Getting disparate representative of various interest groups to come to the table entails them believing that they have some likelihood of obtaining a relatively competitive advantage in doing so. However, successful framing also requires one to exclude from the table those whose only intention is to defeat their ideological opponent on the issue. For framing to work, there has to be a realistic expectation that addressing the issues at hand will require a degree of compromise in the interest of realizing a better (not ideal) state of affairs following the interaction than could have reasonably been expected prior to it. When it comes to understanding the future of timber in the Pacific Northwest, we are fortunate that a rather in-depth psychosocial analysis has been conducted that tells us a lot about the motivations (interiorities) and behavior (exteriorities) of the significant players in the policy debate.

William Dietrich in his now well-known book *The Final Forest* (1992) was employed as a reporter by the *Seattle Times* when he began investigating the spotted owl controversy in the forests of the Pacific Northwest. In the interest of developing as nuanced a perspective as possible, Dietrich decided to become fully familiar with an established logging community in the crosshairs of the owl controversy and understand the values that motivated the various interest groups. That community – Forks, Washington – is the site around which Dietrich identified all the key players involved in the conflict around owls and timber.

The interest groups he interviewed and came to know well included loggers (those who fell the trees in the forest), cutters (those who take the timber and saw it into lumber and other timber products), biologists (scientists employed to either represent the interests of timber companies or the federal and state government in terms of regulating forests and forest habitats), endangered species (in this case the northern spotted owl), the local community (Forks, WA), forest management reformers (staff of the Forest Service seeking better approaches to forest and habitat management), the timber industry (broadly writ to include the saw mill owners, importers, exporters and those who own or manage timberland), truckers (those who transport the logs from the forest to the sawmills), environmentalists (those who seek to protect the northern spotted owl and its habitat principally by banning logging of old-growth forests), and the local foresters (those who manage forests for either public or private interests). For the sake of this case study we will focus upon loggers, regulators (foresters and forest managers), environmentalists and the timber industry.

## Loggers

If you were to visit Forks, Washington – or for that matter any number of logging communities scattered throughout Northern California, Oregon and Washington - today you might find a sweatshirt for sale in a local store emblazoned with a saying similar to those Dietrich found back in 1992 (Dietrich, 1992, p. 33).

> My Family Is Supported By Timber Dollars.
> Support Your Local Spotted Owl: From A Rope.

> If We'd Kicked The Shit Out Of The Preservationists
> We Wouldn't Have This Problem Today.

While it is clear from historical and research data that timber economics is much more complex than the influence of spotted owls and "preservationists," it is important to realize that for those engaged at a hands-on level in logging and the timber business the immediacy of their economic exigencies are experienced in their interactions with spotted owls, governmental regulators representing state and federal agencies and environmentalists representing local, state and national organizations and constituencies. Understanding this simple but important perspective requires one to recognize how precarious the existence of a logger, cutter or timber hauler is. For instance, cutters typically work for low wages (in 1992 at levels of $150 to less than $100 daily) and can only find work on timber stands that have not been tied up by preservationist boycotts or litigation. Consequently, according to Dietrich, they are forced to "take work where it comes" (Dietrich, 1992, p. 38).

Logging is one of the most dangerous occupations to be found in the U.S. Between 1870 and 1910 one study concluded that the life expectancy of a logger was only seven years – though more current estimates suggest that the mortality rate among loggers is around 30% (Dietrich, 1992, p. 36). According to statistics from the U.S. Bureau of Labor Statistics (BLS) logging is the second most dangerous occupation, narrowly following commercial fishing. In 2011, the fatal work injury rate among commercial fisherman was 121.2 per 100,000 full-time workers as compared to 102.4 per 100,000 full-time workers for loggers. Third in the ranking were commercial pilots with a fatal work injury rate of only 57 per 100,000 full-time pilots (BLS, 2012, p. 5). Regardless of how one looks at the data, the inescapable reality is that logging is extremely dangerous and pays low wages lacking pension, accident and health insurance coverage. Appreciating the hazards of logging requires considering the various roles that loggers assume to include the "cutter" (those who cut trees down) and the "choker" (those who tie cables to cut logs to snake them out of the forest).

Dietrich portrays the cutter as "at the top of the logger's pyramid in the way fighter pilots are atop the flier's pyramid" (Dietrich, 1992, p. 38). Consider the case of one cutter, Larry Suslick, from Forks, Washington. According to Dietrich, Suslick "considers himself lucky after a quarter century in the woods with only a broken knee, torn muscles, and blows on the head and side from falling or rolling logs" (Dietrich, 1992, p. 36).

Alternately, consider a typical workday for another logger, Dewey Rasmussen. His daily work requires scaling old-growth timber to cut them down. Accordingly,

> He would strap metal spurs to his ankles and loop a climbing rope up to sixty feet long around the massive trunks. He hitched the rope upward as he climbed using a chainsaw to cut branches out of his way. The purpose of his climbing was to attach a steel cable in the upper part of a tree." "It was a daredevil job, climbing up these giant beanstalks. The climbing rope had a steel center to help guard against accidently sawing through it. Then there was the problem, one hundred feet up, of getting the thick cable that dangled from on hip around the thick trees. Rasmussen would tie heavy fishing weights unto the cable's end and begin swinging it in an increasing arc. When the weighted cable had enough momentum he would snap his arm to hurl it in a circle around the tree's girth. Aim was crucial. He had to take care the whizzing end that whipped around the trunk came near enough to grab, but not so near it would hit the climber in the head. Rasmussen loved this job: the heights, the danger the skill." "It was like a sport. (Dietrich, 1992, p. 37)

Once cut the logs have to be "choked" or bound with steel cables and dragged to a clearing where they are trimmed of branches and loaded on logging trucks that transport their heavy and cumbersome loads along harrowing and narrow mountain roads from the forest floor to the distant sawmills. While the cutters are considered the elite among logging workers, the role of the choker is often perceived as one of the worst – in part because it is so toilsome and dangerous and is one of the lowest paying timber jobs. One logger described the dreary and dangerous nature of the choker's work by asking Dietrich:

> How'd you like to get up in the dark, at four or five in the morning, drive an hour, get out all stiff, look two thousand feed down the hill and then scramble down there and start choking logs? If the sun ain't blazing, and if it ain't one hundred twenty degrees, its pissing rain. (Dietrich, 1992, p. 36)

While the cutter fells the trees and the choker gets the cut logs to the trucks, it is the log truck driver who actually transports the product to the mill. They endure some of the longest workdays and their jobs are some of the most treacherous. In Washington State the number of log truck accidents ranged from120 to 150 annually (2002-2007) (Mason, et al., 2008, p. 71) and according to data from neighboring British Columbia, log truck driver fatalities are second only to cutters (also known as "fallers" in Canada) in overall industry fatalities (Canadian Workman's Compensation Board, 1994, p.8).

Dietrich describes the situation of a log truck driver, Dick Mossman, typifying many log truckers both then and now. Mossman purchased an International Harvester log truck as a new vehicle in 1979 for the price of $75,300 – a steep price even by today's standards. At the time Mossman and his wife were farming and Dick drove a log truck for Weyerhauser (a huge timber conglomerate in the region). Mossman sought additional financial security and independence for his family so he mortgaged the family farm, bought the truck and – thanks to the 1980 economic recession - ultimately sold the farm to keep the truck and keep the Mossman family sheltered and fed.

The truck employs a 350 horsepower diesel engine capable of pulling some 40 tons of timber. It is, however, a very costly vehicle to operate and maintain. Accordingly

> In 1989 it ate $7,200 in tires and more than $10,000 in maintenance and repair, not to mention $14,000 in fuel and $2,300 in road taxes. (Dietrich, 1992, p. 145)

With costs like these, the marginal income for the Mossmans to maintain their existence in the Forks, Washington area is very slim and even small changes in timber prices, regulatory requirements and logging permitting can dramatically and adversely impact their lives and livelihood.

The lifestyle of the truck driving Mossman family with their tenacious and sometimes narrowly maintained grip upon maintaining a family, livelihood and a "sense of place" in the forests of the Pacific is very much shared by the families of cutters, chokers and others who labor on the forest floor with them. For the outside observer who learns of the sometime desperate nature of their lifestyles, it might seem that they could do better employed in other work and perhaps living in other regions. Yet these people are doing what they want to do and living the lives of their choosing in the environment they prefer to reside in. They are accustomed to hardship, at home with danger and uncertainty, and to a great extent gauge their character against their capacity to virtually heroically endure in the face of obstacles and adversity.

In part what motivates these timber workers is their desire to work independently without the constraints of supervision. Moreover, they seem to revel in confronting and defying danger that is ever-present in all of these jobs. As William Dietrich observed in his extensive interviews with loggers engaged in every aspect of their trade it is the danger of their work that in part attracts them. Accordingly, danger "is what makes men fall in love with a hard, dirty, dangerous job" (Dietrich, 1992, p. 38).

This insight is vital in understanding what it is about these unique people that motivates them to desperately cling to their livelihoods, homes, communities and way of life. It is in great part their inability to envision any other life that leaves them feeling so totally alive and vital that binds them to their current way of life. Coaxing or motivating them to pursue other work in a different locale must take into account just who these people are, what they value and what they want in life. In this regard, the forest becomes a vehicle for them to realize a lifestyle.

Motivating them to change their ways entails opening up alternative lifestyles and personal realization that satisfies their character and brings them self-worth and meaning.

Consequently, it would be a grave error to underestimate the character of these forest people and the extent to which they will fight to protect the only lifestyle they know or are likely to ever know. Their exteriorities include their trucks, gear, equipment, earned income, savings, homes, families and associations. Their interiorities largely consist of their sense of rugged and defiant individualism, thirst for independence and autonomy and capacity to endure hardship, danger and risk to provide a life for themselves and their families.

It would also be erroneous to assume that because timber harvesters and haulers cut the timber that they don't also value the forest and its habitat. Moreover, it would be an even graver error to assume that environmentalists love the forests more than those who harvest timber – "as if they had invented love for the outdoors with their weekend hikes" (Dietrich, 1992, p. 51). Dietrich portrays those who labor in the forests as deeply valuing the forest environment not just as an economic resource or as a work-site, but also as a place where they live and recreate. Accordingly, loggers

> live in the woods and work in the woods and play in the woods. They are out in the chill rain and the hot sun. They see deer while driving to the logging job in the morning and eagles on the way home. They fish, they hunt, they hike. The forests are for them a mosaic of memory a city dweller can't imagine, a hundred places cut and regrown. (Dietrich, 1992, p. 51)

The practice of clear-cutting that environmentalists abhor is perceived quite differently by loggers. For loggers "a clear-cut isn't and end. It's a beginning" (Deitrich, 1992, p. 51). Residents of the Pacific Northwest often perceive clear-cuts in a positive aesthetic light when they create space for the sky and sun to be seen and felt.

Consider, for instance, the impenetrable walls of forest that often grips highways throughout the region, rendering them icy and dangerous by blotting out the sunlight that would otherwise penetrate the forest canopy. For those who traverse these dark and dangerous roads driving such roads is like traversing a tunnel and clearing trees brings relief to this dark and claustrophobic sensation. As one resident observed, that when they cut the trees "you could finally see some mountains. I couldn't believe it, it was so pretty" – allowing the now open terrain to "bloom with foxglove and fireweed and black berries" permitting more sunlight and expansive vistas (Dietrich, 1992, p. 260).

## Environmentalists

Who are the environmentalists? Environmentalists involved in the spotted owl habitat controversy include local, national and state-based organizations. Prominent state organizations – in the State of Washington alone – include the Capitol Land Trust, Washington Forest Protection Association, Washington Conservation Corps, Washington Trails Association, Washington's National Park

Fund, Whatcom Land Trust, and the Seattle Audubon Society. National environmental groups that have been prominent in the spotted owl controversy in the state include the Natural Resources Council, Earthjustice, The Sierra Club, and the National Audubon Society. These are the principal environmentalist drivers of the spotted owl and timber controversy as they pursue the elimination of any and all logging operations within old-growth ancient forests. They argue that in the absence of their efforts, the species and habitats of the region are rendered voiceless and completely vulnerable to the economic, political and cultural efforts of their opponents – namely, those who derive a living from forests and forest products.

In the eyes of those who share their values and support them with their time and money, these organizations corporately function as a modern-day "David" taking on the "Goliath" of big timber. Accordingly their efforts are construed as both vital and heroic. Yet, for others either actively involved in the controversy of observing it from afar, these organizations often assume a sinister character. As noted earlier in this narrative, many within the timbering communities view environmentalists as naïve meddlers and respond with hostility to their efforts.

Among others, environmentalist efforts are sometimes construed as being a bit "holier-than-thou." Consider the views of one commentator situated within the environmentalist community who asserts that environmentalists are modern day Puritans. Accordingly,

> Our attitudes reek of Puritanism. We are, often, dour, strict and humorless. We're judgmental. Behind most of life's simple pleasures we see unnecessary consumption, which we ridicule. Because humanity is responsible for environmental problems we are, ipso facto, all sinners and we find little joy in being human. We portray the giant global corporations as occult covens, and we burn their representatives in effigy in our own reenactments of the Salem witch trials. When our neighbors seem too moderate or abstract for our tastes — as the Quakers did to New England's 17th-century Puritans — we whip them out of the colony, at least figuratively, and we're not above discussing executions. To say the least, we're no fun a lot of the time. (Welch, 2008)

In the Pacific Northwest there are no grander environmental villains than the timber companies and the countless cutters, chokers, haulers and processors who work on their behalf. Comparatively, for those employed within the timber industry environmentalists are perceived as those who relate to forests as they would have them be rather than how forests are actually utilized by society.

Sociologist Robert Lee of the University of Washington contends that, loggers have a more realistic view of nature and are willing to both use and enjoy it. Accordingly, "They accept the rules of life. They know somebody has to cut it [the forest] so let's do the best job possible" (Dietrich, 1992, p. 150). In essence, forest workers regard the forest in pragmatic terms while environmentalists relate to the environment in romantic, spiritual and idealistic terms. Forest workers bristle at the suggestion they are environmentally insensitive. As one small farmer and logger in the region observed,

I like to feel I'm as environmentally sensitive as the next guy. On the other hand, I don't like to see my way of life eliminated. Environmentalists have some idealistic notion of the way the world ought to be, and as long as it don't affect their pocketbook, its okay. Well it would be real romantic to think the world can be some kind of paradise, but paper and lumber is going to be needed. The way I feel, it ain't natural, it ain't good. It ain't natural to make things out of synthetics. Wood is natural. This is the most natural alternative we have, plus it's renewable. (Dietrich, 1992, p. 50)

While forest workers relate to the woodlands vocationally and within the context of actually residing within the forests they harvest, most of the principal environmental interests - and many (though not all) of those who advocate for environmental preservation - reside in comparatively distant urban areas and construe the forest as a refuge and natural resource in which human impact should be dramatically curtailed and minimized. Moreover, they value the forests as natural ecosystems serving as habitat for countless creatures whose right to exist is as great or perhaps greater than the right of humans to utilize timber for societal purposes.

This vision is completely at odds with the comparatively local utilitarian economic ethic of the forest workers and the industries that employ them. In fact some environmentalists have adopted such a totalizing preservationist philosophy toward forest ecosystems that their zeal and ardor has been compared to religiosity in the sense that they pursue a degree of immortality allowing them to participate in something larger and more enduring (Satterfield, 2002). As Dietrich observes forests offer such immortality in that they serve as timeless and "enduring symbols of undisturbed nature" (Dietrich, 1992, p. 151).

While risking over-generalizing what people value and how values influence behavior, it is likely accurate to categorize environmentalists as perceiving ideal outcomes emphasizing the welfare of the forest over the long term whereas forest workers pursue pragmatic and short term outcomes maximizing the utility of the forest to benefit human communities while not employing these natural resources beyond their natural sustainability levels. This is the classic "eco-centric" versus "anthropocentric" philosophical dichotomy between environmentalists and so-called "non-environmentalists" - that includes any group that does not affirmatively embrace a narrowly eco-centric position. It also captures the classic dichotomy between traditional preservationism and conservationism.

Sociologist Matthew Carroll is more discriminating in his characterization of the philosophical perspectives of the principal players in the Pacific Northwest environmental debate. He associates environmentalists with a transcendentalist philosophy that is essentially spiritual in nature, stressing "the values of scenery, wildlife, and ecology – the fabric of natural life that offers contrasts and lessons to human philosophy" whereas commercial timber workers and loggers employ a market philosophy in which the "forest's value is set by the price society puts on its tangible products" (Dietrich, 1992, p. 152). By comparison, Carroll describes the values of the regulators – foresters - as being essentially utilitarian, in terms of following the adage of the nation's first forester, Gifford Pinchot, and providing the greatest good to the greatest number of citizens over the long run (USFS, 2009).

As commentator William Wade Keye observed in the *San Jose Mercury News,*

> By philosophy and training, foresters are optimistic about our ability to manage timbered ecosystems with beneficial results." This doesn't just include cutting and planting trees. Forestry must consider other values, such as maintaining or enhancing water quality and biological diversity. Forest management isn't perfect, but it is science-based and active. (Keye, 2003)

By comparison environmentalists' values are more akin to those of Thoreau and Muir where nature is deemed essentially perfect and attempts to improve upon it are deemed arrogant and illegitimate. When these values have been translated into political and economic policies they have produced national parks and wilderness areas and severe restrictions of the application of forest management techniques to produce high timber yields as had historically been the case in national forests.

Managing forests for timber production is in fact antithetical to the identities of most contemporary environmentalists and as a result there is a deeply held antagonism between those whose agendas involve protecting the forest from commercial interests and those, such as loggers, who are deemed to be little more than instruments of forest destruction and transformation – virtual pawns of corporate greed and avarice. As far as many environmentalists are concerned, loggers are on their way to extinction and are part of a tragic and dying epoch in American history that can't end too quickly (McDermott & Nagoki, 1990). Moreover, they are perceived as having in part brought this state of affairs upon themselves by their wasteful harvesting practices (Estrada, Borja & Lee, 2012; Robbins, 2012; Parker, 2007). There is more than a bit of the "they get what they deserve" attitude among those antagonistic to timbering in the Northwestern woods.

Environmentalists and foresters can sometimes find themselves in common cause as in the case of protecting the spotted owl. However when it comes to environmentalists and loggers there is seldom any common cause to be realized. This outcome is in part because environmentalist values all too often separate "work" from nature and work is precisely what loggers, cutters, chokers, haulers and others perform in the deep woods of the Pacific Northwest. It is this work that sustains them economically, socially and frankly psychology – since their hard work and how they master it contributes to a deep sense of self-worth and value. Moreover, the logger doesn't make a sharp distinction between work life and family and recreational life. These distinctions tend to get blurred and become indistinct in the experiences of those who wrest a living from the forest floor.

As Richard White observed in his essay "Do You Work for a Living or Are You an Environmentalist?"

> Environmentalists must come to terms with work because its effects are so widespread and because work itself offers both a fundamental way of knowing nature and perhaps our deeper connection with the natural

world. If the issue of work is left to the enemies of environmentalism, to movements such as wise use, with its single minded devotion to propertied interests, the work will simply be reified into property and property rights. If environmentalists segregate work from nature, if they create a set of dualisms where work can only mean the absence of nature, and nature can only mean human leisure, then humans and nonhumans will ultimately be the poorer. For without the ability to recognize the connections between work and nature, environmentalists will eventually reach a point where they seem trivial and extraneous and their issues politically expendable. (White 1996, p. 174)

In truth, environmentalists are not so much opposed to work per se as they are work such as that conducted in commercial interests like logging, farming, fishing, and ranching. This animus puts environmentalists inescapably at odds with any number of outdoor occupations and businesses.

## Regulators

In the Pacific Northwest regulators largely consist of those who work in the employ of federal and state agencies responsible for managing the forestlands owned or overseen at the national or state level. In great part understanding "who" these regulators are and how they operate requires understanding a bit about the state and federal legislation that brought them into being and dictates their identity and mission. Unlike the other players in the Pacific Northwest timber issue, this constituency is very much a reflection of the laws that created and govern them.

At the federal level, regulators may work for the U.S. Forest Service, the U.S. Bureau of Land Management, the U.S. Fish and Wildlife Service or the Bureau of Indian Affairs. At the state level – in the state of Washington alone – regulatory agencies with jurisdiction in one fashion or another over the state's forest environments are numerous. In fact Washington State government includes more than 20 separate regulatory agencies whose authority in one form or another involves forests and forest habitats to include the State Conservation Commission, the Department of Ecology, Department of Fish and Wildlife, Forest Practice Board, Hardwoods Commission, Office of the Land Commissioner, Department of Natural Resources, and the Northwest Power and Conservation Commission to name but a few. All of these agencies are the product of the legislative intent that produced them and assigned them a statutorily derived mission. For instance, the U.S. Forestry Service alone is governed by at least 80 acts of Congress that serve to direct their daily activities (Brown, 2004).

In theory these agencies and their personnel are charged with dispassionately implementing the legislative intent of the enabling legislation that governs them. Yet, in reality agency administrators and staff are under constant political and economic pressure to accommodate the interests of advocacy groups, industries and political parties and officials. Nor are agency officials devoid of political and philosophical values of their own. Although federal officials are prohibited from engaging in political activism through the Hatch Act and in the State of

Washington state employees are similarly constrained, personal and political values and philosophies often bleed through into agency positions and decisions – thus the considerable effort of interest groups to influence their decisions.

Certainly most of those whose careers involving managing federally and state regulated forests operate out of the conservation ethic of Gifford Pinchot and have sought to manage them in a way that produces "the greatest good for the greatest number in the long run" (Miller, 2001, p. 130, Brown, 1999). Values were also shaped legislatively with the passage in 1937 of the Sustained Yield Act which put the regulators in the position of insuring a sustainable yield of timber by empowering the U.S. Forest Service to both regulate harvest by timber type and volume and insure that new trees were planted to replace those that had been harvested (Dietrich, 1992, p. 100). Moreover, their responsibility involves protecting the forests from needless destruction wrought by wildfires by systematically burning off forestlands in "control-burns" thereby reducing the amount of underbrush and other flammable tender that fueled the worst of the wildfires.

In each instance, the principal benefactor of the forester's efforts were people – either the general public which utilized the forest for employment or recreation, and later the economic interests who depended upon access to state and federal lands to sustain themselves and their customers. However, by the mid 1980's these dominant values began to undergo change under the steady and relentless efforts of powerful environmental groups and organizations whose values suggested that the forests and their inhabitants had rights independent of those possessed by humans. Consequently, what had heretofore been an essentially conservationist value orientation has now found itself being transformed into a bifurcated orientation in which the needs of humans had to be balanced in one fashion or another to accommodate the inherent rights of ecosystems and their species to exist.

What emerged thereafter was a new approach to regulating forest environments. While still oriented in the direction of Pinchot's original conservation ethic, contemporary regulators have also found themselves influenced by the preservationist values of John Muir and are now additionally accountable to environmentalist interests and not to the interests of the timber companies and self-serving political constituencies alone. What has emerged is a "new forestry" seeking to "integrate ecology with wood production" (Dietrich, 1992, p. 106). This new philosophy was in part fueled by yet other changes in federal legislation – particularly the National Forest Management Act of 1976 which directed the U.S. Forest service to manage forest habitats for the purposes of timber production, fire safety, maintenance of sustainable natural habitats and public recreation (USFS, 2013).

The product of this legislatively mandated "new forestry" approach was of course a different mix of professionals becoming involved with forest management and with this change in personnel came a change in the professional values each group brought to the U.S. Forest Service by virtue of their training and background. What resulted was a new hybrid of forest management personnel to include the traditional forester and timber regulator, as well as new professionals such as hydrologists, archeologists, ecologists, geologists, biologists and a host of other professionals whose expertise extended from basic sciences and the social sciences into the realm of public policy and law. What united this diverse group of regulators was their shared commitment to fulfilling the legislative mandates that informed their mission and a fierce dedication to the forest ecosystems and their inhabitants.

The introduction of new professional disciplines into the USFS transformed the culture of the organization and served to

> attract enthusiasts from across the United States, many of them more liberal, worldly and wildlife oriented than their predecessors. (Dietrich, 1992, p. 108)

The net effect of these professional changes was to reorient the USFS closer to the values of the environmentalist community while simultaneously further alienating them from the local timber workers and timber industry interests located within the bounds of the forested region they managed. Evidence of this growing distance and sometime animosity between the regulators and the loggers is evidenced in the lyrics to the tune "Fire Danger" by Buzz Martin and can be seen in the captions to be found in the editorial pages of newspapers and on sweatshirts, tee-shirts, and caps sold in stores throughout the region.

Compared to years past, the schools of forestry that produced the Pacific Northwest's sylvan professionals – from whose ranks the bulk of so-called regulators were drawn – witnessed a decline in funding from timber interests while experiencing a dramatic increase in research and operational funding from the federal government. As Dietrich observed,

> Pacific Northwest forestry schools got most of their donations from the timber industry, and it was natural their research would focus, often narrowly, on the most efficient ways to cut down and regrow trees. When the federal government made money available in 1969 to study the forest ecology, the scale began to tip the other way. (Dietrich, 1992, p. 112)

The source of this funding was the McIntire-Stennis Cooperative Forestry Act of 1962 designed "to increase forestry research in the production, utilization, and protection of forestland; to train future forestry scientists; and to involve other disciplines in forestry research" (USDA, 2013). While the law served to accomplish the various purposes for which it was drafted and enacted, it also served to transform the culture of the U.S. Forest Service and to ultimately shift the valence of regulatory support and sympathy marginally away from the timber interests and their workers and in the direction of the growing environmentalist movement.

This new orientation in schools of forestry ultimately created a dichotomy in the fashion in which scientists chose to orient themselves regarding forest environments. The net effect was a shift away from emphasizing the value of forests in terms of what commodities they produce and a movement in the direction of appreciating forest ecosystems and their inhabitants for their own right. As one commentator observed, scientists tend to split on more abstract lines between the technocrat and the naturalists, between those who like the simplified order of tree farms and those more comfortable with, or appreciate of the seemingly disordered complexity of natural systems. (Dietrich, 1992, p. 112)

Ultimately this shift in emphasis and the diversification of the professional background of the nation's forest service resulted in a new orientation to forest management – the so called multi-use forest – in which goals of timber protection, recreation and habitat protection proceeded concomitantly, though sometimes in a disjointed and ineffective fashion. Underlying this philosophy is a new orientation of what to expect forestland to produce. Under a single use paradigm, such as that which principally dominated the U.S. Forest Service until the sixties and seventies, the chief product of concern was timber and fire protection. However, when a multi-use approach is embraced then the necessary conclusion to be drawn is that now the forest will be expected to produce numerous goods and services, not all of which can be readily quantified in monetary terms. Seemingly, contemporary forest professionals, ecologists and the general public prefer multi-use approaches to managing forestland. Yet others contend that multi-use approaches should be applied to very large geographic areas within which forest production should be directed toward specialized uses such as habitat protection, timber production, recreation, etc. – a perspective principally championed by forest economists (Zhang, 2005).

At issue is the efficacy of the approach. As one early critic of multi-use forestry observed "as an idea, multiple use has met with almost universal acceptance; as a working tool of management, it has had far less success" (Gregory, 1955, p. 7). Moreover, the terms multiple use or "multi-use" may have become mere jargon that no longer adequately describes what is meant as in the observation by Howard Stagner that the term "is sometimes used so loosely that one wonders if it has any meaning at all" (Stagner, 1960, p. 24).

The implementation of a multi-use forest management philosophy has occurred against the backdrop of significant controversy. According to the U.S. Forest Service's historical archive, the period between 1980 and 1995 in which multi-use forest management was first widely introduced was one of great conflict and controversy as timber and labor interests, environmentalists and state and federal officials quarreled over forest management plans and with increasing frequency sought remedies in state and federal courts. Likewise, during this period of time disputes emerged over the proper role of the U.S. Forest Service in combatting forest fires through the use of controlled burns, and in areas where environmentalist interest prevailed, forest biomass accumulated dramatically increasing the risk of catastrophic wildfires. Finally, escalating concerns over the protection of sensitive habitats for endangered species and a more widely shared concern over the maintenance of biodiversity challenged the USFS in terms of how it managed not only forested areas but rangeland as well (Fedkiw, 2009).

Today the multi-use philosophy of U.S. forest management, while still the dominant regulatory philosophy, finds itself competing with a variety of other forest management philosophies both in the U.S. and internationally to include: (Haynes, 2005, p. 3)

1. *Cut-And-Accept-What-Grows-Back Approach*: This is the long-term historical approach to forestry prior to the introduction of the scientifically managed forest of the Pinchot conservation era.
2. *Greatest Good For The Greatest Number*: The original Pinchot forest management approach to managing forests for utilitarian purposes to achieve what today we would refer to as sustainable forest product yields.
3. *Multi-Use Philosophy*: An approach that broadens forest management beyond the goals of fire prevention and timber harvesting to recognizing and accommodating the multiple benefits and services that can be produced by forests, to include non-market benefits and services.
4. *Cross Landscape Management*: This is an approach which seeks to manage ecosystems across a broader range of interrelated landscapes, one that emphasizes the interdependent relationship between one ecological system and related systems both human, biotic and environmental in nature.
5. *Montreal Process*: This is an internationally derived agreement on managing forest landscapes emanating from the 1992 Earth Summit that is developed around the following seven criteria: (Montreal Process, 2009)
    o Conservation of biological diversity.
    o Maintenance of productive capacity of forest ecosystems.
    o Maintenance of forest ecosystem health and vitality.
    o Conservation and maintenance of soil and water resources.
    o Maintenance of forest contribution to global carbon cycles.
    o Maintenance and enhancement of long-term multiple socio-economic benefits to meet the needs of societies.
    o Legal, institutional and economic framework for forest conservation and sustainable management.

Given the emergence of the values associated with the Montreal Process (Ritter, Wickham & Coulston, 2004) and the cross landscape management approach it seems inevitable that the value base of the modern forestry regulator will continue to shift away from the original "cut-and-accept-what-grows-back approach" toward more nuanced and expansive forest management philosophies that cross landscapes, international boundaries and interest groups. As a result it is very likely that the philosophical divide between forest regulators and the logging community will widen while an inevitable convergence of values appears to be forming between environmentalists and regulators.

## The Timber Industry

The final constituency to consider is the timber industry in the Pacific Northwest – particularly in the State of Washington. The timber industry in Washington is experiencing a downturn in demand for timber and timber sales. According to the Washington Department of Natural Resources (WDNR, 2013),

The timber revenue projection for the 2011-2013 Biennium is revised downward four percent from $317.9 million to $306.2 million. For the

2013-2015 Biennium, the projected revenue from timber removals is revised downward two percent from $398.8 million to $392.5 million. Revenues for the 2015-2017 Biennium are predicted to be $415.7 million, down thirteen percent from $478.7 million.

The principal factors associated with the current downturn are changes in demand principally fueled by a decline in the housing industry, a decrease in lumber exports (particularly to China) and increased regulatory oversight of forestlands.

Yet, over the same period U.S. log exports have increased even as first quarter 2013 lumber exports declined by 7% - this according to Xiaoping Zhou, a research economist with the U.S. Forest Service's Pacific Northwest Research Station. Consequently,

> Log exports increased by 16 percent: from 362 million board feet in the first quarter of 2012, to 420 million board feet in the first quarter of 2013. The total value of log exports increased more than 27 percent, from $232 million to $297 million. Meanwhile, lumber exports dropped by 16 million board feet in the first 3 months of 2013 compared to the same time last year. (Zhou, 2013)

Combined log exports from Oregon and Washington accounted for 91% of total Northwest log exports or some 382 million board feet and the bulk of these exports are bound for Asia (Zhou, 2013).

All markets for U.S. timber, both domestic and foreign, are supplied from timber resources situated across the continental U.S. as well as in Alaska. Considered as a whole, the U.S. timber industry consists of timberland owners, timber harvesters, companies and processors, timber and logging mills and exporters. As fourth quarter 2013 trade statistics suggest, today's timber industry is principally fueled by lumber and log exports to Asia. In the State of Oregon alone, the Pacific Lumber Exporters Association encompasses more than 40 members who in one fashion or another are engaged in exporting timber products (PLA, 2013).

Lumber exports are most economically beneficial to the Pacific Northwest region since timber mills are utilized to process the wood before it is overseas. Consequently when lumber exports are high so is the volume of work going through U.S. mills. However when log exports exceed lumber exports then the implication is that U.S. lumber mills are being idled and work that would otherwise have been performed in the U.S. is exported to overseas mills and processors (Kerr, 2012). Asian markets are willing to bear the extra expense of shipping logs across the Pacific Ocean and pay more for Pacific Northwest logs than can many processors in Oregon and Washington, thereby rendering these local processors comparatively uncompetitive.

Virtually all exported logs come from private timberland allowing landowners the discretion to pursue overseas rather than domestic markets and get the best available market price for their product. In an effort to increase the volume of logs processed domestically, local wood processing facilities and mills have been lobbying Congress and The Office of the President to increase timber production on federal lands. They do so principally because they otherwise lack direct access to private lands, leaving only state and federal forests available to them as a resource. Current public policy generally bans exporting logs from federal land – with few exceptions. While this policy is largely derived from a desire to limit logging on public lands given environmental concerns, the net effect is that the banning of log exports on federal lands serves to subsidize exports from private lands where exports are legal (Kerr, 2012).

Two of the largest timber companies and landowners in the U.S. are both located in the State of Washington. Weyerhaeuser, located in Federal Way, Washington, is the largest timber company in the U.S. with net sales of $14.5 billion in 2012 alone. Ranked second in timber sales volume is Plum Creek Timber Company (Seattle, WA) who also holds the distinction of being the nation's largest private landowner. This company's 2012 sales totaled $7.1 billion. Ranked third in sales volume is Rayonier (Jacksonville, FL) located in the Southeast U.S. with $6.2 billion in sales in 2012 (Cummans, 2012). Rayonier's principal land holdings are situated in the Southeastern U.S.

Weyerhaeuser owns approximately 6 million acres of timberlands in the U.S. and Canada and manages another 14 million acres under long-term agreements in Canada (Weyerhaeuser, 2013). Of this total acreage 645,000 acres are located in Oregon and Washington (Njus, 2013). By comparison, Plum Creek Timber Company owns 6.4 million acres in 19 states to include 897,000 in Montana, 383,000 acres in Oregon, 88,000 in Washington (Plum Creek, 2012).

These two forestland owners largely determine how much timber to export and in what form (logs versus lumber) in the Pacific Northwest. Their decisions are derived almost entirely on the basis of where they can secure the best value for their shareholders in the marketplace. Unlike regulators these corporations are only indirectly influenced by federal and state laws and regulations. Like regulators, however, they employ a utilitarian approach but not in the sense implied by Pinchot's "greatest good for the greatest number." Rather they employ "free-market utilitarianism" which essentially implies that "he who can produce most value for others should have a right to the resource" (Bylund, 2006; Rothbard, 2003). This is the credo by which they justify their decisions to their investors, customers and trading partners.

As is the case with all of the principal players in the Pacific Northwest timber and environmental issue, accountability is central. Each group is accountable to a constituency that it identifies with philosophically, economically, and politically. Regulators are accountable to the Congress and state legislators and to the laws and regulations proffered therein. Environmentalists are accountable to their members and to the non-profits and non-governmental organizations they represent, as well as to the countless volunteers and donors who support their causes and agendas. The loggers and those involved at every level for harvesting and processing wood are immediately accountable to themselves and their families to the degree they are the wage earners and financial supporters of their families and businesses. They also find themselves in common cause with municipal and business interests whose livelihoods are indirectly derived by their efforts in the forests of the region. By comparison, the large timber companies are accountable first and foremost to their shareholders. Without the support of these countless investors, their businesses would disintegrate. Consequently, the first principle of accountability for the timber industry is sustained profitability.

Sustainable profits require the timber industry to continually employ the land to bring forth an ongoing supply of timber. The need for a sustainable supply of timber led Weyerhaeuser to introduce a new concept in forest management in 1941 – tree farming. The first of these innovations – Clemons Tree Farm – became a laboratory for the corporation and allowed it to experiment with developing more productive seeds, seedlings, nurseries and techniques for replanting following timber harvests (Dietrich, 1992, p. 138). It also led to the replacement of ancient old-growth forests with comparatively faster growing and more manageable Douglas Fir tree plantations where timber could be harvested over shorter periods of time with less costs and risks than those associated with harvesting timber from native old-growth forests. Moreover, the use of timber plantations allowed for the increased use of mechanized timber harvesting technologies that increased efficiency in part by reducing overall labor costs.

The emergence of timber plantations allowed timber companies to enjoy increased yields and profits and greater per/acre productivity. By the 1980's the productivity on privately owned timber company land dwarfed the harvests from public lands. While owning just 14.6% of the nation's forestland, the timber industry produced 30% of the wood harvested annually and generated per-acre growth "63% higher than on national forest land" (Dietrich, 1992, p. 138). However, this increased yield was being harvested with greater reliance on technology resulting in a concomitant increase in timber-related unemployment. Moreover, since tree farms encompass a single species they proved to be particularly vulnerable to pests such as the bark beetle (Robbins, 2008).

The net effect of timber company practices was that they endeared themselves to their shareholders but not necessarily to the loggers who were displaced by technology or the mill owners whose profits were siphoned overseas with the shipment of logs to Asia. Likewise, timber companies remained the principal target of environmental groups who distrusted them on the basis of their profit motive, their employment of tree farming and the creation of disease susceptible forest monocultures, and on the basis of the environmental damage they did with their road building, clear-cutting and their sometimes indifference to issues associated with ecosystems and endangered species (Rast, 2012; Bonanno & Constance, 2008; Lewicki, Gray & Elliott, 2002). In simplistic terms, these companies were sometimes perceived as the root of all the evil that had befallen Pacific Northwest forests and their inhabitants (Hill, 2000).

## A Language Frame to Accessing Federal Land for Lumber Processing

As noted earlier, a contemporary controversy requiring resolution involves the desire by mill operators to have access to timber from federal lands to process for lumber (Kerr, 2012). Since contemporary research underscores the importance of intuition in decision-making and problem-solving the Frame-logic employed to address this issue should have the capacity to capture the nuance of intuition. For that reason a Frame-logic approach focusing upon how intuitive language – language communicating personal values and experiences (Downs, 2000) - is employed in policy discussions might prove useful. Employing a frame-analysis based upon language orientation is advisable for virtually any assessment since it helps the analysts understand the values and felt experiences of the participants so that this information can be employed in considering how each party might intuitively approach an issue and thereafter employ a reasoned rationale to explain and defend their intuitive positions. Information for developing a language orientation approach to frame-analysis entails determining how the various parties relate to one another and the issue based upon public statements and actions they have made, interviews, research, press coverage and personal experience interacting with the various parties. This is an imprecise process at best, but it can prove useful in aiding the policy analyst in understanding intuitive motivations informing actions and position statements.

Regarding the current issue of expanding timber harvesting on federal land, the rationale for the expansion is based upon the fact that the resources of domestic lumber mills are being underemployed to the extent log exporters are sending timber processing to mills in Asia. Since the bulk of the logs being exported come from private lands over which mill operators have little influence, they are seeking access to logging from federal lands to bolster their lumber output. What follows is a deliberative approach to imaginating in which the responses of contestants to this issue are identified, compared and clustered. In most cases the responses of contestants to this issue are pretty definitive.

Given the behavior of a number of environmentalist groups in 2004 as they protested efforts by the Bush administration (i.e. the Western Oregon Plan Revision (WOPR) to open up public lands to logging), it is clear that not only can these groups be expected to object to the current effort, they would likely do so on the grounds that logging will threaten the spotted owl as well as water quality in adjacent creeks and tributaries (AP, 2004). By comparison timber companies have championed more logging to produce additional timber, generate jobs and prevent wildfires (Bernard, 2013). However, since they stand to realize greater profits by exporting logs harvested on private lands to foreign mills, their support for logging on federal lands does not guarantee that mill owners will be processing more timber from these public lands.

Assuming the controversy over WOPR is indicative of how regulators would support current logging in national forests then their response would tend to mirror the values of the current administration in the White House. For instance during the Bush administration the Bureau of Land Management made arrangements to implement the plan – given that as an extension of the administration their charge was to implement public policy (BLM). Accordingly they conclude that under the plan

> timber harvesting would increase. There would be an increase in jobs and income along with a multiplier as impacts ripple through other sectors in the affected county economies. Economic effects would vary in proportion to increased timber harvest volumes. (BLM, 2008, p. 13)

Moreover the BLM concluded that

> Under all alternatives, the occurrences and habitats of species listed under the Endangered Species Act would be maintained or increased and recovery activities would be implemented. (BLM, 2008, p. 16)

However, in 2009 during the Obama administration the policy stance of the BLM changed and WOPR was withdrawn. Accordingly, Obama Interior Secretary Ken Salazar labeled the plan "legally indefensible" to the degree it had ignored key provisions of the Endangered Species Act consultation requirements. Moreover, he indicated he would ask a federal court that had earlier approved timber cutting under the WOPR to annul their decision (Leber, 2009).

Compounding the economic impact of this decision is a federal decision in 2012 to discontinue subsidies to counties whose revenues had been reduced by federal action limiting logging on federal lands relative to enforcing the Endangered Species Act. As this eleven-year program ended, counties and municipalities find themselves struggling to continue even routine public services (Bernard, 2013). Given the response of the Administration on this issue it seems unlikely that federal regulators within the BLM or within the U.S. Forest Service would be in favor of expanding logging in Northwest forests to accommodate the needs of the mill owners.

Loggers and those who harvest timber are economically harmed as federal subsidies to their communities are eliminated. However, their livelihoods are additionally impacted principally to the degree that log exports to Asia continue at current levels. Since the bulk of exported logs come from private lands, harvesting logs on public lands represents a potential marginal decrease in the capacity of timber companies to export logs (Institute for Culture and Ecology, 2008). Even so, since expanding logging territory serves to potentially increase employment among loggers who as a group have generally supported expanding logging into federal lands and opposed the recall of WOPR (Venetis, 2009).

Given these various positions on the issue or expanding logging on federal land in the face of lumber mill closures, let us consider the problem from several Frame-logic formats, beginning with the one involving frame perspective and language orientation. We will begin with the Frame-logic of the mill owners which will focus upon lament /nostalgia, fear/apocalyptic, justice/equality and pride/control language categories (Table 12).

Those involved in operating and working in timber mills will tend to rely upon the legitimacy derived from having historically harvested and processed timber products from federal land and point to precedent and their skills and acumen to both justify their desire to harvest timber on public land and to assert that in the absence of exercising that right that mills, timber-related employment and even communities will disappear and forest fires will become more frequent and destructive. Some of the interiorities that inform the values of mill owners and workers include a belief that (a) the elevation of the importance of the spotted owl over the importance of their livelihoods is illegitimate and unnecessary, (b) state and federal governments are imposing their will on what should otherwise be a market-driven industry, (c) large timber companies are indifferent to their economic predicament and are perfectly willing to sacrifice the future of timber mills in the region to realize short-term profits from Asian markets, (d) regulators – regardless of the agency – are more sympathetic to the values of the environmentalists and the timber companies than they are to the mill operators and loggers.

Table 12: Frame-logic Paradigm: Mill Owner Frame Perspectives and Language
Orientation

|  | *Diagnostic Perspective* | *Prognostic Perspective* | *Motivational Perspective* |
|---|---|---|---|
| *Lament/Nostalgia Language* | The crisis for mill owners is the product of having been denied access by environmentalists and regulators to timber that can and should be harvested in the interest of employing workers and preventing wildfires. | For generations, timber has been productively harvested from federal land and should be again and if denied a source of timber the industry and communities will die. | Allowing logging on federal land maintains and supports local communities and keeps jobs in America. |
| *Fear/Apocalyptic Language* | Mill owner's livelihoods are threatened by over-regulation of federal forestland, unfair competition from foreign mills and lack of access to timber from public land. | Without regulatory relief and access to public forestland mills will ultimately go out of business. | If communities, citizens and employers in the Pacific Northwest want to thrive and prosper they should lobby for reduced regulation and allowing access to logging on federal lands. |
| *Pride/Control Language* | Nobody knows more about how to safely and sustainably harvest and process timber than experienced Pacific Northwest timber workers and employers. | If environmental obstacles to sustainably harvesting timber on federal lands are not eliminated the Mills will go out of business and the economy and way of life of communities in the Pacific Northwest will be destroyed. | If the best scientifically based methods for harvesting timber are applied on federal lands timber production and employment can be assured conserving and improving upon forest habitats and resources. |
| *Justice/Equality Language* | It is unfair for the welfare of and endangered species to serve to drive timber mills out of business, such that the welfare of a bird is held in higher esteem than the livelihood of a man or a business. | In the absence of international trade protection and access to logging on federal land, mills will ultimately close. | When timber processing plants and mills close not only are jobs lost, so is the expertise and capacity to produce lumber in the U.S. in the future. |

This Frame-logic paradigm reflects what we might reasonably suspect to be the values of mill owners and workers given what has been written in Dietrich's (1992) book, and as reflected in information reported and conveyed in news reports and from interviews and statements from industry representatives. This paradigm is quite different than what one might expect of environmentalists. Table 13 illustrates a comparable Frame-logic paradigm for environmentalists. As before, in this paradigm language is utilized dealing with lament/nostalgia, fear/ apocalypse, pride/control and justice/equality.

Table 13: Frame-logic Paradigm: Environmentalist Frame Perspectives and Language Orientation

|  | *Diagnostic Perspective* | *Prognostic Perspective* | *Motivational Perspective* |
|---|---|---|---|
| *Lament/Nostalgia Language* | Current environmental conditions reflect an utter disregard for environmental values, laws and regulations in the interest of using forest resources as market products. | In the absence of strict regulation, the continued use of forests as marketable resources will forever threaten fragile forest ecosystems and species. | The timber industry is in permanent decline and can be forever removed as a significant environmental threat. |
| *Fear/Apocalyptic Language* | Continued use of forests as a source of marketable commodities will forever doom forest habitats and species. | Market driven management of forests must be replaced with environmentally driven approaches. | Restraining market driven management of forests now insures sustainable forest habitats in the future. |
| *Pride/Control Language* | Environmentalists are the only group that can be counted upon to dispassionately represent the interests of species and habitats. | In the absence of environmentalist advocacy forest habitats and their species will be forever destroyed | Advocacy and political activism continues to prove effective in shaping public opinion and promoting environmental laws and regulation. |
| *Justice/Equality Language* | Endangered species cannot speak for themselves requiring environmental interests to speak and act on their behalf through laws and regulation. | Only when all people and all species are treated equally through law and regulation will there be lasting justice and peace on the planet. | Promoting justice and equality among people and across species creates a more peaceful and sustainable world. |

Environmentalists assert that the timber industry has reached its nadir and must be allowed to dissipate as a serious threat to forest habitats. They associate forest destruction with rampant market forces driving timber harvests across the Pacific Northwest and justify hastening the demise of the cotemporary timber industry culture in the interest of preserving forest habitats and species and extending environmental justice to natural habitats and their endangered species. At least some of the interiorities informing the actions and values of these environmentalists include (1) a profound distrust of corporate culture – particularly in regard to large timber companies, (2) a belief that exploitation of forests and species is the necessary product of profit motives, (3) a belief in the justified role of government to act to curb markets and insure environmental justice, (4) a sense that forest workers don't "really" care for the environment and (5) a sense of confidence that curtailing the timber industry can ultimately be achieved by reducing demand for their products. These interiorities reflect information derived from public statements, interviews, news reports and policy statements emanating from environmental organizations, organizational representatives and from the assertions of environmentalists.

The next interest group in need of review is the timber industry. Table 14 reflects the Frame-logic for this all important and broadly demonized interest group and in the minds of many has driven the environment versus forest use issue. This group makes use of all of the language orientations to include lament/nostalgia, fear/apocalypse, pride/control and justice/equality language modalities. The content of the cells is derived from press releases, public relations statements, news coverage, interviews, the content of lawsuits and the like.

Timber companies decry governmental and environmental interference in their industry. They feel confident they are the most informed and capable interest group in the debate and are best prepared to manage forestland, as demonstrated by the thousands of acres of such land that they own or lease for timber production. They question the motivation and acumen of environmentalists in terms of their ability to sustainably manage forest resources for human benefit and they unashamedly prioritize the generation of profits benefiting their shareholders, employees, managers and the communities who are also enriched by virtue of their activities. While they value the worth of lumber processing mills and plants, they follow a profit motive that demands they maximize income where markets are available, thus prioritizing the profitable overseas log export business over supporting local timber mills.

Table 14: Frame-logic Paradigm: Timber Company Frame Perspectives and Language Orientation

|  | Diagnostic Perspective | Prognostic Perspective | Motivational Perspective |
|---|---|---|---|
| Lament/Nostalgia Language | Communities and workers have benefited from generations of foresting on public lands and fire safety has been enhanced by the activities of timber companies and landholders - now threatened by regulation and environmentalists. | If environmentalists and government regulators continue to interfere with timber harvests and the market forces that drive the industry, communities will die, unemployment will increase and forests will be more at risk to wildfires. | If needless governmental regulation and environmentalists interference and with the activities of timber companies can be eliminated then economic prosperity, forest conservation, and fire safety can be assured in perpetuity. |
| Fear/Apocalyptic Language | Out of control environmentalism and an uncontrolled federal regulatory bureaucracy are significantly threating livelihoods and a way of life in the Pacific Northwest. | Unchallenged and unchecked the actions of regulators and environmentalists will cost thousands of jobs, destroy businesses and threaten communities and their culture. | Resisting the power of government and environmentalists in the courts, legislature/Congress, and in the media can restore economic and conservation reason in the Pacific Northwest. |
| Pride/Control Language | Timber company executives and staff are more attuned to the needs of citizens and shareholders and possess more expertise and insight into sustainable forest management than either regulators or environmentalists. | If environmentalists and regulators destroy the timber industry and the culture of timber that characterizes communities throughout the region will collapse. | Financial investment in the timber industry yields a sustainable source of timber, guarantees employment for workers and supports communities throughout the region. |
| Justice/Equality Language | It is unjust for the welfare of spotted owls to be held as a higher value than human welfare when forest, species and human interested can be balanced. | When human welfare again assumes the primacy in forest conservation the economy and natural resources of the region will fall into balance. | Reprioritizing the value of human work, values, welfare and community in the region will save jobs and ultimately promote the sustainable use of forests. |

Table 15: Frame-logic Paradigm: Logger Frame Perspectives and Language Orientation

|  | *Diagnostic Perspective* | *Prognostic Perspective* | *Motivational Perspective* |
|---|---|---|---|
| *Lament/Nostalgia Language* | Before the intervention of environmentalists, regulators and the development of corporate tree farms loggers had free access to public land that is now mostly unavailable. | Ongoing restricted access to federal forests and restrictions to privately owned land, coupled with technological innovations in timber harvesting threaten to put an increasing number of loggers out of work. | Returning access to logging on federal lands increases the opportunity for work and contributes to the economy of the communities loggers reside in. |
| *Fear/Apocalyptic Language* | Continued regulation of logging and restrictions on where logging can occur threatens the livelihoods of loggers throughout the region. | Unchallenged and unchecked the actions of regulators and environmentalists will cost thousands of jobs, destroy businesses and threaten communities and their culture. | Ongoing regulation that drives forest workers from the region threatens to permanently eliminate requisite industry worker skills and expertise. |
| *Pride/Control Language* | Loggers are the most knowledgeable and skilled group regarding cutting and transporting timber than anyone else and without them the timber industry comes to a stop. | Loss of the expertise and skills of the loggers will lead to the collapse of the timber industry. | Threats to loggers and their way of life threatens the timber industry and transforms regional culture. |
| *Justice/Equality Language* | It is unjust for the welfare of spotted owls to be held as a higher value than the livelihoods and lifestyles of loggers and their communities. | Managing forests should prioritize employing loggers while pursuing environmental goals. | Reprioritizing the value of human work, values, welfare and community in the region will save jobs and ultimately promote the sustainable use of forests. |

Their interiorities include (1) a distrust of the acumen and motivations of environmental groups, (2) an inherent reluctance to surrender autonomy to the political influence of regulators, and (3) a belief that the interests of endangered species and habitats have been overstated and overemphasized needlessly jeopardizing the economic interests of individuals and communities. Likewise (4) they suspect that environmentalists and many regulators harbor a deep-seated animus against free market economics and business interests. These assertions reflect content found in news reports, policy papers, interviews and statements of timber company executives, shareholders and board members.

Next to mill owners and their employees, the group most significantly influenced by the issue of opening logging up on federal land is the loggers themselves – by which we refer to all those engaged in bringing the timber from market to mill. Table 15 reflects the Frame-logic for this interest group that also makes use of all of the language orientations.

From the perspective of the loggers, their well-being is principally dependent upon the volume of timber they harvest – regardless of whether timber is harvested from public or private lands. As the volume of timber demand increases so does demand for their labor. Consequently, when any interest group, albeit environmentalists, regulators or timber companies, acts in a fashion that restricts demand their livelihoods are negatively impacted and they can be expected to resent and resist the action. Their choice is to fight for their jobs and lifestyles or seek other work that leads them away from the region and permanently depletes the workforce needed to support the forest industries. Ideally they would like free and unfettered access to public lands and would assure the public that they are professional and know how to sustainably harvest the timber. Consequently, they can be expected to want to see access to public lands expanded for the purposes of timbering. They can also be expected to believe their welfare and the welfare of their families and communities trumps the importance of protecting the spotted owl. For this reason they can also be expected to object to and even resist the further imposition of regulations and rules that impedes them from the free and open pursuit of their livelihoods.

Some of the interiorities of the loggers include (1) a belief that environmentalists are naïve meddlers who are interfering with their way of life, (2) a belief that timber companies are more interested in their profit margins than they are in the welfare of forest workers, (3) a sense that regulators are little more than representatives of distant bureaucracies that impose rules upon them without real appreciation or concern over the impact these rules will have upon them and their communities and (4) a sense that nobody involved in the controversy has the depth of knowledge or appreciation of the worth of the forest and how to sustainably derive a livelihood from it.

The final group to be submitted to this Frame-logic analytical paradigm is the government regulators employed by a variety of state and federal agencies to manage public lands and resources. As noted earlier, regulators principally work to enforce laws passed by Congress as well as to implement the political values of the presidential administration they work for. Their values are reflected in the Frame-logic portrayed in Table 16. They principally employ the pride/control and justice equality language orientation.

Table 16: Frame-logic Paradigm: Regulators Frame Perspectives and Language
Orientation

|  | *Diagnostic Perspective* | *Prognostic Perspective* | *Motivational Perspective* |
|---|---|---|---|
| *Pride/Control Language* | Regulators serve the public interest and pursue the greatest good for the greatest number and in the absence of regulation environments suffer. | Without strict regulation and oversight timber resources, environmental habitats and inhabitant species will be destroyed. | Employing scientific management of forests and advocating for the interests of people, species and the environment serves to sustain forest resources. |
| *Justice/Equality Language* | Justice and equality are only guaranteed through the law and regulators are the keepers of law and the overseers of equality for people and species. | A breakdown in regulatory control of environmental resources results in natural resource, environmental and species depletion and destruction. | A well-motivated and supported public regulatory service is all that stands between forest and species sustainability and destruction. |

Regulators use the fewest language categories principally because of their accountability to law and to administrative oversight. Even so they tend to reflect many of the values of environmentalists, particularly to the degree environmental concerns and activism have produced legislation favored by environmentalists and enforced by regulators. Their default position on environmental issues is that laws and regulations are required to manage environmental resources and to protect species and they see themselves as the best trained and the most dispassionate group involved in environmental issues for managing these tasks.

The interiorities of regulators include (1) a built in skepticism regarding corporate timber interests believing these entities need to be monitored carefully otherwise they will skirt regulations and laws. While supportive of mainstream environmental groups whose values often correspond with their own regulators are also (2) highly skeptical of environmental radicals who engage in such activities as tree spiking. Finally, (3) they question the motives and knowledge level of politicians who have not made a career of public service and would use the environment as a political tool to gain an advantage. Having discussed the perspectives and language orientations of interest groups involved in this controversy and offered some suggestions on how different interest groups might respond to the Frame-logic paradigm employed in this case study, it is possible to generally anticipate the degree of convergence and divergence among interest groups regarding the issue of relieving mill owner shortfalls by allowing loggers and timber interests to cut trees in national forests. Table 17 illustrates this general convergence and divergence in thought based upon their interiorities and language orientation.

Table 17: Shared Frame-logic Perspectives and Language Orientation

|  | Diagnostic Perspective | Prognostic Perspective | Motivational Perspective |
|---|---|---|---|
| Lament/Nostalgia Language | Environmentalists Vs. Loggers, Timber Companies & Mill Owners | Environmentalists Vs. Loggers, Timber Companies, & Mill Owners | Environmentalists Vs. Loggers, Timber Companies, & Mill Owners |
| Fear/Apocalyptic Language | Environmentalists Vs. Loggers, Timber Companies & Mill Owners | Environmentalists Vs. Loggers, Timber Companies & Mill Owners | Mill Owners Vs. Environmentalists Vs. Timber Companies Vs. Loggers Vs. Regulators |
| Pride/Control Language | Mill Owners Vs. Environmentalists Vs. Timber Companies Vs. Loggers Vs. Regulators | Environmentalists & Regulators Vs. Mill Owners, Timber Companies & Loggers | Mill Owners Vs. Environmentalists Vs. Timber Companies Vs. Loggers Vs. Regulators |
| Justice/Equality Language | Regulators & Environmentalists Vs. Loggers, Timber Owners & Mill Owners | Mill Owners Vs. Environmentalists Vs. Timber Companies Vs. Loggers Vs. Regulators | Mill Owners Vs. Environmentalists Vs. Timber Companies Vs. Loggers Vs. Regulators |

Within this Frame-logic paradigm the greatest convergence among interest groups in terms of diagnosing the nature of the issue can be found within the Justice / Equality diagnostic perspective cell. Therein we find a strong convergence of opinion between loggers, mill owners, and timber owners regarding the nature of the problem to be addressed (i.e. it is unfair for the welfare of humans, human communities and businesses to be sacrificed to promote the welfare of the spotted owl). The contravening argument in that regard is held by the regulators and environmentalists who effectively assert that the welfare of the spotted owl is as valuable that of humans and deserved of special protection.

Loggers, mill owners and timber companies also find themselves in general agreement regarding the diagnostic perspective as expressed in lament/nostalgia language. The overarching theme of the lament and nostalgic diagnostic perspective is essentially that these groups have successfully and productively worked forests for generations contributing to the economic welfare of the region while innovating in forest management practices. Thus they harken back to an era before the ESA created such a high degree of oversight in the forests and mills.

Their nostalgic prognostic perspective is quite simply that if a transition is not made returning more control and discretion to timber workers, mill owners and timber company executives that the lumber and timber product industries will suffer, unemployment will rise, communities will fail and people will be forced to sell their possessions and move on to different locales and different ways of life. This is an outcome that environmentalists are generally comfortable with. Finally, their motivational approach to the issue all centers upon the need to allow logging on federal land so as to encourage employment, lumber processing and timber-related market activities both domestic and foreign.

There is also a strong sense of agreement among loggers, mill owners and timber company owners regarding their use of fear / apocalyptic language. In terms of the diagnostic perspective, all generally agree with the theme that the current regulation of federal land as promulgated by the government and supported by environmentalists is threatening the viability of lumber mills and timber companies and contributing to high unemployment and community disintegration. Their prognostic perspective is similar and asserts that more of the same approach to timber policy will permanently close mills and companies, lead to widespread unemployment and threaten the very existence of many communities dependent upon ongoing access to timber resources. Regarding the motivational aspect of the frame logic perspective all three of these groups agree that encouraging Congress and the Administration to reverse their positions could restore their prospects of continuing their way of life in the forests of the Pacific Northwest.

Regarding the justice / equality language category, loggers, mill owners and timber companies find themselves completely at odds with environmentalists and regulators, who consistently assert that without regulation, advocacy and oversight forests and their endangered species will be forever lost as a natural resource. Consequently, when it comes to this language grouping a general coalescence is observable between loggers, timber companies and mill owners as well as an utterly complete disagreement with the position of environmentalists and regulators. There does not appear to be any room for conversation or compromise between these interest groups regarding these categories.

The remaining categories to be explored is the pride / control language perspective and the prognostic and motivational cells for justice / equality. For pride / control each interest group defined themselves as being unique to every other groups such that there was no convergence of perspectives beyond prognostically agreeing that in the absence of their ability to exercise their own sense of control over the issue of logging on federal land that the future of their group and the economic future of the region was at stake. In every other aspect (diagnostically and motivationally) these groups clearly delineated themselves from one another in terms of the pride / control language set. Regarding language focusing upon justice / equality a similar degree of discordance can be observed.

Once again, the net effect of the divergence of views to be found when framing the issue of logging on federal land from a language perspective is one in which shared interests can be found among interest groups directly engaged in logging and timber production but a clear discontinuity of expectations between these interests and those of environmentalists and regulators. Consequently, successfully framing this controversy in the interest of finding some common ground across all interest groups necessitates applying another framing approach. Having said that, it is worth reiterating that considering the issue from the language orientation perspective is always a good idea since it is very useful in highlighting what people see as the nature of the problem and the solution as well as what serves to motivate participants. However its principle value is the degree to which it facilitates the analyst in understanding the interiorities of each group that drives their values, words, reasoning and actions.

## Identity Framing on the Basis of the Degree of Anthropocentrism

An alternative to using language as a perspective for considering the diagnostic, prognostic and motivational aspects of the logging issue is to consider the responses of the various interest groups in terms of the degree to which they pit the interests of particular species and ecosystems against the interests of human beings – namely the degree to which they recognize the legitimate right of humans to employ natural resources to satisfy human needs and desires. Unlike the language frame perspective previously employed, anthropocentrism (the legitimacy of human utilization of natural resources) can be considered as an identity frame and be construed in terms of degrees anthropocentrism or anti-anthropocentrism rather than as a mutually exclusive characteristic. Consequently one could construe attitudes regarding anthropocentrism as varying from a belief that environmental problems are fully attributable to human activities to believing that environmental issues have virtually nothing at all to do with human use of natural resources.

In considering the principal interest groups discussed to this point one could argue that environmentalists generally tend to identify themselves as extremely anti-anthropocentric in their perspectives meaning they tend to believe human beings typically use natural resources in an exploitative and destructive fashion. Loggers, mill owners, and timber companies could be expected to be pro-anthropocentric in their identities arguing that humans have a legitimate right to use natural resources and that in using these resources ecological destruction need not occur or can me largely mitigated. Regulators, by comparison may be found anywhere between these extreme identities such that those whose values most nearly coincide with the "greatest good for the greatest number" credo of Gifford Pinchot may be somewhat to very pro-anthropocentric in their values whereas more recent employees the U.S. Forest Service of in the Bureau of Land Management whose values more nearly coincide with preservationists and environmentalists tend to be more anti-anthropocentric in their values.

Table18: Frame-logic Paradigm: Logging on Federal Land: Forestry Frame Perspectives
and Anthropocentrism

|  | *Diagnostic Perspective* | *Prognostic Perspective* | *Motivational Perspective* |
|---|---|---|---|
| *Exclusively Anthropocentric* | Humans have an unqualified right to use forest resources as they see fit although they *may* make environmental demands that are unsustainable. | Scientific forest management and employing modern harvesting technology by skilled workers regularly results in productive and sustainable forestry. | Relying upon scientifically sound timber management techniques and employing the latest timber technology can produce sustainable wood supplies, a sound environment and a minimum of environmental destruction. |
| *Somewhat Anthropocentric* | Humans have a qualified right to use forest resources but sometimes fail to recognize that species and ecosystems have a right to exist independently of human needs and desires. | The scientific management of forests and the use of modern harvesting technology by skilled workers sometimes but not always results in productive and sustainable forestry. | Relying upon scientifically sound timber management techniques and harvesting timber by employing the latest technology may or may not produce sustainable wood supplies, a sound environment and a minimum of environmental destruction. |
| *Somewhat Anti-anthropocentric* | Humans have a strictly qualified right to use forest resources as long as they use these resources to meet their needs and reasonable desires. | Scientific forest management and employing modern harvesting technology by skilled workers often produces ecosystem and species destruction. | Relying upon scientifically sound timber management techniques and employing the latest timber technology can't reliably produce sustainable wood supplies or a sound and sustainable environment. |
| *Exclusively Anti-anthropocentric* | Humans have no unqualified right to use forest resources as they see fit and can only legitimately use these resources to meet basic human needs. | Scientific forest management and employing modern harvesting technology by skilled workers inevitably produces habitat destruction to the detriment of ecosystems and species. | Relying upon scientifically sound timber management techniques and employing the latest timber technology can never be expected to produce sustainable wood supplies or a sound and sustainable environment. |

Table 18 illustrates how this Frame-logic might be applied to the logging on federal land issue. When assuming a diagnostic perspective in terms of one's degree of anthropocentrism, values could conceivably be held that range from an extremely anthropocentric perspective that "humans have an unqualified right to use forest resources as they see fit although they may make environmental demands that are unsustainable," to a somewhat anthropocentric perspective that asserts "humans have a strictly qualified right to use forest resources as long as they use these resources to meet their needs and reasonable desires" to a profoundly anti-anthropocentric perspective that "humans have no unqualified right to use forest resources as they see fit and can only legitimately use these resources to meet basic human needs." When these same points along a theoretical continuum of anthropocentric to anti-anthropocentric values is considered one find extremely anthropocentric advocates touting the benefits of scientific technology in managing and harvesting timber optimistically claiming that "scientific forest management and employing modern harvesting technology by skilled workers regularly results in productive and sustainable forestry." By comparison somewhat anthropocentric observers might be expected to speculate "The scientific management of forests and the use of modern harvesting technology by skilled workers sometimes but not always results in productive and sustainable forestry. " However the anti-anthropcentric observer could well be expected to adopt a much more dour perspective on the promise of scientific technology and claim that "scientific forest management and employing modern harvesting technology by skilled workers inevitably produces habitat destruction to the detriment of ecosystems and species."

If the interest groups pertinent to the logging on federal land issue were assigned to a Frame-logic paradigm based upon their degree of anthropocentrism then they might be conceivably distributed as follows (see Table 19). If we only consider those who are either extremely anthropocentric in their identity or extremely anti-anthropocentric, then we are left with a clear balkanization of loggers, mill operators, timber company operators on the anthropocentric extreme and radical environmentalists on the anti-anthropocentric extreme. However if we consider that people may have a range of values regarding anthropocentrism then we see some opportunity for collaboration as we can expect a confluence of some stakeholders from virtually every identity group in and around the mid-range values of "somewhat anthropocentric" and "somewhat anti-anthropocentric." This provides a glimmer of hope that perhaps there are points around which disparate groups might meet and confer.

Table 19: Frame-logic Paradigm: Forestry Frame Perspectives and Anthropocentrism by Interest Group

| | Interest Groups |
|---|---|
| **Exclusively Anthropocentric** | Loggers, Mill Operators, Timber Company Operators |
| **Somewhat Anthropocentric** | Environmentalists, Regulators, Mill Operators, Loggers, Timber Company Operators |
| **Somewhat Anti-anthropocentric** | Environmentalists, Regulators |
| **Exclusively Anti-anthropocentric** | Environmentalists |

This Frame-logic paradigm is more useful since it suggests that (a) there is a midrange of values that might be shared by any number of interest groups and (b) when those with extreme values (anthropocentric or anti-anthropocentric) are excluded from the policy discussion there may be common ground for the remaining interest groups to come to an agreement. That said there are some additional ways in which the logging issue might be resolved but identifying them requires employing frame paradigms such as those proffered by Lewicki et al (2002).

Lewicki et al (2002) concluded that in the interest of resolving policy stalemates most adversaries find themselves encouraged to "reframe" their perspectives such as in

1.  Shifting from specific interests to more general ones,
2.  Narrowing the issues or breaking them into smaller parts,
3.  Translating disputes over values into interests,
4.  Identifying superordinate (or overarching) goals;
5.  Agreeing to disagree. (Lewicki, Gray & Elliott, 2003, p. 34)

When employing any of these approaches within an anthropocentrism Frame-logic paradigm what remains constant is the reality that each interest group will tend to address the logging issue on the basis of their intuitive range of anthropocentric values and act in their self-interest.

While the intuitive factor remains constant for all deliberators, what varies is how they might choose to resolve the logging issue in terms of the specific characteristics of the issue (e.g. impacts upon local communities or economies, opportunities for alternate employment, lifestyle adjustments, etc.), amenability to being considered in smaller parts (e.g. confining this issue to a particular national forest), shared interests where there might be agreement (e.g. maximizing employment opportunities, minimizing risks, supporting municipal and community resources), overarching goals (e.g. maintaining as many people as possible in the region employed in one fashion or another), and agreeability (e.g. moving on to another issue that may be amenable to resolution).

Since intuition drives reason and Haidt's research suggests that both intuition and reason serve to link individual values with those of important reference groups they identify with, we have to assume that any framing effort involving logging on public land will entail individuals seeking to address the issue in a manner concordant with their reference groups. So if anthropocentrism is a continuum of values (meaning one can hold values that are comparatively "more" or "less" anthropocentric) then we can also assume that when it comes to seeing the legitimacy of human involvement in natural ecosystems to satisfy wants and needs that there should be a range of values that different interest groups might be able to agree upon.

The only exception to this assumption involves those who are strident or extreme environmentalists (meaning they see virtually no circumstance in which humans may legitimately utilize a natural reason other than to meet very basic survival needs) or those who are so completely pro-anthropocentric that they will not accept any policy option in which the rights of ecosystems or species are recognized and accommodated for their own sake. Representatives of both of these extreme philosophical positions must necessarily be excluded from the framing process quite simply because they are incapable of compromise and compromise is what framing is all about.

Fortunately, when considering the interest groups attendant to the logging on federal land issue one can assume that there are environmentalists whose values range from being rather firmly anti-anthropocentric to those whose values are more akin to traditional conservationists who see a wide range of acceptable options for human use of forests and in that regard are somewhat pro-anthropocentric. In this regard, the salient factor is not "whether" human activity can be allowed in forested areas but rather "how much" and "what kinds" of activities are acceptable. Framed in this fashion, those who can be brought to the proverbial bargaining table are those who acknowledge the legitimacy of human use of natural resources, but who may disagree on the "what," "how" and in this case the "where" of that utilization.

While environmentalists can be as a matter of course expected to resist the broad employment of forest resources for human use, it would be erroneous to assume that those who labor in forest industries do not share a similar perspective – though holding their values to a differing degree. As Dietrich's (1992) book illustrates among those who labor in the forests as loggers, chokers, truckers etc. many hold the forest as an ecological entity in high regard. This implies they don't subscribe to the unfettered use of forest resources by humans. While they generally tend to be pro-anthropocentric in their outlook to interacting with the forest, there is no reason to believe that they are not also concerned about and even skeptical of the unfettered harvesting of timber resources to the point where many would describe themselves as conservationists and perhaps even environmentalists.

That said we should suspect that there is more common ground between environmentalists and those laboring in the timber industry than otherwise might seem reasonable to assume. We have to assume that among these forest laborers there are at least some who may consider themselves to be environmentalists and hold values in the mid-range of anthropocentrism – being either somewhat anthropocentric or somewhat anti-anthropocentric. Arguably, this very phenomenon also applies to those engaged in running lumber mills and timber companies as well as to regulators.

There is every reason to expect that most of these groups not only economically benefit from the forest but like most everyone else in the Pacific Northwest, utilize the woods for recreation as hunters, anglers, hikers, bikers, whitewater enthusiasts etc. Regardless of whether these people think of themselves as sportsmen and women, conservationists, or environmentalists, the chances are good that they intuitively embrace a set of mid-range anthropocentric values encompassing a shared set of environmental principles embraced by a number of pertinent reference groups including recreational and sport associations, hunting and fishing organizations, professional and industry related organizations, environmental associations and NGOs and the like. Assuming there exists a group of individuals engaged in the dispute over logging on federal land that by some measure agree that humans possess some measure of right to be on that land and utilize it, then the issues become not "whether" they should be there but "in what manner" should they be there, where and to what end. These become, therefore, the points around which the debate over logging on federal land should occur.

It is worth remembering that while the formal process of engaging in a framing process among competitors to address the logging on federal land issue is going on – what we call deliberative imagining – a simultaneous process is also at work in which individuals working through policy conundrums with others employ their gut-reactions to respond to issues and drive reasoned responses, arguments and discussions. This constitutes instinctive or intuitive imagining. Both intuitive and deliberative imagining occur simultaneously and are necessary to arrive at any consensual agreement.

## Employing a Risk Frame-logic: Bargaining to Share Risks

As discussed earlier Lewicki et al (2003) provide a number of frame perspectives that might be employed at this point to further move the framing process toward a conclusion. Two in particular apply to the logging issue – identity frames and risk frames. Identity frames might be employed to the degree that various interest groups in part define themselves in terms of the extent to which they embrace anthropocentric or anti-anthropocentric environmental values. However, as illustrated when the Frame-logic is approached in terms of language style, there is likewise the risk that employing an identity frame set alone (such as the one involving anthropocentrism) will only serve to further Balkanize the groups involved in this controversy.

Risk frames, on the other hand, might prove useful in part because virtually all of the interest groups involved in the logging on federal land issue have expressed concern over risk to one degree or another pertaining either to environmental risks, socio-economic risks or both. Unlike other variables that might be considered in framing this issue, risk is virtually never born by one group alone. Risks tend to be generalized to impact a number of groups. Consequently, when dealing with risk-generating issues, most parties will share or spread the risk so that no party is unduly impacted.

Suppose we create a Frame-logic paradigm to contrast identity and risks frames where identity is defined in terms of the degree of anthropocentrism and risk in terms of the degree of economic risk to the local and regional economy. Such a paradigm might look like this (see Table 20). Given what we know about this particular issue at this point it can reasonably be expected that only the most radical environmentalists would be completely oblivious to the economic risk the Pacific Northwest would face if all logging on federal land were denied and the operators of timber companies continued to export logs to Asian lumber mills. More than likely we should expect to see a range of values among environmentalists regarding the economic risk of failing to support lumber mills by allowing logging on federal lands. Consequently we should expect to see environmentalists who are somewhat anthropocentric or somewhat anti-anthropocentric be willing to acknowledge some degree of risk ranging from low to high risk. The same phenomenon should apply to regulators and to "somewhat" and "exclusively" anthropocentric loggers and timber company operators.

Table 20: Frame-logic Paradigm for NOT Resuming Logging on Federal Land: Degree of Anthropcentrism and Economic Risk Perception

| Interests | Risk Perception | | | |
|---|---|---|---|---|
| | No Economic Risk | Low Economic Risk | Moderate Economic Risk | High Economic Risk |
| *Exclusively Anthropocentric* | | Timber Companies, Loggers | Timber Companies, Loggers | Timber Companies, Mill Owners, Loggers |
| *Somewhat Anthropocentric* | | Environmentalists, Regulators, Loggers | Regulators, Timber Company Operators, Loggers, Mill Owners, Environmentalists | Regulators, Timber Company Operators, Loggers, Mill Owners, Environmentalists |
| *Somewhat Anti-anthropocentric* | | Environmentalists, Regulators | Regulators, Timber Company Operators, Loggers, Mill Owners, Environmentalists | Regulators, Timber Company Operators, Loggers, Mill Owners, Environmentalists |
| *Exclusively Anti-anthropocentric* | Environmentalists | | | |

By comparison, the lumber mill owners and workers should be expected to generally be exclusively anthropocentric in their values and are most likely to fear moderate to severe economic risk to not being able to have access to logs for lumber from federal lands. Regulators and environmentalists are by definition very unlikely to be exclusively anthropocentric in orientation but may be somewhat anthropocentric or somewhat anti-anthropocentric in their values. These individuals and groups may also recognize the potential for moderate or severe economic risk in continuing to bar lumber mills for getting access to logs on federal lands.

That said let's reconsider the logging on federal land issue again for a moment. This is primarily an issue for mill owners because timber companies principally cut timber on land they own or control and since they have the autonomy and authority to do so and choose to maximize their current profits by exporting logs overseas to Asian mills. In so doing they threaten the viability of local mills that one-by-one are going out of business. When mills go out of business so do other related businesses and eventually municipalities and communities are weakened considerably. However, as long as overseas markets for logs remains profitable then there is every incentive for timber companies to continue their export practices.

What happens though if foreign log exports dry up and exporting logs is no longer profitable? Will these timber companies want to turn their attention again to U.S. markets and if they do, who will mill their logs into lumber? Assuming domestic mills are still in business, the answer is those mills that have produced U.S. lumber in the past will do so again. But what if the current export practice continues to shut down lumber mills? If in the future timber companies need to embrace a U.S. market again in a big way, can they count not only on there being mills available to produce the lumber, will there even be the expertise remaining regarding how to operate a lumber mill? The sad reality is that too-often when skilled businesses close on a wholesale level not only are the businesses lost, so are the skills and expertise required to operate the businesses.

Timber companies have a long-term stake in the future of the lumber mills – whether they recognized it immediately or not. Without the presence of lumber mills, the domestic long-term viability of timber companies is compromised. In the interest of avoiding undue future risk of not having lumber mills available when they need them, timber companies have an incentive to send some of their logs to domestic markets to keep these local mills open or decide to invest in lumber mill operations of their own. If they choose to commit to the process of supporting local mills, then their conversations with mill operators principally centers upon "how much" locally and privately grown timber makes its way into local lumber mills not "whether" there will be any whatsoever. If they see a need to open their own mills they must project out the costs associated with capitalizing and running such an operation and compare those costs against the costs of utilizing existing mills. Likewise they must consider where and at what cost will they find the workers with the expertise to sustainably and safely operate these mills. Thereafter they choose the option most beneficial to them – which in this case likely involves using existing mills rather than creating lumber mills on their own.

Depending on the extent of the degree of their perceived economic risk we should find some common ground between the timber companies and the lumber mills, and frankly also with the loggers, chokers, skidders and others who work in the employ of the timber companies to bring wood products from the forest to the consumer. Environmentalists, on the other hand, are not directly impacted by whether local lumber mills remain open or closed, if for no other reason because they typically don't reside in these mill communities. Their principal concern is to deter logging on federal land. However, assuming they are sensitive to the economic plight of local logging communities, they *might* find it in their interests to encourage timber companies to maximize logging on private land and to earmark some portion of those logs for lumber production in local mills. In this way they protect habitats on public land while supporting local forest economies.

In contrast, regulators can be expected to divide themselves pretty evenly between the interests of the troika of timber companies, mills and loggers and the interests of the environmentalists. If their values trend toward conservationism in the tradition of Gordon Pinchot then they might find themselves sympathetic with the interests of the mill owners and operators recognizing that their legislative mandate is in part designed to support the economic needs of the timber industry and related industries. However if their values trend toward some degree of environmentalism that is anti-anthropocentric then they may be prone to being less supportive of the desires of lumber mill owners and operators

By way of contrast, environmentalists tend to intuitively distrust timber companies or any of the group associated with them (such as the loggers and the mill owners) who principally relate to the forest as a commodity that can be bought and sold. However, if they study the dynamics of this particular controversy they will see that logging on federal land became an issue because insufficient timber resources were finding their way from private lands into local lumber mills. The mill's solution was to seek access to federal land to supply new wood supplies for lumber. The solution environmentalists might offer is to ask timber companies to send some of their logs from private land to these mills to keep them open and to assure the region continues to possess the capacity to produce lumber and other timber products. If private lands were more productive in this regard then there would be no need to increase timber demand on federal lands. So approached, risk would be mitigated in that natural environments on federal land would be vouchsafed, risks to mills of closure would be reduced and the future of mills for timber companies would be assured.

The costs of this solution, however, principally fall upon the timber companies who forgo a degree of profitability derived from international log exports in the interest of realizing a marginally smaller profit in selling logs for lumber production. Convincing these companies to follow this course would require persuading them they were getting something of value for their sacrifices. This could be provided in a number of ways. One way would be for regulators and environmentalists to support a contingency plan allowing timber companies to selectively harvest logs from federal land in the event that demand for logs and lumber exceeded the capacity of their lands. Yet another solution would be for the regulators and environmentalists to support the timber companies in lobbying Congress for either a tax credit (to offset a portion of their forgone profits from limiting log exports) for supplying some agreed upon tonnage of logs to domestic mills annually or to ask for tariff relief to insure fair prices in international markets.

In pursuing any of these solution, environmentalists would have been asked to accept a degree of anthropocentricism by actually teaming with timber companies and lumber mills to encourage the expansion logging on private land - all in the interest of protecting public lands from this practice. Moreover, they would have assisted in supporting key components of the timber industry in their region thereby running the risk that these entities might threaten environmental resources on public land again. In so doing they run the risk of alienating themselves from groups they identify with who may not be a party to these negotiations. However if they cooperate in offering such options to timber companies they do so recognizing that there exists some degree of acceptable and even necessary anthropocentrism that must be embraced in the interest of insuring the viability of human communities.

Mill owners would likely appreciate the commitment of timber companies to their long term viability but in the process might begin to feel unduly beholden to and controlled by these companies, especially if timber companies choose to buy or create their own lumber mills to process timber as the market demands. Moreover, mill owners might respond to this "solution" by feeling as if they are eternally going to have to bargain with timber companies and regulators regarding what volume of lumber these two entities are willing to allow. Mill owners should be expected to intuitively want more autonomy from timber companies and regulators alike, while timber companies can be expected to exert more control over the totality of the timber market to include controlling or owning lumber mills.

On the other hand loggers should be happy with this arrangement provided that the combination of domestic and foreign timber production maintained their employment and income levels. Regulators should also like this solution to the degree that it puts logging on private not public land. However, their experience should suggest that as long as there are timber resources on federal land there will be economic interests ready and willing to harvest that timber. Similarly, they should expect that as world and domestic markets for timber fluctuates, so will demand for the timber they manage. They should also be aware that regulations that currently apply to federal land could conceivably be expanded to private lands also and that the net effect of such expansion could be the further constriction of the nation's access to lumber and logs which could pose risks beyond the scope of this case study but risks that would force all parties to address the issue of logging on federal land again.

## Rationale Versus the Process for Achieving a Frame-fit

The preceding is a discussion of a set of motivations, rationales, and options that might be open to the parties involved in this issue, allowing them to come to compromise on the federal land logging issue in the interest of mitigating anticipated risks. It does not however provide a process to pursue these ends. In truth, there are many different processes that could be employed to frame this issue in terms of anthropocentric values and risk. It would seem however that since the parties at greatest risk to being negatively impacted by the continued export of logs to Asia are the lumber mills the process of rectifying this situation should be theirs to initiate.

In the Pacific Northwest lumber mills are typically locally owned and operated (Learn, 2013; Hampton Affiliates, 2013; Committee for Family Forestlands, 2012; Jacket, 2009) – meaning that fighting the current log export policy and restrictions to logging on federal land falls individually on each mill owner's shoulders. However, these independent mills participate in any number of prominent regional and national industry organizations representing their interests (to one degree or another) to include the American Forest Resource Council, American Hardboard Association, Forest Landowners Association, Forest Resource Association, Forest Stewardship Council, Hardwood, Plywood and Veneer Association, National American Wholesale Lumber Association, National Lumber and Building Material Association, Pacific Logging Congress, Western Hardwood Association, Woodworking Machinery Industry Association and the World Forest Institute (Andrzejewski, 2013). These trade associations and nonprofit organizations exist to serve lumber mills, manufacturers, retailers and the forest owners who produce the timber that is later milled into lumber and other wood products consumed domestically and abroad. Without question, these organizations have a stake in the future of domestic lumber mills and may constitute a set of resources that could be employed to harness the individual concerns of the lumber mill owners and operators and provide an organizational counter-weight to the better funded and organized environmentalists and timber companies.

In short, the independent mill owners need advocates to assist them in bringing timber companies and environmentalists to the bargaining table. In truth, some of the organizations cited above undoubtedly also have ties to the timber companies as well, but to the degree that any one of these organizations or a combination thereof could be convinced that it is in their economic interest to support the future of domestic lumber mills then these independent operators would gain strength and be able to seek a better frame-fit of their dilemma. Alternatively, the lumber mills may choose to form their own business association and pool resources to wage a public relations war espousing their values to the community and their need for a compromise. This too might serve to bring the environmentalists, loggers and timber companies to the bargaining table. Likewise, doing so would tend to elevate the significance of their crisis in the eyes of local, state and federal officials and politicians thereby providing yet other venues in which their concerns could be aired and addressed. In the absence of a process such as one of those suggested above, what we have is a rationale for how to go about framing this issue in a way that takes into account both intuitive and deliberative approaches to imagining but no vehicle for actually achieving the desired frame-fit.

For framing to actually occur it is necessary to have both a rationale and process for framing the issue. That process will always be inherently political and negotiated and will always involve a power frame such as those categories identified by Lewicki et al. (2002). In regard to the situation of the lumber mills in the face of increased log exports, the subcategories of power relationships they will want to account for include those involving resources, coalitional/relational power (building advocates to their cause), authority and position (influencing political and economic systems), sympathy and vulnerability (appealing to the good nature of their competitors and the public), force and threat (especially threat as it pertains to risk to the economic viability of the region) moral righteousness (their inherent right to live on the land and prosper from it as long as they do so sustainably) and voice (through public relations).

Most important among these approaches to exercising power is the need to present their case in such a fashion that all parties can intuitively sympathize with their situation and intuitively see a resolution that at best benefits their situation and minimally harms them. Ultimately this process will involve appealing to their intuitive best interests while simultaneously leveraging their position employing some degree of power or coercion that further motivates the participants. In short, framing is unlikely to happen purely on the basis of altruism, sympathy or understanding alone. Ultimately participants will sign on to a deal because they find it in their enlightened self-interest to do so and by virtue of external forces – some persuasive and others coercive.

Recognizing this coercive aspect of imagining is necessary in virtually any frame-fit and is particularly important in this case since one party in the dispute - the environmentalists - should have virtually no interest at all in seeing the lumber mills survive (and indeed have every reason to want to seem the close) while another party – the timber companies – could create their own mills if they chose to and literally run the independent mills out of the market. That leaves the labor force of the forest – the ill-organized loggers, chokers, etc. – as the only uncommitted party to the dispute. However, since lumber mills serve as markets for the logs provided by cutters, chokers and haulers they (the timber workers) can be expected to be supportive of the mills. Moreover, they populate most of the small towns and communities throughout the region they – along with local businesses, residents and politicians –can be expected to constitute a potent force in state and local politics that could also be employed in seeking a forum with the rest of the parties to this issue.

# Chapter 7: Let's Work Together—Individual Freedom and Community Need

Together we'll stand
Divided we'll fall
Come on now people
Let's get on the ball
And work together
Come on, come on
Let's work together

*Let's Work Together*
Canned Heat

## Intuition and Community

As we concluded the previous chapter discussing the conundrum Pacific Northwest timber mills are embroiled in relative to procuring sufficient timber resources to keep their mills in production, it became clear that successfully achieving their aim necessitated them affiliating, organizing and coherently functioning as a community of mill owners cooperatively pursuing shared goals and outcomes. In a nutshell, we were making the argument for solving common issues from the perspective of the community as compared to perpetuating a balkanized process where each competing interests pursue their agendas individually and in competition with every other party to the dispute at hand. In most policy disputes such teamwork and cooperation is a necessity for actually realizing some degree of success in pursuing policy agendas. However doing so requires all involved to become comfortable with the fact that some degree of compromise is required to realize closure to policy issues since in virtually no instance will any party to a policy dispute walk away with everything they were seeking. Likewise, it requires the recognition by all parties that the policy process is fluid and ongoing and that realizing policy goals requires remaining in the thick of the policymaking milieu.

There are, however other important reasons why group and community approaches to policy resolution is not only important but also necessary. Key among these is the realization that since all parties will state their positions based upon intuitive assumptions and beliefs they will inevitably seek outcomes that not only satisfy their personal needs and ambitions, but will additionally do so in a fashion that meets the expectations of the groups and communities that they belong to or strongly identify with. As Lewicki et al. (2003), Lianne Lefsrud and Renate Meyer (2012) suggest identity frames are always important to understand and are inherently useful in resolving frame conflicts: providing that the boundaries around which the identities are defined are not so stringently enforced so as to allow them to become impervious to outside influence thereby prohibiting the capacity of the policy participant to assimilate or assume some of the characteristics of other interest groups and individuals influential to the outcome of the issue.

Unavoidably, intuitive reasoning and action occurs against the backdrop of the constituencies the individual, agency or group belongs to or identifies with. The corollary of this rule is that any attempt to change the agenda or interests of an individual or group must ultimately seek to change the constituency with whom they identify. Once an individual, agency or group comes to identify with a new constituency or begins to incorporate the values of other constituencies into their own values then their sense of who they identify with in the community expands and with that expansion comes a change in what they intuitively hold to be true or valuable.

Consequently, when timber mill operators begin to coalesce and organize as a group around common needs and assets they begin the process of coopting one another's values and interests and to the degree they include other related groups in their circle (e.g. suppliers, retailers, customers, community leaders, etc.) the range of intuitive values and beliefs they hold expands and becomes more inclusive as opposed to exclusive. The more expansive the range of constituencies identified with the greater the range of values and policy options that become feasible and available for consideration.

Chapter seven explores an approach, known as "communitarianism" that is designed to bring policy disputes as close to the community as possible and to create an environment where pressing policy problems are resolved communally, locally, informally and without necessarily involving formal action by legislatures, agencies or the courts. It is also an approach that seeks to expand the range of communities and groups that individuals come to value and identify with. In this fashion, communitarian approaches serve to expand the range of possibilities around which policy issues might be resolved.

The chapter title was drawn from a song by *Canned Heat* that underscores the utter necessity of people finding a way to solve mutual problems. This community-centered approach, most notably championed by the late Nobel laureate, Elinor Ostrom (2009), is we think best illustrated in the work of sociologist Amitai Etzioni who describes "communitarian" approaches as involving an examination of "the ways shared conceptions of the good (values) are formed, transmitted, justified, and enforced" (Etzioni, 2003, p. 224). In this regard, Etzioni calls for promoting and enhancing the capacity of local institutions such as the family, schools and voluntary associations to transmit social values, mores and norms around which conflicts can be avoided or mediated.

Based upon this conceptualization Etzioni believes that generally policy issues should be resolved locally and informally whenever feasible and that individual needs must be balanced against the needs of the community. Etzioni's model is based upon what he refers to as the "new golden rule" which asserts "Respect and uphold society's moral order as you would have society respect and uphold your autonomy to live a full life" (Etzioni, 1997 p. xviii). Etzioni's approach is well grounded in the history of communitarian thought as exemplified by the work of its founder, Alasdair MacIntyre (1988) as well as via the efforts of communitarian ecologist Avner DeShalit (2004;1995).

In articulating a communitarian vision that he believes contributes to environmental sustainability, DeShalit claims that

> Although sentiments and emotional ties are important elements of a community and should be treated as such, I consider the members of a community to be rational: i.e. they subject their membership in the community to critical examination. (DeShalit, 1995, p. 1881)

This insight would seem to imply that rationality ultimately perseveres over emotion and sentiment. Such an assertion is in keeping with how decision-making and policy formulation have historically been construed.

However, in light of the work of moral psychologists such as Jonothan Haidt (2006; 2013) it is compellingly clear that rationality serves intuition that is in great part emotional, instinctive and sentimental in nature. So considered, DeShalit's assertion that members of a community subject their membership in a community to critical examination may not in fact mean that they apply strictly objective and rational criteria to whether they remain committed to the community as much as it means they critically compare what they experience and understand about the community to a set of intuitively held beliefs, experiences and values that were arrived at through earlier interactions within the community. This is of course the stream of consciousness phenomenon William James first described which we believe captures the naturally intuitive process of imaginating.

As Jonathan Haidt (2013) observed, people tend to hold intuitive opinions and values that not only conform to their intuitive sense of what is ethical and functional, they likewise identify and affiliate with groups and organizations that not only share their intuitions but actually shape the values and preferences of their members. This phenomenon is known as group conformity and is necessary in the interest of maintaining a social context for an individual's life, since violating the expectations of the group risks their expulsion and disenfranchisement (Dewar, 2013). Indeed it would seem that the desire for group conformity on the part of individuals is literally hard-wired into the human DNA and evolutionarily programmed into our brains (Morgan & Laland, 2012) since conformity is a human trait that ultimately "drives all other traits to extinction" (Mesoudi, 2011).

Practically speaking what this suggests is that from an evolutionary perspective the dominance of conformity as a basic human trait has literally been perpetuated biologically and culturally such that in the interest of learning how to survive in the world individuals have learned to conform to the mores and expectations of one group or another since individual identity is in great part socially and not just individually derived. This process of group or social identity was central to Wimberley's work in nested ecology (Wimberley, 2009) to the degree that individual identity and values are culturally transmitted. This process hinges around the significant influence of human culture which can be fruitfully defined as "information capable of affecting individuals' behavior that they acquire from other members of their species through teaching, imitation, and other forms of social transmission" (Richerson and Boyd, 2006, p. 5).

Social ecology, as conceptualized by communitarian writers, is to a significant degree based upon the importance of individual conformity to group and community norms and expectations in the interest of insuring social order, cultural development, the fulfillment of human needs and aspirations and the development and maintenance of human identity. Indeed Etzioni's "new golden rule" reflects the expectation that individuality be tempered to the degree needed to realize basic community goals and needs. When applied to policy disputes involving disagreements and conflicts among various groups, an ecologically oriented communitarianism would call for individuals and groups to look for if you will "shared identity."

Shared identity consists of those values and other cultural characteristics that unifies individuals and groups and holds them in common, what has historically been called "common cause" (Ammerman, 1975) or "commonwealth" (Mehrota, 2008). Reframing policy issues, as discussed in the previous two chapters, necessitates identifying common causes in the interest of creating a broad enough group identity to allow for some degree of intuitive consensus to emerge. Of course one of the principal challenges to realizing this goal is the degree to which groups rather narrowly define those issues tailored to their identities – their "signature issues" - and focus so narrowly on such a narrow set of concerns that they no longer see the utility in engaging their ideological opponents around other values where they undoubtedly share a congruence of interests.

## Winning Hearts and Minds

Unavoidably the give and take in policy disputes involves not only convincing the opponent of the so-called "logic" of one's positions – i.e. winning minds – it also and perhaps more importantly must aim to win over hearts first. In truth position-swaying arguments must be directed first toward the admixture of emotion, values and experiences that comprise intuition and hope that having appealed to hearts that minds will soon follow. This is common wisdom of any successful marketing professional, salesman, or politician. Successful appeals for policy positions and most important for change from the status quo always targets the hearts of the listeners – if not the heart of the key opponent in the policy dispute certainly the hearts of that opponent's constituency.

This process is reminiscent of the wisdom of the early French economist Frederic Bastiat's parable of the broken window in his famous monograph *That Which is Seen and That Which is Not Seen* (1850). In this essay Bastiat recounts the tale of the careless shopkeeper's son who accidently breaks a square of glass that could have been used for a window. In analyzing this event Bastiat observes:

> Suppose it cost six francs to repair the damage, and you say that the accident brings six francs to the glazier's trade—that it encourages that trade to the amount of six francs—I grant it; I have not a word to say against it; you reason justly. The glazier comes, performs his task, receives his six francs, rubs his hands, and, in his heart, blesses the careless child. All this is *that which is seen*. But if, on the other hand, you come to the conclusion, as is too often the case, that it is a good thing to break windows, that it causes money to circulate, and that the encouragement of industry in general will be the result of it, you will oblige me to call out, "Stop there! Your theory is confined to that *which is seen;* it takes no account of that *which is not seen*." *It is not seen* that as our shopkeeper has spent six francs upon one thing, he cannot spend them upon another. *It is not seen* that if he had not had a window to replace, he would, perhaps, have replaced his old shoes, or added another book to his library. In short, he would have employed his six francs in some way, which this accident has prevented. (Bastiat, 1850, p. 4)

Bastiat's parable reminds the reader that in the realms of economics and public policy that which is not seen is often as important as that which is immediately perceived. He goes on to apply this insight to the behavior of politicians that, for instance, advocate for taxes observing:

> Have you ever chanced to hear it said: "There is no better investment than taxes. Only see what a number of families it maintains, and consider how it reacts on industry: it is an inexhaustible stream, it is life itself." In order to combat this doctrine, I must refer to my preceding refutation..." "The advantages which officials advocate are *those which are seen*. The benefit which accrues to the providers *is still that which is seen*. This blinds all eyes. But the disadvantages which the tax-payers have to get rid of are *those which are not seen*. And the injury which results from it to the providers, is still that *which is not seen*, although this ought to be self-evident. (Bastiat, 1850, p. 7)

The same insight derived from the broken window can be applied to any "political pitch" by a policy advocate – politician or not – who seeks to win the hearts of one constituency or another. In every case they will present the obvious "seen" benefits and virtues of their position while minimizing any discussion of "what is unseen" – the unavoidable "down-side of any policy option. Bastiat's insight is based upon what economists now refer to as "opportunity costs" which simply means that any decision for any particular policy choice by necessity implies that other options and choices are forgone. These forgone opportunities are realized at a cost and in the ideal situation the benefit derived from one policy choice produces more benefit than the cost experienced by the forgone opportunity.

These calculations work well enough when the issue at hand can be readily resolved by some form of cost-benefit analysis, but in so many cases the issues defy such analyses for a host of reasons to include the comparison of immediate to long term benefit, the realization of value in non-monetary terms or when the issues at hand touch deep philosophical, religious or spiritual values. In fact, it is arguable that whenever those seeking to sway public opinion speak to our hearts and not necessarily to our minds that their intent is to massage those values that are not readily quantifiable. The intent is to get us to respond to the argument on a gut "emotional" level and later employ or rationality to explain and justify newly embraced intuition.

Even so, whenever a policy choice is embarked upon other options are forgone and in virtually every case the supposed benefit of the policy are emphasized while costs or other perhaps less desirable outcomes are de-emphasized or ignored entirely. For instance, in the instance of Colorado's decision to close coal-powered electric generator plants, the benefits touted included cleaner air, less carbon contribution to global warming, the embracing of cleaner burning natural gas and so forth. These were the benefits that proponents promised the public they would be able to literally "see." What proponents of closing the coal plants failed to tell the public was that this policy choice would result in significant coal-related unemployment, the demise of local businesses in and around the communities housing these coal-generation plants, and the bankruptcy of many local governments. Likewise, proponents failed to note that American coal that was not being consumed in comparably environmentally clean U.S. plants would be shipped overseas – much of it to Asia – where it would be burned in less environmentally stringent plants and producing marginally more carbon pollution that would find its way into the atmosphere and eventually make its way into Colorado skies from overseas (Unger, 2013). Moreover, as more coal (and nuclear) power plants are closed and natural gas plants are opened, demand for natural gas will of necessity rise and will likely produce cost increases for this fuel, driven both by demand (particularly demand for heating fuel during winter months) and by variations in pipeline capacity across the nation (IER, 2013).

## Avoiding Analysis Paralysis

A useful parallel to the policy pitch can be found in the business world where capital firms structure investment deals. In a recent interview Ken Lombard, of Capri Capital Partners compared investment dealmakers with financial analysts by endeavoring to arrive at a finance structure "that mitigates your downside— but not to the point of running scared" (Drucker Exchange, 2013). He explains his approach saying that while

> analysis tells you what you need to hear in how you need to structure a deal, there's a difference between deal makers and analysts. Analysts can tell you everything wrong with the deal; the deal maker is going to try to figure out a way to come up with a structure that makes sense. (Drucker Exchange, 2013)

In so doing Lombardi emphasizes focusing upon opportunity first and risk second, doing so however in a fashion that doesn't underestimate risk but that also doesn't needlessly paralyze the deal making effort. What he advocates for is deal making that moves the process forward in prudent and thoughtful terms but which doesn't paralyze the deliberation process by providing too much information or allowing perceived "costs" to unnecessarily stand in the way of reasonably achieved "opportunities."

In presenting an imagining approach to policy deliberation in this text, we too advocate for analysis that is predicated upon an intuitive decision that to some degree is emotionally and value laden, but which doesn't embrace a particular policy option without applying a degree of analytic skepticism to the process. In short, while recognizing that rationality serves intuition and that arguments directed to the heart often inform and shape arguments and rationalizations, we would argue, as Lombardi has above, that the policymaker and the dealmaker are both required to consider not just what is seen and anticipated but also consider that which is unseen and unknown – meaning opportunity costs and risks.

At issue is not whether to engage in this process but rather how to go about it. Analysis paralysis occurs when policymakers take on the mantle of analysts who inform the policy process but don't necessarily make the policy decisions - subjecting each and every policy option to such thorough and detailed scrutiny that they become overwhelmed with a burden of risks that negates recommending taking a definitive policy decision. Policymaking along these lines is known as rational-comprehensive decision-making and it implies a virtually endless search for the ideal option that fully maximizes benefit and minimizes risk. These approaches contribute to policy gridlock and are arguably only justified for issues of overwhelmingly importance where there is both significant time to search for the very best policy alternative and access to the resources to engage in a very thorough deliberation.

On the other extreme are the routine policy decisions that only require consideration of a narrow range of policy alternatives that differ only marginally from current policy. This approach, known as incrementalism, defines the bulk of policy decisions made by legislative bodies at the local state and national level. These are typically policy issues that only require narrowly marginal changes from existing policy. More controversial are issues that, on the basis of timing and importance considerations, require more than typical incremental approaches to policy (i.e. choosing options that are marginally different from current policies to improve policy-related decision-making) but much less than rational-comprehensive methods (Wimberley & Morrow, 1981). The options most often employed are the mid-range strategies of "mixed-scanning" introduced by Amitai Etzioni (Etzioni, 1967) - using incremental approaches for routine policy decisions and more rational-comprehensive approaches for more important decisions - or employing the satisficing approach of Herbert Simon (Simon, 1969). In the interest of engaging in imagining from a communitarian perspective, we recommend employing satisficing.

Satisficing involves developing a tentative sense of the range of policy outcomes that will prove acceptable in addressing the majority of one's policy goals and then proceeding to accept the first alternative presenting itself that meets your basic intuitively derived policy criteria. Satisficing denotes "problem solving and decision making that sets an aspiration level, searches until an alternative is found that is the aspiration level criterion and selects the alternative" (Simon, 1972, p. 168).

Satisficing also calls for a "stop-rule" that the decision-makers employ to end the search for policy alternatives "when a good enough alternative is found" (Simon, 1979, p. 3). Simon defines satisficing as "bounded rationality" in which replaces

> the global rationality of economic man with a kind of rational behavior that is compatible with the access to information and the computational capacities that are actually possessed by organisms, including man, in the kinds of environments in which such organisms exist. (Simon, 1955, p. 7)

Simon, like other contemporary decision scientists of his time (Kahneman & Tversky, 1979, 1984) recognized that decision-making was not a completely rational process and sought to develop a decision model that reflected these "boundaries" to rationality.

To that end Simon's model of bounded rational decision-making (Simon, Newell & Simon, 1972) begins with intelligence gathering, proceeds to the design of possible courses of action and ultimately concludes with choice along the lines described above. Employing this step-wise approach, Simon describes the decision-making processes of the administrative mind, though his insights have been widely applied to policymaking (Kalantari, 2010; Jones, 2003). He does so through the process of empirical observations of how decisions are made in the interest of uncovering the unique logic employed by the decision-maker in solving administrative and policy problems.

In this way Simon describes the manner by which the "logic" of a decision-maker may be perceived by others as lacking in logic, order of purpose. To illustrate his perspective, Simon presents the reader with a short "parable" of the ant that proceeds as follows:

> We watch an ant make his laborious way across a wind- and wave-molded beach. He moves ahead, angles to the right to ease his climb up a steep dunelet, detours around a pebble, stops for a moment to exchange information with a compatriot. Thus he makes his weaving, halting way back to his home. So as not to anthropomorphize about his purposes, I sketch the path on a piece of paper. It is a sequence of irregular, angular segments - not quite a random walk, for it has an underlying sense of direction, of aiming toward a goal." … "Whoever made the path, and in whatever space, why is not straight; why does it not aim directly from its starting point to its goal? In the case of the ant … we know the answer. He has a general sense of where home lies, but he cannot foresee all the obstacles between. He must adapt his course repeatedly to the difficulties he encounters and often detour un-crossable barriers. His horizons are very close, so that he deals with each obstacle as he comes to it; he probes for ways around or over it, without much thought for future obstacles. It is easy to trap him into deep detours." … "Viewed as a

geometric figure, the ant's path is irregular, complex, hard to describe. But its complexity is really a complexity in the surface of the beach, not a complexity in the ant. On that same beach another small creature with a home at the same place as the ant might well follow a very similar path. (Simon, 1969, p. 63f)

This story of the ant and its seemingly erratic meanderings could also describe the fashion with which humans negotiate James's proverbial stream of consciousness as each decision is tempered by the obstacles and opportunities constantly presenting themselves. The lesson to be learned is consistent and the same, namely, the seemingly illogic of one person's behavior can be logically and methodically perceived by another once the underlying method or pattern is understood. Simon's work sought to establish the underlying order in rational terms. However, today decision-makers understand that this underlying order is not so much experienced in rational terms as much as in intuitive ways. This intuitive way of knowing is not simply perceived individually, it is also a group phenomenon and a key component of understanding social ecology.

## Intuition and Social Ecology

Herbert Simon's satisficing approach to decision-making has sometimes been criticized for not accounting for the role of individual and group intuition. Cognizant of this criticism, Simon responded in 1987 with an article on intuition and emotion in decision-making and acknowledged that

> Because I used logic (drawing conclusions from premises) as a central metaphor to describe the decision-making process, many readers of *Administrative Behavior* have concluded that the theory advanced there applies only to "logical" decision-making, not to decisions that involve intuition and judgment. That was certainly not my intent. (Simon, 1987, p. 58)

Some 50 years after the publication of his most recognized book – *Administrative Behavior* – Simon's ideas were further influenced by a popular theory of that era concerning the functioning of the right- and left- quadrants of the brain – one predominantly qualitative and the other quantitative. This "left-right brain" theory suggested that the brain engages in two very different kinds of decision-making – one analytical and logical and the other "non-logical" which is to say creative and intuitive. While contemporary research has since debunked this theory (Nielsen et al., 2013), the once popular notion influenced Simon's decision-making model to the degree he construed rationality as extensively fact and data driven while intuitive knowing is extensively pattern driven – meaning that intuitive know is knowledge based upon recognizing patterns of relationships that are later codified into individual and group habitual behavior.

Arguably, based upon James' theory and much of the work of contemporary moral psychologists, intuitive knowing is indeed pattern driven. Management professor Michael A. Roberto employs this insight in his work suggesting that "intuition is fundamentally about pattern recognition and pattern matching based on our past experience" (Roberto, 2009, p. 12). Roberto bases this insight upon the research of psychologist Gary Klein (2013; 2002) who after reviewing a voluminous amount of research, some dating back to William James and his contemporaries, arrived at an understanding of how "intuition" and "insight" work together to make decision making effective.

Klein distinguishes between these two terms by describing intuition as the employment of learned patterns of behavior and thought while insight involves the discovery of new patterns of association (Klein, 2013, p. 26). Klein then added "connections" to the concepts of intuition and insight to describe how humans go through a seemingly unconscious process of connecting streams of associations to eventually arrive at an awareness that has sometimes been described as an "aha" experience (Bowden & Jung-Beeman, 2003). In fact Klein's understanding of mental connections dated back to a contemporary of William James – Graham Wallas – who's most influential work *The Art of Thought* (1926) best described this process by which seemingly unconsciously formed association suddenly become conscious and available for use. Consequently, on the basis of this body of thought and research, contemporary policy analysts and decision makers construe intuition as knowledge that becomes habitual (Rajkomar & Dhaliwal, 2011; Welch, 2007; Yu & Lai, 2005). In fact, Simon conceives of intuition and judgment as "analyses frozen into habit and into the capacity for rapid response through recognition" (Simon, 1987, p. 63).

Yet others understand intuition in a much different light perceiving it as "understanding without a rationale" or "knowing without knowing how one knows" (Rew & Barrow, 2007; Nyataga & Vocht, 2008). According to Tilman Betsch of the University of Erfurt,

> the output of intuition is a feeling, for instance, the feeling of liking an entity or a feeling of risk. Feelings are a powerful means of communication, not only between individuals (e.g., via facial expressions) but also within the organism. (Betsch, 2010)

Regardless of how intuition is conceptualized or construed it is widely regarded as the product of experiential knowledge acquired over time and compiled in long-term memory.

These long-term intuitive memories are not only maintained and utilized by individuals, they are likewise employed within groups and communities and are enshrined in culture, traditions, history, customs, institutions and "collective memory" (Olick, 2013). Often referred to as group or collective consciousness, this is a form of collective experience and awareness that is produced by experiential knowledge mediated by group awareness, membership, institutions and custom. The sociologist Emile Durkheim in *The Division of Labor in Society,* coined the term "collective consciousness" to describe the idea that "two consciousness's exist within us: the one comprises only states that are personal to each one of us, characteristic of us as individuals, whilst the other comprises states that are common to the whole of society" (Durkheim, 1893, p. 61).

When we consider social ecology, we are dealing with the shared and codified intuitive knowledge, experience and values of a community or culture that serves as the context or gestalt within which individual intuitive values are held and exercised. Of necessity, individual intuitions are held consistent with group and community-wide intuitive values. For instance, deep ecologists embrace a whole set of intuitive values regarding nature and economics that are peculiar to the values of other deep ecologists such that self-identify as a deep ecologist is more or less congruent with a like-minded group identity. Similarly, conservative ecologists embrace beliefs that are uniquely imbued with libertarian values such that their intuitive aversion to excessive governmental regulation in environmental affairs is consistent with the overall resistance to excessive found among the broader community of libertarians (Wimberley & Hobbes, 2013).

Social ecologies embrace an exceedingly wide variety of group values and perspectives such that the process of brokering complex environmental issues necessitates finding shared intuitive values across a number of key reference groups and institutions within the broader social ecological system. For instance, the deep ecologist might well belong to a church that includes libertarian-minded conservative ecologists in their membership and both of these church members – while sharing divergent ecological views – might, by virtue of their membership in the same church, share any number of theological values from among which they might find common ground and common cause to rethink their environmental values. Likewise, one might expect some degree of confluence among yet other community groups and institutions, if not familial or other shared friendship ties. These confluences of group affiliation and belonging are the foundations upon which social ecologists optimistically assert that ecologically sustainable values and practices can be forged since they are shared networks of belonging that ultimately transcend and enable group identity and belonging.

## Balancing Individual Freedom and Community Needs

What makes a communitarian approach to social ecology so useful is that it principally utilizes local institutions, organizations and groups to arrive at consensus regarding pressing issues rather than trying to arrive at a consensus by directly appealing to the interests of individuals. Earlier discussions of framing policy issues presuppose the presence of such community entities around which individuals coalesce and share values and beliefs. As noted before, while sometimes these various "identity groups" may prove useful in bridging policy disputes (as illustrated above), at other times identity group identification can lead to further balkanization and stalemate. However, when more functional connections are forged between groups – say around shared wants or needs or for that matter risks – then possibilities unfold for finding common ground and common cause through shared group and organization identification and affiliation.

Returning to the case in the preceding chapter involving the lumber mill owners in the Pacific Northwest, one can readily see the utility of such a communitarian approach to social ecology evidenced in the options available to independent mill owners to network with like-minded people in their communities with whom they share governance, business, economic, contracting and employment relationships. Likewise, since the mill owners are economically related to literally thousands of downstream retailers, wholesalers and customers, and upstream suppliers, they have significant opportunity to influence the policy process regarding their desire to acquire logs from federal lands by recasting their economic problem as likewise being an economic, product or service problem for others with whom they do business. Moreover, since there are numerous trade groups and associations with whom mill owners interact and share membership, these business and trade organizations also represent sources of shared values and concerns that may be employed to leverage the policy process. The key, however, is that to achieve these ends, individual mill owners must work with other timber mill owners in a concerted way as a group of impacted economic interests rather than as individuals.

The "social" in social ecology requires group effort and initiative over individual initiative and from a communitarian perspective couches timber policy issues not narrowly in terms of the economic and business needs of individual mills or for that matter of timber mills as an entity per se, but rather characterize their issues within the context of the community's welfare – which in this case relates to the very existence of many of the small communities throughout the Pacific Northwest who are to a significant degree economically dependent upon the business of the mill operators. So conceptualized, they can expand upon the economic and labor impacts of mill closings and also talk about such things as the loss of neighborhoods, sources for municipal and government support services, loos of culture and a way of life, displacement of families from their historical homes and the like. These are the ways through which a communitarian approaches to social ecology might be fruitfully pursued to achieve policy ends.

Even so, such an approach – while arguably necessary – is insufficient without clear-cut decision rules on what constitutes acceptable and achievable outcomes to the problem at hand – which in this case entails the economic viability of timber mills made possible by new access to logs to mill. This is where Simon's "satisficing" approach based upon bounded rationality can be useful. When applied in the mill owner's situation, it implies gathering together the interests impacted by the current export practices of timber companies and the regulatory practices of the state and federal government and achieving a consensus regarding what outcomes would be acceptable to as many parties as possible and identifying criteria around which those acceptable outcomes might be gauged and recognized. This process, while at face a rational endeavor is in fact driven by the passions, experiences, biases and perspectives of those most impacted by the current policy impasse. Their intuitive perspectives on the issue at hand will drive what options they pursue and which ones they will ultimately deem to be acceptable. Yet because their "satisficing" goals are a reflection of their shared intuitive perceptions, values and experiences, they will additionally be required to appeal to similar intuitions and values among those with whom they interact to seek resolution. These shared intuitions (as opposed to shared rationality) will be the common ground and the common cause they seek to achieve a suitable resolution. Unavoidably the potential solutions that present themselves will likely not be ideal and will be lacking to one degree or another. That said if the mill owners and their petitioning constituencies (i.e. those seeking a "satisficing" solution) are presented with an option that by one measure or another generally satisfies their criteria for a satisfactory outcome to the issue then they should be willing to accept the "available" or "workable" solution rather than persist in petitioning for an ideal one.

There is one final characteristic of communitarian approaches to socially ecological approaches to policy impasses that is worth mentioning. Such approaches seek to achieve local and whenever possible informal solutions to policy issues while minimally involving governmental or judicial institutions in the process. In other words, communitarian approaches to social ecology seek to reach informal solutions without having the issue necessarily becoming embroiled in legislative, legal or judicial proceedings. In searching for such solutions the intent is to the greatest degree possible to avoid needlessly creating ill-will among policy contestants and substitute shared benefits, shared costs and mutual benefit whenever possible. The net result of avoiding litigation and demonization of interests is that it allows the policy participants to engage one another again in the future as the need for other negotiations and collaborations may require. Moreover it implies pursuing negotiated settlements over laws and regulations.

# Chapter 8: Oil and Water—The Green Tea Coalition

You and I are like oil and water
And we've been trying, trying, trying
Ohhhhhhh... to mix it up.

*Oil and Water*
Incubus

## Imaginating and Communitarianism

Throughout the preceding chapters we have been talking about the importance of finding ways to "walk in another's shoes," "open communication," "re-frame perspectives," and "find common cause with others." In fact the book begins with an open lament that the current state of environmental affairs is one in which balkanization of perspectives has all but halted meaningful policy deliberation in many areas. In an effort to resolve these impasses in deliberation and cooperation we have endeavored to introduce an ecopragmatic approach that focuses upon how intuitive deliberative processes are employed to contrast, compare and integrate new experiences and ideas with what is already perceived as known, believed and true. This ecopragmatic approach which we call imaginating calls upon the decision maker to not only compare current experience with intuitive beliefs, values and knowledge, it also allows the decision-maker to "imagine" how a new or novel approach or action may become actualized to produce an outcome that may be valued or not – depending upon how the imaginator perceives the ultimate outcome playing out.

Yet, as Haidt's (2013) research has so clearly demonstrated, this intuitive process, while psychologically transpiring at the individual level, is in fact socially grounded within group identities and values that the imaginator deeply identifies with. Consequently, the sociological corollary to the psychological process of imaginating is communitarianism, which is to say the pursuit of Etzioni's "golden rule" where individual values, actions and aspirations are to a degree qualified by the need for group identification and belongingness and by the desire to pursue one's individual interests in a fashion that vouchsafes the social commitment to "respect and uphold society's moral order as you would have society respect and uphold your autonomy to live a full life" (Etzioni, 1997, p. 257). Thus individual aspirations and actions are tempered by communitarian expectations and by the unavoidable need to engage others in the pursuit of one's personal agenda. Put more simply, getting what you want as an individual requires working with others to realize their own goals and this process – if preformed with civility – of necessity requires compromise and the capacity to empathize with the needs and desires of others as well as a willingness to try to understand what motivates the desires of others.

If experience in the environmental arena is in any way a guide to what to expect regarding civil discourse, problem solving, accommodation and compromise pertinent to the pressing environmental issues of our day such as climate change, fisheries protection, desertification and sustainable food supplies (to name but a few), then expectations regarding the fruitful application of communitarianism should be significantly tempered if not dampened. Yet, even in the midst of such pessimistic expectations, surprising exceptions occur and none is more surprising or encouraging than the emergence of a coalition in Georgia between environmentalists in the Sierra Club and libertarians associated with the Tea Party known as The Green Tea Coalition.

## Oil and Water: The Green Tea Coalition

It is hard to imagine a more unlikely partnership than the one that has emerged in the State of Georgia between The Sierra Club and the Tea Party to support the expansion of solar energy for utility customers statewide. Thinking of these two groups working cooperatively is akin to imagining a successful admixture of oil and water. Perhaps no two substances are least suited to be in one another's presence than oil and water and by any reasonable measure they should never be expected to "mix" with one another as suggested in the tune "Oil and Water" by the musical group *Incubus*. Similarly, one would never expect the politically progressive Sierra Club to be in partnership with the libertarian minded Tea Party, yet in Georgia, the two groups have arrived at least some consensus despite the fact that on the vast majority of issues they fundamentally disagree. So, one might wonder, how did this fruitful cooperation occur?

The happenstance of how these two groups arrived upon an area for mutual cooperation is an illustration in the best sense of the word of how framing can be employed to resolve seemingly unresolvable policy disputes. Even so, what makes this particular partnership so very special is that they were able to 're-frame' one another's perspective on their own without benefit of an intermediary. Ultimately they did so because each became passionate (employing emotion) about an issue that spoke deeply to their most sacred values while simultaneously appealing to those groups with whom they most closely partner and identify with.

The issue that brought these two strange bedfellows together was access to affordable solar energy in the State of Georgia. Prior to their partnership access to such energy had proved problematic principally because of the resistance of the state's largest electric utility providers -Georgia Power and the Southern Company - who in part resisted the expansion of small-scale solar projects on customer's rooftops because the cumulative impact of such systems threatened their ability to compete with utility-scale solar energy projects. These electric utility providers, while supportive of expanding their own capacity for producing solar powered electricity, sought to limit the capacity of individual homeowners to independently generate solar-derived electricity and sell power they did not consume back to the utilities.

From an historical perspective, Georgia Power had regularly approached the state's Public Service Commission (PSC) over the years predictably asking for rate increases so as to offset the growing costs associated with operating their aging coal-powered electrical generating facilities. Environmental groups to include the Sierra Club, the Southern Alliance for Clean Energy, and the Solar Energy Industries Association had been regularly appealing to the PSC to deny these increases and force the utility to add solar energy to the state's energy resources. At the heart of their appeal was their concern regarding climate change and water and air pollution associated with the combustion of carbon fuels. In 2013 these environmental groups found a strange new supporter in their cause – namely the Georgia Tea Party – which was drawn to the issue on the basis of their libertarian-derived belief in the right of the consumer to "go off the grid" to whatever degree possible and not only reduce their dependence upon utility-provided electricity but additionally insure that consumers who purchased their own solar units would have the prerogative of selling power beyond that they used back to the utilities for fair rates and without being subjected to unreasonable fees or charges. Having found they shared similar desires though based upon differing premises, the two groups – environmentalists and Tea Party members – united to pursue their common concerns via the newly minted Green Tea Coalition.

Meanwhile, the PSC appeared resistant to approving utility-sized solar systems unless it could be demonstrated that these projects could be brought on line without needing to increase public utility rates. On July of 2013 Kevin Green, chief legal counsel for Georgia Power acknowledged before the commission that solar power projects within the state were demonstrating the capacity for increasing power generation in a cost-effective fashion without the need to increase power rates (Chance, 2013). Green was referring to the Georgia Power Advanced Solar Initiative (GPASI) - a solar energy purchase program adding 210 megawatts (MW) of solar capacity over a two year period - and the Large Scale Solar Initiative – another initiative of Georgia Power that entails buying up to 50 MW of additional solar power to be utilized in Georgia annually (Chance, 2013). Based upon this testimony and at the encouragement of both environmental and Tea Part supporters, the PSC approved the development of large-scale solar utilities in Georgia.

## Pertinent State Legislation

The 2013 PSC ruling served to extend the capacity for solar power in Georgia, a commitment building upon the solar capacity earlier achieved by the Georgia Cogeneration and Distributed Generation Act of 2001 (GCDGA 2001) which "provides compensation to customers for any power produced in excess of on-site needs or for all of the power generated from the [solar] system" (USEPA, 2008). Based upon the provisions of this legislation,

Utilities are required to purchase the excess power from an eligible customer generator until the cumulative renewable energy capacity reaches 0.2% of the utility's system peak load. Systems can be interconnected on the customer side of the meter and have a bi-directional meter to measure flows in each direction. In this scenario, net excess generation (NEG) is credited to the customer's next bill. Alternatively, customers may send all power from a system directly to the grid by connecting ahead of the customer meter and essentially selling all power (rather than meeting on-site load with part of the energy and then selling any excess generation). (USEPA, 2008)

The act also permits customers generating their own electricity to use that energy free from most other PSC regulation.

In 2012 and 2013 amendments were brought before the Georgia General Assembly to amend the GCDGA 2001 to "expand consumer choice and economic competition in power production and remove artificial barriers to renewable energy development" (Smith, 2012). In 2012 SB401 was introduced in an effort to "address a fundamental question of customer freedom to use renewable energy such as solar power, to produce and consume electricity on-site, regardless of whether a customer owns or leases/operates the property or utilizes other modern financing mechanisms such as Third Party Purchase Agreements (PPAs)" (Smith, 2012).

The bill met with stiff opposition from both Georgia Power and Southern Power, the other large public electric utility operating in Georgia. Their antagonism involved wanting to narrowly define the capacity of the consumer to sell back power to the utility by limiting such capacity to those who actually owned the solar unit outright. In this way they hoped to spare their companies from paying any additional fees to individual solar providers while increasing their monopoly over solar power generation in the state. The proposed amendments to the GCDGA under SB401 would have liberally broadened the language of the act redefining the term "customer generator" (those who in the original act were permitted to sell power back to the utilities) to include a private person such as "a customer who utilizes the electrical energy from a distributed generation facility, whether the customer finances the distributed generation facility by purchase, lease, loan, or other form of financing, including a power purchase agreement" (Georgia SB401, 2012). The bill also explicitly prohibited the assessment of unreasonable charges on the part of the utilities insisting that charges for metering the power generated by the solar units be "commercially reasonable" (Georgia SB401, 2012). Unfortunately for the bill's supporters, the Georgia General Assembly failed to enact the legislation. In 2013, the bill was reintroduced with virtually identical language as SB51. SB51 remains on the docket for the 2014 session of the Georgia General Assembly.

While it is unclear whether SB51 will finally be enacted, a related bill in the Georgia General Assembly may fair better due to its support by the Green Tea Coalition. HB657, The Rural Georgia Economic Recovery and Solar Resource Act of 2014, seeks to dramatically increase the number of households in the state that can "go solar." When introduced in 2013, only half of the state's households had the capacity to utilize solar power. However under the terms of this legislation the number of households utilizing solar-derived power could be dramatically expanded by developing new "solar farms."

As noted earlier in this discussion, the Georgia Public Service Commission is reluctant to approve any alternative energy project like solar unless it can be assured that there will be absolutely no upward pressure on electric rates. HB657 is designed to not only not decrease utility rates but to additionally create a new statewide solar provider who would sell power to the state's electric utilities that would ultimately be credited to the consumer's bill. Of course the key to this approach is for the solar provider to keep prices low compared to other energy resources so as to earn the consumer's loyalty by holding down solar energy costs while the cost of other fuel sources inevitably rise (Kidd et al., 2013).

The intent of the legislation is to break the effective monopoly that public utilities enjoy derived from the 1973 Georgia Territorial Electric Service Act, which shelters utilities from competition within their defined service areas (Grillo, 2013). This act, in the minds of many observers, is one of the single largest obstacles to the development of solar power in the state. It is also one of the principal legislative projects of Georgia's Green Tea Coalition since the bill only targets "customers that the solar industry can't do work for, namely, those that can't go solar while creating the opportunity for virtually any customer to voluntarily participate in the solar program or not as they see fit (Green Tea Coalition, 2013). As proposed, the program allows consumers to either voluntarily realize a degree of energy savings on their utility bill or opt-out of the program with the stroke of a pen on a program enrollment card. Consequently this bill presents a free market solution that does not restrict the rights homeowners, businesses, or Georgia Power and avoids imposing a customer mandate by promoting consumer choice thereby generating revenues to pay for customers that want to exercise their sovereign rights to be energy independent and install solar panels.

## Utility Scale Solar Energy and the Residential Solar Energy Producer: Costs

The benefits to be realized by consumers from producing and selling solar energy generated on their rooftops and in their back yards however must be considered within the context of the investment by Georgia's utility companies in large-scale solar plants. Arguably, corporate investments in large-scale solar energy must take into account the degree to which solar energy is also generated by private homeowners empowered to produce and sell energy. In fact a recent report by the Edison Electric Institute cites small-scale solar systems as the most significant threat confronting the nation's utilities (Shulman, 2013). From the perspective of the state utility companies homeowners producing solar power are competitors that cut into their "bottom line" and who compete with the utilities for profits. One way to combat this growing competition in solar production is to petition regulators to raise electric rates for residential customers installing solar panels on their property. These prospects in great part drew groups as disparate as the Sierra Club and the Tea Party together to advocate for the citizen/homeowner as well as business who may want to generate a portion of their energy needs with solar cells they own and maintain.

Beyond competitive market concerns between utility-scale and small-scale energy producers, another significant issue involves operational costs for utility-scale solar energy production. Central to this discussion is how long it takes a utility company to recoup its investment in solar facilities. According to recent cost-benefit calculations in Georgia, it would seem that assuming an average energy consumption of 1200 kilowatt-hours annually it would take a full six years for a solar panel to produce more energy than had been consumed in its construction. Likewise, the physical space required to produce large volumes of solar energy is significant and costly. Typically solar utility-scale systems necessitate 5 acres of space to generate a single megawatt of energy, meaning that 500 megawatts of energy production requires 25 acres of space. Moreover this level of production is further compromised depending upon the number of sunny days the state experiences annually. Seasonal variations in sunshine coupled with predictable declines after sundown also necessitates the ongoing operation of coal or natural gas driven plants or power from nuclear facilities which further drives up the cost of power generation (Rust, 2013).

## Solar Energy Waste Products

Toxic waste products involved in the production of solar panels is also of significant concern both for the producers of the panels and for consumers and citizens who ultimately pay the costs of disposing of these byproduct. As recently observed in report from the Rochester Institute of Technology (Goe, Tomazewski & Gaustad, 2013)

> One drawback of policies that expand renewable technology is they do not proactively consider how the waste produced by PV panels is managed once these panels reach the end of their life span. PV cells contain economically valuable materials, such as silver, indium, and gallium, and other materials, such as silicon and tellurium, that are extremely energy intensive to produce because they can require purities as high as 99.99999 percent. An additional concern with materials contained in PV cells is the potential for toxic metals, such as arsenic and cadmium, to leach into groundwater once these materials are in landfills. For these reasons, discarded PV panel materials that become part of the waste stream must be recycled.

Solar panel producers produce millions of pounds of polluted sludge and wastewater (containing silicon tetrachloride, cadmium, selenium and sulfur hexafluoride to name but a few) annually and these contaminates must be transported over considerable distances to disposal sites (Dearen, 2013, Gies, 2013). Consequently calculating the true costs of solar energy for the purpose of realizing a return on economic investment and in the interest of arriving at sustainable utility rates requires considering both the energy costs entailed in disposing of these wastes as well as the energy costs associated with waste transport.

The extent of the problem of solar waste can be best exemplified in the State of California where some 46 million pounds of solar waste has been produced between 2007 and mid-2011 of which 97% has been kept in California and 1.4 million pounds exported to other states (with Montana, Nevada and Arkansas receiving approximately 1 million pounds of solar waste) (Dearen, 2013). In California concerns over waste products associated with the production and disposal of solar panels goes back to 2009 and a report by the Silicon Valley Toxics Coalition entitled "Toward a Just and Sustainable Solar Energy Industry" (SVTC, 2009).

According to their report the manufacture of solar cells results in a number of troublesome pollutants of which only a few can be effectively captured for recycling or disposal. For instance, the production of silicon wafers used to actually generate energy within a solar cell creates silica ($SiO_2$) dust that is mostly absorbed into the air. Similarly, some degree of hydrochloric acid – utilized to create metallurgical grade silicon – can also be absorbed into the air. Solar cell production also produces trichlorosilane ($HSiCl_3$) that is chemically converted to silane gas. Silane gas is an extremely hazardous substance given its explosiveness, meaning that accidental releases of this gas can result in significant explosions. The process of producing silane gas results in the creation of silicone tetrachloride ($SiCl_4$) that ultimately ends up in wastewater. Other toxic byproducts noted in the SVTC report include sulfur hexafluoride ($SF_6$) used to clean the reactors utilized in the production of silicon. Sulfur hexafluoride can chemically interact with silicon to produce silicon tetrafluoride ($SiF_4$) and sulfur difluoride ($SF_2$) or can be further reduced to tetrafluorosilane ($SiF_4$) and sulfur dioxide ($SO_2$). All of these agents are toxic and atmospheric $SO_2$ releases can produce acid rain.

SVTC further cautions regarding the dangers of fugitive air emissions involving trichloroethane, acetone, ammonia, and isopropyl alcohol. The SVTC report cites a truly extensive number of other of toxic substances that require treatment or disposal. These include sodium hydroxide, lead, hexavalent chromium, potassium hydroxide, sulfuric acid, nitric acid, hydrogen fluoride, phosphine, arsine, copper indium selenide, copper indium gallium selenide, phosphorous oxychloride, phosphorous trichloride, gallium arsenide, boron bromide, cadmium telluride and boron trichloride (SVTC, 2009, p. 10-14).

Unfortunately these are not the only hazardous substances associated with producing solar panels. For instance, solar panels consist of multicrystalline silicon wafers. Producing these wafers entails utilizing one of a number of other toxic substances to include "ammonia, copper catalyst, diborane, ethyl acetate, ethyl vinyl acetate, hydrogen, hydrogen peroxide, ion amine catalyst, nitrogen, silicon trioxide, stannic chloride, tantalum pentoxide, titanium, and titanium dioxide" (SVTC, 2009, p. 12).

In the interest of cleaning up the solar industry SVTC proffered the following set of regulations:

- Phase out use of chemicals already restricted by the E.U.'s Restriction of Hazardous Substances (RoHS).
- Develop chlorine-free methods for making polysilicon feedstock that eliminate the use of trichlorosilane.
- Phase out use of sulfur hexafluoride ($SF_6$).
- Phase out use of hydrogen selenide.

- Phase out use of arsenic.
- Phase out phosphine and arsine.
- Reduce fugitive air emissions from facilities (SCTV, 2009, p. 27).

The SVTC report likewise makes some suggestions regarding how recycling of solar materials can be improved to include: (SVTC, 2009, p. 29).

- Investing in recycling infrastructure
- Designing solar panels for recycling.
- Recycling silicon recovered from consumer electronics products.
- Developing additional recycling processes for all rare metals.

To date these suggestions have been mostly disregarded and solar panel production facilities continue to produce a significant amount of waste that is being stored in waste sites across the nation.

Issues associated with managing solar energy waste products dramatically grow as the U.S. use of solar energy explosively increases from approximately 14 GW of power in the first quarter of 2010 to 64 GW in third quarter of 2012 (Energy Manager Today, 2012). What this means is that increasingly the costs associated with controlling solar panel production pollution will increase as will the costs associated with treating and disposing of waste byproducts and discarded solar panels. Ultimately these costs are incorporated into the prices consumers pay to satisfy their energy needs.

## Solar Power in Georgia: Disposal, Treatment and Recycling Considerations

To date the Georgia Public Service Commission has been principally concerned with the rates public utilities charge citizens, the development and siting of new energy facilities and the costs associated with these facilities that will be passed on to Georgia consumers. However, in the future this commission will have to also consider environmental costs associated with solar energy production and consider costs for waste treatment, disposal and recycling in arriving at electric utility rates. This kind of cost-accounting is new to the U.S. energy industry and certainly new to officials, utilities and consumers in Georgia. Nevertheless these cost considerations of necessity will become increasingly common and will ultimately increase the cost of energy use.

Currently, Georgia has only one producer of solar panels in the state – Suniva Inc. located in Norcross, Georgia (Suniva, 2013). Suniva is the leading solar panel producer in the U.S. and they assert that their production process "creates zero "sludge" and zero "contaminated water" (Shea, 2013). Suniva claims their monocrystaline solar modules can be produced using 88% recycled glass and 85% of solar cell material using 55% less wastewater, recycling 100% of silicon wafer scrap and utilizing 60% less raw material input than their competitors (Coker, 2010).

According to USEPA data Suniva's air pollution emissions increased from 45 pounds annually in 2009 to 295 pounds in 2011 while off-site transfers of pollutants increased from 35 to 171 pounds over the same period with total pollution releases and transfers increasing from 80 to 466 pounds over the period. Of these pollutants 295 pounds of hydrogen fluoride were released into the atmosphere and 171 pounds of lead was shipped off-site (USEPA, 2012). This is a remarkably small quantity of waste production, especially when considering that the total production related waste – i.e. the sum of recycled on-site, recycled off-site, energy recovery on-site, energy recovery off-site, treated on-site, treated off-site and quantities disposed of or otherwise released on- and off-site – totaled 39,371 pounds in 2011 (USEPA, 2012). Suniva is actively involved in developing a number of solar projects across Georgia but they are not the only supplier from which consumers purchase solar panels.

Solar panels can also be purchased by Georgia homeowners from manufacturers worldwide and the quality and environmental standards involved in manufacturing these panels can vary significantly with many failing to meet the quality and environmental standards boasted by Suniva. Such panels imported worldwide are those which are most likely to be found on the homes and in the backyards of consumers across Georgia to include solar panels principally manufactured in China, such as CanadianSolar, ReneSola, Hanwha Solar One, Sharp, ET Solar, Yingli Solar, Solarland, Suntech and Talesun as well as by U.S. manufacturers like Suniva, SunEdison, SolarWorld, REC Solar and Kyocera. Solar panels manufactured in the US are regulated by the USEPA while panels manufactured in China and other Asian countries are not environmentally regulated as strictly as in the U.S. or Europe. Consequently toxic wastes associated with solar panels produced in China are a much bigger environmental problem in Asia than in Europe or the U.S. (Nath, 2010).

Admittedly, environmental pollution realized in the production of solar panels in Asia doesn't immediately impact utility consumers in Georgia since that pollution has been externalized out of state and out of the U.S. However, when it comes to disposing of spent solar panels, the costs of recycling and disposal applies to all domestic consumers. With the number of Georgians purchasing solar panels increasing and with public utilities increasing the sizes of their solar operations inevitably significant costs for managing solar waste from spent panels will increase and be passed on to the consumer.

Silicon based solar panels have a functional life of about 25-30 years before they are discarded. The glass and aluminum in the cells can be immediately recycled. In some cases the silicon wafers in the panels can be refurbished. In fact about 90% of the content of a solar panel can be recycled. European nations have been steadily increasing the rate at which they recycle used solar panels led by the efforts of PV Recycle (PV Cycle, 2013). In the U.S. it is estimated that recycling solar panels should prove to be a very lucrative business generating approximately $12 billion by 2035 (Energy Matters, 2012).

In Georgia a new technology developed at Georgia Tech University may one day further improve the environmental safety of solar panels by constructing them with solar cells developed from trees (Cameron, 2013). However at the moment there are no solar panel recycling facilities available in Georgia and the organic cells being developed by Georgia Tech are not readily available on the market. Clearly if solar power is to be expanded in Georgia it will be accomplished through the use of silicon-based panels manufactured domestically and abroad. At some point these panels will become spent and will require disposal and recycling. Clearly, thought needs to be given now to planning for facilities to collect and recycle panels currently being sold and utilized in the state by public utilities and private citizens.

Recent reports on issues associated with defective solar panels manufactured abroad and sold in the U.S. may serve to accelerate public concern regarding the recycling and disposal of spent solar panels. For instance, in the Los Angeles area accounts of defective solar panels marketed with a 25-year warranty but have ceased functioning after only two years have grown in number. This story, reported in the New York Times (Woody, 2013), presents anecdotal accounts of problems that appear to be pervasive throughout the central region of California. Similar issues have been reported in Florida (Johnson, 2013) However in the absence of any well documented study or survey of how solar panels are performing across the rest of the nation and internationally it is hard to know the extent to which plans for solar panel recycling and disposal need to be prioritized.

Indicative of the extent of the problem is a recent audit done by a Massachusetts procurement and quality assurance company, SolarBuryer, of Chinese solar panel factories. SolarBuyer discovered "defect rates of 5.5 percent to 22 percent during audits of 50 Chinese factories" over an 18-month period (Olen, 2013). SolarBuyer's audit, directed by company founders Ian Gregory and Peter Rusch, was based upon their extensive experience with solar panel manufacturing in which they had found "poor quality modules to be so prevalent, we needed to provide buyers with solutions" (Trabish, 2013). In fact up to 17% of solar panels procured from Chinese plants could be conceivably faulty and without a company such as SolarBuyer auditing plants manufacturing these units, the consumer might not be aware for their panel's defects until sometimes years after installation (Trabish, 2013).

Given the experience of SolarBuyer and its clients, it is reasonable to expect that a significant number of solar panels – not just those manufactured in China, but also in Australia, Germany, the U.S. and elsewhere (IER, 2013) – can be expected to cease functioning on a timescale much shorter than the 25-30 year period currently anticipated of newly manufactured panels. This reality puts pressure upon states embracing the expanded utilization of solar panels such as Georgia to begin the process of anticipating the costs associated with recycling and disposing of solar panels manufactured today. These costs of necessity must be considered in expanding solar energy utilization in the state.

## The Adequacy of Georgia's Electric Grid System

A final issue to be considered in expanding Georgia's solar energy capacity is the adequacy of the state and regional power grid to manage intermittent energy sources such as those generated by solar panels. The current electrical grid that was designed for steady-rates of electric generation fueled by coal, diesel and natural gas plants. The introduction of green energy sources from wind and solar produces variable and intermittent rates of power generation that can overwhelm the conduction capacity of the grid when both steady-stream or continuous power are being transmitted simultaneously. Accordingly, managing the flow of power can become problematic when the grid must absorb home-generated solar energy while steadily transmitting utility-based power, particularly when solar-generated power fluctuates such as when cloudy days produce a net draw on the grid, whereas very sunny days may produce a troublesome power surge (Palmer, 2013). Consequently, utility companies are increasingly called upon to develop every more complex synchronization systems to insure the grid is not overloaded producing state and regional power failures (Cardwell, 2013).

The development and maintenance of these systems is costly and is complicated by the reality that alternative sources of energy generated off-grid by homeowners and other energy interests serve to undercut the revenue structure of public utilities while often imposing new costs upon them – such as more sophisticated power synchronization technologies. Concern in this regard has been recently fueled by a report by Peter Kind on behalf of the Edison Electric Institute (EEI) entitled "Disruptive Challenges: Financial Implications and Strategic Responses to a Changing Retail Electric Business" (Kind, 2013). What EEI is concerned about is how the growth of decentralized solar and other renewable energy resources threatens the ability of large energy utilities to maintain the electrical grid that everyone relies upon to transport power from one location to another. According to the EEI report:

> Today, a variety of disruptive technologies are emerging that may compete with utility-provided services. Such technologies include solar photovoltaics (PV), battery storage, fuel cells, geothermal energy systems, wind, micro turbines, and electric vehicle (EV) enhanced storage. As the cost curve for these technologies improves, they could directly threaten the centralized utility model. To promote the growth of these technologies in the near-term, policymakers have sought to encourage disruptive competing energy sources through various subsidy programs, such as tax incentives, renewable portfolio standards, and net metering where the pricing structure of utility services allows customers to engage in the use of new technologies, while shifting costs/lost revenues to remaining non-participating customers. In addition, energy efficiency and DSM programs also promote reduced utility revenues while causing the utility to incur implementation costs. (Kind, 2013, p. 3)

Ultimately, it is feared that with the spread or new energy technologies such as the widespread use of solar cells that consumers will reduce their use of utility-generated power forcing utilities to raise their rates which will disproportionately impact users who aren't participating in these new energy technologies. Ultimately, the EEI report concludes that,

> The threat to the centralized utility service model is likely to come from new technologies or customer behavioral changes that reduce load. Any recovery paradigms that force cost of service to be spread over fewer units of sales (i.e., kilowatt-hours or kWh) enhance the ongoing competitive threat of disruptive alternatives. (Kind, 2013, p. 3)

Illustrative of the technology concerns voiced by EEI are the developments occurring at the home-owned solar panel level where technological innovations are making it possible for consumers to use less electricity from the grid while selling power back to the grid as well as being able to go completely off-grid for extended periods of time. For instance, each home-based solar panel employs a grid-tied inverter that converts direct current (DC) into a grid system based upon alternating current (AC). This inverter assists in protecting the solar panel from surges from the grid, while allowing for reduced grid usage and the transmission of excess power into the grid system. However a problem encountered by many homeowners using a grid-tied inverter is that when the power grid is down for whatever reason, consumers are unable to use the energy being provided by their solar panel. In particular this issue involves net-metered solar energy systems that do not include battery back-up.

Unfortunately the majority of the approximately 300,000 solar systems employed in homes across the U.S. are net-metered and lack batteries – meaning that when the grid is down the functionality of the solar panels is completely lost (IEC, 2014). However, by employing battery back-up systems and employing technology that "islands" the solar generating system such that its power is segregated from the incoming power on the electric grid, consumers are increasingly able to function comfortably both on and off the electrical grid (Wilson, 2013). In this way these "decentralized" electric producers are reducing their reliance on the electrical grid, thereby reducing demand for these energy resources while foisting upon the public utilities the complex and costly problem of synchronizing a grid system being fed by "predictable" utility-based providers and comparatively "variable" decentralized energy providers. While decentralized home solar energy production is of great concern to the viability of the electric industry, some providers are innovatively developing new ways of producing solar energy on a utility-based scale and doing so in a manner that makes that energy easier to synchronize into the electric grid.

For instance, consider the case of the Ivanpah Solar Plant in Ivanpah Dry Lake, California. According to officials at the plant solar energy is now being fed into the Pacific Gas and Electric grid (PG&E) by way of a synchronization system that is built around a large array of mirrors situated in the California desert aimed at a central tower that continuously and uniformly captures solar energy used to power a steam turbine that produces electricity in essentially the same way any conventionally fueled generator would. Accordingly this steady source of energy throughout most of the daylight allows the Ivanpah plant to function in a manner similar to other non-solar facilities (Oswana, 2013). This 392 megawatt facility is a joint venture between developer BrightSource Energy, project owners NRG Energy, BrightSource Energy and Google and the contractor Bechtel Engineering.

Ventures like the one at Ivanpah and the willingness of investors to back such projects suggest that the livelihoods of electric utilities are not going to disappear from the scene and can be expected to provide the bulk of the nation's electric energy over the foreseeable future. However, that said, there is no doubt that the advent of home energy production via solar technology will allow consumers to economize in their energy use and place a smaller demand upon utilities, compelling these large corporate entities to refashion their rate structure, refashion how they produce and transport electricity and reformulate how they manage the electric grid in a manner that insures sustainable power while doing so within a cost / reimbursement structure that the utilities and their customers can financially sustain.

These are the issues that Georgia Power and any other electrical utility operating within the State of Georgia will have to consider in light of the Georgia Public Service Commission's decision to encourage and facilitate the ease with which Georgia consumers can employ solar panels in their homes, businesses and properties. Allowing more players in the electric industry produces more and cleaner power while increasing the autonomy of the consumer. However it does so at a price and that price involves a degree of destabilization of the state's utilities, a marginal increase in energy costs for customers who are not using solar panels, and additional grid management costs for the state's electric utilities as a result of the changing nature of the electricity being transmitted across the grid (i.e. intermediately generated power versus stead electric generation).

## Environmental Communitarianism at Work

Given the plethora of issues to be addressed in expanding solar energy in Georgia, it is noteworthy that the Public Service Commission finally agreed to pursue a course of action that empowers consumers to both conserve energy and produce power that can be re-directed back into the electric grid. There is no doubt, however, that the Georgia Public Service Commission's decision to make solar energy more available to consumers is in great part the result of the influence of Georgia's Green Tea Coalition. The Green-Tea Coalition is a wonderful example of environmental communitarianism at work as two very philosophically disparate groups – the progressive Sierra Club and the libertarian-leaning Tea Party – came together around seemingly vastly different intuitive values to accomplish a common goal: the expansion of solar energy in Georgia.

While their intuitive reasons for entering into an agreement with one another (environmental protection versus entrepreneurism and consumer choice in the production of solar energy) emanated from very different sources their shared vision of expanded solar energy via homeowner and public utility owned solar generation made it possible for them to agree to disagree on any number of other policy issues in the interest of coming together to promote outcomes they both favored. This is classic environmental communitarianism as predictably heterogeneous intuitive group values ultimately coalesce to promote homogeneous community outcomes.

However, as valuable and functional as these partnerships can be they require ongoing compromise and the willingness to accept satisficing outcomes rather than ideal ones. Such partnerships also require that each party refrain from demonizing their ideological opponent/partner in recognition of the need to be able to negotiate future issues as they arise. Finally, partnerships such as that illustrated by the Green-Tea Coalition must commit themselves to ever-expanding their boundaries to include others into their midst recognizing that the broader the range of constituencies incorporated within their group the greater degree to which the realm of conceivable and acceptable policy options expands and the greater the probability of arriving at outcomes that are both considered to be feasible and which enjoy community support.

In the case of the Green-Tea Coalition we see a group that has already successfully formed and been influential in the solar energy policy process in the State of Georgia. Yet as the case narrative illustrates, winning support from the public utility commission and the state legislature to expand solar power only sets the stage for creatively dealing with a whole host of other related policy issues such as the appropriate level of financial benefits homeowners should receive for producing solar power, how public utilities will be regulated and paid in terms of their share of solar energy production, what are reasonable solar energy rates for Georgia consumers, how quality control will be introduced in terms of the quality and safety of solar panels sold and manufactured in Georgia and how solar wastes will be dealt with both in the production of solar panels and in the recycling and disposal of spent solar panels. Unavoidably, coalitions such as the one between the Tea Party and The Sierra Club necessitate the creation of ever-broader coalitions encompassing stakeholders involved in the evolving issue at hand – which in this case involves producing more solar power in Georgia and reducing the state's reliance upon fossil fuels.

Clearly there are other constituencies that will need to be brought into the policy debate (or debates) in Georgia regarding solar energy. If the quality and safety of products is an issue then retailers, installers and suppliers will have to be drawn into the conversation regarding issues such as product safety, safe installation, product upgrading and recycling of spent panels, etc. The governor and the state assembly will also have to be included in the policy process as demand increases for the licensed and certified solar-panel technicians, as the accumulation of spent panels increases demand for waste disposal and product recycling and as public-safety and fire fighters cope with extinguishing fires and rescuing victims from burning or damaged homes with potentially lethal solar panels (Wong, 2014; Trabish, 2013; Riggs, 2013).

Nor are these the only issues flowing from the decision to expand the use of solar energy in Georgia. As demand for solar energy increases so will the growth of companies producing solar panels – either in terms of silicon-based panels or at some point in terms of organically engineered solar panels. With the growth of these companies comes demand not only for more workers but also for workers with the requisite education and skills to function in the solar energy. Thus public school district, community colleges and universities will find their niche in the solar market. Likewise as solar panels are produced and shipped to customers state- and nationwide as well as abroad, issues of quality assurance and safety will increasingly emerge as well as issues involving the appropriate levels of tax-levy versus tax-credit should be applied to these products.

While solar energy use is on the upswing in Georgia, it is not the only state to also be moving in this direction. Western and sun-belt states nationwide are also embracing solar power and are expanding their utility-based solar capacity as well as expanding the use of homeowner solar panels. This means that increasingly solar-produced energy will cross state lines meaning that the Congress of the United States, the federal court system and agencies within the federal executive branch will also become involved in the growth of solar power visa vi the interstate commerce clause in the U.S. Constitution. Consequently state-based coalitions such as the Green-Tea Coalition will also have to contend with federal regulators, the Congress and the courts in tailoring solar policy issues to best serve local communities.

That said, a communitarian approach to environmental policy starts at the local level and expands ever outward. While it is true that international, national and interstate concerns will impact states and local communities seeking to fashion their energy policies and practices, ultimately the creation and utilization of solar energy will happen locally and not nationally. Communitarian approaches to energy policy seek to achieve local ends despite national and international constraints and just as "all politics is local" (Oneil & Hymel, 1995) so is all public policy. Policy actions occur locally despite the origin of the policies themselves.

As the efforts of the Green-Tea Coalition continues to unfold in Georgia, so will the array of solar-energy related issues that will present themselves (such as product safety, installation regulation, waste-disposal, solar related employment, training and education, economic development, etc.) as will the number of policy participants that representatives of the Sierra Club and The Tea Party will have to contend and work with. Also expanding is the number of venues within which the Green-Tea Coalition will seek influence. Of necessity the range of venues within which the Coalition will pursue policy outcomes will significantly expand beyond the Georgia Public Service Commission to the General Assembly (where all new state laws and policies will emanate), the Georgia Secretary of State's office (where corporations are formed and regulated and where professional licensure and certification occurs), the Georgia Department of Community Affairs (that oversees housing and community development and provides local government assistance including waste disposal, state and regional planning and economic development), the Georgia Department of Labor (where the solar-energy workforce will be drawn), the Georgia Office of Insurance and Safety Fire Officer (where issues of public safety and insurability are administered particularly in regard to fire safety), the Georgia Department of Education (where education and training for a solar-energy workforce will occur), and the Georgia Department of Economic Development (which concerns itself with all forms of economic development in the state to include business investing in energy resources as well as marketing Georgia-made products to the nation and world).

Conceivably the Georgia Department of Agriculture, and the Georgia Forestry Commission may also become of interest to the Green-Tea Coalition as utility-scale solar energy farms expand into agricultural and forested areas of the state as well as in regard to the emergence of organically produced plastic polymer solar cell energy along the lines of that being developed at the Georgia Institute of Technology (Hicks, 2012). Similarly, the Georgia Department of Natural Resources (GADNR) may likely become involved in regard to waste treatment, recycling and disposal activities involved with either the production of solar panels or their eventual disposal. These activities will be specifically a function of the Environmental Protection Division of GADNR but will also involve the U.S Environmental Protection Agency (USEPA).

In summary, the Green-Tea Coalition is a successful partnership between divergent interest groups to accomplish shared goals. To date it has proved itself to be a substantive force in Georgia energy politics and its continued successes will guarantee that it becomes more involved in policy issues relating to solar-energy that will necessitate interaction with a growing number of agencies and community groups. While current leadership is drawn from the Sierra Club and the Tea Party its continued influence and success will require it to team with a growing number of public interests and organizations to realize success. It will pursue its interests in a growing array of policy venues, will seek to influence the policy and political process with the support of a growing array of other interest groups and as a result will inevitably begin to widen its scope of values and policy possibilities to reflect the pragmatic forces that make policy changes possible and sometimes thwart them.

# Chapter 9: Going Home—From Olmsted to the Carolina Thread Trail

Country roads, take me home,
To the place I belong.

*Take Me Home Country Roads*
John Denver

## On Being Unwittingly Pragmatic

In this the final chapter of *Ecopragmatics*, we would like to pull together many the ideas associated with William James and what we call imagining. To that end we have identified a case study where the principles of imagining were unwittingly but effectively employed – especially in regard to framing and reframing issues and problems, satisficing in decision-making, and approaching issues from a distinctly communitarian perspective. The case study we just completed is also a good example of how pragmatics, common sense and community purpose can be served by the joint contributions of very different groups such as those reflected in the Green Tea Coalition of Georgia. Even so, we were not able to gain personal access to the individual stakeholders and players that were a part of the Green Tea Coalition, which meant that much of the nuance and the "back story" of the case laid beyond our ability to explore and access.

Luckily, In the neighboring state of North Carolina we found yet another remarkable case unfolding that is driven by the cooperation of a really diverse group of stakeholders representing environmentalists, businesses, local and state governments, non-profits and regular citizens. In this instance we were able to gain direct access to many of the stakeholders and participants involved in the case, conduct a number of interviews and access personal files and correspondence. Given this more extensive and in-depth access, we were able to develop the case study in a way that allowed us to learn much more about the history, development and processes of the case, as well as having the opportunity for those key informants to review our preliminary take on their history and development and help us fill in gaps in the story and correct misinterpreted facts and history.

This fascinating case involves the deep-seated interest among a large number of community leaders and interest to push back against the seemingly endless march of urbanization by linking communities to nature and to one another with a set of trails and greenways that bring nature into communities and communities into nature. What follows is the story of the Carolina Thread Trail encompassing a web of trails and greenways traversing a 15 county regions spanning two states. We describe how this greenway system came into being and analyze the processes that created the trail and sustain it today. This case study provides a marvelous illustration of how difficult environmental and social concerns and issues can be fruitfully addressed by a large number of interested parties and how environmental policymaking can be conducted locally to realize a regional, state, and interstate region.

## A Tradition of Greenways

For the purposes of this narrative we define greenways as: "networks of land that are planned, designed and managed for multiple purposes including ecological, recreational, cultural, aesthetic, or other purposes compatible with the concept of sustainable land use (Ahern, 1996, p. 131). Greenways have long been employed in Europe and more recently in the U.S. as examples of cultural landscape designed to create and maintain protected lands within urban regions. Moreover, greenways have historically served the purpose of making people and communities feel at home amidst nature. They are the modern extensions of the historical development of city and regional parks and park systems dating in the U.S. back to the work of Frederick Park Olmsted (Martin, 2012, Olmsted, 1852) and in Europe to the "garden cities" of Ebenezer Howard (Howard, 1898). The term "greenway," dates back to the 1930's when the Greater London Regional Planning Committee proposed the Metropolitan Green Belt around London and coined the term by combines the "parkway" or carriage trails and "greenbelt" denoting an area usually surrounding urban areas where further urban growth is resisted (Amati & Yokahari, 2007). In Britain the greenway concept is principally associated with the work of Ebenezer Howard – an urban designer and landscaper who designed "garden cities" in which urban areas of human habitation and commerce were separated by a series of greenways to insure that the stress of urban living would be reduced by providing citizens ready access to pastoral natural environments (Howard, 1898).

The "greenway" concept was first introduced in the U.S. by William Whyte in *Securing Open spaces for Urban America* (White, 1959) where he identified five different greenbelt formats (Little, 1990) to include urban riverside or waterfront greenways, recreational greenways, ecological corridors, scenic and historic routes and a comprehensive greenway system or network. Since then greenways have proliferated across the American landscape spurred in part by the National Trail System Act of 1968 and expanded on the basis of countless state legislative acts and administrative provisions as well as by the concerted efforts of local government, environmental organizations and community foundations and sponsors nationwide. Presently, the National Trails System alone encompasses 30 separate national trails spans every state and exceeds 53,599 miles. Meanwhile the number and extent of state, regional and local trails defies ready estimation (U.S. National Park System, 2014).

Researchers who have investigated the utility of greenways have concluded these corridors connecting urban and surrounding regions are employed principally because they achieve the following objectives:

- *Spatial efficiency* by providing egress to corridors where environmental resources are concentrated thereby serving to protect the greatest proportion of these resources while utilizing very little land area,
- *Attract political support* and consensus providing mutual benefits to a variety of community interests such as enhancing biodiversity, clean water, recreational opportunity and economic development;
- *Contribute to regional connectivity* ecologically, physically and culturally. (Ahern, 2004 p. 37)

Beyond these benefits, trails and greenways produce an economic benefit to the regions they traverse.

According to a study conducted by the U.S. National Park Service (1995) the nation's trails and greenways have produced a number of local economic benefits to include: helping local governments and other public agencies reduce long term costs for services such as roads and sewers, reduce risks associated with hazards such as flooding; and avoid potential costly damages to natural resources such as water and fisheries (U.S. National Park Service, 1995, p. VI). Moreover trails have been demonstrated to achieve a number of other valuable economic benefits to communities to include improving property values, stimulating local economies and businesses, encouraging tourism, attracting corporate relocations, reducing public expenditures relating to pollution and environmental damage, and by promoting the intrinsic natural and community values and assets of communities (Table 21): (U.S. National Park Service, 1995; Wagner, 2013)

Table 21: Trail-Related Economic Benefits to Communities

| | |
|---|---|
| **Real Property Values** | Studies demonstrate that parks, greenways and trails increase nearby property values. In turn, increased property values can increase local tax revenues and help offset greenway acquisition costs. |
| **Support Local Businesses and Economies** | Spending by local residents on greenway related activities helps support recreation oriented businesses and employment, as well as other businesses that are patronized by greenway and trail users. |
| **Tourism** | Greenways are often major tourist attractions that generate expenditures on lodging, food, and recreation oriented services. Greenways also help improve the overall appeal of a community to perspective tourists and new residents. |
| **Corporate Relocation** | Evidence shows that the quality of life or a community is an increasingly important factor in corporate relocation decisions. Greenways are often cited as important contributors to quality of life. |

| Pubic Cost Reduction | The conservation of rivers, trails, and greenways can help local governments and other public agencies reduce costs resulting from flooding and other hazards. |
|---|---|
| Intrinsic Value | While greenways have many economic benefits it is important to remember the intrinsic environmental and recreation value of preserving rivers, trails and other open spaces corridors. |

## Regional Stewardship and the Carolina Thread Trail

It is against this historical backdrop of greenways in America that the Carolina Thread Trail was conceived and developed in and around the Charlotte / Mecklenburg County North Carolina region. Occurring as it did in the midst of one of the fastest growing urban regions in the country, the Carolina Thread Trail or "Thread" initiative served to not only reclaim, preserve and recreate much of the region's green spaces, it also served the purpose (among many others) of providing a respite for the inhabitants of the region from the hustle and bustle of urban life, allowing them to return to a simpler and more nature-imbued lifestyle - very much like "going home" as described in John Denver's popular anthem *"Take Me Home Country Roads"* that celebrated similar habitat in the Blue Ridge Mountains of neighboring West Virginia. Consequently the impetus to developing the Carolina Thread trail was at once environmentally, aesthetically, economically, socially and health oriented.

The fact this initiative took form within the Charlotte area is a remarkable achievement but the manner in which it happened is even more noteworthy, not simply as a testament to the commitment of those who conceived it, planned it and brought it to fruition but additionally as a guide to other communities interested in pursuing similar initiatives. Perhaps one of the lasting legacies of the Carolina Thread Trail is the manner in which divergent interests and constituencies were brought together to realize a variety of objectives within this single community environmental and economic development project.

Tracing the origins of the Carolina Thread Trail inescapably entails considering the efforts of the Alliance for Regional Stewardship and their influential 2000 report "Regional Stewardship: A Commitment to Place" (Henton et al., 2000). This report would ultimately prove to be very influential nationwide and particularly in North Carolina where it would motivate what the report referred to as "the responsibles" across the region to take matters into their own hands in the interest of:

- Developing strategies to enhance the quality of community life across Carolina,
- Pursuing a variety of initiatives to promote a "sense of place" by restoring and maintaining natural environs,
- Providing access to natural areas for recreation,
- Facilitating community egress,
- Promoting an aesthetic appreciation of natural habitats and their inhabitants and

- Connecting environs that would otherwise have been disparate and disconnected.

At the heart of these efforts and initiatives are "the responsibles" - those who the report describes as coming from "all walks of life including neighborhood leaders, housewives, professionals, executives, educators, union members and other citizens" (Henton et al., 2000, p. 1).

Such "responsibles" are typically known to virtually everyone in the community and in earlier times may have been referred to as affluent members of an "establishment" elite who largely assume responsibility for community affairs. However, these contemporary leaders are more diverse in background and interests than was the case in earlier times while sharing a joint commitment to pursuing the not so glamorous task of maintaining and improving the quality of civic life in their communities. Although historically community leaders have been recognized for their efforts in local communities the "responsibles" drawn to regional stewardship are motivated in part by their inability to solve many problems locally as well as by the realization that regional cooperative efforts can often prove more sustainable and effective than would be the case if each community acted independently. Indeed at the heart of the pursuit of regional solutions to community problems is the recognition that as communities grow – particularly in regard to the urban/suburban sprawl surrounding many large cities – communities and natural resources become fragmented and disjointed.

According to the 2000 Report of the Alliance for Regional Stewardship,

> Regional stewards are leaders who are committed to the long-term well-being of places. They are integrators who cross boundaries of jurisdiction, sector, and discipline to address complex regional issues such as sprawl, equity, education, and economic development. They see the connection between economic, environmental, and social concerns and they know how to "connect the dots" to create opportunities for their regions. Regional stewards are leaders who combine 360 degree vision with the ability to mobilize diverse coalitions for action. (Henton et al., 2000, p.3).

In essence, regional stewards are best understood in terms of their commitment "to bringing the fragments together" and "fostering the shared understanding and priorities that will permit community solidarity in pursuit of goals" (Henton, et al., 2000, p.2).

Understanding the nature of these "responsibles" who embrace the role of regional stewardship is extremely important if not central to understanding the key participants and players who would collaborate to create the Carolina Thread Trail. These are the leaders who by virtue of their commitment to transforming fragmented communities and services into a coherent, functional and pleasing sense of community wholeness have ultimately achieved a "sense of place" among communities and within the region. Accordingly, they have been drawn to their regional stewardship responsibilities by virtue of the attributes they bring to bear upon the task of making whole a fragmented region. These attributes include:

- *Civic Entrepreneurship*: "Applying the same entrepreneurial spirit and persistence to solving regional challenges that business entrepreneurs apply in building a business.
- *Integrative Thinking*: Recognizing "the need for more connected regional approaches to addressing economic, environmental and social objectives."
- *Boundary Crossing Thought and Action*: Boundary crossers demonstrate a willingness to "work beyond traditional governance and consistently collaborate across organizational boundaries and political jurisdictions."
- *Coalition Building*: Coalition builders "build support from leaders, citizens, interest groups and policy professionals toward a shared regional vision."

Ultimately the skills these stewards bring to the task of integrating communities and regional resources is crystalized in a framework for regional stewardship (Figure 7) where local governments, philanthropists, entrepreneurs, local neighborhoods and representatives of the environmental community are brought into a cooperative partnership to integrate neighborhoods into a regional whole, invigorate and transform local and regional economics, effect governmental reform via regional governmental bodies (such as councils of government) and cooperate with federal, state and local governments and environmental transformation to promote livable and sustainable communities. As a consequence a variety of policy initiatives are promoted to include environmental justice, smart growth, accessible government and better community integration.

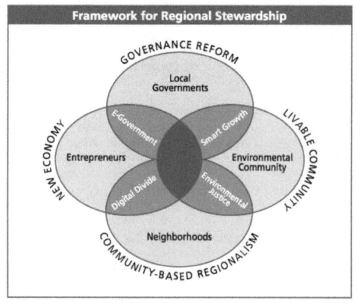

Figure 7: A Framework for Regional Stewardship
(Henton et all, 2000, p. 14)

## From Environmental Summit to Open Spaces Framework Plan: Voices & Choices

The framework for regional stewardship proffered by the Alliance for Regional Stewardship was well received in North Carolina by an organization with a short-lived but very influential track record for promoting regional solutions to environmental problems. Known as Voices and Choices of the Central Carolinas (a.k.a. Voices & Choices), this advocacy organization was founded in 1997 shortly after the 1995 Citistates Report inspired regional conferences (Neal & Johnson, 1995). The Citistates Report was developed through the efforts of four regional organizations - Foundation for the Carolinas, the *Charlotte Observer*, Carolinas Regional Partnership (currently known as Charlotte Regional Partnership) and the Urban Institute of the University of North Carolina Charlotte. These organizations convened to sponsor and commission the Citistates Report authored by the nationally recognized writers/reporters Neal Peirce and Curtis Johnson (Pierce & Johnson, 1995).

This report sought to provide an independent assessment of the issues and opportunities facing the greater Charlotte area. The report was published in piecemeal format in the pages of the *Charlotte Observer* from September 17 through October 8, 1995 (Henton, Melville & Walesh, 2007, p. 37). Chief among the recommendations to be found within its pages was the need for "multiple forums – region-wide and locally – to put the decisions about your physical growth, your educational future, your parks, towns and neighborhoods into the hands of thousands of citizens" (Henton, Melville & Walesh, 2007, p. 37). What followed was a truly spirited civic debate and conversation about the impacts of regional growth.

One of the central products to come out of that debate was the creation of a "new platform for civic engagement: Voices & Choices" (Henton, Melville, & Walesh, 2007, p. 37). Voices and Choices of the Central Carolinas (originally known as Central Carolina Choices) was created in 1997 and its first task was to assist the Mecklenburg County Commission conduct the 1998 Environmental Summit. The 1998 Environmental Summit, the first of its kind in the metro Charlotte area, was initially conceived of by the Mecklenburg County Commission and later developed and implemented by a steering group of 35 community leaders.

Preceding the summit a diverse group of 45 community leaders (a.k.a. "responsibles") conferred to develop a series of future scenarios for the Charlotte area to include "a future in which we do little to change and make no effort to plan; a future in which we make all the right choices with harmony and prosperity abounding; and a future in which our region overcomes tremendous obstacles to finally land on its feet environmentally and economically" (Freedman, 1998). Shortly thereafter a group of 450 participants attended four regional open meetings to discuss the various "future scenarios" (which had been widely published in local newspapers and magazines) and identify challenges and opportunities.

The input from these community participants was documented and became part of the proceedings for the Environmental Summit that convened in Charlotte on November 13, 1998. The event was the attended 500 community leaders representing businesses, local governments and the public to develop a regional environmental vision. Following the summit "volunteer action teams" were developed who spent a year designing action plans around a number of environmental quality categories to include: air quality and transportation, water quality, resource recovery/recycling, land use and open spaces. One of the central objectives to come out of the 1998 Environmental Summit in Charlotte was the realization of an interconnected system of open spaces by the year 2020. This goal became the chief focus of Voices and Choices and was thoroughly incorporated fully into its vision and mission statements (Freedman, 2008, UNCC, 2007, p. 48).

Voices and Choices proved influential despite its relatively brief existence (1997-2004). The organization pursued a variety of approaches to protecting shared environmental resources throughout Central North and South Carolina. In 2003 they published their "Open Spaces Framework Plan" that began with a statement of who they were and what their vision for the region entailed. They stated their organizational intent clearly, declaring:

- We are citizens of Central North and South Carolina who care about the place in which we live, and we have a shared vision of our region's future in which economic and environmental interests are balanced.

- We see a region where the Broad, Catawba and Yadkin/Pee Dee River basins and their tributaries are clean, where the air is pollution-free, and wise use is made of the land across county and state lines. *We envision a growing, thoughtfully planned 15-county area with abundant open spaces and parks, where you can still leave Mecklenburg urban bustle to wind through rolling Stanly County farmland.*

- We see a comprehensive transportation system integrated with land use that gets people to where they want to go, whether they bicycle to school in Rock Hill or ride a train to work from Spencer. We see a place where recycling is a part of everyday life in cities such as Albemarle and Hickory, reusing resources and reducing waste.

- We see a Central Carolinas in which future quality of life is a higher priority than short-term gain, and where active citizens in Monroe and Cherryville get involved in making community decisions. While our larger cities like Charlotte are our economic engines, our small towns retain unique identities – from Shelby to Wadesboro, from Harmony to Lancaster.

- We look at a region full of opportunity, where choices have to be made about our future, and we invite others to let their voices be heard – help us make the vision real. (Voices & Choices, 2003, p.1)

Note the italicized language in the second bullet of their declaration of intent, namely their vision of "a growing, thoughtfully planned 15-county area with abundant open spaces and parks, where you can still leave Mecklenburg urban bustle to wind through rolling Stanly County farmland." This assertion is a reaffirmation of one of the principal objectives coming out of the 1998 Environmental Summit and is one of the earliest public declarations calling for what later would become the Carolina Thread Trail. This vision is in fact consistent with the basic components of the Voices and Choices "framework plan" which included natural habitat, wetlands and floodplains, farmland and timberland, rural heritage and scenic areas, urban green space, parks and recreation.

The open spaces framework developed and published by Voices and Choices in 2003 envisioned "a way to coordinate and implement open spaces conservation across the region" (Voices & Choices, 2003, p. i). So perceived they articulated a conceptual plan,

- "Regional in scale, strategic in intent, and collaboratively developed;"
- Reliant upon "local plans and efforts for detailed scale and implementation;"
- Designed to "comprehensively address six types of open spaces" (i.e. natural habitats, wetlands and floodplains, farmland and timberlands, rural heritage and scenic areas, urban green space and parks and recreation);
- Articulating a "shared regional values in the form of principles and criteria for open spaces protection;"
- Illustrating "these principles in a Vision Map;" and
- Specifying "guidelines for inter-local application and adaptation" that "can be used to leverage funding resources." (Voices & Choices, 2003, p. 2).

The open spaces framework incorporated a three-part conceptual process to design, construct, and ultimately implement a structure designed around a set of three key objectives:

- Engage regional open spaces professionals, the business community, and environmental and citizen groups in defining a common open spaces framework for the region,
- Comprehensively address all six types of open spaces, including how they overlap and either complement or conflict with each other, and
- Provide a sound foundation upon which to build the Framework, utilizing proven approaches and accepted practices from elsewhere in the US. (Voices & Choices, 2003, p. 5)

As Voices and Choices laid the groundwork for their open spaces framework they collaborated with the Urban Institute of the University of North Carolina at Charlotte who maintains a regional indicators database measuring the region's quality of life across a number of parameters to include social, economic and environmental indicators. At the time of the development of the Carolina Open Spaces Framework UNC's Urban Institute had identified some 106,000 acres of land that was protected in one fashion or another within the region's 4.4 million acre expanse. Voices and Choices also collaborated in another effort that included UNC Charlotte as well as three regional Councils of Government (Western Piedmont, Centralina, and Catawba Regional) known as the Piedmont Green Plan Urban Growth Model. This effort sought to predict future land use by developing predictions based upon 1998 land use plans and population predictions through 2020 in order to project the amount of open spaces would be annually developed -

which at the time of the publication of the Open spaces Framework amounted to 41 acres yearly.

Voices and Choices developed a vision map as a tool to realizing an interconnected open system by the year 2020 – a goal first articulated at the 1998 Regional Environmental Summit. The vision map – which is quite literally a topographical map identifying priority open spaces areas throughout the region through the year 2020 - incorporates a comprehensive description of the six open spaces elements of the framework plan including:

- Existing green assets as of 2000—protected open spaces of five acres or more, both public and private,
- Proposed habitat, wetlands/floodplains, rural heritage, and waterfront-access park areas— a major feature of the interconnected system, these areas often naturally overlap and are represented together as one element in the system,
- Primary agricultural areas—areas where the highest concentrations of sustainable farming and timbering are envisioned,
- Urban green-space—all municipal areas within which an urban greenspace network exists or will exist that could connect to other open spaces system elements,
- Proposed new regional parks—parks that would bring the average travel time to a regional park to under 30 minutes for all areas of the region,
- Water supply watershed critical areas—areas in which development is allowed and most land is privately held, but intensity of development and impervious surface area is regulated to protect water quality;
- Linkages connecting the other elements—connections that could include public access trails as well as wildlife or water quality corridors that are not accessible to the public. (Voices & Choices, 2003, p. 11)

The vision map then targeted specific areas found from among these open spaces elements; doing so on the basis of a set of objective and subjective criteria. The objective criteria included:

- Water-supply watershed regulated critical areas identified via the wetlands/floodplains criteria,
- Stream banks of the major tributaries to the region's three rivers as identified via the wetlands/floodplains criteria,
- Sites identified through the Natural Heritage Inventory in the natural habitat criteria;
- Rural heritage and urban greenspace locations identified through those respective criteria. (Voices & Choices, 2003, p. 12)

Subjective criteria employed included:
- Large blocks of undeveloped land identified through the natural habitat criteria that help provide linkage to other open spaces system elements or balance the distribution of open spaces across the region,

- Proposed new regional park locations meeting the parks/recreation criteria that improved the drive time to a regional park from 60 minutes or less to 30 minutes or less for all regional residents,
- Potential waterfront-access park locations meeting the parks/recreation criteria, based on distance from existing parks and potential linkages
- Primary agricultural areas meeting the farmland/timberland criteria where both good soils and good concentrations of farming or timbering activity currently occur. In the absence of necessary GIS data on locations of good soil or activity concentrations, local agricultural and silvicultural experts were asked to define these areas. (Voices & Choices, 2003, p. 12)

Beyond these objective and subjective criteria, planners also employed a set of three overarching criteria throughout the visioning process being mindful to include:

- Land that represents compatible co-location or adjacency of more than one type of open spaces,
- Land that enhances the total system's connectivity and regional balance;
- Land that fits the regional scale required of a vision map. (Voices & Choices 2003, p. 12)

Upon completing this phase of developing their vision map, Voices and Choices staff recognized that the process of building an open spaces framework at a regional level entails developing consensus regarding common held values. Consequently they set about developing a set of shared principles and criteria that all participants could embrace in developing and implementing the framework. Accordingly through meetings, conferences and surveys they arrived at a set of shared values (principles) and criteria that could be comfortably applied and embraced by participants within the framework to identify open spaces deemed worthy of protection.

The principles are conceptual and nature so as to be flexibly applied regionally to accommodate local flexibility. They were designed to reflect the region's values regarding open spaces and environmental protection and included:

- Significant natural habitat areas are a critical part of our regional ecosystem and should be preserved.
- Habitat areas that are large in size, of high quality, of a rare type (or containing rare species), or are critical to the long-term viability of an ecosystem, are "significant." They provide food, water, shelter, and breeding grounds for native plant and animal species, preserve the biodiversity of our region, and teach us about the physical environment we depend upon.
- The lands that contribute to the long-term viability of those significant natural habitat areas should be protected.

- The long-term viability of habitat areas refers to the ability of the area to sustain the plant and animal populations in it over the long-term without experiencing local extinctions of those species within the habitat area.
- Factors contributing to the long-term viability of habitat areas include:
  o  Quality (degree of food, shelter, and breeding grounds provided),
  o  Size (population size of the species supported by the area),
  o  Buffering (the degree of protection provided from intrusion or human disturbance around the edges of the core habitat area), and
  o  Connectivity (the degree to which it is connected to other areas of the same habitat type). (Voices & Choices, 2003, p. 18)

The open spaces criteria served to identify specific lands to be incorporated into a regional open spaces system. These criteria are grounded in a scientific rationale designed to insure a comprehensive and planned approach to system development. Moreover, these criteria were designed for regional and local implementation recognizing that local conditions require flexible application. Their principle, purpose however, is to assist examining and critiquing the effectiveness of open spaces plans. The selected criteria for the open spaces framework include:

- Natural Heritage Inventory sites, GAP priority sites, or sites identified through other inventories developed through an equally scientific process.
- Large blocks of undeveloped land, especially those containing intact, viable ecosystems with high diversity of animal and plant populations.
- Undeveloped lands adjacent to protected natural habitat areas (particularly those habitat areas that by themselves may lack long-term eco-system viability), specifically adjacent land that can:
  o  Enlarge the protected habitat area, or
  o  Buffer the protected habitat area with transitional uses.
- Undeveloped lands that serve as important wildlife corridors connecting protected habitats and providing access to water (i.e. continuous stream corridors).
- Small habitat areas or wildlife refuges within development that can act as "stepping stones" to habitat corridors or between protected habitat areas

## A State of the Region Report, Open Spaces Conservation and the Carolina Thread Trail

Having published their "Open Spaces Framework" in 2003 Voices and Choices immediately followed up with a second report in 2004 entitled "2004 State of the Region Report: Central Carolinas Region" (Taylor, 2004). This proved to be the last and the most influential of the work produced and published by Voices and Choices and is in part noteworthy because of the broad range of constituents brought together to financially sponsor and disseminate its findings. A truncated list of these contributors included Bank of America, Duke Energy, Wachovia, Bell South, Goodrich, The Foundation for the Carolinas and the Z. Smith Reynolds Foundation. When considered within the context that the report had already garnered support from conservation and environmental groups as well as from municipal and county governments across the 15 county region, the additional support from the region's principal banking, energy and foundation interests is even more remarkable. To its credit Voices and Choices demonstrated and unusual ability to integrate a very disparate set of community interests to pursue an ambitious set of regional objectives.

This "2004 State of The Region Report" presents a regional perspective on air quality, transportation, land use, water quality, municipal solid waste management and economic health and does so in a manner that sets it apart from previous assessments and reports in that it:

- Addresses a 15-county region defined by growth and change, not by political boundaries."
- "Assembles hard data measuring both our economic and environmental health."
- "Uses indicators to be tracked over time revealing trends that can be managed."
- "Reveals the interconnected effects of the six topic areas: air quality, transportation, land use, water quality, solid waste management and economy."
- "Makes clear that economic health, environmental health and quality of life depend on each other."
- "Offers recommendations and "good works" to learn from and emulate" (Taylor, 2004, p. ii).

As subsequent events would demonstrate the "2004 State of the Region Report" proved to be enormously significant for the 15 county region of central North and South Carolina because "For the first time, a document combining research and recommendations for six major topic areas affecting our quality of life is offered to the Central Carolinas region" (Taylor, 2004, p. vii).

This State of the Region Report drove home the point that environmental and economic health across the region are intertwined and that improving the life for citizens in the region of necessity required investing in promoting environmental health. To that end it specified a set of goals that had been pursued in making the report to include:

1. Providing baseline quality of life indicators that could be measured and tracked longitudinally,
2. Educating citizens and leaders regarding important trends relative to the six areas critical to the region's economic and environmental health,
3. Identifying challenges to realizing environmental and economic improvement and suggesting strategies for resolution,
4. Providing examples of best practices to be emulated and applied regionally;
5. Encouraging and facilitating regional collaboration requisite for producing sustainable growth, prosperity and an ever-improving quality of life (Taylor, 2004, p. viii).

The report evaluated the state of the region relative to air quality, transportation, land use, water quality, municipal solid waste management and economic health and articulated a set of findings for each target area.

While reporting on all of these findings and recommendations is beyond the scope of this paper, there were three overall findings that are important to subsequent initiatives as well as in regard to the development of the Carolina Thread Trail. These include,

1.  As rapidly as the 15 county region was growing the per capita impact of that growth on the environment had progressed at an even faster rate to the point where the average citizen in the region was generating almost twice as much waste as the national average,
2.  A regional vision for growth and quality of life was lacking and "unless we find ways to agree on hard goals for open spaces conservation, waste reduction, air and water quality, and in training and educating our workforce, we will have foreclosed many of our options leaving us with expensive—and sometimes federally mandated— after-the-fact solutions to avoidable problems;"
3.  The data and information requisite to implementing a shared vision and regional planning was not being collected, analyzed and disseminated and the absence of this data undercuts cooperative efforts and compromises the region's ability to understand the region's current problems, let alone trend the data to plan for the future (Taylor, 2004, p. ix).
4.  Ultimately the "responsibles" who would develop the Carolina Thread Trail chose to focus upon developing a regional vision regarding the need to conserve open spaces by creating a network of interconnected parks, trails and greenways that would not only conserve and expand green-space within the region, but would additionally link and integrate communities economically, aesthetically, environmentally and socially.

Upon assuming an historical perspective on the development of the Carolina Thread Trail, one would have to attribute the historical philosophy and vision of open spaces, greenways and parks to Olmsted and Whyte while crediting the Alliance for Regional Stewardship for developing a regional approach employing what they called the "responsibles" to address local and regional concerns. In a similar fashion, the 1995 "Citistates Report," and the efforts of Voices and Choices relative to the 1998 Environmental Summit held in Charlotte also contributed to the historical development of open spaces management and connectivity and indirectly contributed to efforts such as the Carolina Thread Trail.

However that influence was limited primarily because of the extent to which local community leaders tend to harbor a degree of skepticism and reluctance toward uncritically adopting ideas or plans that emanate from outside their local jurisdiction. This particularly applied to the concept of regionalism. Paradoxically, the very attribute (regionalism) of Voices and Choices that brought it to the forefront in civic leadership in 1997 ultimately contributed to its demise in 2004. It seems that while the "responsibles" in the 15 county region valued cooperative regional effort, they preferred doing so by first considering the values of needs of local communities, thereafter proceeding outward to embrace shared needs in the communities of the region. What emerged was a simple but valuable lesson in building regional consensus – think locally, actively engage local leaders and empower local communities to imagine a regional vision in terms that enfranchise their interests, needs and values.

This is one of the principal lessons that The Carolina Thread Trail founders learned from the demise of Voices and Choices. While in theory a commitment to regional approaches to common problems is a good idea, in practice those who developed the Thread discovered that focusing upon local needs and issues best guaranteed cooperation and participation in the Carolina Thread Trail. There is a paradox here in that while the Carolina Thread Trail has clearly made a significant regional impact, it has done so by engaging one locality and constituency after another rather that gaining sponsorship by embracing a regional vision.

In retrospect founders of the Thread concluded that despite the fact that the Citistates Report and the 1998 Environmental Summit facilitated and enabled the larger conversation that would in part be reflected in the Carolina Thread Trail, their focus upon regionalism proved to be antithetical to how the Thread was actually developed. Ultimately "localism" proved to be a so much more productive community value and selling point for participation in the Thread. Likewise, while the North Carolina General Assembly's 1998 "Million Acre Initiative" (MAI, 2001) designed to foster statewide partnerships among public and private interests to protect and plan for the use of open space was an important foundational event contributing to open space management, the act was not central to development of the Thread. MAI had a statewide focus whereas The Carolina Thread Trail effort was always local first, then regional.

Like the Million Acre Initiative and the Environmental Summit of 1998, the two reports of Voices and Choices significantly contributed to the regional conversation toward linking open spaces and communities. Without doubt these reports informed the early planning phase of the Carolina Thread Trail. However, this influence was proscribed to the degree that Voices and Choices championed a regional vision that often served as impediments to those championing the development of the Thread in local communities. While the Carolina Thread Trail envisioned a regional network of trails, the practical creation of those trails required a "local" as opposed to a "regional" emphasis. What the planners of the Thread principally took away from the Voices and Choices report was the need for a regional trail system. This became the practical focus of the planners and this trail system was pursued with officials and landowners across the region by consistently emphasizing local self-determination and control. That said, Voices and Choices would have to be given credit for being the midwife to an idea that – in the form of the 2004 State of the Region Report – provided a process and a vision that would later be taken up by a wide range of "responsibles" within the region.

## The Charlotte-Mecklenburg Community Foundation's
## Environmental Committee

In 2004 when Voices and Choices finally closed its doors a void was created in the effort to engage in regional planning to promote economic, social, recreation, health and environmental integration and cooperation within the 15 county Charlotte, North Carolina region. It was at that point the Charlotte-Mecklenburg Community Foundation's Environmental Committee stepped into the void to determine in part what had been lost with the demise of Voices and Choices and what steps could be taken to continue much of the regional stewardship goals that the now defunct organization had once promoted. In so doing the committee members, consisting of influential regional philanthropists, principally sought to be strategic in their approach and identify a high impact investment for the Foundation's funds rather than diminishing their investment capacity by dividing it among smaller and perhaps less consequential efforts. To that end the Foundation employed The Lee Institute of Charlotte - a non-profit organization that "provides facilitation, civic engagement, consulting and leadership training to nonprofits, governments and community groups across the Charlotte region" – to conduct a key informant survey among notable regional "responsibles" to include representatives of the environmental / conservation community, businesses, foundations, and governments.

The Lee Institute began its efforts with a preliminary survey of existing successful collaborative networks for the purpose of identifying those that might be emulated. These preliminary findings were reported back the Charlotte-Mecklenburg Community Foundation's Environmental Committee who ultimately concluded that:

- Successful collaborative networks must be timely and collaboration must include a sense of urgency,
- Network collaborators must be unfailingly committed and consistent with participants assuming clearly identifiable roles and functioning on the basis of clear operating norms,
- Collaborative processes must be consistently inclusive with equal voice and member participation insured,
- Collaborative networks must also be open, supported by sufficient staff and be convened and facilitated by a neutral party,
- Desired outcomes and milestones should be clearly and specifically delineated and associated with visible and measurable progress indicators;
- Deliberative and collaborative efforts must recognize that ultimately the enlightened self-interest of the participants must be acknowledged and met and that leadership would necessarily emerge from among members of the network. (Lee Institute, 2004, p. 23)

Based upon these preliminary conclusions, The Lee Institute began its regional survey interviewing a total of 240 key informants to include a draft survey sent to some 50 business, governmental and environmental leaders, followed by a final survey sent to 108 organizations that "protect, educate about, or advocate for the quality of land, water or air" in the region and another 82 surveys sent to environmentally influential business, foundation and governmental leaders (Lee Institute, 2004, p. 5). Surveys consisted of a series of questions developed around the background of the responding organization, the nature of their collaborative efforts, their perspective on the Voices and Choices State of the Region Report (2004) to include a ranking of that organization's recommendations in terms of its importance to regional quality of life, and suggested roles the Foundation for the Carolinas (FFTC) might assume to improve the region's environment (Lee Institute, 2004, p. 6).

The findings from these surveys ultimately concluded that the Foundation should initiate a process to:

- Identify "big" ideas rather than generating endless "studies" without "action,"
- Identify and document existing collaborative relationships among the various constituent groups included within the survey and look for both shared and divergent opinions and options for implementation;
- Explore existing collaborations between the constituent groups and identify areas where they either agreed or disagreed regarding problems and solutions.

The survey findings likewise surmised the existence of common concern regarding land use planning and conservation as well as a consensus that:

- There appeared to be a ripe opportunity for the Charlotte-Mecklenburg Community Foundation and Foundation For The Carolinas to exercise a leadership role in building consensus and action plans around land use planning and conservation that could be realized by bringing environmental and conservation groups together several times annually to network and collaborate. Doing so however required being sensitive to the reasons why some groups identified themselves as conservationist while others were self-described environmentalists.
- Likewise it was believed that the foundations could also be useful in educating the public about the interrelationship between environmental conservation, quality of community life and economic growth and vitality.

Although respondents to the survey were seriously invested in seeing the Charlotte-Mecklenburg Community Foundation and Foundation For The Carolinas assume a leadership role around an important regional environmental issue, at issue was *which* issue should be principally pursued. In the interest of answering this question, The Lee Institute surveyed respondents and conducted focus groups to rank the six environmental issues described in the Voices and Choices 2004 State of the Region Report. The result of this ranking process demonstrated that land use dominated every other issue, consequently the Charlotte-Mecklenburg Community Foundation concluded that "The idea of preserving open spaces, which has some strong support already in the region because of work by Voices and Choices, the Urban Institute, Crescent Resources,

Land Trusts, and other non-profits, has surfaced as the number one idea for further leadership by the EC (environmental committee)" (Lee Institute, 2004, p. 19).

## The Carolina Thread Trail

The findings forthcoming from the Lee Institute served to contribute to the conceptual framework undergirding the Carolina Thread Trail. However the Thread came into being as a function of Foundation For The Carolinas and its subsidiary organization, The Charlotte-Mecklenburg Foundation, whose environmental committee helped form the Carolina Thread Trail Governing Board first chaired by former Duke Energy CEO Ruth Shaw in 2005 (FFTC, 2009). So conceived, the Carolina Thread Trail developers set about creating a vast network of trails and greenways throughout the 15 county Charlotte – Mecklenburg region by working with local jurisdictions and engaging civic and community leaders to determine community priorities, preferred locations for the trail and service areas. In 2007 the Thread was successfully launched (Carolina Thread Trail, 2014). The name "Carolina Thread" reflects the cultural history of the region and the Thread's logo incorporates the "eight-point star" quilt pattern to capture the metaphor of a group of disparate yet related communities woven together like pieces of cloth in an old-fashioned Southern quilt. The intent of the logo pattern is to reflect an effort to weave the social, ecological, economic and recreational resources of the region into one multi-colored and unique community quilt (Carolina Thread Trail, 2014).

The Thread is principally influenced by two organizations: The Catawba Lands Conservancy - the lead organization for the trail - and the Foundation For The Carolinas that serves as its philanthropic arm. The Thread was launched with private capital with the intent of leveraging local, state and federal funds. As of 2013 the Carolina Thread Trail achieved the following milestones:

- Provided $3 million in private grant awards to communities,
- Collaborated with 14 counties to adopt master plans with Thread routes,
- Collaborated with 76 local governments,
- Opened 132 miles of trails, greenways and pathways;
- Funded and initiated another 28 miles of trails near term completion.

The Carolina Thread Trail has additionally secured some $16.8 million in private capital, $7.3 million in donated land and in excess of $23.7 million by way of publicly committed funding. Today "The Thread" spans includes 119 miles of trails across two states to include the counties of Anson, Cabarrus, Catawba, Cleveland, Gaston, Iredell, Lincoln, Mecklenburg, Rowan, Stanly and Union in North Carolina and Cherokee, Chester, Lancaster and York counties in South Carolina. As of 2013 there were 14 other corridors for trails and greenways under development or construction (Carolina Thread Trail, 2013).

The Thread has been developed through a public/private funding model in which private donations – used to leverage public matching funds - serve to fund catalytic community grants for planning and actually constructing the trail as well as providing for supportive expenses. The Foundation for the Carolinas, serving as The Thread's philanthropic partner, receives contributions and places them in The Carolina Thread Trail Fund that they maintain and manage. Thereafter they employ those and other funds for the purpose of leveraging local, state and federal funds as available. As of 2012, the Carolina Thread Trail had awarded a total of Total $642,544 in community grant awards and $3,044,519 in cumulative private grants (Carolina Thread Trail, 2012).

The Catawba Lands Conservancy is the administrative home for the Carolina Thread Trail. Staff assigned to the Thread by the conservancy promote and manage the trail system and negotiate with landowners and communities to gain access to land through which the trail traverses and connects. In some cases land is donated to the Conservancy but in many cases it remains in the hands of landowners or communities and is developed (via grants and awards to acquire easements) into greenways and trails that are subsequently maintained by landowners, communities and/or the conservancy. That said the Carolina Thread Trail is overseen by a governing board responsible for fundraising and trail development as well as strategic planning for the future of the Carolina Thread Trail system (Carolina Thread Trail, 2012). However the specific locations and routes of the trail are locally determined. Such local involvement has served not only to garner cooperation and participation but to achieve one of the key principles of the Carolina Thread Trail – self determination.

The original vision of the Carolina Thread Trail was to "preserve, protect and connect open spaces through a 500+ mile "green ribbon" of parks, trails and conservation corridors, touching 2.3 million people in our region" and its core principles include:

- Invitation to communities to participate,
- Active listening,
- Communities self-determine trail locations,
- Bias toward action,
- Respect for land;
- Respect for land ownership. (Carolina Thread Trail, 2009)

Ultimately the mission of The Carolina Thread Trail entails "energizing, connecting, and enhancing" the region and the lives of its inhabitants. It does so by promoting:

- *Healthy Families and Kids*: Providing outdoor recreation resources through the creation of trials and open spaces as "key ingredients to healthier communities," that positively contribute to a higher quality of life. The Carolina Thread trail also provides "opportunities for families and children to get healthy, play outdoors, connect with nature and explore our natural surroundings."
- *Economic Development and Sustainability:* Creating outdoor trails and greenways that attract visitors thereby aiding businesses by attracting customers and additionally contributing to the economic health of communities. Accordingly, "The real estate industry cites walking and biking trails as the #1 desired amenity for prospective homeowners. According to the Outdoor Industry Association, at least 48% of North

Carolinians and 54% of South Carolinians participate in outdoor recreation each year. In North Carolina, the association says outdoor recreation generated approximately $1.3 billion in state and local tax revenue in 2011 and 2012."

- *Water Quality and Conservation:* "The Thread is making a permanent legacy of conservation and connectivity with 1,300 acres of preserved land to contain trails, thanks to Funding from the North Carolina Clean Water Management Trust Fund and support from out land trust partners like the Catawba Lands Conservancy."
- *Community Engagement:* The Thread engages some 78 local governments, 500 volunteers and countless community partners to create and maintain the regional trail network. (Carolina Thread Trail, 2012).

The Carolina Thread Trail's 19 member governing board consists of philanthropists, community and business leaders from across the region that work together to govern the Carolina Thread Trail and promote the financial support of the organization. The Carolina Thread Trail serves as a supporting organization of Foundation for the Carolinas and philanthropic efforts are collaboratively approached via a contract for service with the Catawba Land Conservancy – thus avoiding the need to establish a new organization with additional financial overhead. The Conservancy staff assigned to the Carolina Thread Trail consists of seven persons to include a director and executive director, two development officers, an outreach coordinator, a community affairs coordinator, and a research director.

## What Makes the Carolina Thread Trail Unique and Worthy of Emulating?

At a time when other communities are finding themselves Balkanized regarding environmental problems and issues it is refreshing and a bit surprising to encounter communities like the Charlotte-Mecklenburg region that are actually addressing pressing environmental issues in a proactive collaborative fashion. That said, the reality of such cooperation and the very existence of the Carolina Thread Trail begs the issue: how is it this community is successfully addressing its environmental issues when other regions are not? The answer to that question is at once complex and simple.

The Thread's development has been rendered complex by pursuing priorities and approaches that vary from community to community across North and South Carolina. Comparatively it has been simplified by focusing upon the "responsibles" in each community and fostering cooperation among them rather than seeking to invite participants who might not be as invested in reaching realistic solutions to environmental problems as they are in posturing and discouraging the actions of their ideological opponents. Likewise, the core principles adopted by the developers of he Thread have also served to contribute toward simplifying the policy environment and consensus building in that they have been developed around a set of core principles:

- Invitation to communities,
- Active listening,
- Communities self-determine trail locations,
- Bias toward action,
- Respect for land;
- Respect for land ownership. (Carolina Thread Trail, 2009)

All of this is to say that the dominant philosophical principle which seems to unite all of the efforts surrounding the Carolina Thread Trail is that of pragmatism – which is to say pursuing those outcomes which build the strongest consensus around addressing values and concerns of greatest importance to local communities. In studying the history of this environmental effort in North and South Carolina it is instructive to note that the impetus for the bulk of the efforts that resulted in the Carolina Thread Trail project began in community foundations.

For those who are unfamiliar with the work of community foundations, they principally serve to link those with resources to give with causes and concerns in need of financial support and investment. At their best community foundations seek to elicit the values and concerns of those with resources to give and then try to present them with a range of projects that by one measure or another match the interests of philanthropists. Likewise, being aware of who is interested in funding particular interests and issues, the community foundation works with those who would apply for financial support to aid them in tailoring their proposals to meet the needs and objectives of funders. In this way the staff or community foundations quite literally play the role of "match maker" (Goodman, 2005).

This orientation that kicked off what later would become the Carolina Thread Trail is critical in that it entailed a facilitating organization that sought out people who liked to collaborate. This orientation and the deliberative processes that flowed naturally from it tended to attract and engage people with a predilection to collaboration and compromise while generally discouraging the participation of people of less flexible character who would prioritize manipulation and the dictation of a policy agenda rather than eliciting and shaping the outcome. In fact, it is worth noting that the Lee Institute prioritized employing a fair, inclusive and transparent process of surveys and gatherings designed to elicit a diverse array of perspectives as well as seeking to assist participants in identifying areas of agreement. Without question, utilizing a neutral party such as the Lee Institute enabled the "responsibles" involved in the process to participate fully without assuming responsibility for the engagement process. More importantly the approach utilized by the Lee Institute attracted a group of influential community leaders with the capacity to approach policy as process rather than outcome and to be willing to suspend their vision of where their mutual policy vision should culminate and instead pursue the policy process in anticipation that the ultimate consensual outcome will be an improvement upon the prior state of affairs, even though it is not necessarily an "ideal" outcome.

To a significant degree it would seem that the success of the Carolina Thread effort rests upon the extent to which it was conceived and operationalized as a pragmatic and collaborative endeavor that would recognize the diversity of values and interests in communities and pursue a course of environmental and community development that would sensitively reflect the particular concerns of communities while pursuing the more broadly shared interests of the region. According to Dave Cable, the first Director of the Carolina Thread Trail, a key to the Thread's success "was our grants process and local control." These two factors were not priorities for the Voices and Choices organizational efforts.

By comparison, Cable observes, the Carolina Thread Trail embodied a "bias toward action, local control and money to back up grants" which rendered the Thread as a winning initiative for local communities within the region. Participating communities plan their own trail locations with a 90% grant for consulting services to make the planning efficient, with only one stipulation – they consult with their neighboring communities and ensure that all trails connect across political boundaries. Furthermore, communities found the Thread attractive not simply or perhaps not even principally because it was a "trail" so much as it promoted water quality, riparian protection, connectivity of conservation corridors and wildlife habitat. It is the Thread's prioritization of these outcomes that facilitated access to public funding such as North Carolina's Clean Water Management Trust Fund. Had the process been less discriminating in terms of who was engaged and how these voices were vetted in the policy process, it could have easily resulted in a balkanized situation where ideology and action stymied one another. In short, the collegial and interactive approach to the policy process coming out of the community foundations served to prevent the pursuit of "ideal" outcomes from standing in the way of "good" and "better" ones.

While such a collaborative spirit and vision is undoubtedly one of the key reasons why the Carolina Thread Trail effort is working, it would mean little if it were not for a vision of the environment and communities as "wholes" rather than one of "parts." This philosophical foundation, coupled with a pragmatic and cooperative spirits, is without question what made this unique Carolina initiative work. As this narrative has illustrated, the idea that communities and the environment exist as parts of a larger "whole" dates back to Europe and Ebenezer Howard's "garden cities" and to the early cities of the United States and the work of Fredrick Law Olmsted. These values were transfused into the "open spaces" environmental perspective and in the Carolinas were embodied in the efforts of Voices and Choices among other organizations. Thankfully, this penchant to see communities and environments as "wholes" is serving the Charlotte-Mecklenburg area well and hopefully has become a given in any future environmental or community development.

That said organizations like Voices and Choices and The Carolina Thread Trail must rely upon the inculcation of succeeding generations into the wisdom of thinking in wholes and acting locally, cooperatively and pragmatically. As time progresses on and the cast or "responsibles" in the region changes and is transformed, it is imperative that future "responsibles" continue to find themselves principally focused upon the "wholes" of regional environments and communities rather than becoming isolated advocates for self and community interests alone. Without doubt, the dedicated folks who fashioned the Carolina Thread Trail made their effort look a lot easier than it was. In the future, especially in a future of scarce resources, such cooperation and vision can be expected to be a lot harder to secure – meaning that the values of the Thread need to be nurtured and promulgated along the length of its expanse to current and future cadres of hikers, bikers, residents and responsibles.

## Imaginating the Carolina Thread Trail

The concept of imaginating has been developed throughout this narrative in the interest of describing an intuitive process by which routine and more consequential decisions are made. The text's narrative has been developed around the stream of consciousness perspective of William James and has concluded that for effective policymaking to occur it must take into account that decision makers act intuitively and use reason to both justify their decisions as well as to win others over to their perspective. Among other conclusions, the narrative thus far has emphasized the necessity of negotiating difficult environmental policy issues within and among those who are both intuitively and practically willing to be available for deliberation. Of necessity, bringing people to the negotiating table that are available for deliberation necessitates excluding to the greatest degree possible those who have no investment in negotiating or compromising on issues. Such an assertion may sound overly simplistic or painfully obvious. However for policy development to progress fruitfully such rigid and unyielding ideologues must be either eliminated or marginalized if the deliberative process is to prove successful.

The Carolina Thread Trail initiative illustrates this point to the degree that the development of the entire project emerged from among a divergent group of "responsibles" residing throughout central North and South Carolina. What distinguishes this group of community leaders is not the degree to which they shared a vision for their region (coming as they did from a wide variety of constituencies) but rather degree to which they felt responsible for the welfare of their local communities and were willing to enter into conversations and deliberations with other leaders who shared a sense of civic and community responsibility, albeit from a variety of motivational perspectives.

In so doing these "responsibles" engage in a satisficing approach to decision making and policy deliberation by demonstrating a willingness to develop a tentative sense of the range of policy outcomes that will prove acceptable in addressing the region's needs and then embracing the available alternatives that meets their intuitively held policy values. This is a process each of the responsibles participates in until – as a group – they arrive at a shared consensus around an acceptable (not ideal) set of approaches that will be employed regionally.

There are, however, two forms of imaginating: intuitive and deliberative. The process just described is intuitive in form and occurs almost without conscious reflection among those who have learned to habitually approach complex issues in a pragmatic way. There is however a more formal process that has been proposed in this text which outlines a deliberative process or discipline that decision makers or policy analysts might want to employ to insure that the intuitive process (which will occur even in the midst of a deliberative effort) is systematically applied in the interest of clarifying problem definitions, identifying stakeholders and their motivations and in the interest of identifying, working through and compensating for bias. Briefly, here is a step-by-step recap of the principles of deliberative imaginating:

1. *Carefully Consider the Case:* Consider the case's interiority and exteriority, tentatively define the problem, clarify issues, identify stakeholders, perspectives, note key process, opportunities, biases, compare new-stock and old-stock ideas, in preparation for framing.
2. *Reconsider the Five Attitudinal Principles of Ecopragmatics Derived From James:*
   vi.   *Be Outcome Oriented*
   vii.  *Be Mindful*
   viii. *Discriminate*
   ix.   *Be Grounded in Past Experiences*
   x.    *Be Open to New Experiences*
3. *Metaphorically Frame and If Necessary Re-Frame the Case:* Frame and reframe the case – to include interior and exterior dimensions -in metaphorical terms that serves to help explain the case and suggest solutions to problems.
4. *Specify the Thematic Perspective on the Problem and Develop Tentative Conclusions:* Identify emerging themes, elements, forces and possible outcomes suggested by the way the case has been framed. Consider reframing where necessary. Empathetically put yourself in the position of each stakeholder and consider the range of conclusions they might consider (or not) and project the worst, likely and ideal outcomes on the basis of your analysis.
5. *Develop a Strategy for Pursuing a Resolution to the Case Problem:* Identify an achievable and acceptable outcome supported by your analysis and develop a satisficing strategy of realizing this outcome in a fashion consistent with broad citizen participation and investment.
6. *Review Your Analysis and Conclusion*s: Review efforts and complete a checklist specifying that all six steps have been addressed and answer the following questions:
   e.   How will you and the stakeholders know whether "old-stock" ideas and values are superior or inferior to the "new-stock" ideas and values presenting themselves in the case study?
   f.   How will you and the stakeholders identify bias (theirs and others) and account for it in their deliberations and those of others?
   g.   How will you and the stakeholders go about addressing the policy issue at hand within the confines of local communities and regions (i.e. utilizing communitarian approaches)?
   h.   How will you and the stakeholders know when they have arrived at an acceptable conclusion to the issue at hand?

Given this framework, let's consider how these principles were unwittingly but effectively applied in the Carolina Thread Trail case.

1. *Carefully Consider the Case:* The Carolina Thread Trail was developed within the context of open spaces management and the issues surrounding the region's approach to open spaces was vetted by various organizations over a number of years with broad input from public, private, philanthropic, environmental, and regulatory interests. Voices and Choices and the Foundation for the Carolinas played particularly important roles in terms of identifying problems, clarifying the motivations of participants to deal with the problems, eliciting possible solutions and partnerships, identifying and developing a process for dealing with these problems and consistently demonstrating a willingness to listen and consider ideas that challenged the "old-stock" ideas and values each participant held. In virtually every way conceivable those involved with the progression of events that culminated in the Carolina Thread Trail engaged in an analytical and deliberative process that fully considered the issues at hand and proffered consensually derived actions to deal with these issues.

2. *Reconsider the Five Attitudinal Principles of Ecopragmatics Derived From James:*

   a. **Outcome Orientation:** The deliberative processes beginning with Voices and Choices and culminating in the creation of The Carolina Thread Trail were at every point designed toward problem identification (lack of connection between open spaces), input from stakeholders, a statement of priorities and an action plan tied to specific outcomes – such as the creation of a network of trails and greenways throughout the 15 county Mecklenburg County North Carolina regions.

   b. **Mindfulness:** Throughout the multi-year, multi-organizational history culminating in the creation of the Thread, significant effort was made to develop plans in consultation and coordination with other entities, organizations and communities – meaning that the process was ever mindful of the reality that outcomes to be employed regionally and locally of necessity required a constant commitment to mindfully developing consensual rather than individually conceived courses of action and policies. Moreover, the process of deliberation and action was ever mindful to prioritize the needs of the region within the context of local needs and discretion. Finally throughout the process that culminated in the Carolina Thread Trail consistent care was made to recognize and compensate for the bias each participant brought to the deliberation to insure that preconceived biases of what might or might not be effective were tempered against new experience and information, as well as by a willingness to try something new and judge its effectiveness based upon the outcomes achieved. This pragmatic approach applied locally and with an emphasis upon self-determination is undoubtedly what led an ever-growing number of communities to want the Thread to come through their neighborhoods and communities.

c.  **Be Discriminating:** Discrimination was central to the creation
    of the Thread to the degree that short-term problems and
    solutions were distinguished from long- term needs and
    approaches. Likewise, discrimination was employed to sort out
    bias from reality as well as a willingness on the part of many to
    temporarily suspend preconceived notions to allow new
    processes and outcomes to emerge that could be used to
    confirm or change biases. Discrimination was most importantly
    applied as the Thread came under development as Conservancy
    staff pursued a regional vision by focusing on local values and
    local control.

d.  **Grounded in Past Experiences:** The process that led to the
    creation of the Carolina Thread Trail were in every cases built
    upon prior experiences, as documented in this case study to
    have dated back to the work of Fredrick Law Olmsted and
    beyond. This was particularly the case when the Foundation for
    the Carolina's Environmental Committee made it a priority to
    build upon the prior work done by Voices and Choices as it
    pursued regional solutions to an environmentally and
    economically sustainable regional community. It is likewise
    illustrated in the lessons that founders of The Thread took from
    the demise of Voices and Choices as they learned the value of
    creating regional programs locally – one community at a time.

e.  **Remaining Open to New Experiences:** While participants
    drew upon experiences from the past the broadly inclusive
    approach to engaging business, environmental, governmental
    and community leaders – the responsibles - in the deliberative
    process all but guaranteed that every individual participant was
    given the opportunity to see, hear and consider how problems
    differ depending upon one's perspective and how divergent
    ways and conceptual approaches to framing and resolving
    problems created opportunities for problem resolution that were
    novel and in many cases beyond what any one individual
    stakeholder may have conceived. The willingness to think of
    problems and solutions in new ways and to act on these new
    perspectives has been the hallmark of The Carolina Thread
    Trail effort. Nowhere is this more clearly illustrated than in the
    recognition by Conservancy staff in developing the Thread of
    how past efforts had failed by prioritizing regionalism over
    localism. Having learned from past experiences these staff have
    successfully expanded the Thread through consistent
    negotiations with local leaders based upon a commitment to
    local self- determination.

3.  **Metaphorically Framing and Re-Framing the Problem and Possible
    Solutions:** Had the historical events that culminated in the Carolina
    Thread Trail been narrowly experienced locally or within the scope of
    individual organizations or communities then there is little doubt that a
    network of regional trails and greenways would have never been

forthcoming. The very fact of their existence today is testimony to the degree each participant was willing to frame and reframe the nature of the problems and the scope of the possible solutions in terms of how other deliberators conceived of the issues and solutions. In essence, all of the participants, to one degree or another, "walked in the shoes" of other participants in the interest of seeing things in a new light, and as this process continued over many years across several organizations and institutions, participants did so repeatedly. This is the essence of what framing and reframing policy issues is about. However, that said, participants remained true to local values and concerns and participated in the Thread in ways that supported those values and concerns. Fortunately for the founders of the Thread, the very concept of a set of greenways and trails that connected disparate communities and environs created a palate or infrastructure around which a diverse set of community interests could be organized and conceptualized.

4. *Specify the Thematic Perspective on the Problem and Develop Tentative Conclusions:* Throughout the process of problem identification and the pursuit of strategies and solutions the participants sought perspectives and approaches that could be used to better frame and understand the issues at hand and how to solve them. For instance, they asked themselves if the issues at hand were principally those of urban sprawl versus waste management, or was it one of economic development versus environmental sustainability. Likewise they explored the degree to which the problems entailed rural-agrarian interests versus urban-suburban interests or whether the issues had to do with natural resources exploitation versus natural resources preservation and development. Each paradigm offered the participants an opportunity to think of the issues at hand within the context of different problem-issue themes and with each theme came a different set of constraints, opportunities and potential solutions. Ultimately the participants developed a thematic approach involving open-spaces versus built environments and developed a set of conclusions and action plans based upon that thematic decision. These conclusions – particularly the commitment to having built and natural environments locally and regionally coexist together, led to the development of a network of trails and greenways that became The Carolina Thread Trail.

5. *Develop a Strategy for Pursuing a Resolution to the Case Problem:* Obviously the development of the Carolina Thread Trail constitutes one of many strategies that regional bodies, governments and organizations have embraced to address the pressing problems threatening environmental and economic sustainability. Even so, The Thread is one of a set of ongoing and emerging strategies that emanated from a particular set of historic events. That said, a quick review of the environmental practices of communities throughout the region reinforces the fact that many communities utilized the outcomes of Voices and Choices and other environmentally active organizations to improve the economic and environmental sustainability of their local communities benefiting local residents and the region.

## Necessary Anthropocentrism and Householding Principles

In the introduction to the text an emphasis was made upon "necessary anthropocentrism" (the recognition that out of necessity all humans will think about and experience the environment from the perspective of a human being residing in the world) and "householding" (the need for every human to make a home and community for themselves) as foundational principles in ecopragmatics. These principles are clearly illustrated throughout the development of the open spaces concept in North Carolina and in the development of the Carolina Thread Trail. These efforts, while benefiting the natural environs of the region, all begin with human concerns and issues that transcend narrow environmental issues to include economic and physical health, community development, democratic participation, quality of life, recreation, aesthetics and more. This is what environmental policy looks like when it is pragmatically developed within the context of human concerns and within human communities.

Likewise, the Carolina Thread Trail is in great part built around the concept of linking homes, communities and regions with a set of trails and greenways connecting natural and built environments. It is also about the creation of a unique sense of space that unites urban, rural and natural environments. In these ways efforts such as those involved in the trail pragmatically make "householding" a central concern. In fact the process of getting local communities to "buy-into" the Thread required those pursuing land acquisition agreements to recognize that the trails went through people's homes and communities and because of this they needed to give local people and communities every opportunity to exercise their right to self-determination and plan those trails and greenways in a manner that complimented their sense of community and "householding." It could legitimately be argued that any successful effort at melding diverse interests around a common environmental concern incorporates the importance of householding whereas virtually every failed effort probably underestimated the importance of this need – the natural need of every human being to make a place for themselves and their families in the world.

## A Communitarian Approach to Regional Economic and Environmental Planning

That said, communities and individuals can often find themselves at odds over environmental issues precisely because the perceive differential impacts of potential policies on their homes and communities. Too often negotiating policy issues turns into a standoff between various constituencies that insist upon only considering issues from within the confines of their narrow "identity" group. Thus environmental groups can only consider ideas that are "environmental" in nature while businesses can narrowly consider what benefits them economically and municipalities and counties consider tax revenue and reelection. In truth it is the nature of every constituency group to develop its agenda to garner the support of its supporters and members. This is necessary and healthy for any organizational entity.

While, there are times when developing policy around organizational or community identity may prove necessary, too often narrowly conceived identity group identification produces balkanization and stalemate. However, when cooperative relationships are developed across constituencies then opportunities emerge for forging common ground and common cause through shared valuation and outcome development efforts. This constitutes the communitarian component of ecopragmatics that owes more to the democratic impulses of John Dewey than to the psychological orientation of William James.

The fact that the story of the Carolina Thread Trail is not one characterized by stalemate and balkanization serves as a powerful testimony of the degree to which participants from across the region participated in an informal, democratic and intuitive set of deliberative practices over many years in the interest of identifying regional needs that could be met locally and with local-determination. In fact it is this emphasis upon local-determination and involvement that probably best explains the success of the Carolina Thread Trail. Such an approach not only acknowledges and recognizes the legitimacy of local people having control over their lives and communities, it is also a testament to the degree that policymakers have faith in the decision of local communities in terms of how they value their communities and the surrounding environment. While many within the larger environmental community harbor an inherent distrust of such local thinking, the fact that it has worked so well in the case of the Thread is a testimony to the validity of the work of the late Elinor Ostrom (2001) whose Nobel winning work illustrated that important environmental problems could in fact be effectively dealt with on the basis of local involvement and control. The fact that the organizers and planners of the Thread successfully created a network of community involvement defined by nature trails and greenways is in itself a remarkable accomplishment. To the degree the Thread's planners forged a regional vision from among local priorities and values stands as testimony to the power of making the whole a reflection of its parts rather than compelling local communities to succumb to a distant regional vision. In short, participants throughout the process pursued the common good in such a way as to allow for local discretion in how common goals would be addressed.

Exemplary of this are the various ways in which land can be included in the greenways and trails developed as a part of the Thread. In some instances land has been contributed to one of the region's land trusts for the purpose of being included in the Thread. In other cases private owners maintain ownership of their property but agree to create and maintain trails and greenways on it. In yet other instances municipalities and counties own land to be included in the Thread and so designate the land for such use as well as maintain it with taxpayer funds. These various approaches to acquiring and maintaining land in the Thread network illustrates that while constituents share a common goal – namely the expansion of the Thread – they leave it up to landowners and local governments to decide how that land will be incorporated, developed and sustainably maintained.

## Conclusion

The inclusion of the Carolina Thread Trail case study provides an ideal illustration of how pragmatic environmental decision-making can occur and how stalemate and balkanization can be avoided in civil policy discourse. At the heart of such an approach is (1) a commitment to a method (pragmatics) over an particular ideology, (2) the recognition that not everyone in the community can be expected to fruitfully enter into a collaborative effort, and (3) a willingness to – as much as possible - exclude narrow ideologues from the policy process while actively identifying and engaging the "responsibles" within the community who can and will productively enter into pragmatic and collaborative policymaking. Finally, and perhaps most important is the realization that ultimately all policy deliberations are intuitive with reason and rationality playing an explanatory, exculpatory and persuasive role. That said one should always expect and explore bias – one's own as well as that of others – and seek to learn not only what others would do or say but more importantly understand the reasons why people say and do the things they do.

While being mindful of these basic principles, policy makers have an opportunity to "imaginate" (consider a value, idea or course of action and project a set of scenarios forward in time that might suggest possible outcomes) intuitively as well as through a formal deliberative process in the interest of first drawing tentative conclusions and eventually more formal ones regarding possible definitions of problems and issues and thereafter possible solutions. Ideally one would hope that representatives of various interested constituencies would come together in a true spirit of cooperation and respect for the perspective of others as well as recognizing that feelings and intuitive experiences are important and usually drive policy preferences. If these conditions are met, then chances are good that those gathered around the deliberation table will be successful in developing an ongoing cooperative relationship that produces a broad and nuanced community and regional perspective on problems and generates mutually supported plans and programs for dealing with issues and problems as well as the capacity to continue assessing outcomes and ever broadening the circle of "responsibles" invited into the deliberative process. It is in this hope that *Ecopragmatics* was written – not so much in the interest of presenting a broad and brand-new theoretical approach as explaining why good policy initiatives like the Carolina Thread Trail succeed while other efforts fail under the pressure of identity politics and balkanization. Hopefully this text will prove useful for those who prioritize better community and environmental outcomes over environmental posturing and stalemate politics.

# Chapter References

## Introduction: Introduction to Ecopragmatics

Angle, Jim (2012) "EPA Blasted for Requiring Oil Refineries to Add Type of Fuel that's Merely 'Hypothetical'," *Fox News*. (June 21), Retrieved from the Worldwide Web June 23, 2012 at http://www.foxnews.com/politics/2012/06/21/regulation-requires-oil-refiners-use-millions-gallons-fuel-that-is-nonexistent/.

Barth, Karl (1947) *Church Dogmatics*. Volume 1-14. Grand Rapids, MI: William B. Erdmans, Publisher.

Bearden, David M. (2002) "National Environmental Education Act of 1990: Overview, Implementation and Reauthorization Issues," *CRS Reports for Congress*. (February 26), Order Code 97-97 ENR.

Bookchin, Murray (2005) *The Ecology of Freedom: The Emergence and Dissolution of Hierarchy*. Oakland, CA: A. K. Press.

Bookchin, Murray (1987) "Social Ecology versus Deep Ecology: A Challenge for the Ecology Movement," *Green Perspectives: Newsletter of the Green Program Project*, nos. 4-5 (summer 1987).

Bureau of Labor Statistics (US) (2012) *Occupational Outlook Handbook*. Washington, DC: U.S. Department of Labor.

Callicott, J. Baird (1999) "Silencing Philosophers: Minteer and the Foundations of Antifoundationalism," Environmental Values. Vol., p. 499-516.

Clark, John (1996) "How Wide is Deep Ecology?" *Inquiry*. Vol. 39, No. 2, p. 189 – 201.

Cohen, Bonner (2009) "Tiny Fish Threatens to Turn California's Central Valley into Dust Bowl," Committee for a Constructive Tomorrow. (August 31), Retrieved from the Worldwide Web June 27, 2012 at http://www.cfact.org/a/1581/Tiny-fish-threatens-to-turn-Californias--Central-Valley-into-Dust-Bowl.

Cramer, Philip F. (1998) *Deep Environmental Politics: The Role of Radical Environmentalism in Crafting American Environmental Policy*. Westport, CT: Praeger Press.

DeShalit, Avner (2004) *Red-Green: Democracy, Justice and the Environment*. Tel Aviv, IR: Babel Publishers.

DeShalit, Avner (1995) *Why Posterity Matters: Environmental Polices and Future Generations*. Florence, KY: Routledge.

Dunlap, Riley (2010) "At 40, Environmental Movement Endures, With Less Consensus," *Gallup Politics*. (April 22), Retrieved from the Worldwide Web April 3, 2012 at http://www.gallup.com/poll/127487/environmental-movement-endures-less-consensus.aspx

Ehrlich, Paul H. and Ehrlich, Anne R. (1998) *How Anti-Environmental Rhetoric Threatens Our Future*. Florence, KY: Island Press.

Esbjörn-Hargens, Sean and Zimmerman, Michael E. (2009) *Integral Ecology: Uniting Multiple Perspectives on the Natural World*. New York, NY: Random House/Integral Books.

Etzioni, Amitai (2003) "Communitarianism," in K. Christensen's and D. Levinson (eds.) *Encyclopedia of Community: From the Village to the Virtual World*. Vol. 1, A-D, Los Angeles, CA: Sage Publications, pp. 224-228.

Etzioni, Amitai (1997) *The New Golden Rule: Community and Morality in a Democratic Society*. New York, NY: Basic books.

Etzioni, Amitai (1967) "Mixed-Scanning: A Third Approach to Decision-Making," *Public Administration Review*. Vol. 27, No. 5, p. 385-392.

Farber, Daniel A. (1999) *Eco-Pragmatism*. Chicago, IL: University of Chicago Press.

Fox, Warwick (1989) "The Deep Ecology-Ecofeminism Debate and its Parallels," *Environmental Ethics*. Vol. 11, No. 1, p. 5-25.

Gallup, 2012 "Environment," Retrieved from the Worldwide Web March 31, 2012 at http://www.gallup.com/poll/1615/environmeont.aspx

GfK Roper Consulting (2011) *The Environment: Public Attitudes and Individual Behavior - A Twenty Year Evolution*. Nuremburg, GR, Retrieved from the Worldwide Web March 31, 2012 at http://www.scjohnson.com/Libraries/Download_Documents/SCJ_and_G fK_Roper_Green_Gauge.sflb.ashx.

Greenwood, Keith and Idlet, Ezra (1992) "You Can't Get There From Here," *Over the Limit*. Dublin, IR: Trout Records.

Guggenheim, Davis (Director) (2006) *An Inconvenient Truth*. Hollywood, CA: Paramount Pictures.

Guha, Ramachandra (2005) "Movement Scholarship," What's Next for Environmental History? *Environmental History* Vol. 10, (January) No. 1, p. 40-41

Gunns, Bill (2006) "The American Environmental Values Survey: American Views on the Environment in an Era of Polarization and Conflicting Priorities," EcoAmerica and SRI Consulting, (October), Retrieved from the Worldwide Web April 2, 2012 at http://ruby.fgcy.edu/courses/twimberley/EnviroPol/AEVS.pdf

Haider, Sylvia and Jax, Kurt (2007) "The application of environmental ethics in biological conservation: a case study from the southernmost tip of the Americas," *Biodiversity and Conservation*. Vol. 16, No. 9, p. 2559-2573.

Haidt, Jonathan (2013) *The Righteous Mind: Why Good People Are Divided by Politics and Religion*. New York, NY: Vintage.

Haidt, Jonathan (2006) *The Happiness Hypothesis: Finding Modern Truth in Ancient Wisdom*. New York, NY: Basic Books.

Hanson, Victor Davis (2009) "A Fishy Tale," *National Review Online*. (September 24), Retrieved from the Worldwide Web June 27, 2012 at http://www.nationalreview.com/articles/228295/fishy-tale/victor-davis-hanson.

Hassoun, Nicole (2011) "The Anthropocentric Advantage? Environmental Ethics and Climate Change Policy," *Critical Review of Social and Political Philosophy*. Vol., 1, No. 2, p. 235-257.

Hoffman, Andrew J. and Sandelands, Lloyd E. (2005) "Getting Right with Nature: Anthropocentrism, Ecocentrism, and Theocentrism." *Organization & Environment*, Vol. 18, No. 2, p. 141-162.

Houlder, Vanessa and MacCarthy, Clare (2003) "Bjorn Lomborg: Danish Writer Cleared of Scientific Dishonesty," *Financial Times (London)*. December 18, Retrieved from the Worldwide Web April 4, 2012 at http://www.eskimo.com/~rarnold/lomborg_cleared.htm.

Imagineers, (1998) Walt Disney Imagineering: A Behind the Dreams Look At Making the Magic Rea

Imagineering Academy (2012) "Imagineering," Retrieved from the Worldwide Web April 4, 2012 at http://www.imagineeringacademy.nl/about-imagineering.

Jacques, Peter J., Dunlap, Riley E. & Freeman, Mark (2008) "The Organization of Denial: Conservative Think Tanks and Organizational Scepticism," *Environmental Politics*. Vol. 17, No. 3, p. 349-385.

James, William (1912) "Absolutism and Empiricism," Chapter 12 in *Essays in Radical Empiricism*. New York, NY: Longman Green and Company, p. 266-279.

James, William (1911) *Memories and Studies*. New York, NY: Longman Green and Company.

James, William (1909) *The Meaning of Truth*. New York, NY: Longmans Green and Company.

James, William (1907) *Pragmatism: A New Name for Some Old Ways of Thinking*. New York, NY: Longman Green and Company.

James, William (1903) *Varieties of Religious Experience, a Study in Human Nature*. New York, NY: Longman Green and Company.

James, William (1900) *Talks to Teachers on Psychology and To Students on Some of My Life's Ideals*. Boston, MA: George H. Ellis Company, Inc.

Jensen, Eric; McBay, Aric and Keith, Lierre (2011) *Deep Green Resistance: Strategy to Save the Planet*. Westminster, MD: Seven Stories Press.

Jones, Jeffrey M. (2011) "Americans Increasingly Prioritize Economy Over Environment: Largest margin in favor of economy in nearly 30-year history of the trend," *Gallup Politics*. Retrieved from the Worldwide Web April 1, 2012 at http://www.gallup.com/poll/146681/americans-increasingly-prioritize-economy-environment.aspx.

Hirokawa, Keith (2002) "Some Pragmatic Observations About Radical Critique in Environmental Law," *Stanford Environmental Law Journal*. Vol. 21, No. 2, p. 252-263.

Katz, Eric and Light, Andrew (1996) *Environmental Pragmatism*. Florence, KY: Routledge.

Keulartz, Jozef (1999) "Toward a Post Naturalist Environmental Philosophy," Prologue, Struggle For Nature: A Critique Of Radical Ecology. Florence, KY: Routledge Press, p. 1-120.

Kovak, Matt (2007) "Word Origins: Imagineering," *Paleo-Future*. (May 15), Retrieved from the Worldwide Web April 4, 2012 at http://paleo-future.blogspot.com/2007/05/word-origins-imagineering-1947.html.

Lewin, Kurt (1976) *Resolving Social Conflicts in Field Theory in Social Science*. (Kindle Edition), Washington, DC: American Psychological Association.

Lindenberg, Siegwart (2008) "Social Rationality, Semi-Modularity and Goal Framing: What is it All About?" *Analyze & Kritik*. Vol. 30, p. 669-687.

Lindenberg, Siegwart (2001) "Social Rationality as a Unified Model of Man (Including Bounded Rationality)," *Journal of Management and Governance.* Vol. 5, No. 3, p. 239-251.

Linkola, Penne (2009) *Can Life Prevail?* London, UK: Arktos Media Ltd.

Lomborg, Bjorn (2001) *The Skeptical Environmentalist.* Cambridge, UK: Cambridge University Press.

Luke, Timothy W., (2002) "Deep Ecology: Living as if Nature Mattered Devall and Sessions on Defending the Earth," *Organization and Environment.* Vol. 15, No. 2, p. 178-186.

MacIntyre, Alasdair, (1988) *Whose Justice? Which Rationality?* South Bend, IN: University of Notre Dame Press.

Mappin, Michael J. and Jorhnson, Edward A.(2005) "Changing perspectives of ecology and education in environmental education," In Edward A. Johnson and Michael J. Mappin's *Environmental Education and Advocacy: Changing Perspectives on Ecology and Education.* Cambridge, UK: Cambridge University Press.

Middleton, Brandon (2012) "Feds And NRDC File Responsive Briefs In 9th Circuit Delta Smelt Litigation," Pacific Legal Foundation Liberty Blog. (April 30), Retrieved from the Worldwide Web June 27 2012 at http://blog.pacificlegal.org/2012/feds-and-nrdc-file-responsive-briefs-in-9th-circuit-delta-smelt-litigation/.

Minteer, Ben (2012) *Refounding Environmental Ethics: Pragmatism, Principle and Practice.* Philadelphia, PA: Temple University Press.

Minteer, Ben (2009) *The Landscape of Reform: Civic Pragmatism And Environmental Thought in America.* Boston, MA: MIT Press.

Naess, Arnie (1973) "The Shallow And The Deep, Long-Range Ecology Movements: A Summary" Inquiry. Vol. 16, p. 95-100.

Naik, A. M. (2007) "Larsen and Tourbro Limited: Investor Presentation," Retrieved from the Worldwide Web April 4, 2012 at http://www.larsentoubro.com/lntcorporate/uploads/L&T_Investor_Prese ntation_Sept_07.pdf

Norton, Bryan G. (2005) *Sustainability: A Philosophy of Adaptive Ecosystem Management.* Chicago, IL: University of Chicago Press.

O'Hara, Craig (2001) *The Philosophy of Punk: More than Noise.* Oakland, CA: AK Press.

Ostrom, Elinor (2001) *The Drama of the Commons.* Washington, DC: National Academies Press.

Parker, Kelly (1990) "The Values of Habitat," *Environmental Ethics.* Vol. 12, p. 353-368.

Peirce, Charles Sanders (1878) *"How to make our Ideas Clear," The Writings of Charles Sanders Peirce. Bloomington, IN: Indiana University Press.*

PollingReport.com (2012) "Environment," Retrieved from the Worldwide Web March 31, 2012 at http://www.pollingreport.com/enviro.htm

Ray, Jannise (2007) "Altar Call for True Believers," *Orion Magazine.* September/ October, p. 58-63.

Rosebraugh, Craig (2004) *Burning Rage of a Dying Planet: Speaking for the Earth Liberation Front.* Herndon, VA: Lantern Books.

Rosenthal, Sandra B. and Buchholz, Rogene (1999) *Rethinking Business Ethics: A Pragmatic Approach*. New York, NY: Oxford University Press.

Schon, Donald A. and Martin Rein (1994) *Frame Reflection: Toward the Resolution of Intractable Policy Controversies*. New York, NY: Basic Books.

Sessions, George (1995) "Deep Ecology for the 21$^{st}$ Century," *Inquiry*. Vol. 16, p. 311-312.

Simon, Herbert A. (1957): *Models of Man - Social and Rational*. New York, NY: John Wiley and Sons.

Sisco, Annette (2009) "LSU Ouster Of Ivor Van Heerden Removes Most Honest Appraiser Of City's Levee Failures," *Picayune-Times*. (May 15), Retrieved from the Worldwide Web April 7, 2012 at http://blog.nola.com/guesteditorials/2009/04/worried_about_funding_lsu _oust.html.

Steiner, Gary (2010) *Anthropocentrism and Its Discontents: The Moral Status of Animals in the History of Western Philosophy*. Pittsburgh, PA: University of Pittsburgh Press.

Sullivan, Collin (2009) "California Water Agency Changes Course on Delta Smelt," *The New York Times, Energy & Environment*. (May 12), Retrieved from the Worldwide Web June 27, 2012 at http://www.nytimes.com/gwire/2009/05/12/12greenwire-calif-water-agency-changes-course-on-delta-sme-10572.html.

Sussman, Brian (2012) *Eco-Tyranny: How the Left's Green Agenda Will Dismantle America*. Blue Springs, MO: WND Books.

Taylor, Bron R. (2008) "The Tributaries of Radical Environmentalism," *Journal for the Study of Radicalism*. Vol. 2, Vol. 1, p. 27-61.

Taylor, Bron R. (2000) "Deep Ecology as Social Philosophy: A Critique." In Eric Katz, Andrew Light and David Rothenberg (eds.) *Beneath the Surface: Critical Essays on Deep Ecology*. Cambridge, MA: MIT Press, p. 269–99.

Tversky, Amos and Kahneman, Daniel (1981) "The Framing of Decisions and Psychological Choice," *Science*, New Series, Vol. 211, No. 4481, (Jan. 30), p. 453-458.

White, Lynn (1967) "The Historical Roots of Our Ecological Crisis," *Science*. Vol. 155, p. 1203-07.

Wilber, Ken (1997) "An Integral Theory of Consciousness," *Journal of Consciousness Studies*. Vol. 4, No. 1, p. 71-92.

Williamson, Timothy (2007) "Anthropocentrism and Truth," *Philosophia*. Vol. 17, No. 1, p. 33-53.

Wimberley, Edward T. (2009) *Nested Ecology: The Place of Humans in the Ecological Hierarchy*. Baltimore, MD: Johns Hopkins University Press.

Wimberley, Edward T. and Hobbs, Bradley K. (2012) "The Conservative Ecologist: Classical Liberalism Revisited," *The International Journal of Environmental, Cultural, Economic and Social Sustainability*. Vol. 8 (In Press).

Wray-Lake, Laura; Flanagan, Constance A. and Osgood, D. Wayne (2008) "Adolescent Environmental Attitudes, Beliefs, and Behaviors across Three Decades," The Network to Transition to Adulthood Working

Paper, Funded by the John D. and Catherine T. MacArthur Foundation Grant No. 00-00-65719-HCD, Pennsylvania State University, Department of Human Development and Family Studies,113 South Henderson Building, University Park, PA, 16802.

Zimmerman, Michael E. (2003) "On Reconciling Progressivism and Environmentalism," In J. Kassiola's *Explorations in Environmental Political Theory: Thinking About What We Value.* Armonk, NY: M.E. Sharpe Publisher, p.149-177.

Zimmerman, Michael and Taylor, Bron (2005) "Deep Ecology," in Bron Taylor's Encyclopedia of Religion and Nature. New York, NY: Continuum, p. 456-460.

Zwick, Steve (2012) "A Tennessee Fireman's Solution to Climate Change," *Forbes.* (April 19) Retrieved from the Worldwide Web at http://www.forbes.com/sites/stevezwick/2012/04/19/a-tennessee-firemans-solution-to-climate-change/

Zygmunt J.B. Plater (2006) "Keynote Speaker, Environmentalists & Cultural Relativity: the Challenges of Being Effective in a Polarized, Balkanized, Commoditized, Lobotomized Political World" 24th International Public Interest Environmental Law Conference. Eugene, OR. March 3.

## Chapter 1: Straight Talk

Anscombe, G. E. M. (1958) "Modern Moral Philosophy". *Philosophy.* Vol. 33, No. 124, p. 1–19.

Berger, Peter L. and Luckman, Thomas (1966) *The Social Construction of Reality: A Treatise in the Sociology of Knowledge.* New York, NY: Anchor.

Bjork, Daniel W. (1983) *The Compromised Scientist: William James in the Development of American Psychology.* New York, NY: Columbia University Press.

Bromley, Daniel W. (2004) "Reconsidering Environmental Policy: Prescriptive Consequentialism and Volitional Pragmatism," *Environmental and Resource Economics.* Vol. 28, p. 73-99.

Collins, Gary R., Johnson, Eric L. and Jones, Stanton L. (2000) *Psychology & Christianity: Four Views.* Westmont, IL: IVP Academic.

Collinge, William (1998) *Subtle Energy: Awakening to the Unseen Forces in Our Lives.* New York, NY: Warner Books.

Crowder, George (2006) "Value Pluralism and Communitarinism," *Contemporary Political Theory.* Vol. 5, p. 405-427.

Dewey, John (1946) "Democracy and Educational Administration" In John Dewey's *Problems of Man.* New York, NY: Philosophical Library.

Dewey, John (1938) *Logic: The Theory of Inquiry.* New York, NY: Holt, Rinehart and Winston.

Dewey, John (1934) *The Late Works,* Vol. 10, Carbondale, IL: Southern Illinois University Press.

Dewey, John (1929) *Experience and Nature.* LaSalle, IL: Open Court Press.

Dewey, John (1927) *The Public and its Problems.* New York, NY: Henry Holt and Company.

Dewey, John (1920) *Reconstruction in Philosophy*. New York, NY: Henry Holt and Company.

Dewey, John (1916) *Experience and Education*. New York, NY: Simon and Schuster.

Dewey, John (1910). *How We Think*. Boston, MA: D.C. Heath & Co.

Dewey, John (1904) *The Late Works*. Vol., 2, Carbondale, IL: Southern Illinois University Press.

Dorrien, Gary J. (1995) *Soul in Society: The Making and Renewal of Social Christianity*. Minneapolis, MN: Fortress Press.

Etzioni, Amitai (2002) "Individualism Within History," *The Hedgehog Review*. (Spring), p. 49-56.

Etzioni, Amitai (1998) *The Essential Communitarian Reader*. Lanham, MD: Rowman & Littlefield Publishers.

Etzioni, Amitai (1995) *New Communitarian Thinking: Persons, Virtues, Institutions, and Communities*. Charlottesville, VA: University Press of Virginia.

Firebraugh, Joseph J. (1953) "The Relativism of Henry James," *Journal of Aesthetics and Art Criticism*. Vol. 12, No. 2 (December), p. 237-242.

Fischer, Constance T. (1994) *Individualizing Psychological Assessment: A Collaborative and Therapeutic Approach*. New York, NY: Routledge.

Fish, Stanley (1995) "What Makes and Interpretation Acceptable?" In Russell B. Goodman's (Ed.) *Pragmatism: A Contemporary Reader*. New York, NY: Routledge. p. 253-265.

Gotkin, George (1985) "William James and the Cash-Value Metaphor," *Et Cetera*. (Spring), p. 37-46.

Haidt, Jonathan (2013) *The Righteous Mind: Why Good People Are Divided by Politics and Religion*. New York, NY: Vintage.

Haidt, Jonathan (2006) *The Happiness Hypothesis: Finding Modern Truth in Ancient Wisdom*. New York, NY: Basic Books.

James, William (1884) "Absolutism and Empiricism," *Mind*. Vol. IX, No. 34 (April), p. 281-286.

James, William (1898) "Philosophical Conceptions and Practical Results," *University Chronicle*. Vol. 1, No. 4 (September), p. 287-310.

James, William (1892) "Streams of Consciousness," In William James's *Psychology*. (Chapter XI), New York, NY: World Publishing.

James, William (1890) *Principles of Psychology*. Boston, MA: Henry Holt.

James, William (1900) Preface to Ferrari's Italian Translation" Appendix III of *The Principles of Psychology,* Vol. III, Cambridge, MA: Harvard University Press, (1981), p.1484.

James, William (1904) "A World of Pure Experience," *Journal of Philosophy, Psychology, and Scientific Methods*. Vol. I, No. 20, p. 589-597.

James, William (1907) *Pragmatism*. New York, NY: Longman Green and Company.

James, William (1908) *The Meaning of Truth*. New York, NY: Longman Green and Company.

James, William (1910) ""Pluralism, Pragmatism, and Instrumental Truth," In William James's *From A Pluralistic Universe*. New York, NY: Longman Green and Company, pp. 321-4

James, William (1912) *Essays in Radical Empiricism*. New York, NY: Longman Green and Company.

Kivinen, Osmo and Piiroinen, Kivinen (2006) "Toward Pragmatist Methodological Relationalism: From Philosophizing Sociology to Sociologizing Philosophy," *Philosophy of the Social Sciences*. Vol. 36, No. 3, p. 303-329.

Lewis, Clarence Irving (1929) *Mind and the World Order: Outline of a Theory of Knowledge*. Mineola, NY: Dover Publications.

Lossky, Nikolay (1928) *The World as an Organic Whole*. London, UK: Oxford University Press.

Lossky, Nikolay (1924) *Foundations of Intutitivsm*. Berlin, GR: Humboldt University of Berlin.

Margolis, Joseph (1998) "Peirce's Fallibilism," *Transactions of the Charles S. Pierce Society*. Vol. 34, No. 3, p. 535-569.

Minteer, Ben (2012) *Refounding Environmental Ethics: Pragmatism, Principle and Practice*. Philadelphia, PA: Temple University Press.

Minteer, Ben (2009) *The Landscape of Reform: Civic Pragmatism And Environmental Thought in America*. Boston, MA: MIT Press.

Morgan, David L. (2007) "Paradigms Lost and Pragmatism Regained: Methodological Implications of Combining Qualitative and Quantitative Methods," *Journal of Mixed Methods Research*. Vol. 1, No. 48, p. 48-76.

Murphy, Joseph (2008) *The Power of Your Subconscious Mind*. Radford, VA: Wilder Publications.

Mustain, Megan Rust (2006) "Metaphor as Method: Charlene Haddock Seigfried's Radical Reconstruction," William James Studies. Vol. 1, Retrieved from the Worldwide Web April 11, 12 at http://williamjamesstudies.org/1.1/mustain.html.

Nevid, Jeffery S. (2011) Essentials of Psychology: Concepts and Applications. Independence, KY: Wadsworth Publishing.

Norris, Christopher (1998) "Treading Water in Neurath's Ship: Quine, Davidson, Rorty," *Principia – An International Journal of Epistemology*. Vol. 2, No. 1, p. 227-279.

Peirce, Charles Sanders (1878) *"How to make our Ideas Clear," The Writings of Charles Sanders Peirce. Bloomington, IN: Indiana University Press.*

Perley, David (2006) "Explosive Metaphors and Vagueness: Seigfried's Contribution to James Scholarship and its Significance Beyond the Field of Philosophy," William James Studies. Vol. 1, Retrieved from the Worldwide Web April 11, 12 at http://williamjamesstudies.org/1.1/perley.html.

Putnam, Hilary (1995) "The Question of Realism," in *Words and Life*, Cambridge, MA: Harvard University Press.

Putnam, Hilary (1995) *Pragmatism: An Open Question*. Hoboken, NJ: Wiley-Blackwell.

Richardson, Robert E. (2006) *William James: In the Maelstrom of American Modernism: A Biography*. Boston, MA: Houghton-Mifflin Harcourt.

Rorty, Richard (2003) "Richard Rorty: Philosopher," The Believer. (June), Retrieved from the Worldwide Web April 21, 2012 at http://www.believermag.com/issues/200306/?read=interview_rorty.

Rorty, Richard (1982) *Consequences of Pragmatism: Essays 1972-1980.* Minneapolis, MN: University of Minnesota Press.

Schon, Donald A. and Martin Rein (1994) *Frame Reflection: Toward the Resolution of Intractable Policy Controversies.* New York, NY: Basic Books.

Scotton, Bruce W., Chinen, Allan B. and Battista, John R. (1996) *Textbook of Transpersonal Psychology and Psychology.*

Seigfried, Charlene Haddock (2006) "Is James Still Too Radical for Pragmatic Recognition? William James'ss Radical Reconstruction of Philosophy–Fifteen Years Later, William James Studies. Vol. 1, Retrieved from the Worldwide Web April 11, 12 at http://williamjamesstudies.org/1.1/seigfried.html.

Serafin, Steven R. and Bendixen, Alfred (2005) The Continuum Encyclopedia of American Literature. New York, NY: Continuum.

Shur, John J. (2009) "Looking Toward Last Things: James's Pragmatism Beyond Its First Century," In John J. Shur's (Ed.) *100 Years of Pragmatism: William James's Revolutionary Philosophy.* Bloomington, IN: Indiana University Press.

Stephens, Piers H. G. (2012) "The Turn of the Skew: Pragmatism, Environmental Philosophy and the Ghost of William James," *Contemporary Pragmatism.* Vol. 9, No. 1, p. 25-52.

Stephens, Piers H. G. (2009) "Toward a Jamesian Environmental Policy," *Environmental Ethics.* Vol. 31, p. 227-244.

Thayer, H.S. (1975) "Introduction," in William James, Fredson Bowers and Iignas Skrupskelis's *The Meaning of Truth.* Cambridge, MA: Harvard University Press.

Thayer-Bacon, Barbara J. (2002) "Using the "R" Word Again: Pragmatism as Qualified Relativism," *Philosophical Studies in Education.* Vol. 33, p. 93-102.

Townshend, Peter (1969) Pinball Wizard. [The Who], On Tommy, Gelfen Records.

Wilber, Ken (2010) "Toward A Comprehensive Theory of Subtle Energies," *Ken Wilber Online.* Boston, MA: Shambhala Publications, Retrieved from the Worldwide Web April 11, 12 at http://wilber.shambhala.com/html/books/kosmos/excerptG/part3.cfm.

Witmer, Gene (2011) "On Making Everything Boring," *Florida Philosophical Review.* Vol. XI, No. 1 (Summer), p. 1-16.

Zimmerman, Barry J. and Schunk, Dale H. (2003) *Educational Psychology: A Century of Contributions.* New York, NY: Routledge.

## Chapter 2: The L&N Don't Stop Here Anymore

Adams, Sean Patrick (2010) "The US Coal Industry in the Nineteenth Century," *EH.Net.* Economic History Association, (April 2) Retrieved from the Worldwide Web April 24, 2012 at http://eh.net/encyclopedia/article/adams.industry.coal.us.

Atlantic Legal Foundation (ALF) (2012) "EPA Slammed by the Supreme Court,"
    *ALF News Archive*. (March 21), Retrieved from the Worldwide Web
    April 28, 2012 at http://www.atlanticlegal.org/newsitem.php?nid=288.
American Coalition for Clean Coal Electricity (ACCCE) (2010) "ACCCE
    Statement on Colorado House Bill 1365 Passage," (April 1), ACCCE
    Press Release, Retrieved from the Worldwide Web April 26, 2012 at
    http://www.cleancoalusa.org/press-and-media/press-releases/accce-
    statement-colorado-house-bill-1365-passage.
Associated Governments of Northwest Colorado (AGNC) (2009) "Energy
    Development Policy," (November 12), Retrieved from the Worldwide
    Web April 26, 2012 at http://agnc.org/policy.html.
Associated Press (AP) (2010) "Xcel Energy Unveils Plan To Cut Plant
    Emissions," *The Daily Sentinel,* Grand Junction Colorado, (August 13),
    Retrieved from the Worldwide Web April 28, 2012 at
    http://www.gjsentinel.com/news/articles/xcel-energy-unveils-plan-to-
    cut-plant-emissions.
Bannister, Craig (2013) "Senator Calls on Holder to Investigate EPA's Armed
    Raid on Gold Mine," *CNS News*. (October 22), Retrieved from the
    Worldwide Web June 25, 2014 at http://cnsnews.com/mrctv-blog/craig-
    bannister/senator-calls-holder-investigate-epas-armed-raid-gold-mine
Barraso, John (2009) "Culture of Intimidation" Rules EPA," Office of U.S.
    Senator John Barraso (R-WY), Press Release, (July 7), Retrieved from
    the Worldwide Web June 25, 2014 at
    http://www.barrasso.senate.gov/public/index.cfm?FuseAction=PressOffi
    ce.PressReleases&ContentRecord_id=56688E7F-F9BB-0142-9D8E-
    EE57BB867F21&IsPrint=true
Batasch, Michael (2013) "Senators Slam EPA for Leaking Farmer's Personal
    Data to Environmentalists," *Daily Caller*. (June 6), Retrieved from the
    Worldwide Web June 25, 2014 at
    http://dailycaller.com/2013/06/06/senators-slam-epa-for-leaking-
    farmers-personal-data-to-environmentalists/
Begos, Kevin (2012) "Electric Power Plants Shift From Coal To Natural Gas,"
    *The Huffington Post*. (April 29) Retrieved from the Worldwide Web
    April 29, 2012 at http://www.huffingtonpost.com/2012/01/16/electric-
    plants-coal-natural-gas_n_1208875.html.
Berger, Judson (2014) "Watchdog: EPA Officials Obstructed Justice Through
    'Intimidation'," *FoxNews.com*. (February 27), Retrieved from the
    Worldwide Web at
    http://www.foxnews.com/politics/2014/02/27/watchdog-epa-officials-
    obstructed-probes-through-intimidation/?intcmp=latestnews
Black, George (2012)"Dirty Industry, Dirty Fight," *OnEarth Magazine*. (March
    2) Retrieved from the Worldwide Web May 3, 2012 at
    http://www.onearth.org/article/dirty-industry-dirty-fight.
Bowe, Anthony (2010) "An Unlikely Coalition for Clean Air Act: A Lesson in
    Political Bipartisanship and Coalition Building," *The Colorado
    Statesman*. (April 23) Retrieved from the Worldwide Web April 24,
    2012 at http://coloradostatesman.com/content/991786-an-unlikely-
    coalition-clean-air-act.

Chen, Jim (2005) "Conduit-Based Regulation of Speech," *Duke Law Journal*. Vol. 54, p. 1359-1457.

Colman, Zack (2014) "Winter Blackouts Could Hit Midwest, Mid-Atlantic Regional Operator Warns," *Washington Examiner*. August 27, 2014, Retrieved from the Worldwide Web August 27, 2014 at http://ruby.fgcu.edu/courses/twimberley/10199/blackout.pdf.

Cox, Clara (1983) "Comparing the Studies of Coal Slurry Pipeline," *Special Report*. Virginia Water Resources Research Center, Virginia Polytechnic Institute and State University, Blacksburg, VA, (December), Retrieved from the Worldwide Web May 3, 2012 at http://vwrrc.vt.edu/pdfs/specialreports/sr171983.pdf.

Davidson, Steve (2014) "U.S. Coal-Fired Electric Power Dying Faster Than Expected: New Forecasts Expected," *Communities Digital News*. (February 15), Retrieved from the Worldwide Web June 25, 2014 at http://www.commdiginews.com/health-science/u-s-coal-fired-electric-power-dying-faster-than-expected-new-forecasts-expected-8894/

DeAngelis, Jackie (2014) "Natural Gas Prices Seen Flaring Higher," *CNBC*. (May 29)

Denning, Liam (2012) "A Lump of Coal for Gas Bills," The Wall Street Journal. (March 29) Retrieved from the Worldwide Web April 28, 2012 at http://online.wsj.com/article/SB100014240527023041771045773114900 76867340.html?mod=ITP_moneyandinvesting_5.

Deninston, Lyle (2012) "Obama EPA About to Get Kneecapped by the Supreme Court," *Fox News*. (January 10) Retrieved from the Worldwide Web April 28, 2012 at http://nation.foxnews.com/epa/2012/01/10/obama-epa-about-get-kneecapped-supreme-court.

DeWitt, Bog and Meyer, Rob (2005) *Strategy Synthesis: Resolving Strategy Paradoxes to Create Competitive Advantage*. London, UK: Thomson Learning.

Energy Information Administration (2011) "Quarterly Coal Report," (July) U.S. Energy Information Administration, Washington, D.C., Retrieved from the Worldwide Web May 2, 2012 at http://www.eia.gov/coal/production/quarterly/pdf/tes1p01p1.pdf.

Eves, Robin T. (2011) "CEO Letter to Shareholders," Clean Coal Technologies, Inc., New York, NY, Retrieved from the Worldwide Web April 29, 2012 at http://www.cleancoaltechnologiesinc.com/contact.php.

Etzioni, Amitai (1997) *The New Golden Rule: Community and Morality in a Democratic Society*. New York, NY: Basic Books.

Futch, Matt, Flaherty, Phil and Gilbert, Carly (2011) *Colorado's Clean Air-Clean Jobs Act A Holistic Approach to Energy, Economy and Environment*. Boulder, CO: State of Colorado, Governor's Energy Office.

Goodell, Jeff (2007) *Big Coal: The Dirty Secret Behind America's Energy Future*. New York, NY: Houghton Mifflin Harcourt

Goss, Sara (2009) "Obama Said He Would Bankrupt the Coal Industry," American Thinker. (February 27) Retrieved from the Worldwide Web April 26, 2012 at http://www.americanthinker.com/blog/2009/02/obama_said_he_would_bankrupt_t.html.

Harder, Amy (2012) "What's Really Causing Coal's Decline?" *National Journal.* (April 9) Retrieved from the Worldwide Web May 2, 2012 at http://energy.nationaljournal.com/2012/04/whats-really-causing-coals-dec.php.

Helman, Chris (2012) "EPA Official Who Sought To 'Crucify' Oil Companies Has Resigned," *Forbes.* (April 30), Retrieved from the Worldwide Web June 25, 2014 at http://www.forbes.com/sites/christopherhelman/2012/04/30/epa-official-who-sought-to-crucify-oil-companies-has-resigned/

Hemphill, Thomas A. and Perry, Mark J. (2012) "How Obama's Energy Policy Will Kill Jobs," *The American.* (March 8), The American Enterprise Institute, Retrieved from the Worldwide Web June 25, 2014 at http://www.american.com/archive/2012/march/how-obamas-energy-policy-will-kill-jobs/article_print

Hoffmeister, John (2011) Keynote Address: 2011 KPMG Global Energy Conference. (May 25), Houston, Texas, Retrieved from the Worldwide Web April 26, 2012 at http://www.kpmginstitutes.com/global-energy-institute/insights/2011/pdf/global-energy-conference-recap-2011.pdf.

Holland, Jesse (2012) "High Court Criticizes 'Heavy Hand' of EPA," Buffalo Law Journal. (January 12), Retrieved from the Worldwide Web April 28, 2012 at http://www.lawjournalbuffalo.com/news/article/current/2012/01/12/103688/high-court-criticizes-heavy-hand-of-epa.

Hurdle, Jon (2014) "Advocates See US Gas Exports Spurring Major Job Growth," *MNI: Financial Market News.* (June 24) Retrieved from the Worldwide Web June 25, 2014 at https://mninews.marketnews.com/print/981723

Inhofe, James M. (2012) "Inhofe Floor Speech: President Obama's War on Domestic Energy Production: "Crucify Them," U.S. Senate Committee on Environment and Public Works, (April 25), Retrieved from the Worldwide Web April 25, 2012 at http://epw.senate.gov/public/index.cfm?FuseAction=Minority.Speeches&ContentRecord_id=ea800426-802a-23ad-4e25-9051360ff8fc&IsPrint=true.

Institute for Energy Research (IER) (2010) "Colorado Energy Facts," Retrieved from the Worldwide Web September 10, 2014 at http://instituteforenergyresearch.org/media/state-regs/pdf/Colorado.pdf.

Investors Business Daily (IBD), 2012 "EPA's Heavy Hand Seen in Gas Crisis," IBD Editorials. Retrieved from the Worldwide Web April 28, 2012 at http://news.investors.com/articleprint/605348/201203221853/epa-partly-to-blame-for-gas-crisis.aspx.

James, William (1907) *Pragmatism: A New Name for Some Old Ways of Thinking.* New York, NY: Longman Green and Co.

James, William (1890) *The Principles of Psychology.* New York, NY: H. Holt Publisher.

Janowiak, Jim (2012) "The Town EPA Says Must Close," The Daily Accountant. (March 4) Retrieved from the Worldwide Web April 24, 2012 at http://thedailyaccount.com/The-Town-EPA-Says-Must-Close.html.

Kuhn, Thomas (1962) *The Structure of Scientific Revolutions.* Chicago, IL: University of Chicago Press.

Langley, Ann (1995) "Between 'Paralysis by Analysis' and 'Extinction by Instinct'" *Sloan Management Review.* (Spring) Vol. 36, No. 3, p. 63-76.

Leeb, Stephen (2011) *Red Alert: How China's Growing Prosperity Threatens the American Way of Life.* New York, NY: Business Plus.

Long, Gary (2010) "U.S. Crude Oil, Natural Gas, and Natural Gas Liquids Reserves," U.S. Energy Information Agency, (November 30), Retrieved from the Worldwide Web July 5, 2012 at http://www.eia.gov/oil_gas/natural_gas/data_publications/crude_oil_nat ural_gas_reserves/cr.html.

MacIntosh, David L. and Spengler, John D. Spengler (2011) "Emissions of Hazardous Air Pollutants from Coal Fired Power Plants," Paul Billings Vice President for National Policy and Advocacy American Lung Association 1301 Pennsylvania Ave., NW Suite 800 Washington, DC, Retrieved from the Worldwide Web May 3, 2012 at http://www.lung.org/assets/documents/healthy-air/coal-fired-plant-hazards.pdf.

Malewitz, Jim (2012) "Coal States Uncertain of Industry's Future," *Governing View.* (April 20) Retrieved from the Worldwide Web May 20, 2012 at http://www.governing.com/blogs/view/coal-states-fear-for-future-of-the-industry.html.

Marton, Kati (2011) "The Weapons of Diplomacy and the Human Factor," *New York Times* (Opinion and Editorial), (April 19) Retrieved from the Worldwide Web April 8, 2012 at http://www.nytimes.com/2011/04/20/opinion/20iht-edmarton20.html?pagewanted=all

McCarthy, James E. and Copeland, Claudia (2011) "EPA's Regulation of Coal-Fired Power: Is a "Train Wreck" Coming? *CRS Reports for Congress.* Congressional Research Service, (August 8), 7-5700, R41914, Retrieved from the Worldwide Web April 26, 2012 at http://www.fas.org/sgp/crs/misc/R41914.pdf.

McGregor, Douglas (1969) *The Human Side of Enterprise.* New York, NY: McGraw Hill.

Medarova-Bergstom, Keti; Baldock, David; Volkery, Axel and Withana, Sirini (2011) "When Financial Needs Meet Political Realities: Implications for Climate Change in the Post-2013 EU Budget," *Directions in Environmental Policy.* (June) Institute of European Environmental Policy, London, UK, Retrieved from the Worldwide Web April 8, 2012 at http://www.ieep.eu/assets/805/DEEP_EU_budget-_financial_needs_political_realities.pdf.

Mica, John L. (2011) "Hearing Highlights EPA Overreach Impacts on Mining in U.S. and Appalachia," Report from Chairman Rep. John L. Micah, U.S. House of Representatives Transportation and Infrastructure Committee, (May 5) Retrieved from the Worldwide Web May 2, 2012 at http://transportation.house.gov/hearings/hearingDetail.aspx?NewsID=12 59.

Miller, Steve (2012) "New EPA Regulations are the Latest Attempt to Shutter America's Coal Industry," *America's Power*. (March 27) American Coalition for Clean Coal Energy (ACCCE), Retrieved from the Worldwide Web April 28, 2012 at http://www.americaspower.org/new-epa-regulations-are-latest-attempt-shutter-america's-coal-industry.

Minteer, Ben (2012) *Refounding Environmental Ethics: Pragmatism, Principle and Practice*. Philadelphia, PA: Temple University Press.

Minteer, Ben (2009) *The Landscape of Reform: Civic Pragmatism And Environmental Thought in America*. Boston, MA: MIT Press.

Morgan, David L. (2007) "Paradigms Lost and Pragmatism Regained: Methodological Implications of Combining Qualitative and Quantitative Methods," Journal of Mixed Methods Research. Vol. 1, No. 48, p. 48-76.

News New Mexico Staff (2012) Heavy Hand of EPA Continues Obama Assault on Coal, Electric Bills Likely to Rise," *News New Mexico*. (March 2) Retrieved from the Worldwide Web May 2, 2012 at http://newsnewmexico.blogspot.com/2012/03/heavy-hand-of-epa-continues-obama.html.

Nielsen, John (2010) "Clean Air, Clean Jobs Bill Becomes Law with WRA's Support," *Western Views*. Vol. 21 (Spring), A publication of the Western Resources Association, Boulder, CO.

Papachristodoulou, George Lazarou and Trass, Olev (2009) "Coal Slurry Fuel Technology," *The Canadian Journal of Chemical Engineering*. Vol. 65, No. 2, p. 177-201.

Pickens, T. Boone (2011) "The Plan," PickensPlan. Retrieved from the Worldwide Web May 1, 2012 at http://www.pickensplan.com/theplan/.

Podesta, John (2011) "Statement on EPA's Proposed Mercury and Air Toxics Standards: CAP President and CEO Commends Agency," Center for American Progress, Washington, DC, (March 16) Retrieved from the Worldwide Web April 29, 2012 at http://www.americanprogress.org/issues/2011/03/podesta_epa_rules.htm l.

Pyle, Thomas (2012) "Ghost Town? How onerous regulations are killing a Craig, Colorado," American Energy Association Press Release. (February 21) Retrieved from the Worldwide Web April 24, 2012 at http://www.americanenergyalliance.org/2012/02/1916/.

Raloff, Janet (2008) "Scientific Interference: Complaints at the EPA," *Science News*. (May 8), Retrieved from the Worldwide Web June 25, 2014 at https://www.sciencenews.org/blog/science-public/scientific-interference-complaints-epa

Rascalli, Ann (2010) "Ritter Signs Clean Air Clean Jobs Act into Law," Colorado Energy News. (April 19) Retrieved from the Worldwide Web April 24, 2012 at http://coloradoenergynews.com/2010/04/ritter-signs-clean-air-clean-jobs-act-into-law/print/.

Richardson, Valerie (2014) "Obama Administrations 'Culture of Intimidation' Seen in Nevada Ranch Standoff," Washington Times. (April 15), Retrieved from the Worldwide Web June 25, 2014 at http://www.washingtontimes.com/news/2014/apr/15/culture-of-intimidation-seen-in-nevada-ranch-stand/

Rowe, John (2011) "Energy Policy: Above All, Do No Harm," American Enterprise Institute. (March 8), Retrieved from the Worldwide Web April 25, 2012 at http://www.exeloncorp.com/assets/newsroom/speeches/docs/spch_Rowe _AEI2011.pdf.

Rugaber, Christopher S. and Wiseman, Paul (2012) "US economic growth too sluggish to drive down unemployment," *Associated Press*. (April 27) Retrieved from the Worldwide Web May 2, 2012 at http://www.news-sentinel.com/apps/pbcs.dll/article?AID=/20120427/NEWS/120429586/1 010/CELEB.

Safer States (2014) "Adopted Policy," Retrieved from the Worldwide Web June 25, 2014 at http://www.saferstates.org/bill-tracker/

Schon, Donald A. and Rein, Martin (1984) *Frame Reflection: Toward the Resolution of Intractable Policy Controversies*. New York, NY: Basic Books.

Shanahan, Elizabeth A., McBeth, Mark K., Hathaway, Paul L., Arnell, Ruth J. (2008) "Conduit Or Contributor? The Role Of Media In Policy Change Theory," *Policy Science*. Vol. 41, No. 2, p. 115-138.

Sheesley, Timothy (2010) "Economic Impacts of Implementing the Colorado Clean Air-Clean Jobs Act under different scenarios" Exhibit No. TJS-3, October 6 Testimony before the Public Service Company of Colorado, Docket No. 10A-245E.

Singer, Roger (2010) "Clean Air and Clean Jobs," *Denver Post*. (March 26) Retrieved from the Worldwide Web April 24, 2012 at http://www.denverpost.com/headlines/ci_14758586.

Slaughter, Nathan (2012) "Could This be the Death Knell for Coal Stocks?" *Townhall.com* (May 2) Retrieved from the Worldwide Web May 2, 2012 at http://finance.townhall.com/columnists/nathanslaughter/2012/04/17/coul d_this_be_the_death_knell_for_coal_stocks/page/full/.

Smith, Craig (2010) "Clean Air, Clean Jobs Act Signed into Law," The Craig Daily. (April 20) Retrieved from the Worldwide Web April 25, 2012 at http://www.craigdailypress.com/news/2010/apr/20/clean-air-clean-jobs-act-signed-law/.

Sweet, Bill (2010) "Old-Time Coal," *Energy Wise*. (September 10), Institute of Electrical and Electronics Engineers (IEEE), Retrieved from the Worldwide Web April 8, 2012 at http://spectrum.ieee.org/energywise/energy/fossil-fuels/oldtime-coal.

Talamani, Jonathan (2010) "Colorado's "Clean Air-Clean Jobs Act": Encouraging Conversion Of Coal Plants To Natural Gas," *Climate Law Blog: Center for Climate Change Law, Columbia University*. Retrieved from the Worldwide Web April 24, 2012 at http://blogs.law.columbia.edu/climatechange/2010/10/19/colorado's-clean-air-clean-jobs-act-encouraging-conversion-of-coal-plants-to-natural-gas/.

Taylor, Rebecca (2011) "Reconsidering the Transformative Potential of Dialogue," *Philosophy of Education Yearbook*. p. 199-202.

Thrasher, Ernie (2012) "US coal exports to China may double in 2012 - Xcoal," *SteelGuru*. (April 23) Retrieved from the Worldwide Web May 2, 2012 at http://www.steelguru.com/sfTCPDF/getPDF/MjYwNDI3/US_coal_expo rts_to_China_may_double_in_2012_Xcoal.html.

Trembath, Alex; Luke, Max; Shellenberger, Michael and Nordhaus, Ted (2013) "Coal Killer: How Natural Gas Fuels the Clean Energy Revolution," Breakthrough Institute White Paper. (June), Retrieved from the Worldwide Web June 25, 2014 at http://thebreakthrough.org/images/main_image/Breakthrough_Institute_ Coal_Killer.pdf

Tremoglie, Michael P. (2012) "Alaska AG says EPA's actions 'unlawful'" *LegalNewsline.com*. (April 30) Retrieved from the Worldwide Web May 2, 2012 at http://www.legalnewsline.com/spotlight/235995-alaska-ag-says-epas-actions-unlawful.

Tri-State (2012) "Base-load Resources: Craig," Tri-State Generation and Transmission Association. Retrieved from the Worldwide Web April 24, 2012 at http://www.tristategt.org/aboutus/baseload-resources.cfm.

True, Robert (2011) "Colorado Air Quality Control Commission Report to the Public 2000-2001," Colorado Department of Public Health and Environment. (October 1) Retrieved from the Worldwide Web April 25, 2012 at http://www.cdphe.state.co.us/ap/down/rttp00-01fullreport.pdf.

U.S. Department of Energy (DOE) (2014) "July 28 Stakeholder Meeting on Natural Gas – Electricity Interdependence," Background Memo for the Quadrennial Meeting of the Energy Review Task Force Secretariat and Energy Policy and Systems Analysis Staff, United States Department of Energy, (Released July 24), Washington, D.C., Retrieved from the Worldwide Web September 10, 2014 at http://energy.gov/sites/prod/files/2014/07/f17/qermeeting_denver_backg roundmemo.pdf.

Walsh, Bryan (2011) "Natural Gas Can Save the Climate? Not Exactly," *Time Magazine: Ecocentric*. (September 9), Retrieved from the Worldwide Web April 28, 2012 at http://ecocentric.blogs.time.com/2011/09/09/natural-gas-can-save-the-climate-not-exactly/.

Webber, Michael (2009) "Coal-To-Liquids: Can Fuel Made From Coal Replace Gasoline?" Earth. (April 8), Retrieved from the Worldwide Web June 25, 2014 at http://www.earthmagazine.org/article/coal-liquids-can-fuel-made-coal-replace-gasoline

Wu, Song; Bergins, Christian; Kikkawa, Hirofumi; Kobayashi, Khironobu and Kawaski, Terufumi (2010) "Technology Options For Clean Coal Power Generation With Co2 Capture," XXI World Energy Congress, September 12 – 16, Montreal, Canada, Retrieved from the Worldwide Web April 25, 2012 at http://www.worldenergy.org/documents/congresspapers/226.pdf.

Yeatman, William and Cooke, Amy Oliver (2010) "Colorado's Clean Air Clean Jobs Act Will Accomplish Neither Government Officials and Special Interests Pushed HB 1365 on a Foundation of Fallacies," *CEI nPOINT*.

(October 28), No. 171, Retrieved from the Worldwide Web April 24, 2012 at http://cei.org/sites/default/files/William%20Yeatman%20and%20Amy%20Oliver%20Cooke%20-%20Colorado's%20Clean%20Air%20Jobs%20Act%20Will%20Accomplish%20Neither%20-%20HB%201365.pdf.

Ziegler, Kirk (2010) "Clean Air Plan Prompts Outcry in Colorado Coal Counties," KUNC Community Radio for Northern Colorado (August 12) Retrieved from the Worldwide Web April 24, 2012 at http://www.publicbroadcasting.net/kunc/news.newsmain?action=article &ARTICLE_ID=1734661.

## Chapter 3: Simplify

Arnold, Dean E. (1991) "Diversion Wells - A Low-Cost Approach To Treatment Of Acid Mine Drainage," *Twelfth Annual West Virginia Surface Mining Drainage Task Force Symposium Proceedings,* Morgantown, WV (April 3-4), Retrieved from the Worldwide Web May 24, 2012 at http://wvmdtaskforce.com/proceedings/91/91ARN/91ARN.HTM.

Centers for Disease Control (CDC), (2012) "Faces of Black Lung," National Institute for Occupational Safety and Health (NIOSH), Centers for Disease Control and Prevention, Atlanta, GA, Retireved from the Worldwide Web May 24, 2012 at http://blogs.cdc.gov/niosh-science-blog/2008/08/mining/.

Coleridge, Samuel Taylor (1798) "The Rime of the Ancient Mariner," in William Wordsworth and Samuel Taylor Coleridge's *Lyrical Ballads, With a Few Other Poems.* London, UK: J. & A. Arch, Publishers.

Egan, Tom (2008) "Mountain into Molehills," *New York Times Sunday Book Review.* (January 20), Retrieved from the Worldwide Web May 24, 2012 at http://www.nytimes.com/2008/01/20/books/review/Egan-t.html?_r=1.

Esbjörn-Hargens, Sean and Zimmerman, Michael E. (2009) *Integral Ecology: Uniting Multiple Perspectives on the Natural World.* New York, NY: Random House/Integral Books.

Integral Institute (2009) "The Integral Institute," Retrieved from the Worldwide Web May 20, 2012 at http://www.integralinstitute.org/.

Festinger, Leon (1957). A Theory Of Cognitive Dissonance, Evanston, IL: Row & Peterson.

James, William (1909) *A Pluralistic Universe,* New York, NY: Longman and Green.

James, William (1892) "Streams of Thought," in *Principles of Psychology.* (Vol. 1), New York, NY: Holt.

Kaslev, Allan M. (2005) "The Development of Ken Wilber's Thought: Phase 4 – All Quadrants, All Levels," Retrieved from the Worldwide Web May 20, 2005 at http://www.kheper.net/topics/Wilber/Wilber_IV.html.

Lyengar, Shanto (2009) *Framing Public Issues.* Washington, DC: Framework Institutes,

Maher, Kris (2009) "Black Lung on Rise in Mines, Reversing Trend," Wall Street Journal. (January 15), Retrieved from the Worldwide Web May 24, 2012 at http://online.wsj.com/article/SB126083871040391327.html.

Maslow, Abraham (1934) "A Theory of Human Motivation," *Psychological Review*. Vol. 50, No. 4, p. 370-96.

Mead, George Herbert (1913) "The Social Self," *Journal of Philosophy, Psychology, and Scientific Methods*. Vol.10, p. 374-380.

McFarlane, Thomas J. (2000) "A Critical Look at Ken Wilber's Four Quadrant Model," *Sangha: The Newsletter of the Franklin Merrell-Wolff Fellowship*. (January), Retrieved from the Worldwide Web May 20, 2012 at http://www.integralscience.org/wilber.html.

Meyers, Richard (2005) "The 1927 Strike," in Lowell May and Richard Meyers' *Slaughter in Serene: The Columbine Coal Strike Reader*. Denver, CO: Bread and Roses Workers' Cultural Center & Industrial Workers of the World.

Mineral Information Institute (2012) "Mining Reclamation Success - Coal Mining Reclamation," Retrieved from the Worldwide Web May 24, 2012 at http://www.mii.org/Rec/coal/coal.html.

National Mining Association (2012) "Safety," Retrieved from the Worldwide Web May 24, 2012 at http://www.nma.org/statistics/safety.asp.

National Mining Association (2011) "Mining Industry Employment In The United States By Sector, 1985 – 2010," Retrieved from the Worldwide Web May 24, 2012 at http://www.nma.org/pdf/e_sector.pdf.

Philibert, Cedric and Podkanski, Jacek (2005) *International Energy Technology Collaboration and Climate Mitigation: Case Study 4 – Clean Coal Technologies*. Paris, FR: OECD/IEA.

Quinn, Daniel (1996) *The Story of B*. New York, NY: Bantam.

Reese, Stephen, Gandy, Oscar Grant, August (2001) *Framing Public Life*. Hillsdale, NJ: Lawrence Erlbaum Associates.

Ruf, Frederick (1991) *The Creation of Chaos: William James and the Stylistic Making of a Disorderly World*. Albany, NY: State University of New York Press.

Shaynerson, Michael (2008) *Coal River*. New York, NY: Farrar, Straus & Giroux.

Skousen, Jeff (2011) "Acid Mine Drainaige," Acid Drainage Technology Initiative, West Virginia University, Morgantown, WV, Retrieved from the Worldwide Web May 24, 2012 at http://wvwri.nrcce.wvu.edu/programs/adti/publications/adti_handbook.html.

Umemoto, Karen (2001) "Walking in Another's Shoes: Epistemological Challenges in Participatory Planning," *Journal of Planning Education Research*. Vol. 21, p. 17-31

U.S. Department of Labor (2012) "Wage Base History," Division of Coal Mine Workers' Compensation (DCMWC), Washington, DC, Retrieved from the Worldwide Web May 24, 2012 at http://www.dol.gov/owcp/dcmwc/exh609.htm.

Vonnegut, Kurt Jr. (1969) *Slaughterhouse Five*. Cranston, RI: Thomason Books

Wilber, Ken (2012) "The Integral Operating System. Part II: States and Stages," *The Integral Post.* (February 19), Retrieved from the Worldwide Web May 20, 2012 at http://integrallife.com/member/ken-wilber/blog/integral-operating-system-part-ii-states-and-stages.

Wilber, Ken (2011) *A Brief History of Everything.* (Second Edition), Boston, MA: Shambala.

Wimberley, Edward T. (2009) *Nested Ecology: The Place of Humans in the Ecological Hierarchy.* Baltimore, MD: Johns Hopkins University Press.

World Energy Council (2004) *Sustainable Global Energy Development: The Case of Coal.* (July) London, UK: World Energy Council.

## Chapter 4: Cool Water

Allaben, Kathryn (2013) "Is There a Way to Stop the Floridan Aquifer Depletion?" *WUFT News.* Gainesville, FL (November 6), Retrieved from the Worldwide Web July 8, 2014 at http://www.wuft.org/news/2013/11/06/is-there-a-way-to-stop-floridan-aquifer-depletion/

Arroyo, Jorge and Shirazi, Saqib (2009) "Cost of Water Desalination in Texas," Analysis Paper 10-02, Innovative Water Technologies Texas Water Development Board.

Bennett, Lanetra (2007) "Judge Makes Ruling, River Restoration Underway?" WCTV Television, Tallahassee, Florida (March 7) Retrieved from the Worldwide Web June 9, 2012 at http://www.wctv.tv/home/headlines/6368227.html

Buckeye Technologies (2011) "Profitable Sustained Growth: 2011 Annual Report, Buckeye Technologies," Retrieved from the Worldwide Web July 8, 2012 at http://www.bkitech.com/images/document/2011_annual_report.pdf.

Carriker, Roy R. (2012) "Florida's Water: Supply, Use and Public Policy," Document FE 207, a publication of the Department of Food and Resource Economics, Florida Cooperative Extension Service, Institute of Food and Agricultural Sciences, University of Florida, Retrieved from the Worldwide Web June 13, 2012 at http://edis.ifas.ufl.edu/fe207.

Chamlee, Virginia (2011) "Environmentalists: State Water Pollution Rules 'Less Protective' Than No Standards At All," The Florida Independent. (December 1), Retrieved from the Worldwide Web June 11, 2012 at http://floridaindependent.com/58883/florida-water-coalition-nutrient-criteria.

Cunningham, Ron (1980) "Decline in Quality of Water Blamed on Phosphate, Pollutants," The Lakeland Ledger. (April 27), Retrieved from the Worldwide Web June 12, 2012 at http://news.google.com/newspapers?nid=1346&dat=19800427&id=j44s AAAAIBAJ&sjid=JPsDAAAAIBAJ&pg=6875,4266170.

Curry, Christopher (2011) "Water Districts Chastised For Not Protecting Groundwater," *The Gainesville Sun.* (November 29), Retrieved from the Worldwide Web June 7, 2012 at http://www.gainesville.com/article/20111129/ARTICLES/111129496.

Dutzik, Tony and Baliga, Nina (2004) "Phosphorous Pollution in Florida's Waters: The Need for Aggressive Action to Protect Florida's Rivers and Streams from Nutrient Runoff," Florida Public Interest Research Group Education Fund, (Winter), Tallahassee, Florida.

Earthjustice (2011) "Earthjustice Files Suit to Protect Floridians' Right to Clean Water," Retrieved from the Worldwide Web June 11, 2012 at http://earthjustice.org/print/news/press/2011/earthjustice-files-suit-to-protect-floridians-right-to-clean-water.

Earthjustice (2010) "Comments by Earthjustice on Behalf of the Florida Wildlife Federation et al." (January 26), Retrieved Sept. 10, 2014 at http://crca.caloosahatchee.org/crca_docs/FL_Nutirent_Stnds_Comments _ID%20EPA-HQ-OW.pdf.

Earthjustice (2004) *Reckless Abandon: How the Bush Administration is Exposing America's Waters to Harm.* Washington, DC: A Publication of Earthjustice, National Wildlife Federation, Natural Resources Defense Council, and Sierra Club

Environmental Law Reporter (1989). "An Annotated Legislative History of the Superfund Amendments and Reauthoritization Act Of 1986 (SARA)," In *Superfund Deskbook.* Washington, DC: Environmental Law Institute.

Festinger, Leon (1962) *A Theory of Cognitive Dissonance.* Evanston, IL: Row, Peterson.

Florida Administrative Code (FAC) (2010) Chapter 62-302

Florida Administrative Code (FAC) (2005) Water Resource Implementation Rule, Chapter 62-40.

Florida Agricultural Statistics Service (FASS) (2012) "Florida Crops and Produce," Florida Department of Agriculture and Consumer Services, Retrieved from the Worldwide Web June 2, 2012 at http://www.ers.usda.gov/StateFacts/fl.HTM.

Florida Department of Agriculture and Consumer Services (FDACS) (2012) "Florida Crops and Products," Division of Marketing and Development, Retrieved from the Worldwide Web June 12, 2012 at http://www.florida-agriculture.com/consumers/crops/agoverview/.

Florida Department of Environmental Protection (FDEP) (2012) "Water Management Districts," Retrieved from the Worldwide Web June 1, 2012 at http://www.dep.state.fl.us/secretary/watman/.

Florida Department of Environmental Protection (FDEP) (2011) "Regional Water Supply Planning: Annual Report 2011," Retrieved from the Worldwide Web June 1, 2012 at http://www.dep.state.fl.us/water/waterpolicy/docs/2011-regional-water-supply-planning-ap.pdf.

Florida Department of Environmental Protection (FDEP) (2010) "Water Use Trends in Florida," Retrieved from the Worldwide Web June 1, 2012 at http://www.dep.state.fl.us/water/waterpolicy/docs/factsheets/wrfss-water-use-trends.pdf.

Florida Department of Environmental Protection (FDEP) (2009) "Development of Numeric Nutrient Criteria for Florida's Waters," Retrieved from the Worldwide Web June 11, 2012 at http://www.dep.state.fl.us/water/wqssp/nutrients/.

Florida Groundwater Association (FGA) (2012) "FGA Home Page," Retrieved from the Worldwide Web June 1, 2012 at http://www.fgwa.org/.

Florida Pulp and Paper Association (2012) "Welcome to the Florida Pulp and Paper Association," Retrieved from the Worldwide Web June 14, 2012 at http://www.fppaea.org/.

Florida Springs Institute (2012) "Mission and Goals," Retrieved from the Worldwide Web June 11, 2012 at http://floridaspringsinstitute.org/pages/mission-and-goals.

Florida State Statures, Chapter 24952-No. 1338, 1947.

*Gainesville Sun* (2012) "Get on With It," Editorial, (June 3) Retrieved from the Worldwide Web June 11, 2012 at http://www.gainesville.com/article/20120603/OPINION01/120609925?t c=ar.

Georgia Department of Environmental Protection (GDEP) (2010) "River Basin Characteristics: Satilla River," Atlanta, GA.

Glasser, Douglas (1998) *Death in the Air - Phosphoric Acid Production and Airborne Fluorides*. Retrieved from the Worldwide Web June 12, 2012 at http://sonic.net/kryptox/environ/m/death.htm.

Glassman, Jim (2012) "The State of Florida's Economy," (March 31), J. P. Morgan Florida Report, Retrieved from the Worldwide Web June 18, 2012 at http://www.summary/prices/quotes/statistics.

Grubbs, J.W. and Crandall, C.A. (2007) *Exchanges of Water Between the Upper Floridan Aquifer and the Lower Suwannee and Lower Santa Fe Rivers, Florida*. Professional Paper 1656, U.S. Geological Survey and the Suwanee River Water Management District, Live Oak, FL.

Hardin, Gerald (1988) *Extension of the Tragedy of the Commons*. Washington, DC: American Association for the Advancement of Science.

Horning, Gloria G. (2005) *Social Network and Environmental Justice, A Case Study in Perry, Florida*. (Doctoral Dissertation), Retrieved from the Worldwide Web June 9, 2012 at http://etd.lib.fsu.edu/theses/available/etd-03302005-181859/unrestricted/Horning.pdf.

James, William (1880) "Great Men, Great Thoughts and the Environment," *Atlantic Monthly*. (October), p. 441-449.

Johnston, Richard H. and Bush, Peter W. (1988) "Summary of the Hydrology of the Floridan Aquifer System in Florida and in Parts of Georgia, South Carolina and Alabama," *U.S. Geological Survey Professional Paper 1403-A*, Washington, D.C." U.S. Government Printing Office.

Katz, Brian G. (1992) "Hydrochemistry of the Upper Floridan Aquifer, Florida," Water Resources Investigations Report 91-4195, U.S. Geological Survey, Retrieved from the Worldwide Web June 3, 2012 at http://library.fgcu.edu/chnep/236a.pdf.

Knight, Robert (2012) "Commercial Lawn Pumping Drying Up Florida's Springs," *Times-Union Point of View*. (May 20) Retrieved from the Worldwide Web June 10, 2012 at http://jacksonville.com/opinion/columnists/2012-05-20/story/point-view-commercial-lawn-pumping-drying-floridas-springs.

Lake City Journal (2011) "Columbia County To Take Legal Action To Prevent Area Springs, Rivers And Wells From Running Dry," (August 6) Retrieved from the Worldwide Web June 7, 2012 at http://www.lakecityjournal.com/m/Articles.aspx?ArticleID=7711.

Ledger.com (2012) "Santa Fe River: Pumping, Pollution, Privation," The Lakeland Ledger. (June 2) Retrieved from the Worldwide Web June 11, 2012 at http://www.theledger.com/article/20120602/EDIT01/120609937?p=1&tc=pg.

Maehr, David S. (1981) "Bird Use of a North-Central Florida Phosphate Mine," *Florida Field Naturalist.* Vol. 9, No. 1, p. 28-32.

Marella, Richard L. (2014) "Water withdrawals, use, and trends in Florida, 2010," *U.S. Geological Survey Scientific Investigations Report 2014–5088,* http://dx.doi.org/10.3133/sir20145088.

Marella, Richard L. (2008) "Water Use in Florida, 2005 and Trends 1950–2005," *USGS Factsheet* 2008-3080. Retrieved from the Worldwide Web June 1, 2012 at http://pubs.usgs.gov/fs/2008/3080/.

Marella, Richard L. (1992) *Factors that Affect Public-Supply Water Use in Florida, with a Section on Projected Water Use to the Year 2020.* Denver, CO: U.S. Geological Survey, Water-Resources Investigations Report 91-4123.

McGhee, Mike (2007) "Georgia-Pacific's St. Johns River Enhancement Project," White Paper prepared on behalf of Georgia-Pacific by consultant Mike McGhee (Retired USEPA Water Administrator, Region IV), Retrieved from the Worldwide Web June 14, 2012 at http://www.gp.com/stjohns/pdfs/enhancementProject.pdf.

McGovern, Bernie (2008) *Florida Almanac: 2007-2008.* Miami, FL: Pelican Publishing.

Miller, James A. (1990) "Ground Water Atlas of the United States: Alabama, Florida, Georgia, and South Carolina," HA 730-G, U.S. Geological Survey, Retrieved from the Worldwide Web May 31, 12 at http://pubs.usgs.gov/ha/ha730/ch_g/index.html.

Mosaic, 2012 "Florida Phosphate's Economic Impact," The Mosaic Company, Lithia, Florida, Retrieved from the Worldwide Web June 12, 2012 at http://mosaicfla.com/about-mosaic/economic-impact.aspx.

Mussey, Orville D. (1955) "Water Requirements of the Pulp and Paper Industry," Geological Survey Water Supply Paper 1330-A, U. S. Geological Survey, Washington, D.C.: Government Printing Office.

North Central Florida Regional Planning Council (NCFRPC) (2011) "Council Minutes," (June 30), Holiday Inn Hotel and Suites, Lake City, FL.

Our Santa Fe (2012) "Home Page," Retrieved from the Worldwide Web June 10, 2012 at http://www.oursantaferiver.org/more.htm.

Peter G. Peterson Foundation (2010) "Federal Budget Primer," (November 8), New York, NY, Retrieved from the Worldwide Web June 18, 2012 at http://www.pgpf.org/Special-Topics/The-Federal-Budget-Primer.aspx.

Phillips, Kevin (2012) "Personal Communication," Suwannee River Water Management District, Live Oak, Florida.

Pittman, Craig (2013) "Florida's Aquifer Model Full of Holes, Allowing More Water Permits and Pollution," *Tampa Bay Times*. (January 27), Retrieved from the Worldwide Web July 8, 2014 at http://www.tampabay.com/news/environment/water/floridas-aquifer-models-full-of-holes-allowing-more-water-permits-and/1272555

PotashCorp (2012) "Who We Are," Retrieved from the Worldwide Web June 9, 2012 at http://www.potashcorp.com/about/facilities/phosphate/white_springs/.

Rab, Lisa (2011) "Rick Scott's Quiet Campaign Against the Environment," *Broward / Palm Beach NewTimes.com*. (May 7), Retrieved form the Worldwide Web June 13, 2012 at http://blogs.browardpalmbeach.com/pulp/2011/07/rick_scotts_quiet_ca mpaign_against_environment_department_community_affairs.php.

Rabchevsky, George A. (1997) "Phosphate Rock," U.S. Geological Survey Mineral Information.

Roberts, Diane (2007) "The World's a Dirty Place When You're Poor," *Tampa Bay Times*. (September 9), Retrieved from the Worldwide Web June 1, 2012 at http://www.sptimes.com/2007/09/09/Opinion/The_world_s_a_dirty_p.sh tml.

Save Our Suwannee (SOS) (2012) "About Us," Retrieved from the Worldwide Web June 10, 2012 at http://www.saveoursuwannee.org/about-us/.

Scott, Rick (2011) "Governor's Statement Regarding Water Management District Budgets," Office of the Governor, State of Florida, (August 24), Tallahassee, Florida, Retrieved from the Worldwide Web June 13, 2012 at http://www.dep.state.fl.us/secretary/watman/files/082411/gov_statement _wmd_budgets.pdf.

Simmons, D. (1999) Lobbyist for Procter & Gamble in the State of Florida. (Personal Conversation as reported by Florida State University doctoral candidate Gloria Horning).

Smith, Stanley K. (2005) "Florida Population Growth, Past, Present and Future," Bureau of Economic and Business Research, University of Florida, Gainesville, FL Retrieved from the Worldwide Web June 1 at http://www.bebr.ufl.edu/files/FloridaPop2005_0.pdf.

Sousa, Gregory D., Greenfield, J.M., Peene, S. J., and Rodriguez, H.N. (2000) "Fenholloway River and Estuary TMDL Development Taylor County, Florida," A study funded by the USEPA and conducted by Tetra Tech, Inc., 2110-202 Powers Ferry Road, Atlanta, GA, Retrieved from the Worldwide Web June 1, 2012 at https://docs.google.com/viewer?a=v&q=cache:RPTJ_ZGNvbgJ:www.c wemf.org/workshops/TMDLToolbox/Fen

Spear, Kevin (2014) "Do Lake County's Shrinking Lakes Portend Florida's Future," Orlando Sentinel. (April 24), Retrieved from the Worldwide Web July 8, 2014 at http://articles.orlandosentinel.com/2014-04-24/news/os-low-lakes-climate-change-20140419_1_lakes-lake-minnehaha-lake-county-water-authority

Strickler, Karen (2011) "Climate Challenge Media with Joy Towles Ezell," *Climate Challenge Media*. Retrieved from the Worldwide Web June 10, 2012 at http://vimeo.com/channels/166952.

Suwannee Democrat (2005) "PCS Phosphate named the winner of 2003," (December 21) Retrieved from the Worldwide Web June 12, 2012 at http://suwanneedemocrat.com/branford/x1765737150/PCS-Phosphate-named-the-winner-of-2003-quot-Sustainable-Florida-Award-quot/print.

Suwannee River Water Management District (SRWMD) (2012) "Consolidated Annual Report: 2012," (March 1), Retrieved from the Worldwide Web June 1, 2012 at https://docs.google.com/viewer?a=v&q=cache:NT5Mww-l2YkJ:www.srwmd.state.fl.us/DocumentVi.

Suwannee River Water Management District (SRWMD) (2011) "Water Use Statistics 1995-2011," Provided June 5, 2012 by Megan Wetherington, Senior Engineer, District Office, Live Oak, FL.

Suwannee River Water Management District (SRWMD) (2010) "2010 Water Supply Assessment Report, " Retrieved from the Worldwide Web June 1, 2012 at http://www.srwmd.state.fl.us/DocumentView.aspx?DID=1759

Suwannee River Water Management District (SRWMD) (2004) "Water Supply Assessment 2004," Retrieved from the Worldwide Web June 1, 2012 at http://www.srwmd.state.fl.us/DocumentView.aspx?DID=548.

Tao, Jill L. (2002) "Endogeneity and Environmental Policy: How Local Institutions Structure Local Demand," International Journal of International Development. (July-October), Vol. 4, No. 3-4, Retrieved from the Worldwide Web June 6, 2012 at http://www/spaef.com/file.php?id=672..

U.S. Census Bureau (2012) "State and County Quick Facts: Florida," Retrieved from the Worldwide Web June 1, 2012 at http://quickfacts.census.gov/qfd/states/12000.html.

U.S. Census Bureau (2005) "U.S. American Community Survey," (ePodunk), Retrieved from the Worldwide Web June 7, 2012 at http://www.epodunk.com/cgi-bin/popInfo.php?locIndex=8534.

United States Environmental Protection Agency (USEPA) (2010) "Comments By Earthjustice On Behalf Of Florida Wildlife Federation, St. Johns Riverkeeper, Sierra Club, Conservancy Of Southwest Florida, And Environmental Confederation Of Southwest Florida On United States Environmental Protection Agency Proposed Rule On Water Quality Standards For The State Of Florida's Lakes And Flowing Waters," EPA Docket I.D. No. EPA-HQ-OW-2009-0596 Proposed Rule Published: 75 Fed. Reg. 4174 (Tuesday, January 26, 2010).

U.S. Geological Survey (USGS) (2010) "Water-Use Facts for 2005 and Trends," Retrieved from the Worldwide Web May 31, 2012 at http://fl.water.usgs.gov/infodata/wateruse/waterusefacts2005.html.

U.S. Geological Survey (USGS) (2007) "Total Water Withdrawal in Florida, 2005," Florida Integrated Science Center, Tallahassee, FL, Retrieved from the Worldwide Web June 7, 2012 at http://www.dep.state.fl.us/water/waterpolicy/docs/learning-from-drought-final-report.pdf.

Vinyard, Herschel (2011) "DEP Secretary Announces $700 Million in Water Management Districts' Budget Reductions," (August 24), Florida Department of Environmental Protection, Tallahassee, Florida, Retrieved from the Worldwide Web June 13, 2012 at http://content.govdelivery.com/bulletins/gd/FLDEP-103486.

Waters, Clay (2011) "

Wetherington, Megan (2012) "April 2012 Hydrologic Conditions Report for the District," (May 5), Suwannee River Water Management District, Live Oak, FL.

Wilber, K. (1995) *Sex, Ecology, Spirituality*. Boston, MA: Shambhala.

Williams, Ted (2003) "The Ungreening of America: Down Upon the Suwannee River," Mother Jones. (September/October), Retrieved from the Worldwide Web June 12, 2012 at http://www.motherjones.com/politics/2003/09/ungreening-america-down-upon-suwannee-river.

Wurth, Emily; Grant, Mary; Grass, Alison and MacMillan, Hugh (2009) *Unmeasured Danger America's Hidden Groundwater Crisis*. Washington, DC: Food and Water Watch.

## Chapter 5: Stand Inside My Shoes

American Sportfishing Association (ASA) (2008), *Sportfishing in America*. (January Revision), Alexandria, VA: American Sportfishing Association, Retrieved from the Worldwide Web February 20, 2013 at http://asafishing.org/uploads/Sportfishing_in_America_Jan_2008_Revised.pdf

Amit, Elinor, Wakslak, Cheryl and Trope, Yaacov (2013) "The Use of Visual and Verbal Means of Communication Across Psychological Distance," *Personality and Social Psychology Bulletin*. Vol. 39, No. 1, p. 43-56.

Avineri, Erel and Waygood, E. Owen (2011) "Applying Goal Framing to Enhance the Effect of Information on Transport-Related CO2 Emissions," A Paper Presented at the 9th Biennial Conference on Environmental Psychology, (September), Eindhoven, The Netherlands.

Benford, Robert D. and Snow, David A. (2000) "Framing Processes and Social Movements: An Overview and Assessment," *Annual Review of Sociology*. Vol. 26, p. 611-639.

Bennet, Alex and Bennet, David (2008) "The Decision-Making Process for Complex Situations in a Complex Environment," in Burstein, F. and Holsapple, C.W. (Eds). *Handbook on Decision Support Systems*. New York, NY: SpringerVerlag.

Berger, Peter and Luckman, Thomas (1967) *The Social Construction of Reality: A Treatise in the Sociology of Knowledge*. New York, NY: Anchor.

Bermúdez, José Luis (2009) *Decision Theory and Rationality*, Oxford, UK: Oxford University Press.

Birkinshaw, Julian, Foss, Nicolai J. and Lindenberg, Siegward (2013) "Combining Purpose with Profits," MIT Sloan Management Review.

(February 19) Vol. 55, No. 3, Retrieved from the Worldwide Web July 8, 2014 at http://sloanreview.mit.edu/article/combining-purpose-with-profits/

Bourdieu, Pierre (1985) "The Social Space and the Genesis of Groups," *Theory and Society*. Vol. 14, p. 723-744.

Cairney, Paul (2012) "How Can Policy Theory Inform Policy Making (and vice versa)?" Political Studies Association, Belfast, Ireland, Retrieved From the Worldwide Web February 14, 2013 at http://www.psa.ac.uk/journals/pdf/5/2012/148_112.pdf

Carnegie, Dale (1936) *How to Win Friends and Influence People*. New York, NY: Simon and Schuster.

Chong, Dennis and Druckman, James N. (2007) "Framing Theory," *Annual Review of Political Science*. Vol. 10, p. 103-126.

Corvalan, Carlos, Hales, Simon and McMichael, Anthony (2005) *Ecosystems and Well-Being – Health Synthesis*. Washington, DC: World Health Organization.

Damasio, Antonio (2005) *Descartes' Error: Emotion, Reason, and the Human Brain*. New, NY: Penguin Books.

Drew, Dennis M. (1985) "Beware of Simplistic Solutions," *Air University Review*. (January-February), p. 102-104.

Emery, F. E. and Trist, E. L. (1965) "The Causal Texture of Organization Environments," *Human Relations*. Vol.18, p. 21-32

Eng, Erling (1978) "Looking Back on Kurt Lewin: From Field Theory to Action Research," *Journal of the History of the Behavioral Sciences*. Vol. 14, p. 228-232.

Etienne, Julien (2010) "Compliance Theory: A Goal Framing Approach," A Paper Presented at Third Biennial Conference of the ECPR Standing Group on Regulatory Governance, University College Dublin, (June 17-19), Retrieved from the Worldwide Web July 9, 2014 at http://regulation.upf.edu/dublin-10-papers/3I3.pdf

Festinger, Leon (1957) *A Theory of Cognitive Dissonance*. Stanford, CA: Stanford University Press.

Festinger, Leon (1959) "Some Attitudinal Consequences of Forced Decisions. *Acta Psychologica*, Vol. 15, 389-390.

Figueres, Christina (2012) "Environmental Issues: Time to Abandon Blame-Games and Become Proactive," *The Economic Times*. (December 15) Retrieved from the Worldwide Web February 14, 2013 at http://ruby.fgcu.edu/courses/twimberley/EnviroPhilo/blame.pdf

Fine, Michelle (1991) *Framing Dropouts: Notes on the Politics of an Urban Public High School*. Albany, NY: SUNY Press.

Frame, J. Davidson (2013) *Framing Decisions: Decision-making that Accounts for Irrationality, People and Constraints*. San Francisco, CA: Jossey-Bass.

Gazzanigia, Michael (2005) *The Ethical Brain*. New York, NY: Daina Press.

Haidt, Jonathan (2013) *The Righteous Mind: Why Good People Are Divided by Politics and Religion*. New York, NY: Vintage.

Haidt, Jonathan (2006) *The Happiness Hypothesis: Finding Modern Truth in Ancient Wisdom*. New York, NY: Basic Books.

Hulme, Mike (2009) "On his book *Why We Disagree About Climate Change: Understanding Controversy, Inaction and Opportunity,"* Rorotoko. (October 9), Retrieved from the Worldwide Web February 12, 2013 at http://rorotoko.com/interview/20091009_hulme_mike_disagree_climate _change_controvers_inaction_opportunity/?page=1

Hume, David (1896) *A Treatise of Human Nature.* L.A. Selby-Bigge, (Tr.) Oxford, UK: Clarendon Press.

James, William (1948) *Psychology.* Cleveland, OH: World Publishing.

Kacelnik, Alex (2006) "Meanings of Rationality," In Matthew Nudds and Susan Hurley's (Eds.) Rational Animals? Oxford, UK: Oxford University Press.

Kahneman Daniel (2003) A Perspective on Judgment and Choice. *American Psychologist.* Vol. 58, p. 697-720.

Kahneman, Daniel and Tversky, Amos (1979) "Prospect Theory: An Analysis of Decision under Risk," *Econometrica.* Vol. 47, No. 2, (March) p. 263-292.

Kant, Emanuel (1900) *Fundamental Principles of Metaphysical Ethics.* Translated by Thomas Kingsmill, London, UK: Longmans, Green and Company.

Kemp, David D. (2004) *Exploring Environmental Issues: An Integrated Approach.* New York, NY: Routledge.

Klein, William M. P. and Goethals, George R. (2010) "Social Reality and Self-Construction: A Case of "Bounded Irrationality?" *Basic and Applied Social Psychology.* Vol. 24, No. 2, p. 105-114.

Knickerbocker, Brad (1997) "Is Environmental Education Just Green Propaganda?" *The Christian Science Monitor.* (April 4) Retrieved from the Worldwide Web February 14, 2013 at http://www.csmonitor.com/1997/0404/040497.us.us.4.html

Knight, Eric (2012) *Reframe: How to Solve the World's Trickiest Problems.* Collingswood, AU: Black, Inc.

Kohlberg, L (1969) "Stage and Sequence: The Cognitive-Development Approach to Socialization," In D.A. Goslin's (Ed.) *Handbook of Socialization Theory and Research.* Chicago, IL: Rand-McNally, p. 347-480.

Köhler, Wolfgang (1947) *Gestalt Psychology.* New York, NY: Liveright.

Lazarus, Richard S. (1996) *Passion and Reason: Making Sense of Our Emotions.* London, UK: Oxford University Press.

Lefsrud, Lianne M. and Meyer, Renate E. (2012) "Science or Science Fiction? Professionals' Discursive Construction of Climate," *Organizational Studies.* Vol. 33, No. 11, p. 1477-1506.

Lercher, Aaron (2004) "Is Anyone to Blame for Pollution?" *Environmental Ethics.* Vol. 26, p. 403-410.

Levy, Jack (1992) "An Introduction to Prospect Theory," *Political Psychology.* Vol. 13, No. 2, p. 171-186.

Lewicki, Roy J., Gray, Barbara and Elliott, Michael (2003) *Making Sense of Intractable Environmental Conflicts: Frames and Cases.* Washington, DC: Island Press.

Lewin, Kurt (1976) *Resolving Social Conflicts in Field Theory in Social Science.* (Kindle Edition), Washington, DC: American Psychological Association.

Lindenberg, Siegwart (2008) "Social Rationality, Semi-Modularity and Goal Framing: What is it All About?" *Analyze & Kritik.* Vol. 30, p. 669-687.

Lindenberg, Siegwart (2001) "Social Rationality as a Unified Model of Man (Including Bounded Rationality)," *Journal of Management and Governance.* Vol. 5, No. 3, p. 239-251.

Lindenberg, Siegwart and Steg, Linda (2007) "Normative, Gain and Hedonic Frames Guiding Environmental Behavior," *Journal of Social Issues.* Vol. 63, No. 1, p. 117-137.

March, James G. (2003) "A Scholar's Quest," *Journal of Management Inquiry.* Vol. 12, No. 3, p. 205-207.

Margolis, Howard (1987) *Patterns, Thinking, and Cognition: A Theory of Judgment.* Chicago, IL: University of Chicago Press.

Mayo, James M. (1978) "Propaganda with Design: Environmental Dramaturgy in the Political Rally," *JAE.* Vol. 32, No. 2, p. 24-32.

McAdam, D., & Scott, W. R. (2005). "Organizations and Movements," In D. McAdam & W. R. Scott (Eds.), *Social Movements and Organization Theory.* (pp. 4-40). New York, NY: Cambridge University Press.

McKibben, Bill (2008) "Green Fantasia," *New York Times Review of Books.* Retrieved from the Worldwide Web July 3, 2013 at http://www.nybooks.com/articles/archives/2008/nov/06/green-fantasia/?pagination=false

Mehan, Hugh (1981) "The Role of Language and the Language of Role in Practical Decision-making," In Sandra Christian's (Ed.) *Current Research on Psychoeducational Assessment and Decision-making.* St. Paul, MN: Institute for Research on Learning Disabilities, University of Minnesota.

Todd McElroy and Seta, John J. (2003) "Framing Effects: An Analytic–Holistic Perspective," *Journal of Experimental Social Psychology.* Vol. 39, p. 610-617.

Mohr, John W. (2005) "Implicit Terrains: Meaning, Measurement, and Spatial Metaphors in Organizational Theory," In Marc Ventresca and Joseph Porac's (Eds.) *Constructing Industries and Markets.* New York, NY: Elsevier.

Peacock, Mark S. (2006) "Rationality and the Language of Decision-making: Bringing Language into the Foreground in Economic Theory, " *International Journal of Social Economics.* Vol. 33, No. 9, p. 604-614.

Rogers, Heater (2010) *Green Gone Wrong: How Our Economy Is Undermining the Environmental Revolution.* New York, NY: Scribner.

Scheiring, Gabor (2007) "The Political Economy of Environmentalism: Framing Ecopolotics and Building Ideology in the Zengô-Conflict (Hungary)," *Anthropolis.* Vol. 3, No. 2, p. 6-19.

Scheler, Max (1980) *Problems of a Sociology of Knowledge.* (Manfred S. Frings, translator), New York, NY: Routledge & Kegan Paul.

Schön, Donald A. and Rein, Martin (1994) *Frame Reflection: Toward the Resolution of Intractable Policy Controversies*. New York, NY: Basic Books.

Simon, Herbert A. (1955) "A Behavioral Model of Rational Choice," *The Quarterly Journal of Economics*. Vol. 69, No. 1, (Feb.) p. 99-118

Simon, Herbert A. (1956) "Rational Choice and the Structure of the Environment," *Psychological Review*. Vol. 63, No. 2, p. 129-138.

Simon, Herbert A. (1978) "Rational Decision-Making in Business Organizations," Nobel Memorial Lecture 8, (December) in Assar Lindbeck's (ed.) (1992) *Nobel Lectures*. Singapore, CH: World Scientific Publishing Co., p. 343-371.

Simon, Herbert A (1979) *Models of Thought*. New Haven, CT: Yale University Press.

Sinclair, Marta (Ed.) (2011) *Handbook of Intuition Research*. Cheltenham, UK: Edward Elgar Publishing Limited.

Sionnach, Liam (2009) *Earth First Means Social War*. Frederick, MD: After The Fall Publications.

Tversky, Amos and Kahneman, Daniel (1986) "Rational Choice and the Framing of Decisions," *The Journal of Business*. Vol. 59, No. 4, p. S251-S278.

Tversky, Amos and Kahneman, Daniel (1981) "The Framing of Decisions and Psychological Choice," *Science*, New Series, Vol. 211, No. 4481, (Jan. 30), p. 453-458.

van Trijp, Hans C.M. (Ed.) (2013) *Encouraging Sustainable Behavior: Psychology and the Environment*. East Sussex, UK: Psychology Press.

Waitzkin, Howard, Yager, Joel and Santos, Richard (2012) "Advancing the Business Creed? The Framing of Decisions About Public Sector Managed Care," *Sociology of Health and Illness*. Vol. 34, No. 1 (Jan), p. 31-48.

Wallen, Are (2011) *Factors Influencing Actors At The Interface Between The Socio-Technical And The Ecological Systems - The Case Of On-Site Sewage Systems And Eutrophication*. (Masters Thesis) Gothernburg, SW: Chalmers University of Technology.

Wang, X. T. (2004) "Self-Framing of Risky Choice," *Journal of Behavioral Decision-making*. Vol. 17, p. 1-16

Wilber, Ken (1997) "An Integral Theory of Consciousness," *Journal of Consciousness Studies*. Vol. 4, No. 1, p. 71-92.

## Chapter 6: Gyppo Loggers and Spotted Owls

American Forest Resource Council (AFRC) (2011) "WOPR In the Courts," (August 19), *AFRC News*. Portland, OR, Retrieved from the Worldwide Web March 7, 2013 at
http://www.amforest.org/images/pdfs/AFRC_Newsletter_8-19-11.pdf

Andrzejewski, Walter (2013) "Associations," *Independent Sawmill & Woodlot Management Magazine*. Retrieved from the Worldwide Web July 15, 2013 at https://www.sawmillmag.com/app/associations/index

Associated Press (AP) (2004) "Environmentalists Sue Over Forest Policy," The
New York Times. (May 28), Retrieved from the Worldwide Web July 3,
2013 at http://www.nytimes.com/2004/05/28/national/28forest.html

Bernard, Jeff (AP) (2013) "Bringing Back Good Old Days of Logging Difficult,"
*Yamhill Valley News-Register*. (June 30), Retrieved from the Worldwide
Web July 3, 2013 at
http://www.newsregister.com/article?articleTitle=bringing-back-good-
old-days-of-logging-difficult--1372661694--8398--

Blumm, Michael C. and Wigington, Tim (2013) "The Oregon & California
Railroad Grant Lands' - Sordid Past, Contentious Present, and Uncertain
Future: A Century of Conflict," *Boston College of Environmental Affairs
Law Review*. Vol., 40, No. 1, p. 1-76.

Bonnanno, Allesssandro and Constance, Douglas H. (2008) *Stories of
Globalization: Transnational Corporations, Resistance and the State*.
College Station, PA: Pennsylvania University Press.

Brown, Amie M. (2004) "Selected Laws Affecting Forest Service Activities,"
USDA Forest Service, Legislative Affairs, Washington, DC, Retrieved
from the Worldwide Web June 24, 2013 at
http://www.fs.fed.us/publications/laws/selected-laws.pdf

Brown, Jane (2012) "Federal Judge Puts Final Nail in Coffin of Bush-era
Logging Plan for Oregon," Western Environmental Law Center Press
Release, (March 21), Retrieved from the Worldwide Web March 7, 2013
at          http://www.westernlaw.org/article/federal-judge-puts-final-nail-
coffin-bush-era-logging-plan-oregon-press-release

Brown, Susan Jane M. (1999) "The Forest must Come First:" Gifford Pinchot's
Conservation Ethic and the Gifford Pinchot National Forest-the Ideal
and the Reality," *Fordham Environmental Law Journal*. Vol. 11 (Fall),
p. 137-142.

Bureau of Land Management (BLM) (2008) "FEIS Revision of the Western
Oregon RMP's: Summary," U.S. Department of the Interior, Retrieved
from the Worldwide Web July 3, 2013 at
http://www.blm.gov/or/plans/wopr/final_eis/files/Volume_1/Vol_I_Sum
mary.pdf

Bylund,   Per   (2006)   "A   Utilitarian   Defense   for   Free   Markets,"
LewRockwell.Com. Retrieved from the Worldwide Web June 26, 2013
at http://www.lewrockwell.com/orig6/bylund5.html

Campbell Group (2013) "Global Timber Supply," Timber As An Investment –
Global Supply, Retrieved from the Worldwide Web March 7, 2013 at
https://www.campbellgroup.com/timberland/primer/global-supply.aspx

Canadian Workman's Compensation Board (1994) "Report of Fatalities in the
Logging Industry (1983-1994)," Workman's Compensation Prevention
Divisions, (September 2).

Carollo, Dominic (2011) "Timber Industry Sues BLM to Increase Logging in
Western Oregon," *Natural Resource Updates*. (July 13), Dunn Carney,
Allen Higgins and Tongue, LLP, Retrieved from the Worldwide Web
March 7, 2013 at
http://dunncarneynaturalresourcesupdates.com/2011/07/13/timber-
industry-sues-blm-to-increase-logging-in-western-oregon/

Center for Biological Diversity, Center for Sierra Nevada Conservation, Natural Resources Defense Council and the Sierra Nevada Forest Protection Campaign vs. Gale A. Norton, Secretary of the Interior and Marshall P. Jones, Acting Director, U.S. Fish and Wildlife Service, 2003, United States District Court for the Northern District of California, San Francisco Division, Retrieved from the Worldwide Web March 7, 2013 at http://earthjustice.org/sites/default/files/library/legal_docs/OwlandFisher Complaint.pdf

Center for Effective Government (2008) "Bush Administration Tries to Reverse Old-Growth Forest Protection Plan," Retrieved from the Worldwide Web March 7, 2013 at http://www.foreffectivegov.org/node/3501

Charnley, Susan (2013) "Managing Forest Products for Community Benefits," (January 9 draft), U.S. Forest Service, Pacific Northwest Research Station, Retrieved from the Worldwide Web March 15, 2013 at http://www.fs.fed.us/psw/publications/reports/psw_sciencesynthesis2013 /psw_sciencesynthesis2013_9_5.pdf

Clary, David (1987) "What Price Sustained Yield? The Forest Service, Community Stability and Timber Monopoly Under the 1944 Sustained-Yield Act," *Journal of Forest History.* Vol. 31, No. 1, p. 4-18.

Committee for Family Forestland (2013) "RE: Malheur Lumber Mill Closure Threat," (October 19), Letter addressed to John Blackwell, Chair, Oregon Board of Forestry, Retrieved from the Worldwide Web July 15, 2013 at http://www.oregon.gov/odf/BOARD/CFF/MalheurLumberMillClosure.p df

Conway, F. D. L. and Wells, G. E. (1994) *Timber in Oregon: History and Projected Needs.* Corvalils, OR. Oregon State University Agriculture Extension Service.

Cummans, Jared (2012) "Top 3 Timber Stocks by Market Cap," *Commodity HQ.* (September 18), Retrieved from the Worldwide Web June 26, 2013 at http://commodityhq.com/2012/top-3-timber-stocks-by-market-cap/

Dietrich, William (1992) *The Final Forest: Big Trees, Forks, and the Pacific Northwest.* Seattle, WA: University of Washington Press.

Downs, William (2000) "The Language of Felt Experience: Emotional, Evaluative and Intuitive," *Language and Literature.* Vol. 9, No. 2, p. 99-121.

Estrada, Hector, Borja, Delicia H., and Lee, Luke (2012) "Sustainability in Infrastructure Design," in Ravi Jain and Luke Lee's *Fiber Reinforced Polymer (FRP) Composites for Infrastructure Applications.* New York, NY: Springer Science.

Fedkiw, John (2009) *Managing Multiple Uses On National Forests, 1905-1995 A 90-Year Learning Experience And It Isn't Finished Yet.* Washington, DC: U.S. Department of Agriculture, Forest Service, Published by the Forest History Society http://www.foresthistory.org/ASPNET/Publications/multiple_use/

Ficken, Robert E. (1987) *The Forested Land: A History of Lumbering in Western Washington.* Seattle, WA: University of Washington Press.

Food and Agricultural Organization of the U.S. (FAO) (2010) "Global Forest Resource Assessment: Country Report - The United States," Rome, Italy, Retrieved from the Worldwide Web March 7, 2013 at http://www.fao.org/docrep/013/al658E/al658E.pdf

Gorte, Ross W. (1998) "Clearcutting in the Nation's Forests: Background and Overview," *CRS Reports*. Congressional Research Service, Washington, DC, Retrieved from the Worldwide Web March 15, 2013 at http://cnie.org/NLE/CRSreports/Forests/for-21.cfm

Greber, Bryan J. (1993) "Impacts of Technological Change on Employment in the Timber Industries of the Pacific Northwest." *Western Journal of Applied Forestry*. Vol. 8, No. 1, p. 34-37.

Gregory, Robinson G. (1955) "An Economic Approach To The Multiple Use," *Forest Science*. Vol. 1, No. 1, p. 6-13.

Hampton Affiliates (2013) "Company History" Retrieved from the Worldwide Web July 15, 2013 at http://www.hamptonaffiliates.com/subcontent.aspx?SecID=6

Haynes, Richard W. (2005) "Developing an Agenda to Guide Forest Social Science, Economics, and Utilization Research," U.S. Department of Agriculture, Forest Service, Pacific Northwest Research Station, General Technical Report PNW-GTR-627, (January), Retrieved from the Worldwide Web June 26, 2013 at http://www.fs.fed.us/pnw/pubs/pnw_gtr627.pdf .

Hill, Julia (2000) "Getting Burned by the Timber Industry," *The Thistle*. Vol. 13, No. 2, Retrieved from the Worldwide Web July 2, 2013 at www.mit.edu/~thistle/v13/2/timber.htm

Industrial Economics Incorporated (ICE), (2012) "Economic Analysis Of Critical Habitat Designation For The Northern Spotted Owl," Prepared for the U.S. Fish and Wildlife Service, (Draft, May 29), Retrieved from the Worldwide Web June 4, 2013 at http://www.fws.gov/oregonfwo/species/data/northernspottedowl/Docum ents/DraftEconAnalysis.5.29.12.3.pdf

Institute for Culture and Ecology (2008) "Comments on Western Oregon Plan Revision (WOPR) Draft Environmental Impact Statement," Bureau of Land Management positing, Retrieved from the Worldwide Web July 3, 2013 at http://www.blm.gov/or/plans/wopr/pub_comments/forum/UploadedFiles /a4a3a7c1-f36e-4f3b-8fed-c0b94ba0b734.PDF

Jacket, Ben (2009) "Trouble In Timber Town," Decades After an Industry Downfall, Towns Still Grapple with What's Next?" *Oregon Business*. (November), Retrieved from the Worldwide Web July 15, 2013 at http://www.oregonbusiness.com/articles/72-november-2009/2478-trouble-in-timber-town

Jones, Edward Gardner (1894) *The Oregonian's Handbook of the Pacific Northwest*. Portland, OR: The Oregonian Publishing Company.

Kerr, Andy (2012) "Oregon and Washington Raw Log Exports: Exporting Jobs and a Subsidy to Domestic Mills," *Larch Occasional Paper #10*. (February), The Larch Company, Retrieved from the Worldwide Web

June 26, 2013 at http://www.andykerr.net/storage/conservation-uploads/LOP%2010%20Log%20Exports.pdf

Keye, William Wade (2003) "Environmentalists vs. Forestry: Stopping Attempts to Clean Up Flammable Timber Leads to Wildfires," *The San Jose Mercury News*. (October 7), Retrieved from the Worldwide Web June 19, 2013 at http://www.maninnature.com/Forestry/Forest1d.html

Learn, Scott (2013) "Closure of Rough & Ready mill in Josephine County highlights logging stalemate in Congress," *The Oregonian*. (April 18), Retrieved from the Worldwide Web July 15, 2013 at http://www.oregonlive.com/environment/index.ssf/2013/04/closure_of_r ough_ready_in_mill.html

Leber, Jessica (2009) "Obama Admin Scraps Logging Plan in Oregon Carbon Sinks," *The New York Times (Energy & Environment)*. (July 17, 2009), Retrieved from the Worldwide Web July 3, 2013 at http://www.nytimes.com/cwire/2009/07/17/17climatewire-obama-admin-scraps-logging-plan-in-ore-carbo-10938.html

Lehner, Josh (2012) "Historical Look at Oregon's Wood Product Industry," Oregon Office of Economic Analysis, (January 23) Retrieved from the Worldwide Web March 15, 2013 at http://oregoneconomicanalysis.wordpress.com/2012/01/23/historical-look-at-oregons-wood-product-industry/

Lewicki, Roy J., Gray, Barbara and Elliott, Michael (2002) *Making Sense of Environmental Conflicts: Concepts and Cases*. Washington, DC: Island Press.

Marcot, Bruce G. and Thomas, Jack Ward (1997) "Of Spotted Owls, Old Growth and New Policies: A History Since the Interagency Scientific Committee Report," Green Technical Report PNW-GTR-408 (September), USDA, U.S. Forest Service, Pacific Northwest Research Station, Portland, OR, Retrieved from the Worldwide Web March 13, 2013 at http://www.treesearch.fs.fed.us/pubs/3018

Mason, C. Larry, Casavant, Kenneth L., Lippke, Bruce R. Nguyen, Diem K. and Jessup Eric (2008) "The Washington Log Trucking Industry: Costs and Safety Analysis," The Rural Technology Initiative University of Washington and The Transportation Research Group Washington State University, Report to the Washington State Legislature, (August).

Mcdermott, Terry and Nagoki, Sylvia (1990) "Once A Great Notion -- Decline Of The Timber Industry Marks The Death Of The Old Northwest," *The Seattle Times*. (December 16), Retrieved from the Worldwide Web June 14, 2013 at http://community.seattletimes.nwsource.com/archive/?date=19901216& slug=1109757

Miller, Char (2007) "A Sylvan Prospect: John Muir, Gifford, Pinchot and Early Twentieth Century Conservationism," in Michael Lewis's (Ed.) *American Wilderness: A New History*. London, UK: Oxford University Press.

Montreal Process (2009) "Criteria and Indicators," Montreal Process Home Page, Retrieved from the Worldwide Web June 26, 2013 at

http://www.montrealprocess.org/Resources/Criteria_and_Indicators/inde
x.shtml

Myers, Gary D. (1991) "Old-Growth Forests, the Owl, and Yew: Environmental
Ethics Versus Traditional Dispute Resolution Under the Endangered
Species Act and Other Public Lands and Resources Law," *Boston
College Environmental Affairs Law Review*. Vol. 18, No. 4, p. 623-668.

Njus, Elliott (2013) "Weyerhaeuser to pay $2.65 billion for Oregon, Washington
Timberlands," *The Oregonian*. (June 17), Retrieved from the Worldwide
Web June 26, 2013 at
http://www.oregonlive.com/business/index.ssf/2013/06/weyerhaeuser_p
ays_265_billion.html

Pacific Lumber Exporters Association (PLEA) (2013) "PLEA Members,"
Retrieved from the Worldwide Web June 26, 2013 at
http://www.lumber-exporters.org/plea/01/members.asp

Parker, Ron (2007) "Defending the Timber Industry," *Political Outdoors*. The
Pioneer Press, (August 8), Retrieved from the Worldwide Web June 19,
2013 at
http://klamathbucketbrigade.org/PioneerPress_Defendingthetimberindust
ry080907.htm.

Plum Creek (2012) "Acres by State," Plum Creek Timber Company, Retrieved
from the Worldwide Web June 26, 2013 at
http://www.plumcreek.com/Timberland/AcresbyState/tabid/65/Default.a
spx

Rast, Rebekah (2012) "Environmentalists Target Even Private Logging,"
*American Clarion*. (November 28), Retrieved from the Worldwide Web
July 2, 2013 at
www.americanclarion.com/14934/2012/11/28/environmentalists-target-
even-private-logging/

Ritters, Kurt H., Wickham, James D. and Coulston, John W. (2004) "A
Preliminary Assessment of Montreal Process Indicators of Forest
Fragmentation for the United States," *Environmental Monitoring and
Assessment*. Vol. 91, p. 257-276.

Robbins, Jim (2008) "Bark Beetles Kill Millions of Acres of Trees in West," New
York Times. (November 17), Retrieved from the Worldwide Web July 2,
2013 at
http://www.nytimes.com/2008/11/18/science/18trees.html?pagewanted=
all&_r=0

Robbins, William (2012) "People, Politics, and the Environment Since 1945:
Criticizing the Industry," *The Oregon History Project*. Portland, OR:
Oregon History Society.

Rothbard, Murray N. (2003 *The Ethics of Liberty*. New York, NY: NYU Press.

Satterfield, Terre (2002) *Anatomy of a Conflict: Identity, Knowledge, and
Emotion in Old-Growth Forests*. Ann Arbor, MI: Michigan State
University Press.

Six, Amanda (1995) *Nature and Culture in Two Pacific Northwest Timber-
Dependent Communities. Masters Thesis*. (M.A. Applied Anthropology),
Corvalis, OR: Oregon State University.

Stagner, Howard (1960) "A Second Look At Multiple Use," *American Forests*. Vol. 66, p. 24-25.

Stritholt, James R., Dellsala, Dominick A. and Jiang, Hong (2005) "Status of Mature and Old-Growth Forests in the Pacific Northwest," *Conservation Biology*. Vol. 20, No. 2, p. 363-374.

Thomas, Jack Ward, Franklin, Jerry F., Gordon, John, and Johnson, K. Norman (2006) "The Northwest Forest Plan: Components, Implementation Experience, and Suggestions for Change," *Conservation Biology*. Vol. 20, No. 2, p. 277-287.

U.S. Bureau of Labor Statistics (BLS), (2012) "National Census Of Fatal Occupational Injuries In 2011," *BLS News Release*. Thursday, September 20, 2012, USDL-12-1888, Retrieved from the Worldwide Web June 14, 2013 at http://www.bls.gov/news.release/pdf/cfoi.pdf

U.S. Department of Agriculture (USDA) (2013) "McIntire-Stennis Cooperative Forestry Research Act M/S Program," Cooperative Forestry Research, Catalog of Federal Domestic Assistance, Retrieved from the Worldwide Web June 24, 2013 at
https://www.cfda.gov/?s=program&mode=form&tab=step1&id=fd7a39 2f5655d5ec9fdde7b240722e27

U.S. Department of Technology Assessment (USTA) (1983) "Wood Use: U.S. Competitiveness and Technology," Vol. 1, August, NTIS order #PB84-109925, retrieved from the Worldwide Web June 4, 2013 at http://govinfo.library.unt.edu/ota/Ota_4/DATA/1983/8332.PDF

U.S. Forest Service (USFS) (2013) "National Forest Management Act of 1976," Ecosystem Management Protection, Retrieved from the Worldwide Web June 24, 2013 at
http://www.fs.fed.us/emc/nfma/includes/NFMA1976.pdf

U.S. Forest Service (USFS) (2009a) "Gifford Pinchot: 1865-1946," U.S. Forest Service History, Retrieved from the Worldwide Web June 19, 2013 at http://www.foresthistory.org/ASPNET/people/Pinchot/Pinchot.aspx

U.S. Forest Service (USFS) (2001) "Sierra Nevada Forest Plan Amendment Environmental Impact Statement," (January) Washington, D.C., Retrieved from the Worldwide Web March 7, 2013 at http://www.sierraforestlegacy.org/Resources/Conservation/LawsPolicies Regulation/KeyForestServicePolicy/SierraNevadaFramework/Framewor k-FSROD01.pdf

U.S. Forest Service (USFS) (1993) *Forest Ecosystem Management: An Ecological, Economic, and Social Assessment - Report of the Forest Ecosystem Management Assessment Team*. Washington, DC: United States Forest Service.

Venetis, Kyriaki (2009) "Oregon Loggers Outraged Over Secretary's Decision to Cut the WOPR," *Green Vitals*. (July 20), Retrieved from the Worldwide Web July 3, 2013 at
http://www.greenvitals.net/greenvitalsnet/2009/7/20/oregon-loggers-outraged-over-secretarys-decision-to-cut-the.html

Warren, Debra D. (2010) *Production, Prices, Employment, and Trade in Northwest Forest Industries, All Quarters 2009*. U.S. Department of Agriculture, Forest Service, Pacific Northwest Research Station,

(September), Resource Bulletin PNW-RB-259, Retrieved from the Worldwide Web June 4, 2013 at http://www.fs.fed.us/pnw/pubs/pnw_rb259.pdf

Washington Department of Natural Resources (2013) "Economic and Revenue Forecasts," (June 10 Update), Retrieved from the Worldwide Web June 26,                        2013                        at http://www.dnr.wa.gov/BusinessPermits/Topics/EconomicReports/Pages /econ_timb_rev_forcsts.aspx

Welch, Bryan (2008) "The Problem with Environmentalists," *Mother Earth News.* (November 10), Retrieved from the Worldwide Web June 19, 2013 at http://www.motherearthnews.com/nature-and-environment/problem-with-environmentalists.aspx#axzz2Wiwb3mwT

Weyerhaeuser, 2013 "Weyerhaeuser To Purchase Approximately 645,000 Acres Of Unique, High-Value Timberlands In Washington And Oregon," Weyerhaeuser News Release, (June 16), Retrieved from the Worldwide Web June 26, 2013 at http://www.weyerhaeuser.com/Company/Media/NewsReleases/NewsRel ease?dcrId=2013-06-16_WYLongviewTimber

White, Richard (1996) "Are You an Environmentalists or Do You Work for a Living?: Work and Nature," in William Cronon's (Ed.) *Uncommon Ground: Rethinking the Human Place in Nature.* New York, NY: Norton & Norton.

Zhang, Yaoqi (2005) "Multiple-Use Forestry Vs. Forestland-Use Specialization Revisited," *Forest Policy and Economics.* Vol. 7, p. 143-156.

Zhou, Xiaoping (2013) "West Coast Lumber Exports Decrease – Total U.S. Log and Lumber Exports Increase in First Quarter of 2013," News Release: May 30, 2013, U.S. Forest Service, Pacific Northwest Research Station, Retrieved from the Worldwide Web June 26, 2013 at http://www.fs.fed.us/pnw/news/2013/05/lumber-exports.shtml

## Chapter 7: Let's Work Together

Ammerman, David (1975) *In The Common Cause: American Response To The Coercive Acts Of 1774.* New York, NY: Norton Publishing.

Bastiat, Frederic (1850) *That Which is Seen and That Which is Not Seen.* Paris, FR: Guillaumin Edition, Libraries-Editeurs.

Betsch, Tilmann (2010) "The Nature of Intuition and Its Neglect in Research on Judgment and Decision Making," In Henning Plessner, Cornelia Betsch and Tilman Betsch's (Eds.) *Intuition in Judgment and Decision Making.* New York, NY: Taylor & Francis, p. 3-22.

Boyd, Robert and Richerson, Peter J. (2006) *Not By Genes Alone: How Culture Transformed Human Evolution.* Chicago, IL: University of Chicago Press.

Bowden, E. M. and Jung-Beeman, M. (2003) "Aha! Insight Experience Correlates With Solution Activation In The Right Hemisphere," *Psychonomic Bulletin and Review.* Vol. 10, No. 3, p. 730-737.

DeShalit, Avner (2004) *Red-Green: Democracy, Justice and the Environment.* Tel Aviv, IR: Babel Publishers.

DeShalit, Avner (1995) *Why Posterity Matters: Environmental Polices and Future Generations.* Florence, KY: Routledge.

Dewar, Gwen (2013) "The Curse of the Herd," *Psychology Today.* (January 6).

Drucker Exchange (2013) "Analysis Paralysis," *Time Business and Money.* (July 10), Retrieved from the Worldwide Web.

Durkheim, Emile (1893) *The Division of Labor in Society.* Paris, FR: University of Paris.

Etzioni, Amitai (2003) "Communitarianism," in K. Christensen's and D. Levinson (eds.) *Encyclopedia of Community: From the Village to the Virtual World.* Vol. 1, A-D, Los Angeles, CA: Sage Publications, pp. 224-228.

Etzioni, Amitai (1997) *The New Golden Rule: Community and Morality in a Democratic Society.* New York, NY: Basic Books.

Etzioni, Amitai (1967) "Mixed-Scanning: A "Third" Approach to Decision-Making," *Public Administration Review.* Vol. 27, No. 5, p. 385-392.

Haidt, Jonathan (2013) *The Righteous Mind: Why Good People Are Divided by Politics and Religion.* New York, NY: Vintage.

Haidt, Jonathan (2006) *The Happiness Hypothesis: Finding Modern Truth in Ancient Wisdom.* New York, NY: Basic Books.

Institute for Energy Research (2013) "The Dilemma Caused by Low Cost Natural Gas," IER Press Release. (February 22), Retrieved from the Worldwide Web September 12, 2013 at http://www.instituteforenergyresearch.org/2013/02/22/the-dilemma-caused-by-low-cost-natural-gas/

Jones, Bryan D. (2003) "Bounded Rationality and Political Science: Lessons from Public Administration and Public Policy," *Journal of Public Administration Research and Theory.* Vol. 13, No. 4, p. 395-412.

Kahneman, D., and Tversky, A. (1979) "Prospect theory: An Analysis Of Decisions Under Risk," *Econometrika.* Vol. 47, p. 263–291.

Kahneman, D., and Tversky, A. (1984) "Choices, Values, And Frames," *American Psychologist.* Vol. 39, p. 341–350.

Kalantari, Behrooz (2010) "Herbert A. Simon on making decisions: enduring insights and bounded rationality", *Journal of Management History,* Vol. 16, No. 4, pp.509 – 520.

Klein, Gary (2013) *Seeing What Others Don't: The Remarkable Ways We Gain Insights.* PublicAffairs.

Klein, Gary (2002) *Intuition at Work: Why Developing Your Gut Instincts Will Make You Better at What You Do.* Doubleday.

Lefsrud, Lianne M. and Meyer, Renate E. (2012) "Science or Science Fiction? Professionals' Discursive Construction of Climate," *Organizational Studies.* Vol. 33, No. 11, p. 1477-1506.

Lewicki, Roy J., Gray, Barbara and Elliott, Michael (2003) *Making Sense of Intractable Environmental Conflicts: Frames and Cases.* Washington, DC: Island Press.

Mehrota, S. R. (1963) "On The Use Of The Term 'Commonwealth,'" Journal of Commonwealth Political Studies. Vol. 2, No. 1, p. 1-16.

Mesoudi, Alex (2011) *Cultural Evolution: How Darwinian Can Explain Human Culture and Synthesize the Social Sciences*. Chicago, IL: University of Chicago Press.

Morgan, T. J. H. and Laland, K. (2012) "The Biological Bases of Conformity," *Frontiers of Neuroscience*. Vol. 6, No. 87, p. 1-7.

Nyatanga, Brian and de Vocht, Hilde (2008) "Intuition In Clinical Decision-Making: A Psychological Penumbra," *International Journal of Palliative Nursing*. Vol. 4, No. 10, p. 492-296.

Newell, Allen and Simon, Herbert A. (1972) *Human Problem Solving*. Englewood Cliffs, NJ: Prentice-Hall.

Nielsen, Jared A., Zielinski, Brandon A., Ferguson, Michael A. Lainhart, Janet E., Anderson, Jeffrey S. (2013) "An Evaluation of the Left-Brain vs. Right-Brain Hypothesis with Resting State Functional Connectivity Magnetic Resonance Imaging," *PLOS One Online Journal*. Retrieved from the Worldwide Web September 16, 2013 at http://www.plosone.org/article/info%3Adoi%2F10.1371%2Fjournal.pon e.0071275

Olick, Jeffrey K. (2013) "Collective Memory," In M. J. Smelser and P. B. Baltes (Eds.) *International Encyclopedia of the Social Sciences*, (2nd Edition), Oxford, UK: Pergamon Press, p. 7-8.

Ostrom, Elinor (2001) *The Drama of the Commons*. Washington, DC: National Academies Press.

Rajkomar, Alvin and Dhaliwal, Gurpreet (2011) "Improving Diagnostic Reasoning to Improve Patient Safety," *The Permanente Journal*. Vol. 15, No. 3, p. 68-73.

Rew, Lynn and Barrow, Edward M. (2007) "State of the Science: Intuition in Nursing, a Generation of Studying the Phenomenon," *Advances in Nursing Science*. Vol. 30, No. 1, p. E15-E25.

Roberto, Michael A. (2009) *The Art of Critical Decision Making, (The Great Courses)*. New York, NY: Scribner's The Teaching Company.

Simon, Herbert A. (1997) *Administrative Behavior: A Study of Decision-Making Processes in Administrative Organizations* (Fourth Edition). New York, NY: The Free Press.

Simon, Herbert A. (1987) "Making Management Decisions: The Role of Intuition and Emotion, *The Academy of Management Executive* (1987-1989). Vol. 1, No. 1., p. 57-64.

Simon, Herbert (1979) *Models of Thought*. (Vol. 1). New Haven, CT: Yale University Press.

Simon, Herbert A. (1972) "Theories of Bounded Rationality," In Radner, C. and Radner, R. (Eds.) *Decision and Organization*, Amsterdam, NE: North-Holland Publishing Company, pp.161-76.

Simon, Herbert A. (1969) *The Sciences of the Artificial*. Cambridge, MA: MIT Press.

Simon, Herbert A. (1960) *The New Science of Management Decision*. New York, NY: Harper & Row.

Simon, Herbert A. (1955) "A Behavioral Model of Rational Choice," *The Quarterly Journal of Economics*. Vol. 69, No. 1, p. 99-118.

Unger, David (2013) "Record U.S. Coal Exports Fuel Climate Change Debate," Christian Science Monitor. (June 20). Retrieved from the Worldwide Web September 12, 2013 at http://www.csmonitor.com/Environment/Energy-Voices/2013/0620/Record-US-coal-exports-fuel-climate-change-debate

Wallas, Graham (1926) *The Art of Thought*. New York, NY: Harcourt Brace.

Welch IV, James (2007) "The Role of Intuition in Interdisciplinary Insight," *Issues in Integration Studies*. No. 25, p. 131-155.

Wimberley, Edward T. (2009) *Nested Ecology: The Place of Humans in the Ecological Hierarchy*. Baltimore, MD: Johns Hopkins University Press.

Wimberley, Edward T. and Hobbs Bradley (2013) "The Conservative Ecologist and Free-Market Environmentalism: Classical Liberalism Reasserted," *The International Journal of Sustainability Policy and Practice*. Volume 8, No. 1, p. 1-18.

Wimberley, Terry and Morrow, Allyn (1981) "Mulling Over, Muddling Through, Again," *International Journal of Public Administration*. Vol. 3, Issue 4, p. 483-505.

Yu, P. L. and Lai, T. C. (2005) "Knowledge Management, Habitual Domains, and Innovation Dynamics," *Data Mining and Knowledge Management*. Vol. 3327, p. 11-21.

## Chapter 8: Oil and Water

Cameron, Charley (2013) "Researchers Create Efficient, Recyclable Solar Cells from Trees," *Inhabit*. Retrieved from the Worldwide Web November 13, 2013 at http://inhabitat.com/researchers-create-efficient-recyclable-organic-solar-cells-from-trees/

Cardwell, Diane (2013) "Intermittent Nature of Green Power Is Challenge for Utilities," *The New York Times (Energy & Environment)*. (August 14), Retrieved from the Worldwide Web December 4, 2013 at http://www.nytimes.com/2013/08/15/business/energy-environment/intermittent-nature-of-green-power-is-challenge-for-utilities.html?_r=0&pagewanted=print

Chance, Michael (2013) "A Historic Day for Solar Energy in Georgia," *RenewableEnergyWorld.Com*. (July 12), Retrieved from the Worldwide Web October 1, 2013 at http://www.renewableenergyworld.com/rea/blog/post/print/2013/07/why-today-was-a-historic-day-for-solar-energy-in-georgia.

Coker, Anthony A. (2010) "Sustainability at Suniva," Retrieved from the Worldwide Web November 13, 2013 at http://s389705876.onlinehome.us/Joomla/images/PDFBank/Repository/2011/7AnthonyCoker.pdf

Dearen, Jason (2013) "Solar Industry Grapples with Hazardous Wastes," *Associated Press*. Retrieved from the Worldwide Web November 11, 2013 at http://news.yahoo.com/solar-industry-grapples-hazardous-wastes-184714679.html

Energy Manager Today (2012) "More than 6.4 GW Solar Electric Capacity Installed in US," December 17, Retrieved From the Worldwide Web

November 13, 2013 at http://www.energymanagertoday.com/more-than-6-4-gw-solar-electric-capacity-installed-in-us-087753/

Energy Matters (2012) "Solar Panel Recycling Will Be A Multi-Billion Dollar Industry," (January 23), Retrieved from the Worldwide Web November 13, 2013 at http://www.energymatters.com.au/index.php?main_page=news_article&article_id=3001

Etzioni, Amitai (1997) *The New Golden Rule: Community and Morality in a Democratic Society*. New York, NY: Basic Books.

Georgia SB401 (2012) "A Bill Amending the Georgia Cogeneration and Distributed Generation Act of 2001," Georgia General Assembly. Retrieved from the Worldwide Web October 1, 2013 at http://www.legis.ga.gov/legislation/en-US/display/20112012/SB/401.

Gies, Erica (2013) "Solar Waste Recycling: Can the Industry Stay Green?" *SF Public Press*. Retrieved from the Worldwide Web November 11, 2013 at http://spot.us/pitches/352-solar-waste-recycling-can-the-industry-stay-green/story

Goe, Michele, Tomaszewski, Brian and Gaustad, Gabrielle (2013) "Infrastructure Planning for Solar Technology Recycling," ERSI News. Retrieved from the Worldwide Web November 13, 2013 at http://www.esri.com/esri-news/arcuser/winter-2013/~/media/Files/Pdfs/news/arcuser/0113/uncertainty.pdf

Green Tea Coalition (2013) "Very, Very Important Issue," Green Tea Coalition Facebook Blog, Retrieved from the Worldwide Web October 1, 2013 at https://www.facebook.com/permalink.php?id=209442799211781&story_fbid=220386671450727.

Grillo, Jerry (2013) "Sun Dancing," Georgia Trend. (July), Retrieved from the Worldwide Web October 1, 2013 at http://www.georgiatrend.com/July-2013/Sun-Dancing/.

Haidt, Jonathan (2013) *The Righteous Mind: Why Good People Are Divided by Politics and Religion*. New York, NY: Vintage.

Hicks, Jennifer (2012) "New Techniques Creates First Plastic Solar Cell," *Forbes*. (April 25), Retrieved from the Worldwide Web July 12, 2014 at http://www.forbes.com/sites/jenniferhicks/2012/04/25/new-technique-creates-first-plastic-solar-cell/

Institute for Energy Research (IER) (2013) "America's Green Energy Problems: Defective Solar Panels," *IER News*. (June 3), Retrieved from the Worldwide Web November 15, 2013 at http://www.instituteforenergyresearch.org/2013/06/03/americas-green-energy-problems-defective-solar-panels/

International Electrical Commission (IEC) (2014) "Grid-Tied Inverters: How They Work," Angelfire.org. Retrieved from the Worldwide Web January 15, 2014 at http://www.angelfire.com/biz/themill/hydrofiles/grid-tied.html.

Johnson, Ray (2013) "What Role did Florida Solar Energy Play in the ASP Solar Panel Fraud?" *RenewableEnergyWorld.com*. Retrieved from the Worldwide Web November 15, 2013 at

http://www.renewableenergyworld.com/rea/blog/post/print/2013/05/sola
r-panel-fraud-in-florida-what-becomes-of-advanced-solar-photonics-
blue-chip-energy-and-sfinkx-now

Kidd, Rusty, Kirby, Tom, Rogers, Terry, Brockway, Buzz, Frazier, Gloria and
Fullerton, Carol (2013) "Solar Offers Opportunity to Grow Georgia
Economy," Loganville-Grayson Patch. (May 31), Retrieved from the
Worldwide Web October 1, 2013 at
http://loganville.patch.com/groups/going-green/p/solar-offers-
opportunity-to-grow-georgia-economy.

Kind, Peter (2013) "Disruptive Challenges: Financial Implications and Strategic
Responses to a Changing Retail Electric Business," A Report to the
Edison Electric Institute by Energy Infrastructure Advocates, (January)
Retrieved from the Worldwide Web January 15, 2014 at
http://www.eei.org/ourissues/finance/Documents/disruptivechallenges.p
df.

Krusen, Jochen (2004) "Wind: Intermittent, Power: Continuous – Handling an
Electrical Grid

Nath, Ishan (2010) "Cleaning Up After Clean Energy: Hazardous Waste in the
Solar Industry," *Stanford Journal of International Relations*. (Spring)
Vol. XI, No. 2, p. 6-15.

Olen, John (2013) "Defective Chinese Solar Panels are Derailing Green Energy
Efforts," Economy in Crisis. (September 26), Retrieved from the
Worldwide Web November 15, 2013 at
http://economyincrisis.org/content/defective-chinese-solar-panels-are-
derailing-green-energy-efforts

Oneal, Tip and Hymel, Gary (1995) *All Politics is Local: And Other Rules of the
Game*. New York, NY: Adams Media Corporation.

Oswana, Nancy (2013) "Ivanpah Solar Plant In California Starts Energy Feed To
Grid," Phys.org. (Sept. 27), Retrieved from the Worldwide Web January
15, 2014 at http://phys.org/news/2013-09-ivanpah-solar-california-
energy-grid.html.

Palmer, Roseanne (2013) "Solar Power Growing Pains: How Will Hawaii And
Germany Cope With The Boom In Alternative Energy?" *International
Business Times*. (December 23, 2013), Retrieved from the Worldwide
Web January 15, 2014 at http://www.ibtimes.com/solar-power-growing-
pains-how-will-hawaii-germany-cope-boom-alternative-energy-
1518702.

PV Cycle (2013) "PV Cycle Home," Retrieved from the Worldwide Web
November 13, 2013 at http://www.pvcycle.org.uk/

Riggs, Mike (2013) "Why Firefighters Fear Solar Power," *Citylab*. (September
11), Retrieved from the Worldwide Web July 12, 2014 at
http://www.citylab.com/tech/2013/09/why-firefighters-are-scared-solar-
power/6854/

Rust, James H. (2013) "Thoughts About Utility-Scale Solar Energy," *Somewhat
Reasonable: The Policy and Commentary Blog of the Heartland
Institute*. (July 3), Retrieved from the Worldwide Web October 1, 2013
at http://blog.heartland.org/2013/07/thoughts-about-utility-scale-solar-
energy/.

Shea, Stephen (2013) "In response to an article/photo from the Associated Press that appeared in many newspapers," (February 13 memo from Stephen Shea, Ph.D., Chief Engineering Officer, Suniva, Norcross, GA), Retrieved from the Worldwide Web November 13, 2013 at http://www.suniva.com/documents/Response-to-AJC-article.pdf.

Shulman, Seth (2013) "Got Science? A 'Green Tea Party' May Be Brewing," *Huff Post Green*. August 8, Retrieved from the Worldwide Web November 11, 2013 at http://www.huffingtonpost.com/seth-shulman/got-science-a-green-tea-p_b_3726459.html

Silicon Valley Toxics Coalition (SVTC) (2009) "Toward a Just and Sustainable Solar Energy Industry," A SVTC White Paper, January 14, 2009, San Francisco California, Retrieved From the Worldwide Web November 13, 2013 at http://svtc.org/wp-content/uploads/Silicon_Valley_Toxics_Coalition_-_Toward_a_Just_and_Sust.pdf

Smith, Stephen A. (2012) " Georgia Consumer Choice Bill Would Boost Economic Opportunities," *CleanEnergyOrg.* (February 22), Southern Alliance for Clean Energy. Retrieved from the Worldwide Web October 1, 2013 at http://blog.cleanenergy.org/2012/02/22/georgia-consumer-choice-bill-would-boost-economic-opportunities/.

Suniva (2013) "Suniva, Inc. Homepage," Retrieved from the Worldwide Web November 13, 2013 at http://www.suniva.com/

Trabish, Herman K. (2013) "Putting Out the Solar Panel Fire Threat," *Greentechsolar.* (September 18), Retrieved from the Worldwide Web July 12, 2014 at https://www.greentechmedia.com/articles/read/Putting-Out-The-Solar-Panel-Fire-Threat

Trabish, Herman K. (2012) "SolarBuyer: Teaching Firms How to Spot Shoddy Solar Panels," (March 4), *Greentech Media*. Retrieved from the Worldwide Web November 15, 2013 at http://www.greentechmedia.com/articles/read/educating-solars-long-term-risk-takers

United States Environmental Protection Agency (USEPA) (2012) "Facility Profile Report: Suniva, Inc.," Retrieved from the Worldwide Web November 13, 2013 at http://iaspub.epa.gov/triexplorer/release_fac_profile?TRI=3009WSNVN C5775P&year=2011&trilib=TRIQ1&FLD=&FLD=RELLBY&FLD=TS FDSP&OFFDISPD=&OTHDISPD=&ONDISPD=&OTHOFFD=

United States Environmental Protection Agency (USEPA) (2011) "Enforcement and Compliance History Online (ECHO): Suniva, Inc., Norcross, GA," Retrieved from the Worldwide Web November 13, 2013 at http://www.epa-echo.gov/cgi-bin/get1cReport.cgi?tool=echo&IDNumber=110038901864

United States Environmental Protection Agency (USEPA) (2008) "State Incentives for Achieving Clean and Renewable Energy Development on Contaminated Lands: Incentives for Clean and Renewable Energy," Georgia Incentives for Clean Energy. (November), Retrieved from the Worldwide Web October 1, 2013 at http://www.epa.gov/oswercpa/incentives/ga_incentives.pdf.

Wilson, Alex (2013) "Beating the Achilles Heel of Grid-Tied Solar Electrical Systems," BuildingGreen.com. Retrieved from the Worldwide Web January 15, 2014 at http://www2.buildinggreen.com/blogs/beating-achilles-heel-grid-tied-solar-electric-systems.

Wong, Kristine (2014) "What Risks Do Solar Panels Pose for Firefighters?" *SolarEnergy.net.* (February 25), Retrieved from the Worldwide Web July 12, 2013 at http://solarenergy.net/News/tackling-risks-solar-panels-pose-firefighters/

Woody, Tom (2013) "Solar Industry Anxious Over Defective Panels," *New York Times: Business Day.* (May 28) Retrieved from the Worldwide Web November 15, 2013 at
http://www.nytimes.com/2013/05/29/business/energy-environment/solar-powers-dark-side.html?_r=1&pagewanted=all&

## Chapter 9: Going Home

Ahern, Jack (2004) "Greenways in the U.S.A.: Theory Trends and Prospects," Rob Jongman and Gloria Pungetti's (Ed.) *Ecological Networks and Greenways: Concept, Design, Implementation.* New York, NY: Cambridge University Press.

Amati, Marco and Yokohari, Makoto (2007) The Establishment of the London Green Belt: Reaching Concensus over Purchasing Land. *Journal of Planning History.* Vol. 6. p. 318.

American Trails (2011) "National Trail System: History and Facts," (March 4) Retrieved From the Worldwide Web March 27, 2014 at http://www.americantrails.org/resources/feds/40yearfact.html.

Bailey, Layne (2007) "Follow the 'Thread' - Trail Would Be a Signature Resource for Southern Piedmont," (November 7), *The Charlotte Observer – Opinion.* Retrieved from the Worldwide Web March 9, 2014 at
http://www.carolinathreadtrail.org/assets/files/Follow%20The%20Thread%20%2011-11-07.pdf.

Carolina Thread Trail (2014) "About the Name," Retrieved from the Worldwide Web June 2, 2014 at http://www.carolinathreadtrail.org/overview/about-the-name/.

Carolina Thread Trail (2013) "Carolina Thread Trail 2013 Fact Sheet," Retrieved from the Worldwide Web June 2, 2014 at
http://www.carolinathreadtrail.org/wp-content/uploads/2010/10/2013-The-Thread-Fact-Sheet-Summer-Fall-For-Email.pdf.

Carolina Thread Trail (2012) "The Carolina Thread Trail's 2012 Report to Communities," Retrieved from the Worldwide Web June 2, 2014 at http://catawbalands.org/wp-content/uploads/2010/08/CTT-2012-Thread-Trail-Report-to-Communities.pdf

Carolina Thread Trail (2009) "Project Update: 2008 Update and 2009 Priorities," Retrieved from the Worldwide Web June 2, 2014 at
http://www.carolinathreadtrail.org/wp-content/uploads/2011/01/CTT-2008-2009-Project-Update.pdf.

Carolina Thread Trail (2004) "Carolina Thread Trail - Weaving Communities Together," (draft promotional brochure).

Crossroads Charlotte (2014) "About: What Is Crossroads Charlotte?" (February 24) Retrieved From the Worldwide Web March 9, 2014 at http://www.crossroadscharlotte.org/about/.

Fabos, Julius G. and Ahern, Jack (1996) (Eds.) Greenways: The Beginning of an International Movement. Waltham, MA: Elseiver.

Foundation for the Carolinas (FFTC) (2009) "Pioneering Steps on Carolina Thread Trail Significant Progress in 2008 for Greenway Network," A Region Responds: Report to the Community. Charlotte, NC, Retrieved from the Worldwide Web June 2, 2014 at http://www.fftc.org/page.aspx?pid=2003

Freedman, Bob (1998) "Summit to Raise Key Environmental Concerns," *Charlotte Business Journal.* (November 9), Retrieved from the Worldwide Web May 18, 2014 at http://www.bizjournals.com/charlotte/stories/1998/11/09/editorial3.html ?page=all

Gade, Ole, Rex, Arthur B., Young, James E. and Baker, Perry L. (2002) *North Carolina: People and Environments.* Boone, NC: Parkway Publishers, Retrieved from the Worldwide Web March 9, 2014 at http://geo.appstate.edu/department-resources/nc-people-and-environments

Goodman, Andy (2005) "Playing Matchmaker for Grantmakers," *Global Business Network and the Monitor Institute.* Retrieved from the Worldwide Web June 5, 2014 at https://www.summitas.com/system/files/secure/Playing%20Matchmaker %20for%20Grantmakers.pdf.

Henton, Douglas, Melville, John G. and Walesh, Kimberly A. (2007) *Civic Revolutionaries: Igniting the Passion for Change in America's Communities.* San Francisco, CA: Jossey-Bass Publishers.

Henton, Douglas , Melville, John G., Walesh, Kimberley A., Nguyen, Chi and Parr, John. (2000) "Regional Stewardship: A Commitment to Place," (Monograph Series – October), Alliance for Regional Stewardship, Retrieved from the Worldwide Web March 9, 2014 at http://www.coecon.com/assets/monograph1.pdf

Howard, Ebenezer (1898) *To-Morrow: A Peaceful Path to Real Reform.* London, UK: Faber and Faber.

Huntley, Dan (2007) "Weaving a Web of Trails – Campaign Kicks Off Today in Charlotte for Network of Walking and Biking Paths," *The Charlotte Observer.* (November 9, 2007), Retrieved from the Worldwide Web March 9, 2014 at http://www.carolinathreadtrail.org/assets/files/Articles/Article_Observer _WeavingWebTrails.pdf.

Labaree, Jonothan (1992) *How Greenways Work: A Handbook on Ecology.* (2nd Edition) Montreal, CA: Rivers, Trails, and Conservation Assistance Program and National Park Service Quebec-Labrador Foundation's Atlantic Center for the Environment.

Lee Institute (2004) "Report to Charlotte-Mecklenburg Community Foundation's Environment Committee," (Nov. 3), Retrieved from the Worldwide Web March 9, 2014 at http://www.fftc.org/NetCommunity/Document.Doc?id=64.

Little, Charles E. (1990) *Greenways for America.* Baltimore, MD: Johns Hopkins University Press.

Martin, Justin (2012) *Genius of Place: The Life of Frederick Law Olmsted.* Boston, MA: Da Capo Press.

North Carolina Million Acre Initiative (MAI) (2001) "Annual Report: 2001," North Carolina Division of Parks and Recreation, Retrieved from the Worldwide Web March 13, 2014 at http://ruby.fgcu.edu/courses/twimberley/EnviroPol/MAI.pdf.

N.C. Department of Environment and Natural Resources (2010) "2009 Annual Report North Carolina Million Acre Goal," Office of Conservation, Planning and Community Affairs, (Fall), Retrieved from the Worldwide Web March 9, 2014 at
http://www.conservation.nc.gov/c/document_library/get_file?uuid=a5eb dbfd-b2dc-4a12-b18a-4b5a6b6e286e&groupId=5060033.

Olmsted, Frederick Law (1852) *Walks and Talks of an American Farmer in England.* New York, NY.

Olmsted, Frederick Law (1882) "Trees in Streets and in Parks," *The Sanitarian* Vol. X, No.114 (September).

Ostrom, Elinor (2001) *The Drama of the Commons.* Washington, DC: National Academies Press

Pierce, Neal and Johnson, Curtis (1995) "The Citistate Report," (AKA "The Pierce Report"), *The Charlotte Observer.* (September 17 – October 8, 1995), Retrieved from the Worldwide Web July 14, 2014 at http://www.catawbariverkeeper.org/issues/land-planning-smart-growth/1995%20Peirce%20Report%20Observer%20Articles.pdf/at_dow nload/file

PR Newswire (2007) "The Carolina Threat Trail Receives Nearly $15 Million for Groundbreaking Regional Project," Retrieved from the Worldwide Web March 9, 2014 at http://www.prnewswire.com/news-releases/the-carolina-thread-trail-receives-nearly-15-million-for-groundbreaking-regional-project-58870557.html.

University of North Carolina Charlotte (UNCC) (2007) "The Charlotte Regional Indicators Project: Environmental Indicator Profile 2007," Urban Institute, Retrieved from the Worldwide Web May 19, 2014 at http://ui.uncc.edu/sites/default/files/pdf/EnvironmentIndicators.pdf

U.S. National Park Service (2014) National Trail System. Retrieved from the Worldwide Web March 27, 2014 at http://www.nps.gov/nts/nts_faq.html.

U.S. National Park Service (1995) *Economic Impacts Of Protecting Rivers, Trails And Greenway Corridors: A Resource Book.* Washington, DC: U.S. Department of the Interior, Retrieved from the Worldwide Web March 27, 2014 at http://www.nps.gov/pwro/rtca/econ_all.pdf.

Voices and Choices of the Central Carolinas (2003) "Open spaces for the Carolinas: The Framework Plan," Retrieved from the Worldwide Web March 9, 2014 at http://ruby.fgcu.edu/courses/twimberley/EnviroPhilo/openspace.pdf.

Taylor, Vicki (Editor) (2004) "2004 State of the Region Report," A Report by Voices and Choices of the Central Carolinas, Retrieved from the Worldwide Web March 9, 2014 at http://ruby.fgcu.edu/courses/twimberley/EnviroPol/voices2004rpt.pdf

White, William H. (1959) *Securing Open spaces for Urban America.* Washington, DC: Urban Land Institute.

Wagner, Jeffrey (2013) "Greenways Linking it All Together," USC Citizens for Land Stewardship, Upper St. Clair, PA, Retrieved from the Worldwide Web March 27, 2014 at http://www.usccls.org/Stewardship/Greenways.html.

CPSIA information can be obtained
at www.ICGtesting.com
Printed in the USA
LVHW062036040219
606351LV00003B/15/P